50 Years of Community Development Vol I

This 50th anniversary publication provides a comprehensive history of community development. Beginning in 1970 with the advent of the Community Development Society and its journal shortly thereafter, *Community Development*, the editors have placed the chapters in major themed areas or issues pertinent to both research and practice of community development.

The evolution of community development as an area of scholarship and application, and the subsequent founding of the discipline, is vital to capture. At the 50-year mark, it is particularly relevant to revisit issues that reoccur throughout the last five decades and look at approaches to addressing them. These include issues and themes around equity and inclusion, collective impact, leadership and policy development, as well as resilience and sustainability. Community change over time has much to teach us, and this set will provide a foundation for fostering understanding of the history of community development and its focus on community change.

The chapters in this book were originally published in the journal *Community Development*.

Norman Walzer is Senior Research Scholar at the Center for Governmental Services, Northern Illinois University, DeKalb, USA.

Rhonda Phillips is Dean, Purdue University Honors College, West Lafayette, USA.

Robert Blair is Professor of Public Administration and Urban Studies at the College of Public Affairs, University of Nebraska, Omaha, USA.

The Community Development Research and Practice Series

Volume 13
Series Editor: Rhonda G. Phillips, Purdue University, USA

Editorial Board:
Mark Brennan, Pennsylvania State University, USA
Jan Flora, Iowa State University, USA
Gary P. Green, University of Wisconsin, USA
Brian McGrath, National University of Ireland
Norman Walzer, Northern Illinois University, USA
Patricia A. Wilson, University of Texas, Austin, USA

As the series continues to grow with the ninth volume, it is our intent to continue to serve scholars, community developers, planners, public administrators, and others involved in research, practice and policymaking in the realm of community development. The series strives to provide both timely and applied information for researchers, students, and practitioners. Building on a long history since 1970 of publishing the Community Development Society's journal, *Community Development* (www.comm-dev.org), the book series contributes to a growing and rapidly changing knowledge base as a resource for practitioners and researchers alike. For additional information please see the series page at http://www. routledge.com/books/series/CDRP/.

The evolution of the field of community development continues. As reflected in both theory and practice, community development is at the forefront of change, which comes to no surprise to our communities and regions that constantly face challenges and opportunities. As a practice focused discipline, change often seems to be the only constant in the community development realm. The need to integrate theory, practice, research, teaching, and training is even more pressing now than ever, given rapidly transforming economic, social, environmental, political and cultural climates locally and globally. Current and applicable information and insights about effective research and practice are needed.

The Community Development Society, a nonprofit association of those interested in pushing the discipline forward, is delighted to offer this book series in partnership with Routledge. The series is designed to integrate innovative thinking on tools, strategies, and experiences as a resource especially well-suited for bridging the gaps between theory, research, and practice. The Community Development Society actively promotes continued advancement of the discipline and practice. Fundamental to this mission is adherence to the following core Principles of Good Practice. This book series is a reflection of many of these principles:

- Promote active and representative participation towards enabling all community members to meaningfully influence the decisions that affect their lives.
- Engage community members in learning about and understanding community issues, and the economic, social, environmental, political, psychological, and other impacts associated with alternative courses of action.
- Incorporate the diverse interest and cultures of the community in the community development process; and disengage from support of any effort that is likely to adversely affect the disadvantaged members of a community.

- Work actively to enhance the leadership capacity of community members, leaders, and groups within the community.
- Be open to using the full range of action strategies to work towards the long-term sustainability and well-being of the community.

We invite you to explore the series, and continue to do so as new volumes are added. We hope you will find it a valuable resource for supporting community development research and practice.

Other books in the series:

Knowledge Partnering for Community Development
Robyn Eversole

Social Capital at the Community Level
An Applied Interdisciplinary Perspective
John M. Halstead and Steven C. Deller

Arts and Community Change
Exploring Cultural Development Policies, Practices and Dilemmas
Max O. Stephenson Jr. and Scott Tate

Community-Built
Art, Construction, Preservation, and Place
Katherine Melcher, Barry Stiefel, Kristin Faurest

Using Collective Impact to Bring Community Change
Norman Walzer and Liz Weaver

Addressing Climate Change at the Community Level in the United States
Paul R. Lachapelle and Don E. Albrecht

The Heart of Community Engagement
Practitioner Stories from Across the Globe
Patricia A. Wilson

Culture, Community, and Development
Rhonda Phillips, Mark A. Brennan, Tingxuan Li

Community Capacity and Resilience in Latin America
Paul Lachapelle, Isabel Gutierrez-Montes, Cornelia Butler Flora

50 Years of Community Development Vol I
A History of its Evolution and Application in North America
Norman Walzer, Rhonda Phillips and Robert Blair

50 Years of Community Development Vol II
A History of its Evolution and Application in North America
Norman Walzer, Rhonda Phillips and Robert Blair

50 Years of Community Development Vol I

A History of its Evolution and Application in North America

Edited by
Norman Walzer, Rhonda Phillips and Robert Blair

Routledge
Taylor & Francis Group

LONDON AND NEW YORK

First published 2021
by Routledge
2 Park Square, Milton Park, Abingdon, Oxon, OX14 4RN

and by Routledge
52 Vanderbilt Avenue, New York, NY 10017

Routledge is an imprint of the Taylor & Francis Group, an informa business

British Library Cataloguing-in-Publication Data
A catalogue record for this book is available from the British Library

ISBN13: 978-0-367-43969-9

Typeset in Times New Roman
by codeMantra

Publisher's Note
The publisher accepts responsibility for any inconsistencies that may have arisen during the conversion of this book from journal articles to book chapters, namely the inclusion of journal terminology.

Disclaimer
Every effort has been made to contact copyright holders for their permission to reprint material in this book. The publishers would be grateful to hear from any copyright holder who is not here acknowledged and will undertake to rectify any errors or omissions in future editions of this book.

Contents

Citation Information

The following chapters were originally published in various issues of *Community Development*. When citing this material, please use the original page numbering for each article, as follows:

Chapter 1
Observed Community Development Patterns: 1950–1970
Huey B. Long
Community Development, volume 3, issue 1 (1972) pp. 112–120

Chapter 2
The Basics: What's Essential about Theory for Community Development Practice?
Ronald J. Hustedde and Jacek Ganowicz
Community Development, volume 33, issue 1 (2002) pp. 1–19

Chapter 3
Theorizing Community Development
Jnanabrata Bhattacharyya
Community Development, volume 34, issue 2 (2004) pp. 5–34

Chapter 4
The Power of Community
M.A. Brennan and Glenn D. Israel
Community Development, volume 39, issue 1 (2008) pp. 82–98

Chapter 5
Theories of Poverty and Anti-Poverty Programs in Community Development
Ted K. Bradshaw
Community Development, volume 38, issue 1 (2007) pp. 7–25

Chapter 6
The Community Capitals Framework: an empirical examination of internal relationships
Kenneth Pigg, Stephen P. Gasteyer, Kenneth E. Martin, Kari Keating and Godwin P. Apaliyah
Community Development, volume 44, issue 4 (2013) pp. 492–502

For any permission-related enquiries please visit:
http://www.tandfonline.com/page/help/permissions

Contributors

Theodore R. Alter Department of Agricultural Economics and Rural Sociology, Penn State University, USA.

Martin G. Anderson Extension Community Resource Development Specialist, Cornell University, USA.

Godwin P. Apaliyah The Ohio State University Extension, Columbus, USA.

Janet Ayres Department of Agricultural Economics, Purdue University, West Lafayette, USA.

David Barkley Department of Applied Economics and Statistics, Clemson University, USA.

Jnanabrata Bhattacharyya Department of Political Science and Department of Community Development, Southern Illinois University at Carbondale, USA.

Robert Blair is Professor of Public Administration and Urban Studies at the College of Public Affairs, University of Nebraska, Omaha, USA.

Andy S. Blanke Centre for Governmental Studies, Northern Illinois University, DeKalb, USA.

Ted K. Bradshaw Department of Human and Community Development, University of California, Davis, USA.

M.A. Brennan Department of Family, Youth, and Community Sciences, University of Florida, Gainesville, USA.

Jeffrey C. Bridger Department of Agricultural Economics and Rural Sociology, Penn State University, USA.

Ralph A. Catalano University of California, Irvine, USA.

Tom Daniels Department of Geography and Planning, State University of New York at Albany, USA.

Mary Emery North Central Regional Center for Rural Development, Iowa State University, Ames, USA.

Cornelia Flora North Central Regional Center for Rural Development, Iowa State University, Ames, USA.

David Freshwater Department of Agricultural Economics, University of Kentucky, Lexington, USA.

Jacek Ganowicz Department of Anthropology, Sociology, and Social Work, Eastern Kentucky University, Richmond, USA.

Stephen P. Gasteyer Sociology, Michigan State University, East Lansing, USA.

Willis J. Goudy Department of Sociology and Anthropology, Iowa State University, Ames, USA.

Beth Walter Honadle School of Planning, College of Design, Architecture, Art and Planning, University of Cincinnati, USA.

Otto G. Hoiberg Community Development, University Extension Division, University of Nebraska, USA.

Ronald J. Hustedde Department of Community and Leadership Development, University of Kentucky, Lexington, USA.

Glenn D. Israel Department of Agricultural Education and Communications, University of Florida, Gainesville, USA.

Kari Keating Agricultural Education Program, University of Illinois, Urbana, USA.

Nailya Kutzhanova School of Urban and Public Affairs, University of Louisville, USA.

Larry Leistritz Department of Agricultural Economics, North Dakota State University, Fargo, USA.

Gregg A. Lichtenstein President, Collaborative Strategies LLC.

Huey B. Long Department of Adult Education, University of Georgia, USA.

Thomas S. Lyons Community Development, School of Urban and Public Affairs, University of Louisville, USA.

Deborah Markley Centre for Rural Entrepreneurship, USA.

Kenneth E. Martin The Ohio State University Extension, Columbus, USA.

Rhonda Phillips is Dean, Purdue University Honors College, West Lafayette, USA.

Kenneth Pigg Rural Sociology, University of Missouri, Columbia, USA.

Glen C. Pulver Department of Agricultural Economics, University of Wisconsin-Madison, USA.

Donald C. Reitzes Department of Sociology, Georgia State University, Atlanta, USA.

Dietrich C. Reitzes Department of Sociology, Roosevelt University, Chicago, USA.

Ron Shaffer University of Wisconsin-Madison/Extension, USA.

Kenneth Stone Department of Economics, Iowa State University, Ames, USA

John L. Tait Department of Sociology and Anthropology, Iowa State University, Ames, USA.

Norman Walzer is Senior Research Scholar at the Center for Governmental Services, Northern Illinois University, DeKalb, USA.

Kenneth P. Wilkinson Department of Agricultural Economics and Rural Sociology, Pennsylvania State University, USA.

Kimberly Zeuli Department of Agricultural and Applied Economics, University of Wisconsin-Madison, USA.

INTRODUCTION: AN OVERVIEW OF 50 YEARS OF COMMUNITY DEVELOPMENT

A History of Its Evolution and Application in North America

Norman Walzer, Robert Blair, and Rhonda Phillips[1]

This two-volume set presents a wide range of topics and issues covered over five decades in the journal, *Community Development (CD)*, the journal of the Community Development Society, published since 1970. By doing so, attention is drawn to both the complexity and relevance of community development as a field of study and practice. There can be little question that community development has changed during this time period, with many issues and challenges emerging.

An especially important aspect of *CD* as a publication is that it provides outlets for interactions between academic researchers and practitioners with definite advantages to each group. In fact, this interaction is often mentioned in discussions at Community Development Society (hereafter referred to as the "Society") meetings as a major reason for continued participation. For example, it is often the case that practitioners identify topics that need additional study and researchers apply scientific methods in identifying and evaluating potential strategies to address them. This teamwork contributes to effective practices and improvements in quality of life in communities. Interactions along these lines are what motivated launching the *Journal of Community Development* in 1970. It has continued for 50 volumes and, in the process, grew to the current five issues per year spanning a broad range of topics.

To create this book set on the history and evolution of community development, numerous articles were selected across several categories to illustrate the importance and impact of community development research and practice. While many contributions from around the globe have contributed to community development scholarship, the focus of these books is on North American practices and research. During the past several years, the authors (past editors of *CD*) compiled a list of articles published with the aim to generate a collection of representative contributions that the journal has made to the literature over five decades. Key researchers were surveyed, and presentations with discussions were held at Community Development Society conferences along with download counts in recent years. These efforts produced a list of articles by decade and topic that provide an overall picture of how issues changed, as seen by journal authors and contributors. The books are organized into two volumes, the first containing two sections: Community history and theory, and planning and policy development. The second volume presents three sections: Leadership development; justice, inclusion, and participation; and healthy and resilient communities. Each section includes an introduction.

The coverage by the journal reflects an aspect that community development as a discipline has had to address. The early focus was on rural development issues with the major focus in the early 1970s on this area as a priority. The range of topics soon moved from economic development to much broader topics such as poverty, housing, health, and other social issues that community leaders in both rural and metro areas had to address. Especially important is the recognition that these issues are intertwined and require collaboration among practitioners, public leaders, and academics trained in many disciplines. The journal continues to provide an outlet for these discussions making the editing process somewhat complex.

The journal remains broad enough in coverage to include contributions from disciplines that might not be included in outlets with a narrower and more focused coverage. Consequently, this broader and interdisciplinary perspective sometimes made it more difficult for community development to earn recognition as an independent academic and professional field of study by both scholars and practitioners. The Society still wrestles with this issue and is working to define topics and a field of study that should be covered in academic programs designed to train practitioners. Likewise, a debate continues whether a professional certification is appropriate, and, if so, what topics should be included to maximize the value to practitioners.

Throughout these discussions, *Community Development*[2] (CD) as a journal promoted the credibility and expertise of community development professionals and helped them guide communities to select policies based on tested theories and approaches used elsewhere. Because *CD* is a peer-refereed publishing outlet, it can command respect by scholars and its articles are cited in many other journals so is able to advance the knowledge on community development issues. As an outlet for interdisciplinary research and discussions, *CD* created its niche and continues to be used by a variety of both academics and practitioners. Practitioners identify relevant issues and concerns while scholars explore and document contributing factors and potential remedies. This teamwork provides direction to community development practices and boosts the credibility of community developers as they address a myriad and changing set of issues in their practices.

CHANGING COMMUNITY DEVELOPMENT TOPICS

Time and space do not permit an intensive discussion of these myriad changing topics; rather, several topics are discussed in the following sections along with references to articles during specific time periods to illustrate how ideas progressed. Defining community development precisely is difficult but a suitable place to start is with the Principles of Good Practice (POG) endorsed by the Community Development Society that sponsors the publication of *Community Development*. These principles include the following:

- Promote active and representative participation toward enabling all community members to meaningfully influence the decisions that affect their lives.
- Engage community members in learning about and understanding community issues, and the economic, social, environmental, political, psychological, and other impacts associated with alternative courses of action.
- Incorporate the diverse interests and cultures of the community in the community development process, and disengage from support of any effort that is likely to adversely affect the disadvantaged members of a community.
- Work actively to enhance the leadership capacity of community members, leaders, and groups within the community.

- Be open to using the full range of action strategies to work toward the long-term sustainability and well-being of the community (CDS, 2020, p. 1).

The Principles encompass a broad range of research and practice topics in *CD*. For many reasons, this breadth of topics has enabled *CD* to be a platform for active discussions among Society members – scholars as well as practitioners. The topics covered have changed with both community development issues and interests by scholars/practitioners in researching these topics.

Rural Development. The journal began in an era that focused on addressing rural concerns through regional solutions. For example, the Appalachian Rural Development Act (1965) recognized concerns in many low-income areas and funded agencies to address them. The U.S. Economic Development Administration, under the Public Works and Economic Development Act (1965), took a broader approach to rural issues in general and with financial assistance for regions to design overall economic development strategies. These and other issues motivated early discussions by both Society founders and researchers, and affected the types of topics published in the journal.

Thus, during the 1970s and 1980s, much research and interest by practitioners centered on issues facing rural areas including those resulting from the farm crises in that period (Pulver, 1989). Rural planning approaches with a more organized and consistent set of strategies were also researched in attempts to manage some of the rural concerns addressed. These concerns brought research that was reported in *CD* on a variety of rural-related planning issues (Blakely & Bradshaw, 1982).

Research on these topics was stimulated further by passage of the federal Rural Development Act (1972) that promoted efforts to find ways to help rural areas design a new future. Grant funds and technical assistance by federal agencies such as the U.S. Department of Housing and Urban Development provided opportunities, often with funding for local agencies in rural areas to expand planning and other efforts to address local issues and concerns. These strategies were sometimes based on research published in *CD* as federal financial support enhanced the need for solid research and a theoretical base for planning efforts in both rural and metro areas.

The topics published were expanded as the Society's clientele and interests broadened into finding new ways to address both urban and rural concerns and as community development became more accepted as a discipline based on solid research with a theoretical base and documented practices (Shaffer, 1990). The latter 1970s and early 1980s brought articles that integrated research with local development programs, examined participatory evaluation as a tool to bring community members into finding solutions, and looked for new approaches to long-term solutions (Goudy & Tait, 1979).

Consistent through these discussions was a need to focus on finding solid theoretical foundations that explain the inner workings of community development to continue enhancing its respect and acceptance as a discipline to study and pursue (Bhattacharyya, 2003). This basic direction for *CD* continues as is true of most scholarly outlets that try to link scholarship and practice.

Journal at 25 Years. A useful way to trace the changing topics in community development, especially in the early years of the journal, is to examine issues summarized 25 years ago by Blair and Hembd for the 25th anniversary volume. The editors at that time intended the volume to "reflect on and gauge the progress made in community development." The theme of the 25th volume – "What We Have Learned" – was a way to "reflect on the past and build for the future in community development...[providing] a forum to share important insights gained by people participating in community development the past quarter century." While many submitted manuscripts focused on theory, most emphasized practice. This emphasis reflects the ongoing purpose of *CD*: "to disseminate information on theory, research and practice" of community development. Manuscript reviewers for the special edition included practitioners, researchers, and community development educators. The reviewers emphasized the reflective nature of the 25th anniversary. The articles selected by the reviewers and editors were grouped into three broad categories: the community as an entity, the changing practice of community development, and development of small or rural communities.

It is an enlightening exercise to compare the three general themes of 25 years ago to community development in the 21st century. Community development, for instance, increasingly has taken an urban and neighborhood focus. The community, as the building block of society, which is part of the Society's Mission Statement, was examined in the first set of articles in the special edition. This emphasis has not changed in the subsequent 25 years. Authors explored the nature and structure of community development as a collective and inclusive collaborative process of the community residents.

The second set of articles examined both the practice and the process of community development, focusing on the facilitative role of community development practitioners. It is safe to conclude that the role of the community developer changed in the community development process with the growth in professionalism and knowledge of practices.

While the POG maintain their relevance, community development has become more complex. Several authors in the 25th edition anticipated that controversy would increasingly impact the practice of community development, as is clearly the case in the current environment. Other articles discussed ways that the profession of community development could be improved. The last general topic in the special edition addressed rural and small community development, a continued focus of the profession in its diamond anniversary. As we know, that is now the case with recent population declines and economic stagnation in many rural areas challenging their continued viability.

The 25th edition editors concluded from the scope of the articles that the theory and practice of community development had made significant strides from the birth of the Community Development Society (1969) to 1995, but admittedly more progress was needed in several areas. While much has been learned about community development since 1995, the scope of the profession has expanded to addressing urban issues and challenges, and the quality of community development research has contributed to a more robust set of applied theories of community development. However, essentially the same conclusion can be reached: We need to keep working and learning about community development.

Community and Economic Development. The early economic development literature devoted much attention to job creation and especially the use of financial incentives to lure manufacturing and other high-paying industries. These jobs, in turn, have local multiplier efforts that would stimulate local development. Of increasing importance was investing in workers (human capital) through education programs and workforce development to increase their capacity and make an area more attractive to private investment.

However, it also became clear that effective development practices required a strong community development focus, namely, how to build and strengthen broader community participation and contributions to finding remedies (Green, 2008). The many links between community and economic development capacities, factors, and functions emerged as increasingly important to both process and achieving desired outcomes (Pittman et al., 2009).

Equally clear was that society had changed as shown in discussions by Putnam in *Bowling Alone* in 1995. Residents now engaged in different types of activities, and membership/participation in traditional organizations was declining. Key to local development was to find new ways to engage these groups in community decision--making practices and betterment programs. With technology changes, residents spent less time in traditional group activities but, nevertheless, participated in other endeavors with special interest. In some respects, this scenario had contributed to a centralized decision-making "top-down" environment. This environment has begun to change more recently with more use of social media in community development.

Inclusion. Community development practitioners recognized that under-engaged populations such as minorities, females, and other groups were important contributors to local decision-making. Residents were shifting in how they interacted with groups so new ways to engage these residents in decisions about community issues and projects were discussed in more detail as an essential component of the community development process to enhance social well-being.

During the 1980s, *CD* articles described ways to better engage females and other groups in these processes (Lackey & Burke, 1984; Scott & Johnson, 2005). Much attention has been paid to approaches, tools, and techniques for resident or stakeholder participation. Given community development's roots in social change, issues around inclusion, participation, social justice, and related continued to evolve throughout the past five decades.

Small Business Emphasis. In addition, economic development thinking shifted from focusing mainly on attracting large plants to communities through incentives to finding ways to help local investors launch new businesses. Interest grew in finding ways to stimulate these efforts by focusing on entrepreneurship, small business finance, and related approaches (Lichtenstein, Lyons, & Kutzhanova, 2004). These initiatives were supported by federal agencies such as the Small Business Administration and were part of a national focus and local initiatives.

Local Leadership. The growing professionalism of community development recognized that effective local leaders are key to community sustainability and prosperity. *CD* contained an active discussion (1990s and later) of how to generate local leaders as well as the effects or outcomes when it does not exist. Issues were discussed such as the existence of community lifecycles, and ways to alter it through aggressive external and local intervention via active leadership.

Importance of the Capitals. Social capital grew in importance as an essential ingredient of community development which was crucial to effective local development – both business and industrial development. The five capitals such as financial, natural, produced, human, and social were recognized as elements that could be actively built and maintained in communities and, in fact, are essential for sustainability. Discussions of ways to engage a broad participation by residents in a community became an important part of effective community development (Emery & Flora, 2006). Strategies to deal with these issues were developed and empirically tested under different scenarios. Building and maintaining social capital are critical to community development, and these topics were an important part of discussions in *CD* during the 2000s.

The foundational concepts provided by the community capitals, especially in the context of asset-based community development, also helped in developing scholarship regarding sustainable, healthy, and resilient community approaches and applications. Resilience builds on assets to respond to shocks to community systems, such as those promulgated by natural or human-made disasters. A special issue on resilience provided resources for exploring the connection between sustainability, community development, capitals, and resilience (Cafer, Green, & Goreham, 2019; Kirkpatrick, 2019).

Measuring Outcomes. Measuring the outcomes from community development practices became increasingly important in discussions with both academics and practitioners as necessary to enhance the credibility of community development. The multi-dimensional nature of community issues complicates measuring outcomes but without solid information regarding effectiveness of strategies it is more difficult for practitioners to select and implement effective approaches. Thus, *CD* published many articles documenting the effects of development strategies to learn in which circumstances and scenarios they are effective and how they have a sound theoretical basis (Brennan & Brown, 2008).

Successful and lasting community change has been difficult to measure as well as to document successful strategies. This concern has been pursued by academics, practitioners, and agencies such as foundations that for many years invested in local groups interested in bringing about community change (Blanke & Walzer, 2013). The growth in Collective Impact and similar approaches that provide a framework to bring lasting change was an outcome of these discussions. The debate on measuring community change and factors that are important will continue as new approaches are formulated and implemented by community leaders in efforts to make desired and sustained community improvements. These discussions are at the heart of overall community development practice and are key to maintaining the credibility that community development practices have earned over the years.

THEMES IN THE 50TH ANNIVERSARY COLLECTION

Five major themes are explored in the two-volume book set. As previously mentioned, there are myriad topics, issues, challenges, and opportunities to discuss in community development but these five were selected via scan of articles present in *CD* since 1970. The following discussions provide information and insights about these areas: community history and theory; planning and policy development; leadership development; justice, inclusion, and participation; and healthy and resilient communities. Surely, other topics could have been included, and it is the editors' intention to encourage more exploration, scholarship, and application of these and many more areas of interest.

Community History and Theory

Community development evolved during the past 50 years both as a theoretical discipline and an important field of practice as the need for a better understanding of ways to enhance quality of life and living conditions grew. This evolution was even more complex because multiple academic and professional disciplines are involved in research about the importance of critical issues and best practices. Thus, a challenge facing community development involves incorporating research in each discipline and forging it into a comprehensive set of programs or tools to help improve quality of life and promote economic development vital to the future of an area.

Early discussions focused on economic development and creating employment using successful best practices in the past. As the study of development issues advanced, there was a better understanding that quality of life and living conditions are essential to business attraction and investment – both from internal and external sources. The shift from direct employment generating strategies to providing a conducive investment climate brought a need for a discipline that helps both explain and improve living conditions. Quality of life helps make an area attractive not only to current or potential residents but also entrepreneurs interested in starting or expanding businesses.

Understanding how local governance and strategies make the difference between prosperous and stagnant communities became more important. But was there a theory, or set of theories, to help explain how these conditions develop? More was known about industrial location factors or other economic development considerations than about determinants of quality of life and the importance of what is now termed social capital. This focus continued to change with discussions of community capitals that can be used to monitor and evaluate community change processes.

At the same time, there was growing interest in how Federal programs could help local government agencies create strategic plans with strong potential for development including job creation. This interest went beyond job creation only. It also recognized the need to work with populations disadvantaged in ways that prevented them from participating effectively in development efforts and to bring them more actively into local decision-making processes.

Poverty and housing issues gained more attention, and Federal programs offered technical assistance and incentives to local agencies for housing plus helped provide opportunities for disadvantaged residents to build skills through education and training programs. Some of these efforts might be considered more under the realm of community development than economic development, but they all are vital to the growth and prosperity of communities.

One outcome of this evolution was a better understanding that research on these activities was underway in many disciplines including sociology, economics, housing, and political science or others, but those literatures were not readily accessible to policymakers and even scholars working on a specific issue. In essence, there did not yet exist a clear discipline called community development.

The Community Development Society was an outgrowth of the need to incorporate the research and practice from related disciplines and to host discussions among representatives from each field around issues facing communities. Early discussions often focused on rural communities with limited technical expertise that were losing populations and facing economic stagnation. However, during the 1960s and 1970s, social unrest in large cities reinforced an understanding that neighborhoods in these areas function much like a community and must be better understood to design policies to alleviate some of the conditions. While many policies and practices differed from those used in smaller rural areas, the principles often were similar and based on the current research efforts.

The Society laid out a set of principles and practices, described previously, that could be applied to community development efforts in different scenarios. It also started a journal allowing scholars and practitioners to test their research findings in applications. Practitioners, in turn, can share their findings and further stimulate scholarly research. This multi-disciplinary approach was relatively unique because it reaches a more diverse audience while, at the same time, providing a peer-refereed outlet to evaluate work to add to the literature. The interaction between scholars and practitioner is invaluable in the growth and understanding of community development as an accepted academic discipline that trains future practitioners. The discipline continues to change as conditions in community development evolve.

Articles included in the community history and theory section highlight major contributions that advanced our understanding of important community formation and development components. Central to the early discussions was a need for a solid theoretical foundation that could give the discipline of community development credibility. The fact that diverse academic disciplines contribute to this body of knowledge complicated the development and understanding of this literature but strengthened the outcomes as scholars from multiple disciplines evaluated the work.

Especially noteworthy in advancing community development as a discipline and policy tool was recognizing the importance of "community" in addressing both rural and urban social needs (Pulver, 1989). A community is not necessarily a locality; rather, it is a group of people pursuing a common goal as noted by Brennan and Israel (2008). Understanding the role of the community casts a different perspective on policy formation. Likewise a focusing on outcomes or results became more important as a policy issue (Bhattacharyya, 2004). Top-down leadership may not always yield the most effective results. A broad cross-section of residents must engage in finding solutions that will work in the community. This participation in building or finding the solution is essential to make it work.

Another major contribution to community development thinking was viewing community as having as set of capitals that can be managed somewhat as in a business venture (Emery & Flora, 2006). The capitals, unless maintained, can reduce the sense of community and contribute to the decline of an area. Recognizing the importance of social capital, for instance, has spawned extensive research and many discussions regarding ways in which this component of community development can be advanced. Policies changed in approach because of this research.

Perhaps even more important is a widespread recognition of social capital as a necessary ingredient in a healthy community. It builds on previous work which differentiated community from a geographic location. This understanding enabled community development to embrace the work of several academic disciplines and opened the doors to new policies addressing social issues. Community development took a more holistic approach with scholars applying cutting-edge research in their separate disciplines.

The professional literature also emphasized the importance of internal communication within a community regarding policy issues. Informed constituents are more effective in leadership positions and in policy selection and implementation. The journal contributes to this communication process by providing information about policy options and issues at a professional, as well as academic level to help advance effective local decisions with lasting positive outcomes.

While poverty reduction continues as a major issue in community development discussions, the topics broadened to include housing, job creation, workforce training, transportation, and others that directly affect welfare of residents. Many of these issues interact and policies to address them must be coordinated. Community development as a field of study made serious contributions to policy development, and *CD* is a vehicle to share research and best practices on these initiatives by providing interactive discussions. In this way, it remains a reservoir of best practices along with theoretical bases for their effectiveness.

Because of these contributions, community development is on a par with economic development in creating livable communities where people want to live and work. Policies to improve quality of life and investment are in play around the world, and many factors leading to effective policy development have been discussed in the journal.

Planning and Policy Development

As noted, community development processes include a set of interconnected activities designed to improve a community and enhance the quality of life of its residents. These activities may include community demographic and economic information, analyses of trends, identification of community assets and challenges, formulation of sustainable development strategies, and the creation and an action plan implemented by area residents and entities. This is a time-consuming and strenuous undertaking involving a range of community stakeholders. Essential to this process are the planning and development of strategies and policies for the betterment of the community.

Articles in the planning and policy development section of this volume connect the principles, practices, and theories of planning and policy development to the process of community development. Not only do these articles provide a conceptual foundation to the art and craft of community development, they emphasize a critical component of the Community Development Society, namely, the importance of engaging residents in the community development process. The POG advocates that the community developer needs to facilitate meaningful engagement by promoting participation, involving community members, incorporating diverse interests, and enhancing community leadership, and be open to a full range of development strategies.

Meeting the objectives of the POG is not an easy task. However, the articles in the section on planning and policy development provide community developers with a range of tools, methods, and perspectives consistent with the Principles. At the same time, the guidance and information in this set of articles provide community developers with the practical and realistic skills required to assist the residents in the complex process of community development.

While articles in this section clearly address the community and resident engagement dimension as the foundation to the community development process, they also furnish valuable insights and cutting-edge research on other aspects of the process. Perhaps most importantly, the authors give community developers the ability to perform various aspects of their professional orientation and responsibility: a facilitator, a technical expert, and a community advocate.

On the other hand, because of the diversity of communities, the authors in this section note that there is no perfect approach to community development. Adaptability, then, becomes a key operating principle, as many obstacles and challenges will present themselves. Unfortunately, not every community development initiative meets with success, and the process of community development takes time and effort, as the articles discuss.

In addition to advocating community engagement as the foundation to the community development process, several key themes arise in the articles. Arguably, one key theme in several articles is the notion that community development includes a range of strategies and policies. This idea promotes a more comprehensive and holistic view of community development at a time when researchers began to question the viability of targeted and specific industrial development strategies. Working with community developers, then, residents have a range of development choices. The Community Capitals Framework provides residents with the ability to evaluate and select viable and diverse development strategies. Several articles provide guidance on this aspect of community development.

Organizational collaboration is another key theme discussed in several articles. The authors provide community developers with the ability to craft regional collaborative structures and partnerships among a range of public, private, and nonprofit entities. A community needs a number of partners to succeed in crafting and implementing development strategies.

Finally, several articles give the readers of *CD* insights into innovative approaches to the community development process. Authors address emerging community development issues and challenges, such as sustainability and urban sprawl, while others offered new information on improving community development tools of interactional techniques, collaborative strategies, and program evaluation.

The articles in the section on planning and policy development demonstrate that *CD* in the past 50 years has offered critical guidance on this important aspect of the community development process. *CD*, as an interdisciplinary journal, provides support not only to the community development profession, but also to other groups devoted to improving the quality of life in communities, such as planners, city managers, economic developers, public administrators, and developers of public policy.

Leadership Development

Local leadership is prominent throughout discussions of community development and change. It is essential in both identifying important issues and selecting among policies that will generate lasting results. Creating effective leadership can be difficult even when opportunities exist because it involves engaging a broad cross-section of residents, many with little or no past leadership experience. In some cases, a lack of sufficient credibility may hinder acceptance by others with more vested interests or experiences.

Leadership within a community often involves a process where long-time residents or groups experienced in past initiatives or investments in the community are elected or appointed to leadership roles. Self-interest, in some cases, may encourage a willingness to serve. While this model is fairly common, it can lead to status quo development approaches with less inclination to consider new development approaches or directions. It also can tend to overlook the needs or opportunities of groups not active in discussions or, for other reasons, are overlooked in the community.

A distributed leadership approach, for many reasons, can be more effective but it is also harder to implement. Finding highly qualified or motivated residents with the confidence to take leaderships roles is often difficult. In some instances, they also may not have the time and resources or be able to spend time away from work to participate in leadership roles. Without positive past leadership experiences, they may lack confidence to run for office or apply for appointed positions. The result is that significant groups in the community or development opportunities are overlooked or dismissed.

Important to understand is that community development projects are more likely to succeed when they have been built by and involve broad groups of residents. Residents must accept both the goals and strategies to commit and participate effectively. Without this support, local efforts are less likely to achieve strong results. A main leadership issue, then, is finding ways to engage diverse groups in determining objectives and projects that the community can achieve in light of resources available.

The leadership section in this volume begins with an article reporting types of local self-development strategies used across the US. High on the list of strategies implemented were tourism and cultural activities, business expansion and retention, industrial development, and historic preservation and restoration projects. Locally organized development groups complemented efforts by more traditional economic development organizations. This collaboration and focus on cultural activities and historic preservation and restoration enhances quality of life and living conditions as well as stimulates job creation.

The importance of a holistic approach to community and economic development justifies time spent working with groups in a locality to guide their collaborative efforts to reach community goals. Many different groups and organizations must be brought to the table with significant roles to play. Sometimes overlooked in leadership discussions are the roles played by nonprofit organizations. They provide essential services to both residents and business so are important to success. At the same time, however, these organizations assemble groups around key social issues and give them a voice in community discussions. They also can create less threatening leadership opportunities for residents who might otherwise be overlooked or ignored. Thus, the supportive roles played by nonprofits are key to leadership successes.

Much attention has been paid to ways to build local leadership and qualities that make it function. Robinson (1994) identified 10 basic principles or opportunities for leadership development. At the core, he suggests leadership opportunities exist in most organizations, but it is a matter of matching opportunities with people who have both the ability and interest. This highlights the importance of finding people who traditionally have not participated in these opportunities even though they may have had the potential.

Identifying potential leaders is the first step but equally important is to build support within the community for them to succeed. While they often have knowledge about a specific issue or have support from small groups of residents, they may not have sufficient experience or exposure to be accepted community-wide. Helping them succeed in a distributed leadership approach requires commitment from many players and may be one of the more difficult aspects of local leadership development. When it works well, though, it may create a positive contagion effect within the community that encourages others to be involved in discussions.

The literature on leadership also provides analyses about which approach is most likely to succeed. Top-down approaches often occur automatically on some issues, and this approach may work because leaders are focused on specific outcomes or directions. In other instances, though, a broader-based leadership model offers opportunities for community involvement in both setting goals and designing approaches to address specific issues. Thus, operationally, specific issues and circumstances are important in selecting the most suitable leadership approach for successful outcomes. At the very least, building leadership opportunities and engaging broader population groups are likely to enhance both interest and engagement in successful community development outcomes.

The political establishment plays an especially important role(s) in leadership development. While elected leaders have support from many groups, they cannot always commit residents to actions on specific issues. What they can provide, however, are opportunities to appoint knowledgeable residents who have not been active in these discussions in the past. Thus, elected leaders not only are responsible for designing and implementing effective community development policies, they also can build an active infrastructure for leadership engagement in the future.

An article in the section on leadership studied attitudes of minority residents regarding key factors that are considered important in community development decisions. These groups sometimes have not actively participated in past discussions. The findings from focus group discussions reveal that minorities, an often overlooked group in communities, place trust in program outcomes as highest in motivating people to participate. In other words, the program must have credibility that positive outcomes will happen in order to be accepted by these groups.

Also important is that development process and outcomes are driven by residents further supporting the importance of community engagement processes. Sense of community was also highly rated because greater acceptance of a project and engagement by residents lead to longer-lasting involvement and increase the prospects for success.

The importance of effective leadership in community development projects and outcomes cannot be overstated. Equally important to understand is that while leadership opportunities exist, they also must be developed and nurtured to engage broad-based support within the community. This sometimes means a concerted effort by elected leaders to actively engage affected residents even those with little past experience and established credibility.

The literature on leadership development is extensive and continues to growth as new opportunities arise and strategies are found. The articles in the leadership section are only the beginning but can help guide readers to find ways to stimulate and maintain community development projects.

Justice, Inclusion, and Participation

As noted, community development evolved from deep roots in social change, so issues of justice, inclusion, and participation have long been an important focus. This section of the book set recognizes the need to include all members of a community, especially those who are underrepresented. As part of the need to be more inclusive, much attention has been paid to approaches, tools, and techniques for resident or stakeholder participation. Both inclusion and participation may help foster better social justice processes and outcomes in community development.

The history of development is laced with responses to oppression and social ills; many examples exist where an injustice is the motivating factor to embark on the path of social change making. There is also an underlying foundational concept in community development that has existed since its earliest efforts and that is participation. As discussed previously, participation is a way for residents of a community to engage in decision-making. It represents more too – the idea and opportunity for people to be free to express themselves and participate in their own governance (Phillips & Kraeger, 2018).

Social justice is often discussed in efforts to enhance community development. Less clear is how it translates into processes and approaches for effecting desirable changes. In many cases, a sense of normative (or what should be) imperative may fuel desire for addressing social injustices directly. This normative standard is something to strive for in community development applications. It can also be thought of as a way of "giving voice, or agency, to the unrepresented (as)...a vital function of community development" (Phillips & Kraeger, 2018, p. 3).

Paul Davidoff was an urban planner and social justice and equity activist. He describes the need to rouse the nation to rectify racial and other social injustices, describing social inequalities and the need for greater inclusion in planning and development decision-making. He wrote of this need 55 years ago, and it still holds true today. Davidoff described a world in upheaval around the distribution of resources of nations and the inequities this was causing. While many things have changed since the 1960s, some have remained – by some metrics, there is more unequal distribution than ever before, with widening gaps between the richest and poorest people across the globe.

How then are scholars and practitioners of community development to respond? Given the enormity of the situation where structural barriers exist that divide people along social, economic, political, and other lines, how can communities move forward? Again, the underlying foundations of participation and inclusion are central. By more accessible decision-making and residents being a part of the processes for decisions that impact their lives, issues around social justice have a better chance of being addressed. In other words, inclusion and participation can aid in improving situations for residents. If community development processes are striving to be inclusive, then more people are represented across differences.

An example that can illustrate the connection between participation, inclusion, and striving for social justice improvements can be found in the arts. Artists may be among the first to call attention to social injustices or oppression in communities or societies. Indeed, social justice movements have arisen from efforts first initiated by artists calling attention and fueling desire for change. Culture is also an element influencing community connection that is so central to achieving desirable community development outcomes. It is often seen as "a motivating factor in the creation of social identity and serves as a basis for creating cohesion and solidarity," and these elements are crucial for connecting and enabling community members to take action (Brennan & Phillips, 2020, p. 5). Arts, artists, and culture are indeed a motivating force and are seen throughout the journal's history with both theoretical and applied works.

There are many at work in communities striving for improvements in quality of life and to foster a more just and inclusive environment. With works spanning 50 years, our hope is that the articles included in the section on justice, inclusion, and participation will inspire more attention to these crucial components of community development.

Healthy and Resilient Communities

Since the 1990s especially, ideas about healthy communities have been included in discussions of community development. It is an outgrowth of the desire to make improvements in quality of life, and since health is a major determinant, it is a well-deserved area of study. Health at the individual and collective, or community, level should be a central consideration of community development practices as it relates to health of the natural environment (water and air quality, for example), fresh food supply, and supporting infrastructure such as access to health care.

There is also a connected concept, that of community well-being, that is rapidly gaining more attention. Because well-being of communities is deeply and intricately connected with community development, it would be difficult to imagine that well-being at the collective or community level can be achieved without effective and just practices in community development. Community well-being typically describes a state of conditions, or assessment of health and related aspects. Health and resilience both are domains that connect community development and community well-being, and, as such, are important to include.

As mentioned, efforts began in the 1990s to make health a featured consideration of development processes. The World Health Organization launched the Healthy Cities Program, including indicators such as air quality, access to medical care, and nutrition. One of the first responses to this call to action in the US at the community level was that of Hampton, Virginia. With their Healthy Families Partnership, the city focused on improving parenting skills of residents, including prenatal and postnatal health and education to encourage healthy childhood experiences (Phillips, 2003). The results were impactful and helped to improve health outcomes in the community; these efforts were connected to other community development programs as well.

A second area of interest in this section is that of resilient communities. This is an area that continues to be of high interest, given the many anthropogenic and natural disasters that strike communities. With climate change bringing more incidences, resilience is a focus of many communities located in areas of high risk. This aspect of community development will continue to gain momentum and scholarship as need increases, it is often deeply connected with the disaster management and risk assessment field.

Resilience provides some contextual grounding for connecting to community development. For example, communities that are more prepared will be able to respond more quickly and efficiently. Often, indicators are used as part of the tool set in resilience planning, such as those for quality of life and for identifying, measuring, and monitoring conditions. Indicators and other tools can help communities expand or develop capacity to effectively plan for and respond to need; those communities with social capacity are better able to respond to need (Phillips, 2015). In many ways, resilience can be thought of as social community capacity as it influences adaptability and ability to recover.

As noted in the section on healthy and resilient communities in Volume 2, there are many aspects to consider, ranging from isolation and loneliness, to access to health care and education, to how to build ability to recover from disaster. Certainly, these aspects will play an even bigger role in community development in the future.

SUMMARY

Community Development: Journal of the Community Development Society (now known as "*Community Development*") continues to provide an outlet for researchers on many aspects of community development. Growth from two issues per year to five issues increased its status as a research journal but it still faces challenges as it works to gain an even higher ranking among other journals as measured by number of citations and other factors. Achieving this status will attract additional authors and increase the flow and quality of submissions to *CD*.

At the same time, *CD* must cater to interests of both academics and practitioners in a diversity of associated disciplines. Meeting the needs and interests of diverse markets will continue to be a challenge but addressing the core market for a journal such as *CD* is essential in meeting its market niche. The range of topics included in *CD* will widen in the future as new topics gain importance. This trend is likely to make managing *CD* more difficult yet rewarding as future needs and challenges unfold.

Community development is a growing field of interest as the complexity of managing projects increases. Workforces adjusting to demographic changes with an aging population; housing market changes as well as shrinking retail markets due to internet competition; the inclusion and impact of rapidly evolving technology; overall community well-being and quality-of-life concerns; and changes in transportation demands are only a few of the issues community developers will face in the future.

CD also must adjust to competition from electronic publishing outlets that can respond to interest in specific topics quickly and inexpensively. Many, if not most, major journals offer electronic access to publications. A growing number of private outlets can offer a quicker turnaround. If they are accepted in university or business promotion and advancement schemes, they will represent competition for journals such as *CD*.

Nevertheless, community development is growing in professionalism and relevance for public policy development. *CD* has a definite market niche in serving both academics and practitioners. Combined with an annual conference that attracts an international audience, the future looks bright for both *CD* and the Society as an organization that offers a ready source of information about current effective policies and practices. This two-volume set on the history of community development via the lens of the journal, *CD,* hopefully will deepen the understanding of both research and practice. By doing so, a new generation of practice and scholarship will be informed by learning from the past 50 years.

NOTES

1. Walzer is Senior Research Scholar, Center for Governmental Studies, Northern Illinois University, and served as *CD* co-editor from 2005 to 2007. Blair is Professor of Public Administration and Urban Studies, University of Nebraska at Omaha, and served as *CD* editor from 1992 to 1997. Phillips is Professor of Agricultural Economics and Dean of the Honors College at Purdue University and served as *CD* editor from 2007 to 2012, transitioning publication to Taylor & Francis.

2. In 2006, the *Journal of Community Development* was renamed *Community Development: Journal of the Community Development Society* to reduce confusion by rating agencies with the *Community Development Journal* published in the UK.

REFERENCES

Bhattacharyya, J. 2004. Theorizing community development. *Journal of the Community Development Society* 34(2): 5–34, DOI: 10.1080/15575330409490110

Blakely, E.J. & Bradshaw, T.K. 1982. New roles for community developers in rural growth communities. *Journal of the Community Development Society* 13(2): 101–120, DOI: 10.1080/15575330.1982.9987154

Blanke, A. & Walzer, N. 2013. Measuring community development: What have we learned? *Community Development* 44(5): 534–550, DOI: 10.1080/15575330.2013.852595

Brennan, M.A. & Brown, R.B. 2008. Community theory: Current perspectives and future directions. *Community Development* 39(1): 1–4, DOI: 10.1080/15575330809489737

Brennan, M. & Israel, G. D. 2008. The power of society, *Community Development* 39: 82–98.

Brennan, M. & Phillips, R. 2020. Culture, community, and development: A critical interrelationship. In R. Phillips, M. Brennan & T. Li (eds.), *Culture, Community and Development.* 15–27. London: Routledge.

Cafer, A., Green, J., & Goreham. G. 2019. A community resilience framework for community development practitioners building equity and adaptive capacity. *Community Development* 50(2): 201–216, DOI: 10.1080/15575330.2019.1575442

Community Development Society (CDS). 2020. Principles of good practice. Retrieved 20 January from: https://www.comm-dev.org/about/principles-of-good-practice.

Emery, M. & Flora, C. 2006. Spiraling-up: Mapping community transformation with community capitals framework. *Community Development* 37(1): 19–35, DOI: 10.1080/15575330609490152

Goudy, W.J. & Tait, J.L. 1979. Integrating research with local community-development programs. *Journal of the Community Development Society* 10(2): 37–50, DOI: 10.1080/15575330.1979.9987091

Green, J. 2008. Community development as social movement: A contribution to models of practice. *Community Development* 39(1): 50–62, DOI: 10.1080/15575330809489741

Kirkpatrick, S.J.B. 2019. Using disaster recovery knowledge as a roadmap to community resilience. *Community Development* 50(2): 123–140, DOI: 10.1080/15575330.2019.1574269

Lackey, A.S. & Burke, J.L. 1984. Women in community development 1970–1980: A decade of change. *Journal of the Community Development Society* 15(1): 99–114, DOI: 10.1080/15575338409490077

Lichtenstein, G., Lyons, T.S., & Kutzhanova, N. 2004. Building entrepreneurial communities: The appropriate role of enterprise development activities. *Journal of the Community Development Society* 35(1): 5–24, DOI: 10.1080/15575330409490119

Phillips, R. 2003. *Community Indicators*. Planning Advisory Service, Report Number 517. Chicago, IL: American Planning Association.

Phillips, R. 2015. Community quality-of-life indicators to avoid tragedies. Pp. 293–304 in R. Anderson (ed.), *World Suffering and Quality of Life*. Dordrecht, The Netherlands: Springer.

Phillips, R. & Kraeger, P. 2018. General Introduction. Pp. 1–12 in R. Phillips & P. Kraeger, (eds.), *Community Planning and Development*, Volume 1. London: Routledge.

Pittman, R., Pittman, E., Phillips, R., & Cangelosi, J. 2009. The community and economic development chain: Validating the links between processes and outcomes. *Community Development* 40(1): 80–93, DOI: 10.1080/15575330902918956

Pulver, G.C. 1989. Developing a community perspective on rural economic development policy. *Journal of the Community Development Society* 20(2): 1–14, DOI: 10.1080/15575338909489979

Robinson, J. 1994. Ten basic principles of leadership in community development organizations. *Journal of the Community Development Society* 25(1): 44–48, DOI: 10.1080/15575339409489893

Scott, J. & Johnson, T.G. 2005. Bowling alone but online together: Social capital in e-communities. *Community Development* 36(1): 9–27, DOI: 10.1080/15575330509489868

Shaffer, R. 1990. Building economically viable communities: A role for community developers. *Journal of the Community Development Society* 21(2): 74–87, DOI: 10.1080/15575339009489962

Section 1
Community History and Theory
Introduction

Community development, as a discipline, started as a need to help areas strategize and plan to improve economic and social conditions as well as economic potential. Federal programs in the 1960s and 1970s emphasized the importance for local areas to plan effectively, and, in some instances, it provided federal funds to improve local conditions in distressed areas (Appalachian Redevelopment Act).

More sophisticated state and local planning initiatives focused attention on the importance of capacity-building within a community, namely, strengthening leadership and active engagement by a broad spectrum of residents in efforts to improve housing and living conditions in many local areas. These initiatives also spawned interest in ways to plan more effectively and a greater recognition of the importance of engaging residents in the overall planning and decision-making processes. Interest and study of processes involved and ways to enhance development grew as educational institutions engaged in more instruction and research on these topics.

Hoiberg (1970) describes trends that led to a recognition of the importance of community development principles including an understanding of effective community development as a basis for economic development. Community development agencies were on the increase with a shift in focus from things to people. More attention to inner city problems and urbanization at the national level plus growing interest in professionalization of community development agencies and practices increased interest in building a discipline with theoretical underpinnings.

Many articles (not all included in this volume) contribute to an understanding of how community development issues evolved through time. Cary (1979) described the first decade of the Community Development Society (CDS) and the journal. He provides an excellent discussion of issues raised and their importance for those engaged in community development issues. Blair and Hembd (1994), not included in this volume, compiled a special issue of the journal that capsulized a history of CDS at 25 years plus important issues that had been discussed.

Walzer (2010), not included in this volume, summarized issues facing the CDS at age 40 with a discussion of the evolution of topics as well as expectations regarding future issues and how practitioners building on research reported in the journal can address pending issues. These publications summarize trends and discuss CDS as an organization, rather than focusing on how core issues in community development evolved.

In the 1970s, there was growing recognition that community growth and development often resulted from employment changes decided by groups external to the local area. Long (1972) compared three localities where external groups controlled local investment decisions on projects. The research highlighted the importance of local development groups actively working with, and providing support for, external investors. Essentially, it made the case that these groups can affect their futures by actively participating in development decisions.

Long documented the importance of internal forces and built underlying support for local community development practices, rather than relying external investment decisions. Recognizing this potential helped lay the groundwork for community development as an important contributor to overall local prosperity plus the need to better understand underlying development processes.

As community development components grew in importance, the literature paid more attention to key players and agencies involved plus how they determined, or could affect, development decisions. Could these groups use a common set of principles and practices to guide their actions? How does community development align with economic development which was also undergoing a transition that recognized the growing importance of small businesses in retaining and creating employment? The discussions shifted to the importance of local decisions and engagement in the pursuit of development.

Of special interest was the need for a consistent theory of community development along with ways to measure contributing factors and agree on successful outcomes. An advantage, but also a difficulty, is that many academic disciplines are involved in overlapping social, political, and economic issues. The literatures in these disciplines were not often incorporated in a systematic and holistic framework.

Thus, for community development to provide a solid basis for policy and practice, it needed a sound theoretical and research base for practitioners to use in selecting development strategies and policies. While each major discipline has scholarly and professional outlets for research, community development practitioners and scholars often did not publish in outlets beyond their specific field, making it difficult to incorporate useful advancements in knowledge or understanding of processes.

Early on, the *Journal of Community Development* provided an opportunity to compile, present, and synthesize research from multiple disciplines addressing an integrated concern – community development. This research brought more attention to the need for a consistent development theory that examines community engagement, how power in the community is distributed, and ways to engage an entire community in local decisions. Much research was underway in separate disciplines regarding how the development processes could work and practices that showed signs of having an effect. Alinski, for example, published examples of initiatives used in various communities, in some cases based on conflict strategies. At the same time, he recognized the importance and understanding of advancing social well-being which is a desired outcome of development efforts (Reitzes & Reitzes, 1980).

The strong link between the journal and *Society* members gave applied research a direct audience of practitioners who, by applying the research to local projects, can provide laboratories with opportunities to evaluate the validity of the results. This direct linkage provides a current agenda for researchers as well as direct applications of their findings. These opportunities spurred applied research and provided an opportunity for scholars to publish in a respected peer-reviewed national or international outlet.

Several key articles that discuss the issues raised above are included in this section on community history and theory. The articles will help readers understand how community development issues and thinking evolved through time. The articles were selected for their relevance to the topic through surveys of key informants working in community development, downloads and citations, or other approaches.

The next section provides a brief introduction to the progression of thought on various issues described in Community and History section. Subsequent articles are limited to those published in *Community Development*. Thus, this list is presented as representative, rather than exhaustive in any way. However, citations in subsequent articles provide further guidance to other important contributions in other journals or published sources.

Hustedde and Ganowicz (2002) called for more theoretical concepts (solidarity and agency) to underlie community development discussions because theories help explain behaviors and better inform actions to build solidarity and agency that are vital to capacity-building. They used Gidden's structuration model to illustrate how various groups and attitudes in a community can affect implementation of policies that promote and enhance the community. Understanding how these processes work in different settings provides better guidance for practitioners in selecting strategies for community development that will bring about effective and lasting results.

The need for a more rigorous definition of community development based on theoretical concepts, including solidarity and agency, was stressed further by Bhattacharyya (2004). Especially important is to accurately define community as a concept. Is it a locality, place of work, or something else? Without careful thought, developers and practitioners may be tempted to consider development of a locality rather than focusing on well-being of residents as also was emphasized by Wilkinson (1979). Defining community too narrowly can lead to less effective outcomes than if measured by quality of life or better living conditions.

Wilkinson also found that interaction of social fields with strong linkages is instrumental to improving the well-being of residents. The importance of agencies working in collaborative arrangements rather than using interventionist strategies was also documented. This line of research clearly documented the importance of community with strategies to help build it over the long-term. Interactions among players are important.

Bhattacharyya also distinguished carefully between processes and outcomes by distinguishing between goals, methods, and techniques reinforcing that community development is about creating a satisfying life for residents. By focusing on solidarity and agency, community developers can select and implement various methods consistent with the overall goals rather than immediate outcomes.

Power and authority permeate the evolution in community development discussions, both of which are crucial in designing effective development strategies. Power structures can be classified as elite or plural with elite structures being the most common. A group of residents depending on wealth, position, heritage, or – for another reason – control, or seriously affect, the decision-making structure. They may hold public office, may be large employers, may contribute financially to community agencies, or otherwise may shape the agenda and the resulting outcomes. As noted in the article by Long, sometimes those controlling the power do not even live in the community and have little vested interest.

Brennan and Israel (2008) recognized the absence of a theoretical framework for understanding how local power is generated at the micro level to foster community change, rather than assuming that macro factors create a decision-making structure. They discuss both the importance of the power structure in a community and the sense of community *per se* when the power or authority is distributed equitably among groups from a field theoretical perspective.

A community is a place where people live and work in an interactive setting with associations and networks providing opportunities to advance their social and economic well-being. Leadership opportunities exist within these networks and offer people opportunities to influence actions and outcomes. Networks cross diverse groups and social fields with people participating to different extents. Thus, leadership opportunities are not afforded equally to everyone and can create or encourage disadvantaged groups. Pursuing common interests collectively is what creates a sense of community and can bring better outcomes for all.

Effective channels of communication and formation of linkages among diverse groups are also important in the community-building process. Brennen and Israel analyzed four theoretical scenarios that discuss possible outcomes and impact on local development. Recognition of the social fields in the locality that is crucial to building a strong sense of community is so essential to a successful long-term community change process.

On a practical level, poverty eradication is one of the most common issues addressed in community development efforts but it is elusive due to a multitude of different causes in diverse locations. However, anti-poverty strategies in local situations are often pre-determined by the theory (ies) held by policymakers regarding causes of poverty. Bradshaw (2007) examines five common theories of poverty – including individual irresponsibility, cultural aspects such as nonproductive values, political-economic structure, concentrated social advantages or disadvantages, and cumulative or cyclical conditions.

He makes a compelling case that basing policies on the first four theories is inadequate to significantly reduce poverty conditions. Instead, Bradshaw makes the point that building high levels of community capital is needed with policies aimed at empowering residents and creating associations in environments so that poverty-prone residents can advance. Increasing educational opportunities is one such strategy that is effective in many situations. It helps residents engage in more productive activities where they gain respect and achieve leadership positions by helping to shape policies. This capacity-building approach fits well with the literature on the importance of community capacity in workable solutions.

The Community Capitals Framework (CCF) advanced by Emery and Flora (2006) and others gained acceptance as a way to conceptualize and understand important elements in community using five capitals: Human, Social, Political, Financial, and Built. Pigg, Gasteyer, Martin, Keating and Apaliyah (2013) examine the importance and use of this framework with special attention to interactions between the various capitals to better measure progress in community development.

Building on field theory, the notion is that each capital represents a field of community activity where interactions take place. Thus, it is important to understand how the various capitals connect in a complex way to affect overall community capital and then find approaches to stimulate positive development of these components. The analyses by Pigg et al. are based on 20 sites in five states involving more than 200 projects and activities using focus groups with follow-up interviews.

The analyses show that Human Capital-related activities received most attention followed by Social Capital and then Financial Capital. However, in each case, other capitals were closely aligned, indicating the importance of examining projects in sufficient detail to recognize how the various capitals are interrelated or interact. One main finding is that citizen leaders in communities surveyed understood linkages or interactions between the issues addressed or the fields in which the actions are formed even though they were not necessarily familiar with the CCF.

The findings support the usefulness of the CCF in understanding how community is strengthened. In this study, leaders understood the important elements in building the community and then assembled leaders who could interact positively to improve overall community well-being. Thus, understanding the sectors represented by the community capitals and how they interact in community enhancement processes is important.

SUMMARY

Understanding community and how to improve the well-being of residents has advanced significantly since 1970 and both the CDS and the journal contributed significantly to this progress. Especially important is that practitioners and scholars collaborated to find and test new methods of promoting lasting community change and development. Many other articles in *Community Development* have made similar contributions, and those selected in this volume illustrate significant changes in understanding by both practitioners and scholars how successful communities can be built.

The complexity of development issues makes it difficult to formulate a theory that applies to all aspects. Likewise, it is difficult for policies to address all of the issues. Several important findings result from a review of the articles in this section. First, it is essential to address community-building issues from a broader community development perspective rather than trying to apply single-focused policies addressing a specific concern or need. Local agencies and groups have the power to cause change but they must be energized and sustained.

Second, community-building involves strengthening networks and associations that include all groups in the locality. Not all sectors have the same leadership potential so an effort to build leadership across the community is important. Gaining buy-in from some groups is difficult.

Third, power must be spread across the community and must include the views of groups that, otherwise, might not be heard. Without this approach, it can be difficult to build a consensus on the policies and implement them successfully.

Fourth, the process of community-building is never-ending and needs continual monitoring regarding how policies must adapt to changes. Measuring these changes can be difficult but the CCF is one approach. In monitoring changes, however, it is essential to examine interactions among the capitals, rather than concentrating on one at a time.

Community development, as a discipline, has grown significantly with a consistent body of knowledge to inform and guide practitioners. This section on history and theory illustrates how definitions and concepts have changed, and the significant roles that research reported in *Community Development* contributed to, and even caused, some of that growth.

REFERENCES

Blair, R. & Hembd, J. 1994. What we have learned: A community development symposium. *Journal of the Community Development Society* 25: 1–4.

Brennan, M. & Israel, G. D. 2008. The power of society, *Community Development* 39: 82–98.

Bhattacharyya, J. 2004. Theorizing Community Development. *Community Development*, 34: 5–34.

Cary, L.J. 1979. The community development society: A decade behind—a decade ahead. *Journal of the Community Development Society* 10: 5–12.

Emery, M. & Flora, C.B. 2006. Spiraling-up: Mapping community transformation and community capitals framework. *Community Development: Journal of the Community Development Society* 37: 19–35.

Hoiberg, O. G. 1970. *Perspective in retrospect: Community development during the Sixties, Community Development, Journal of the Community Development Society* 1, 2: 100–103.

Hustedde, R. & Ganowicz, J. 2002. The Basics: what's essential about theory for community development practice? *Community Development; Journal of the Community Development Society* 33: 1–19.

Long, H. B. 1962. Observed Community Development Patterns: 1950–1970, *Community Development* 3: 1, 112–120.

Pigg, K. et al. 2013. The Community Capitals Framework: an empirical examination of internal relationships, *Community Development*, 44: 4, 492–502.

Reitzes, D. & Reitzes, D.C. 1980. Saul D. Alinsky's contribution to community development, *Community Development: Journal of the Community Development Society* 11: 2, 39–52.

Walzer, N. 2010. CDS at 40: The past leading to the future, *Community Development: Journal of the Community Development Society* 41: 1, 401–404.

Wilkinson, K. 1979. Social Well-being and Community, *Community Development, Journal of the Community Development Society* 10:1, 5–16.

Observed Community Development Patterns: 1950 - 1970

Huey B. Long

Augusta, Cape Kennedy, Long Island, Los Alamos, Los Angeles, Houston, Lower Bucks County, Pennsylvania, Marietta, Ga., Oak Ridge, Seattle and a dozen other places reflect post-1945 development trends that are of specific interest to community developers. These trends include (1) the increasing number of decisions made beyond the limits of the geographic areas directly affected by the decisions, (2) the trend toward urbanization and (3) the need for very large installations that require large tracts of land and employ (and often import) large labor forces.

Since the 1970's do not appear to contain the suggestions of drastic alterations among the three trends noted above, it would appear to be instructive to reflect on the experiences of selected areas and see if a pattern emerges. If such a pattern does indeed become observable, community developers may become better equipped to provide assistance in rapidly developing areas.

In order to eliminate the possible influences of a number of decisions three communities affected by *one* major decision making agency and *one* installation were selected for analysis. The three areas selected, Augusta, Georgia-Aiken, South Carolina; Cape Kennedy (Brevard County, Florida) and Lower Bucks County, Pennsylvania are all different. They were changed by different organizations at different times and reflect cultural differences as well as geographic diversity. Yet, the pattern of development and problems faced by the three areas appear to be too similar to have occurred by chance.

THE PROBLEM

Thus, the problem with which this article is concerned is to determine the possibility of developing a matrix that might reveal the pattern of interacting events surrounding the estab-

Dr. Long is an Associate Professor, Department of Adult Education, University of Georgia. Another one of his articles appeared in the Spring, 1971, issue of the Journal.

lishment of a new large installation in a rather undeveloped community.

SIGNIFICANCE OF THE PROBLEM

The identification and ordering of a logical pattern that may visually illustrate both the main community impact events originating with a large installation *and* the community condition or response contains important implications. For example, if such a pattern can be validated, suggestions for improved practice of community development in a rapidly developing area may be forthcoming. Such improved practice could conceivably lead to a clearer understanding of the role of the community developer in relation to the local governmental planner.

Other areas of concern include the possibility that in many areas community development may be rapidly becoming a choice of making *alternate responses* to extra-community events. (An extra-community event is defined as any decision or action that may originate beyond local geographic boundaries.) These extra-community events may be made by the board of directors of a private corporation or by the State or Federal Government.

Further testing and validation of the concept may also suggest that there are critical stages in the developmental sequence that may structurally and/or organically affect later stages, i.e. a zoning decision or lack of decision at one stage may contain the seeds of a problem that must be corrected later.

But first and foremost is the task of developing and validating the concept of a pattern. The above benefits will naturally follow.

SCOPE

This article is restricted to the task of offering a trial matrix based on analyses of three areas. It is not designed to, nor is it proffered as the last word. Neither does the article purport to exhaustively catalog the implications of the use and benefit of such a pattern.

PROCEDURE

The matrix illustrating the perceived pattern of stimulus-response was inductively developed from information generated by numerous research efforts in the selected areas. Specifically the experiences and sequence of events common to Augusta-Aiken, Cape Kennedy and Lower Bucks County were identified and examined.

The data on which the matrix were finally developed is too voluminous to report here. However, the reader may wish to read *The Impact of Large Installations on Nearby Areas* by Gerald Breese, *et al* and *Social Change at Cape Kennedy: 1950-1970* by Huey B. Long and Charles M. Grigg.

THE COMMON EXPERIENCE

Before discussing the common experiences among Augusta-Aiken, Cape Kennedy and Lower Bucks County perhaps major differences may need to be observed.

First, there is considerable difference in geography. Lower Bucks County at the time of the initiation of the steel mill was just on the edge of one of the nation's greatest urban concentrations. Augusta, was an above average southern city and Brevard County was by most standards a rural area on the Atlantic coast.

Next, there was a time difference. While all three growth areas saw their impact installation initiated around 1950 there is considerable difference. The Lower Bucks County crisis was over before Augusta-Aiken felt the full impact. And the Cape Kennedy area experienced two peaks, about 10 years apart, 1956-58 and 1966-68.

Third, the nature and size of the installations were different. Augusta-Aiken felt the influence from a government policy decision. The Atomic Energy Commission, experienced in creating new communities at Los Alamos and Oak Ridge, required 200,000 acres near Augusta. The Cape area was also affected by a governmental installation. Under the direction of the air force, initial land requirements jumped from 15,000 acres to 100,000 acres (under NASA). In contrast Lower Bucks County was affected by U.S. Steel, a private corporation that required 4,000 acres of land.

Thus, there was sufficient difference among the three areas to at least suggest some variations in the pattern of development. However, the differences do not appear to be as substantial as might be expected.

Each area was affected by a large installation that changed land use patterns and residential distribution. The decisions concerning land acquisition and construction schedules were made by individuals located "outside" the affected community.

The character of each area at the time of development could be characterized as rural even though urban areas were not far removed in two instances. Limited expertise in business and government was a rule rather than an exception. Planning, zoning, and development had already been done.

Almost without exception the impact areas experienced difficulties in providing schools, operating the schools, providing recreation, extending water mains, developing additional water supplies and collecting and treating waste water.

Each community lacked efficient social planning agencies. This is not to suggest that charitable and benevolent activities were unknown in the communities prior to the impact. But, it is to note that the customary needs of the communities were met by limited and often direct methods that fell short of the needs of rapidly growing communities.

Retail and commercial activities appear to have generally lagged behind population growth. As a result trips beyond the limits of the local community were required for shopping. Frustrations and dissatisfaction were characteristic among the new residents, who felt that their choice was unduly limited in terms of goods and services.

Generally, then, based on the common experience noted it appears that the establishment of a large installation involves substantial modifications in the host community's economy, government, population, and social structure. Common problems of such areas include: financial stress on local areas for the provision of expanded services; commercial retail outlets and facilities often trailing the population increase; relocation of displaced persons and businesses; disorganization of local society; modification of the economy, and ineffective land use controls.

DEVELOPMENTAL

Based on the experience common to Augusta-Aiken, Cape Kennedy, and Lower Bucks County a tentative developmental matrix is offered to illustrate the interaction of events that may be identified in the development process.

Table 1 is such a matrix. The vertical action column reflects the "stimuli from the large installation" and the horizontal row reflects the "local community response."

Key To Table 1

Stimuli From Large Installation

1. Step one represents the new installation's first consideration of building a new facility in a new area.
2. Step two represents the organization's information collecting phase to determine the feasibility of building a new installation.
3. Step three is when the study team produces detail study that demonstrates to the decision makers the need of the new facility.
4. If other steps follow—the organization makes a positive decision to build.
5. Specific site requirements are defined by the organization's planning task force.

TABLE 1
A HEURISTIC DEVELOPMENT MATRIX

LOCAL COMMUNITY RESPONSE

- A — No Action Stage
- B — Pre-Announcement Rumors
- C — Informal Verification
- D — Legal Verification
- E — Preliminary Speculation
- F — Official Announcement
- G — Community Disbelief
- H — Post Announcement Rumor
- I — Increased Land Values
- J — Increased Speculation
- K — Housing Shortage
- L — Governmental Service Area Stress
- M — Commercial/Service Stress
- N — Social Service Stress
- O — Increased Taxation
- P — Governmental Reorganization
- Q — Community Conflicts
- R — Housing Selection Difficulties
- S — Over-Development (Housing)
- T — Community Apprehension
- U — Contradictory-Self Defeating, Circular Activities

STIMULI FROM LARGE INSTALLATION

	A	B	C	D	E	F	G	H	I	J	K	L	M	N	O	P	Q	R	S	T	U
1. Study Need For New Facility	X																				
2. Collect Data	X																				
3. Demonstrate Need	X																				
4. Positive Decision	X																				
5. Define Site Requirements	X																				
6. Site Search		X																			
7. Rumors		X																			
8. Site Selection		X																			
9. Site Acquisition			X	X	X	X															
10. Displace Former Res.					X		X	X	X	X	X	X									
11. Site Preparation						X	X	X	X	X	X										
12. Import Large Number of construction employees											X	X	X	X	X	X	X	X			
13. Manpower Problems Related to housing and other community problems.											X	X	X	X	X	X	X	X			
14. Liaison With Community by second level decision maker.											X	X	X	X	X	X	X	X			
15. Transportation & Access problems											X	X	X	X	X	X	X				
16. First Wave of Operations Employed											X	X	X	X	X	X	X	X			
17. Lay-Off Construction Crews											X	X	X	X	X			X			
18. Operations Phase Begins (additional employees)											X	X	X	X	X	X	X	X			
19. Full Scale Operations											X	X	X	X	X	X	X	X			
20. Fluctuations In Operations															X		X	X	X	X	
21. Modification Of Operations															X	X	X	X	X	X	X
22. Rumors															X	X	X		X	X	X
23. Close-Out Or Reduction Phase															X	X	X		X	X	X

6. A site search is initiated. (This is the first time that individuals outside the privileged communication circle may learn of the plans).

7. The site search stimulates rumors in areas or states where field inspections are made. Usually the rumors are highly inaccurate.

8. A site is selected by the appropriate organization decision makers.

9. The site is acquired. When acquired by private corporations the site is often acquired through the officer of a local attorney or realtor and even then may use a dummy or "front" corporation. Some information may leak at this stage. Governmental organizations begin negotiations directly with owners.

10. Former residents are displaced.

11. The organization begins to prepare the site.

12. The number of imported construction workers increases.

13. As the number of construction workers increases, the organization may experience worker problems related to housing and leisure activities.

14. To facilitate provision of better housing or cheaper housing and better leisure opportunities an organizational representative is appointed to work with community leaders.

15. As construction activity rises and employees increase, the organization experiences difficulties related to worker transportation and transportion of building materials.

16. Near the end of construction the first wave of operations employees arrive. They are usually imported and add to the number of new residents. But they may be very different from construction employees. For example, construction employees are interested in short term housing whereas the operations employees require permanent housing.

17. After the first wave of operations personnel arrives and near the completion of construction the first large group of construction workers leave.

18. Operations activities begin with additional new employees.

19. More operations employees arrive as more construction workers leave. On the surface this looks like a replacement action. But there may be life style differences that prevent the action from being so simple.

20. Operations fluctuate with economy or national policy decision.

21. Economic-political decisions may modify operations schedule and result in fewer employees.

22. Rumors concerning the future operations grow and affect worker morale.

23. Organization publicly recognizes state of operations and takes corrective action.

Local Community Response

A. Response A has a no-action response on the part of the local community which exists through the fifth step of the stimulation from the large installation.

B. Beginning with the site search initiated by the large installation, pre-announcement rumors may circulate in the local community that may eventually become the site of the large installation. Similar rumors will circulate in other communities. These rumors will persist through step 8 of the large installation or until the site selection is made.

C. After the site has been selected and acquired the rumors may be verified on a limited basis.

D. Verification of the rumors will be made possible at this stage through legal documents.

E. Preliminary speculation will begin in the community by those who have certified the site acquisitions.

F. A community official will make a public official announcement recognizing the purchase of land or site acquisitions.

G. Generally there will be community disbelief and a reluctance to act based on the information available on the community.

H. Post announcement rumors will increase and will likely be highly inaccurate.

I. Local land values will increase.

J. Increased speculation will take place.

K. Housing shortages will begin to be noticeable.

L. There will be pressure placed on provision of governmental services.

M. Community service such as retail business service will begin to feel the pressure.

N. Social services will begin to feel the pressure of increased population.

O. There will be a move to increase the tax base in the community.

P. In an effort to provide service more effectively and more efficiently attempts will be made to reorganize local government.

Q. Conflicts between old timers and new comers will become more prevalent and visible.

R. Housing difficulties will be experienced by a different kind of employee coming into the community.

S. The community will begin to feel the results of over development as there may be more housing and more businesses currently in the community than the economic situation justifies.

T. The community will begin to have some apprehensions about the continued benefits of the installation.

U. Community leaders may become involved in inconsistent, contradictory and self-defeating activities in an effort to respond to the many different demands now being imposed on the community structure.

DISCUSSION

Based on the analysis of the selected areas, the matrix contains data that is arranged to indicate the expected and possible community response to a specific action taken by the outside agency. For example, during steps one-five, taken by the outside agency, no action in the community is taken. In fact the only "action" possible by the community during the first five agency steps is based on previous activity, i.e., existing regulations or general policies that were not specifically originated to handle the specific situation presented by the outside agency's plan. During steps six-eight, the local community action appears to be generally limited to undocumented rumors and only at step nine is evidence available to document the transaction and ultimate plans of the outside agency.

Beginning at step nine the local community is sequentially behind the new installation; everything is a catch-up action. Only by looking ahead and attempting to take several steps at one time can the community gain a semblance of control over the events that have been set in motion.

Several elements appear to mitigate against the community to prevent such action, these elements are:

1. The lack of understanding of the nature of process, i.e., even though Augusta and Bucks County experienced the same kinds of events some 10 years before Cape Kennedy's last phase, pertinent information *was not* analyzed and applied;

2. Local officials do not (in such communities) generally possess the foresight to take long range action;

3. Community development workers are not often involved in such dynamic situations. (The above presumes that the community development specialist would know how to work in such communities.)

There is little question that such a matrix as the one presented in Table 1 could be a highly useful tool. However, the specific steps are not always identified by the headlines in the morning papers. For example, the local community may move from a shortage of housing to a surplus of housing within a few months. Such an important change is not always visible until too late. Building trends and employment data have to be carefully analyzed to pin point when the change occurs. But, it can be done. For example, the writer advised officials in the Cape Kennedy area of a possible peak in development almost two years *before* the condition was publicly recognized. Thus, the development of a specific recommendation based on the general matrix concept would of necessity require astute data collection and analysis. In other words the community developer could only make general recommendations based only on the matrix, but with additional information more specific alternatives could be examined by community leaders.

CONCLUSIONS & SUMMARY

Examination and analysis of development in Augusta-Aiken, Lower Bucks County, Pennsylvania and the Cape Kennedy areas reveals a *pattern* of development that appears to be more than coincidental. It appears that a broad outline of a developmental process may emerge from the analysis. If the process, as identified, is an accurate interpretation of the events and if the process can be generalized to other areas, it appears that it may be possible to construct a matrix that will visually illustrate key interacting events. Identification of these key events should prove instructive to the community developer.

The eventual validation of such a model would provide the community developer with a factual base for analysis and recommendations. Forthcoming problems could be realisticly predicted. Moreover, such a matrix would provide a visual chart of future events that would improve the possibilities that political and social leaders would select the appropriate course of action at the appropriate time.

The theoretical concept of "an orderly developmental sequence" could be also more easily studied. The maintenance of a matrix based on actual events would soon add sufficient knowledge to provide intelligent interpretation. Such interpretation would be useful in identifying possible pathological or retarding results if certain acts are delayed overly long in communities.

The matrix, however, cannot stand alone. Supplementary data must be provided by intelligent data collection and analysis in a variety of areas by competent community developers.

Finally, the concept as offered here, while the result of much thought on the part of the writer, needs additional verification or refutation. Community developers in other communities are encouraged to attempt to develop such a model that may contribute to more successful community development case studies.

THE BASICS: WHAT'S ESSENTIAL ABOUT THEORY FOR COMMUNITY DEVELOPMENT PRACTICE?

By Ronald J. Hustedde and Jacek Ganowicz

ABSTRACT

The major point of this article is that the multidisciplinary field of community development needs some common theoretical concepts for community development practice. The authors examine three major limitations of theory for community development and discuss why theoretical frameworks are important for the field. There are three major concerns that encompass community development practice: structure, power and shared meaning. These concerns are related to three classical theoretical frameworks: structural functionalism, conflict theory, and symbolic interactionism. These seemingly disparate theories take on a deeper meaning when tied to Giddens' structuration theory. Giddens' theoretical perspective is essential for practitioners because of its link between macro and microstructures and the ability of the community to influence macro and micro changes through cultural patterns and norms (modalities). The article includes case studies and examples to illustrate the applicability of key theoretical insights.

INTRODUCTION

There are at least three major limitations of theory for community developers. First, it can be argued that the profession is undergirded with theories from so many disciplines that it is difficult for practitioners to sort through them all. The situation is compounded by disciplines that seldom cross academic boundaries. Community development-oriented anthropologists, community psychologists, sociologists, social welfare professionals, community economists, and others have their own disciplinary approaches and publications. Even interdisciplinary groups such as the Community Development Society and

Ronald J. Hustedde, Associate Professor, Department of Community and Leadership Development, University of Kentucky Lexington Kentucky; and Jacek Ganowicz, Associate Faculty, Department of Anthropology, Sociology, and Social Work Eastern Kentucky University, Richmond Kentucky.

Communication should be directed to Dr. Ron Hustedde, University of Kentucky, Department of Community Leadership and Development, 500 Garrigus Bldg., Lexington, KY 40546-0215. Phone: (859) 257-3186, Fax: (859) 257-1164. E-mail: rhusted@uky.edu. Communication can also be directed to Dr. Jacek Ganowicz, Eastern Kentucky University, Department of Anthropology, Sociology, and Social Work, Keith 223, Richmond, KY 40475.

The authors wish to thank Professors Lori Garkovich and Julie N. Zimmerman from the University of Kentucky, the four anonymous reviewers, and the editor, Ted Bradshaw, for their helpful critiques of our original manuscript.

its publications tend to be dominated by those with a domestic rather than an international perspective. This fragmentation makes it difficult to sort through what is important for community development research or practice.

Second, the balkanization of theory is compounded by theoreticians whose language is cumbersome and fraught with jargon that scares away most practitioners. For example, one of the leading theorists of the day, Jurgen Habermas, has a lot to offer community developers about free and open communicative action. However, his books and articles take so much time to decipher that few practitioners have the time or patience to do so. Further, theoreticians strive to explain the world but do not necessarily apply their theories to day-to-day practices of community development. Unfortunately, this situation leads some practitioners to conclude that theory is irrelevant.

Third, the culture of the community development profession consists of many practitioners who often want to dispense with theory and "get down to earth." They want studies to shed light on issues such as urban slum life, growth versus the environment, globalization or a range of other issues that need immediate attention. Hence, there is more interest in empirical research or practical initiatives than theory itself. The field is supported by classic community development texts, which focus on the philosophical underpinnings of various community development strategies such as Rothman's three approaches (conflict, technical and locality-based) (Rothman, 1987), or the process of doing community development (Biddle and Biddle, 1965; Christenson and Robinson, 1989). If one looks at most community development publications since that time, one might say that the field is theoretically poor because many community development texts tend to focus on process or content rather than theory.[1]

The purpose of this paper is to ask what is essential about theory and to identify several theories that are essential for community development research and practice. Bhattacharyya's (1995) definition of community development as solidarity and agency is offered as a starting point to select theories that are most relevant for the field. We argue that the most important issues for community development theory concern structure, power and shared meaning. These are expressed in functionalism, conflict, and symbolic interaction theory. No single theoretical approach is sufficient on its own because it is argued that societies, communities, and social change are complex.

WHY THEORY?

Theories are explanations that can help us understand people's behavior. Theories can provide a framework to community developers to help them comprehend and explain events. A good theory can be stated in abstract terms and can help develop strategies and tools for effective practice. If community developers want others to conduct relevant research or if they want to be involved in participatory action research, it is important that they have theoretical groundings. Theory is our major guide to understanding the complexity of community life and social and economic change (Collins, 1988; Ritzer, 1996).

The starting point is to offer a definition of community development that is both distinctive and universal and can be applied to all types of societies from the post-industrial to pre-industrial. Bhattacharyya (1995) met these conditions when he defined community development as the process of creating or increasing solidarity and agency. He says solidarity is about building a deeply shared identity and a code for conduct. Community developers sort through conflicting visions and definitions of a problem among ethnically and ideologically plural populations to help groups and communities build a sense of solidarity. Bhattacharyya argues that community development is also agency means the capacity of a people to order their world. According to Giddens, agency is "the capacity to intervene in the world, or to refrain from intervention, with the effect of influencing a process or the state of affairs" (Giddens, 1984, p. 14). There are complex forces that work against agency. However, community development has the intention to build capacity, and that is what makes it different from other helping professions. Community developers build the capacity of a people when they encourage or teach others to create their own dreams, to learn new skills and knowledge. Agency or capacity building occurs when practitioners assist or initiate community reflection on the lessons they have learned through their actions. Agency is about building the capacity to understand, to create and act, and to reflect.

Following this definition of community development, three major concerns involve solidarity and agency building: (1) *structure*; (2) *power*; and (3) *shared meaning*. Figure 1 suggests these concerns are interrelated and influence the direction and impact of community development practice.

Figure 1. Three Key Concerns in the Community Development Field

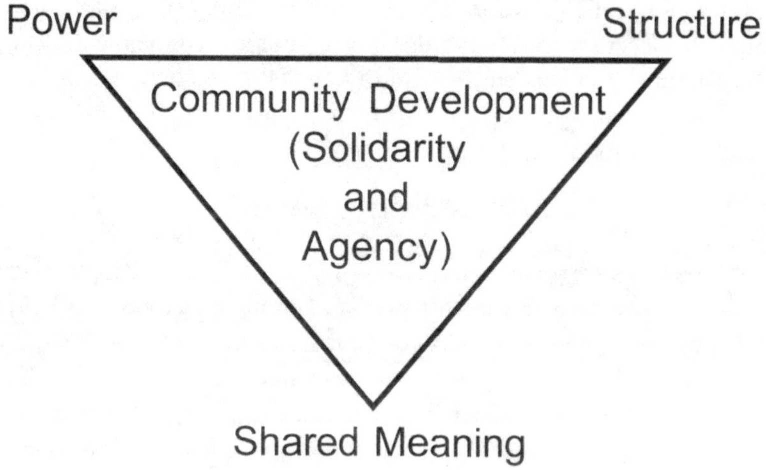

Power   Structure

Community Development
(Solidarity
and
Agency)

Shared Meaning

Structure refers to the social practices or to organizations and groups that have a role to play in solidarity and capacity building and their relationship to one another. Some of these social practices and organizations may have a limited role and there may be a need to build new organizations or expand the mission of existing organizations for solidarity and agency to occur.

Power refers to relationships with those who control resources such as land, labor, capital, and knowledge or those who have greater access to those resources than others. If community development is about building the capacity for social and economic change, the concept of power is essential.

Shared meaning refers to social meaning, especially symbols, that people give to a place, physical things, behavior, events, or action. In essence, solidarity needs to be built within a cultural context. Individuals and groups give different meanings to objects, deeds, and matters. For example, one community might see the construction of an industrial plant as a godsend that will bring prosperity to the town, while another community might see a similar construction as the destruction of their quality of life. Community developers need to pay attention to these meanings if they wish to build a sense of solidarity in a particular community or between communities.

In essence, structure, power, and shared meaning are integral aspects for solidarity and capacity building. These three aspects of the community development triangle (Figure 1) form the basis for essential community development theory. Horton (1992) shared similar concerns about African-American approaches to community development. He emphasized historic power differences and the influence of culture and black community institutions in his black community development model. Chaskin, et al. (2001) focus on neighborhood and other structures and networks in their work on capacity building. However, the authors also include concepts about power and building a sense of community or shared meaning in their interdisciplinary approach. The concepts of empowerment and strengthening community capacity are frequently intertwined in the community development literature (Perkins, 1995; Jeffries, 2000). Beliefs and values evolve in community through daily experiences that lead to pragmatic conclusions about the community's own social reality or shared meaning (Ejigiri, 1996).

What is Essential Community Development Theory for Practitioners and Researchers?

The three key community development issues, structure, power, and shared meaning, have each been a starting point for three key orientations in modern social theory: *functionalism, conflict theory,* and *symbolic interactionism.* The former two originated in the European tradition of macro-structural thinking preoccupied with large scale social phenomena, such as social classes, societal system, culture, norms, i.e., macro objectivity and macro subjectivity, whereas symbolic interactionism, with its roots in the Chicago school of social pragmatism, is considered a micro approach, focusing on individuals and small group behavior, psychological characteristics and properties of interaction.

Conflict theory, going back to the towering figure of Karl Marx, addresses the macro concerns of power. Functionalism, originally laid out in its contours by Auguste Comte, Herbert Spencer, and Emile Durkheim, centers on the macro structural concerns of social cooperation and solidarity. The symbolic interactionists, and the related approaches, followed the opposite tack from both the macro approaches, taking the individuals and their micro behavior as their starting point.

We will look at each of these three theoretical perspectives and how they can be applied to community development practice.

CONCERNS ABOUT STRUCTURE: FUNCTIONALISM

First, let us look at structure, which is about organizations and group capacity to bring about or stop change. In essence, structure is related to the Giddens' concept of agency or capacity building. The theoretical concept concerned with structure is known as *structural functionalism*. It is also called *systems theory, equilibrium theory,* or simply *functionalism*. According to this theoretical framework, societies contain certain interdependent structures, each of which performs certain functions for the maintenance of society. Structures refer to organizations and institutions such as health care, educational entities, businesses and non-profit groups, or informal groups. Functions refer to their purpose, mission, and what they do in society. These structures form the basis of a social system. Talcott Parsons and Robert K. Merton are the theorists most often associated with this theory. According to Merton (1968), social systems have manifest and latent functions. Manifest functions are intentional and recognized. In contrast, latent functions may be unintentional and not recognized. For example, it could be argued that the manifest function of urban planning is to assure well-organized and efficiently functioning cities, whereas the latent function is to allocate advantages to certain interests such as those involved with the growth machine or real estate developers.

Functionalists such as Parsons argue that structures often contribute to their own maintenance, not particularly to a greater societal good. Concern for order and stability also led functionalists to focus on social change and its sources. They view conflict and stability as two sides of the same coin. If the community developer wants to build community capacity, she will have to pay attention to the organizational capacity for stimulating or inhibiting change. Structural functionalism helps one to understand how the *status quo* is maintained. Some critics claim its fallacy is that it does not offer much insight about change, social dynamics, and existing structures (Turner, 1998; Ritzer, 1996; Collins, 1988).

How Can Structural Functionalism Guide Community Development Practice?

Structural functionalism is a useful tool for practitioners. Let us look at a case study of an inner city neighborhood that is struggling to create micro-enterprise businesses that will benefit local people. If one applied structural functionalism to community development practice, one would help the community analyze what organizations are committed to training, nurturing and financing micro-enterprise development and what their latent or hidden functions might be. A functionalist-oriented practitioner is more likely to notice dysfunctions in organizations. If the existing organizations are not meeting local needs in this area, the functionalist would build the capacity of the community by creating a new organization that focuses on small-scale entrepreneurs or adapting an existing organization to meet the same concerns. A functionalist would also want to build links with broader social systems such as external organizations that could help the community's micro-entrepreneurs to flourish. In essence, a functionalist would see structures as important components of capacity-building. While structural functionalism is an important tool for community development, it is limited because it does not fully explore the issue of power that can be found in other theories.

CONCERNS ABOUT POWER AND CONFLICT THEORY

Power is the second key issue for community development. Power is about who controls or has access to resources (land, labor, capital and knowledge). If community development is about building capacity, then concerns about power are pivotal. Insights about power tend to be found in political science or political sociology. Theorists that are more contemporary have added to the richness of the literature. Foucault (1985), in his later writings, argued that where there is power, there is resistance. He examines the struggles against the power of men over women, administration over the ways people live and of psychiatry over the mentally ill. He sees power as a feature of all human relations (Foucault, 1965, 1975, 1979, 1980, 1985; Nash, 2000). It has a fluidity in the sense that power can be reversed and there are different degrees of power. Foucault's focus extends beyond conventional politics at the state level to the organizations and institutions of civil society and to interpersonal relations.

Wallerstein (1984) applied Marxist theory to understand the logic behind the expansion of capitalism to a globalized system, which needs to continually expand its boundaries. "Political states" such as Japan, the UK and the USA are the core-developed states based on higher-level skills and capitalization. These states dominate the peripheral areas, with weak states economically dependent on the "core." The low-technology states form a buffer zone to prevent outright conflict between the core and the periphery. Some have applied Wallerstein's world system theory to regional economics, with places like Appalachia serving as a "periphery" to global market forces. Mills (1959), one of the earliest American conflict theorists, examined some of the key themes in post World War II American politics and argued that a small handful of individuals from major corporations, federal government and the military were influencing major decisions. He believed this triumvirate shared similar interests and often acted in unison. Mill's research on power and authority still influences theories about power and politics today.

However, Mills also had critics such as Dahl (1971), who believed that power was more diffused among contending interest groups. Galbraith (1971) asserted that technical bureaucrats behind the scenes had more power than those in official positions. Neo-Marxists argued that Mills and Dahl focused too much on the role of individual actors. They believed that institutions permit the exploitation of one class by another and that the institution of the state intervenes to correct the flaws of capitalism and to preserve the status quo, which is in their interests.

In essence, conflict theory suggests that conflict is an integral part of social life. There are conflicts between economic classes, ethnic groups, young and old, male against female, or one race versus another. There are conflicts among developed "core" countries and those that are less developed. It is argued these conflicts result because power, wealth, and prestige are not available to everyone. Some groups are excluded from dominant discourse. It is assumed that those who hold or control desirable goods and services or who dominate culture will protect their own interests at the expense of others.

Conflict theorists such as Coser, Dahrendorf, and Simmel have looked at the integrative aspects of conflict and its value as a force that contributes to order and stability. Conflict can be constructive when it forces people with common interests to make gains to benefit them all. Racial inequalities or other social problems might never be resolved at all unless there is conflict to disturb the *status quo*. Simmel discusses how conflict can be resolved in a variety of ways, including disappearance of the conflict, victory for one of the parties, compromise, conciliation, and irreconcilability. (Schellenberg, 1996).

This theoretical framework about power of one party over another and the potential for conflict is not intended to be exhaustive – but, it points to some of the major concerns that can guide community development practice.

How Can Conflict Theory Serve as a Guide for Community Development Practice?

Community organizers tend to embrace more readily conflict theory as a pivotal component of their organizing work. However, we argue that community developers also need conflict theory if their goal is to build capacity. Power differences are a reality of community life and need to be considered as development occurs. Let us take the case of an Appalachian community that is near a major state forest. The Department of Transportation (DOT) wants to build a highway through the state forest. They claim it will lead to more jobs and economic development. A group of local citizens have questioned this assumption. They believe the highway could pull businesses away from the prosperous downtown area to the edge of town, and will lead to sprawling development that will detract from the quality of life. They also believe the proposed highway will lead to the destruction of a popular fishing hole and could harm the integrity of the forest. The DOT has refused to converse with the community; they claim the proposed highway's economic benefits are irrefutable. Conflict theory can serve as a reference point for moving the community's interests further. At first glance, it appeared the DOT was in charge of making the major decisions about the highway. However, the community developer incorporated conflict theory into practice. Community residents were encouraged to analyze the community's political, technical, economic, and social power as well as the power of the DOT. Through its analysis, the group was expanded to include downtown business people, hunters, environmental, and religious groups. In this particular case, the community decided it needed power that is more technical. They were able to secure the services of university researchers (economists, foresters, sociologists and planners) who had the credentials to write an alternative report about the impact of the proposed highway. This report was widely circulated to the media and prominent state legislators from the community. Gradually, external support (power) emerged and the DOT decided to postpone the project.

In a similar situation, the use of conflict theory took another twist. The opponents of a DOT-proposed road sought the role of a mediator/facilitator to help them negotiate with the DOT and other stakeholders. They believed a third-party neutral could create a safe climate for discussion, and that during such discussions power differences could be minimized. In this particular case, their use of conflict theory paid off because the dispute was settled to everyone's satisfaction.

In summary, community developers need conflict theory because it provides insights about why there are differences and competition among groups and organizations within the community. These theories can help us understand why some peoples are silent or have internalized the values of elites even to their own disadvantage. Practitioners and researchers can use Simmel's understanding of conflict to see how people resolve their differences, or they can borrow from Marx and neo-Marxists to see why people believe there are sharp differences that relate to class economic interests, gender, race, culture, and other concerns.

Conflict theory can help communities understand competing interests among groups or if power is concentrated in the hands of a few or more broadly distributed. One can also explore how communities can use conflict to upset the equilibrium through protests, economic boycotts, peaceful resistance, or other ranges of possibilities, especially if competing groups or institutions refuse to budge or negotiate.

While conflict theory is an essential tool for capacity building, it should be noted that critics claim it is limited because it ignores the less controversial and more orderly parts of our society. (Turner, 1998; Ritzer, 1996; Collins, 1988). It does not help us understand the role of symbols in building solidarity. This leads us to another theoretical framework about shared meaning.

CONCERNS ABOUT SHARED MEANING: SYMBOLIC INTERACTIONISM

Shared meaning is the third key concern about community development in Figure 1. If community development is about building or strengthening solidarity, then practitioners must be concerned about the meaning that people give to places, people, and events. Symbolic interactionism is about symbols. Herbert Blumer (1969) gave this name to the theory because it emphasizes that human interaction is symbolic rather than a mechanical pattern of stimulus and interaction. For symbolic interactionists, the meaning of a situation is not fixed but is constructed by participants as they anticipate the responses of others. Mead (1982) explored the importance of symbols, especially language, in shaping the meaning of the one who makes the gesture as well as the one who receives it.

Goffman (1959) argued that individuals "give" and "give off" signs that provide information to others on how to respond. There may be a "front" such as social status, clothing, gestures, or a physical setting. Individuals may conceal elements of themselves that contradict general social values and present themselves to exemplify accredited values. Such encounters can be viewed as a form of drama in which the "audience" and "team players" interact.

In his last work, Goffman (1986) examined how individuals frame or interpret events. It involves group or individual rules about what is to be "pictured in the frame" and what should be excluded. For example, a community developer's framework about a community event might exclude ideas such as "citizens are apathetic." It will probably include our shared "rules" such as "participation is important." The emphasis is on the active, interpretive, and constructive capacities of individuals in the creation of a social reality. It assumes that social life is possible because people communicate through symbols. For example, when the traffic light is red, it means stop, or when the thumb is up, it means everything is fine. Flora, Flora, and Tapp (2000) investigated how two opposing community narratives moved through the stages of frustration, confrontation, negotiation, and reconciliation. Their case study could be viewed as the employment of symbolic interactionism. Among the symbols that humans use, language seems to be the most important because it allows people to communicate and construct their version of reality. Symbolic interactionism contends that people interpret the world through symbols, and they stand back and think of themselves as objects.

For example, a group of Native Americans view a mountain as a sacred place for prayer and healing, and they react negatively when someone tries to develop it or alter their access to the mountain. Developers, foresters, tourism leaders, and others are likely to have other meanings about the mountain.

Different individuals or groups attach a different meaning to a particular event, and these interpretations are likely to be viewed by others as a form of deviance, which may be accepted, rejected, or fought over. Social interactionists contend that one way we build meaning is by observing what other people do, and by imitating them and following their guidance.

How Can Symbolic Interactionism Serve as a Tool for Community Development Practice?

We believe symbolic interactionism is essential for community development because it provides insight about how people develop a sense of shared meaning, an essential ingredient for solidarity.

When a community developer helps a community to develop a shared vision about its future, she is helping to build a sense of unity. A community-owned vision comes about through interaction of people and is told through symbols: pictures, words, or music. A symbolic interactionist would be keen on bringing people together to develop a shared understanding about something.

For example, let us take a case where some citizens have expressed an interest in preserving the farmland adjacent to the city and they have asked a community developer for assistance. If one employed a symbolic interactionist perspective, one would ask them what the presence of farmland means to them. One would link them with farmers and others to see if there is a different or competing meaning; participants would be asked how they developed their meaning about farmland. A symbolic interactionist doesn't ignore the concept of power. Participants would be asked questions such as whose concept of farmland dominates public policy. Through the employment of symbolic interaction theory, a sense of solidarity can gradually be established in a community.

A symbolic interactionist would spot groups that deviate from the dominant meaning about something and would engage them with the others in order to move the community towards solidarity. Symbolic interactionists also use symbols to build capacity. For example, a community may choose to preserve a historic structure because they believe it is beautiful, or they may say it is an important part of a labor, class, racial or gender struggle or some other interest. A community developer can augment their meaning with data about the historical and architectural meaning that external agents see in the structure. Community capacity can be built in other ways, such as providing information about tax credits for historic structures or how to locate grants for preservation. Increasingly, community development researchers and practitioners are asked to help citizens reflect and understand the meaning of their work. We can use the symbolic interactionist concepts to aid us in collective evaluations. Essentially, it all boils down to what it means and who gives it meaning.

Symbolic interactionists probe into the factors that help us understand what we say and do. They look at the origins of symbolic meanings and how meanings persist. Symbolic interactionists are interested in the circumstances in which people question, challenge, criticize, or reconstruct meanings.

Critics argue that symbolic interactionists do not have an established systematic framework for predicting *what* meanings will be generated or for determining *how* meanings persist or for understanding how meanings change. For example, let us say a group of Mexican workers and a poultry processing firm move into a poor rural community that has been historically dominated by Anglo-Saxon Protestants. The event may trigger cooperation, good will, ambivalence, anger, fear, or defensiveness. The cast of characters involved in this event may be endless. What really happened and whose interpretation best captures the reality of the situation? Symbolic interactionists have limited methodologies for answering such questions. In spite of these limitations, we hope we have made a strong case why symbolic interactionism is an essential theory for community development practice.

MOVING BEYOND CLASSICAL THEORY TOWARDS GIDDENS' STRUCTURATION THEORY

We have argued that the classical macro theories of structural functionalism and conflict theory are essential concepts for building community capacity, while the micro theory of symbolic interactionism is important for creating or strengthening solidarity. There are obvious tensions inherent in these classical theories. The dualism of macro versus micro characterizes much of the theoretical thinking in sociology. Sharing the same goal of picturing the social reality, these schools choose to proceed from the opposite directions. The macro thinkers attempt to draw a holistic picture and lay down the workings of "society," whereas the micro theorists hope to arrive at the same results by scrutinizing what happens "in" and "between" the individual people. Neither approach is entirely successful in producing a complete and exhaustive picture for community development practice. In a more recent development, efforts have been made at a "micro-translation," seeking to visualize social reality as made up of individuals interacting with one another and forming "larger interaction ritual chains" (Collins, 1988).

However, it has also been recognized in the recent theory that the issue of social agency itself, pointed out above as a key concern for community development, represents a concern that needs to be theoretically addressed in a way that transcends the established orientations in modern social theory and the whole macro-micro split. In his structuration theory, Anthony Giddens (1984, 1989), offers a perspective that is more fluid and process-oriented than either the macro or the micro approaches. Giddens introduces a third dimension, or an "in-between" level of analysis, which is neither macro nor micro. It has to do with the cultural traditions, beliefs, and norms of society, and how the actors draw upon those in their behavior (Collins 1988: 399). For Giddens, those normative patterns of society exist "outside of time and space" (Collins, 1988, pp. 398-399), meaning they are neither properties of the empirical social system, nor of the individual actors. Their actuality consists in the moments when individuals reach up to that level of society's traditions and norms, in their behavior. People also draw upon and act upon thought patterns or cultural "molds," for example, the notion of reciprocity—getting something in return for something else. Cultural traditions and patterns become modalities by virtue of placing them on Giddens' analytical scheme. They represent a third level, which is in between individualistic behavior and the macro structures. Even though the reality of modalities may be only momentary, when people actually reach up to them in their behavior, we can better visualize the social process and the role of culture and normative patterns. "Actors draw upon the modalities of structuration in reproduction of systems of interaction" (Giddens, 1984, p. 28). Social structure is upheld and existing divisions of society carry on through those "mental molds."

Figure 2: Gidden's Modalities: The Link to Social Change at the Macro and Micro Levels

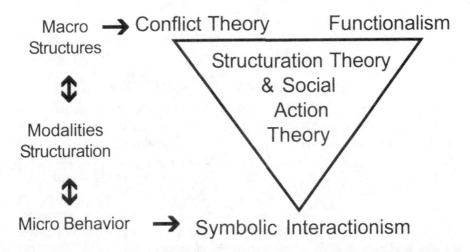

The laying out of society on three theoretical levels serves to better visualize the issue of agency compared to either the macro or the micro theories (see Figure 2). The relationship between those three levels is not necessarily uni-directional or mechanical. Rather, it is a fluid process, in which all three levels interact with each other. Individuals represent the agency whereby interactions between levels take place.

Thus, it becomes easier to grasp how macro structures have an independent existence outside of individuals, people are pictured as free agents exercising their motives and agendas, and yet society continues to exercise an influence on individuals. The notorious problem of Marx's theory and several radical thinkers informed by it, of people being the "puppets of the macrostructure," becomes circumvented.[2]

Coming back to the community development profession and its key concerns, Giddens' model is perhaps best suited to grasp how social agency is exercised and solidarity established amid and often against the existing structural divisions of society. Modalities represent the level whereby solidarity is established by people following the symbolic norms and patterns available to them based on their cultures and traditions. Behavior is neither haphazard nor merely a reflection of the existing social structure and its divisions, but it follows certain paths (modalities) established and available to people through the cultural patterns. Similarly, new rules of behavior also occur through the medium of modalities, in this instance their creative redefinition. This is how the existing divisions can be overcome and new bonds between people forged. For this to take place, a genuine social creativity is necessary, meaning people coming up with solutions and ideas that simultaneously draw on their cultural traditions (common reference point) and transcend those, as a basis for new bonds, new patterns of solidarity to be put into place. Modalities serve not only as the rules for the reproduction of the social system, but also for its transformation (Turner, 1984, p. 494).

Giddens' concept of modalities is the link between macro and micro theories. Modalities are part of the analytical scheme in a particular place. For example, individualism in the United States is a strong modality and can keep citizens from becoming united to take action. The notion of a common good is another American modality, which can be used to transform a divided community into a greater sense of solidarity. Modalities can be used to influence the macro or micro level of social change. There are several substantive analyses of the social processing and the dynamics of social transformation carried out, at least in part, on the level of modalities, looking at cultural patterns and systems of ideas and how they mediate the social process. Gaventa (1980) examines the modalities of Appalachia with a focus on rebellion and quiescence. He analyzes how power is used in the region to prevent or implement decisions. The use of force and threat of sanctions are discussed along with less intrusive aspects such as attitudes that are infused into the dominant culture by elites and internalized by non-elites. For example, there are perspectives such as "you can't change anything around here" or "you don't have to be poor if you want to really work." Gaventa argues there are other modalities in which Appalachian culture has resisted the penetration of dominant social values. Those with less power can develop their own resources for analyzing issues and can explore their grievances openly. He views the "myth of American democracy" as another modality that can set the stage for greater openness and transparency in local government.

Staniszkis (1984) provides further insights about modalities through her ideas about how workers' solidarity emerged in Poland. She saw the working class under the communist regime as a unified bloc, both in a positive hegemonic way and negatively, as subject to the party's control and manipulation. These modalities were taken by Solidarity and its charismatic leader Lech Walesa and transformed through references to workers' common identity as opposed to the party apparatus. Walesa forged workers' strong Christian identification into this new self-understanding and self-image of the workers in Poland to further create a sense of solidarity and unity in opposition to the community party and the system. Through her consistent attention to symbolic meanings and their interplay with the social structure, Staniszkis' work on the transformation of workers' collective identity represents an apt demonstration of how a transformation of modalities may take place.

Analytically, Giddens' structuration theory stands as the middle ground between the micro and the macro theories, where we have also placed the issue of agency and solidarity (see Figure 2). Giddens' structuration theory suggests that the micro theories associated with symbolic interactionism can influence cultural and traditional norms and patterns (modalities) and vice versa. While the symbolic interactionist tend to ignore structure, Giddens' mid-level theory about modalities is a crucial link between symbolic interactionism and the macro conflict and "structural functionalist theories (Giddens, 1984).

Max Weber's social action theory was originally cast at an "in-between level." If his theory were not explicit, it was at least implicit in his intentions.[3] Weber attempted to view society as a fluid process, for analytical purposes dissecting it into various components (Turner, 1998, p. 17) much like Giddens does. Although Weber never attempted an analytical model of society along those lines, some observers have categorized Weber as a micro-theorist because of his subjective interpretation of behavior and its meaning to the actor. Others argue that Weber is a strong macro-theorist. Our understanding is that his intentions actually lie closer to Giddens' perspective that a three-tiered model is better suited to grasp the complexities of social action and the interplay between the symbolic meaning and the structural forces of society. Weber's writings suggest he is constantly preoccupied with the interplay between the symbolic meaning and the structural forces of society. This is especially obvious in his attempts to explain the rise of modern capitalism through the interplay of social structural conditions and the religious beliefs of Protestantism. He followed similar analyses for non-Western societies in his sociology of religion volumes. What Giddens lays down in theory, Weber actually performs in his works, bridging the macro, and the micro dimensions by his attention to society's traditions and norms and how they become transformed, independently of the macro structural forces of society, through people interpreting and reinterpreting them. Similarly, Gaventa and Staniszkis demonstrate how one can connect communities or groups to structure in a way that is not fixed or mechanical.

In contrast to debates about whether structure shapes action to determine social phenomena or the reverse, Giddens believes that structure exists in and through the activities of human agents. He views it as a form of "dualism" in which neither can exist without the other. When humans express themselves as actors and when they engage in the monitoring of the ongoing flow of activities, they are contributing to structure and their own agency. He contends that social systems are often the result of the unanticipated outcome of human action. Giddens viewed time and space as crucial variables. Many interactions are face-to-face, and hence are rooted in the same space and time. However, with the advent of new technologies, there can be interaction across different times and spaces. Community developers are likely to feel some kinship with Giddens because he has a dynamic rather than a static concept of the world. He recognizes the interplay of humans in shaping and being shaped by structure. Critics are likely to argue that he has oversubscribed to the concept about the power of human agency. Our space limits the response to such critiques; we cannot provide a fuller exploration of Giddens' theoretical insights.

How Can Giddens' Structuration Theory Guide Community Development Practice?

Structuration theory provides many theoretical insights (see Ritzer, 1996 p. 433) for those engaged in community development because it links disparate macro theories about structure and conflict with micro theories about individual and group behavior and symbols (symbolic interactionism). Giddens' concept of modalities is essential for community development practice.

Let us revisit the case of the Appalachian community group that is opposing the construction of a road through a nearby state forest. They believe they are overpowered by the Department of Transportation (DOT) that wants to build the road. The community finds it difficult to argue against the DOT report, which contains sophisticated economic, social and natural resource information. Here is what the community developer practitioner did. First, the community's residents identified the strengths of their local traditions – particularly, storytelling and the arts – as a venue for building a sense of solidarity about the integrity of the forest. They examined the modalities of storytelling and the arts as a way to make an impact through the media to the public and elected leaders in the region. The community's strong respect for the local Cooperative Extension Service was identified as another modality that could mobilize the broader informational resources of the land-grant university. The developer was able to draw upon the services of professional economists, sociologists, foresters, and others without spending much money; these professionals developed an alternative to the DOT report that was widely disseminated. Storytelling, the local arts, and links with the local Extension Service influenced broader structures and led to less power imbalances. Eventually, the DOT decided to permanently "postpone" the development of the road. Because the community developer understood the power of modalities (local cultural traditions and patterns), the community was able to develop a sense of shared meaning which led to greater influence on structure and resolution of the conflict.

How do Giddens' structuration theory and the concept of modalities relate to the three classical theories: structural functionalism, conflict theory, and symbolic interactionism?

When one looks at functionalism through the Giddens lens, one sees how structures shape and can be shaped by modalities. From a Giddens perspective, community change agents are not powerless when faced with powerful structures. Cultural patterns can be transformed to influence or break down structural constraints that inhibit solidarity or capacity building.

Giddens' structuration theory illuminates conflict theory because it suggests that communities can influence power imbalances through cultural norms and patterns. It also means that external power can also shape behavior.

Based on a Giddens perspective, the micro theories associated with symbolic interactionism can influence cultural and traditional norms and patterns (modalities), and vice versa. While the symbolic interactionists tend to ignore structure, Giddens mid-level theory about modalities is a crucial link between symbolic interactionism and the macro "conflict" and structural functionalist theories.

Limitations of Giddens' Structuration Theory

Giddens' writing is analytical and abstract to the point of being vague and imprecise. He rarely gives concrete examples, which can be frustrating to those community developers who are more empirically grounded. Giddens' analysis is also difficult because it involves a constant moving between the levels of modalities and societal institutions and the actual actions of individuals.

In spite of these limitations, we believe it is especially useful to community developers because of the potent role of symbolic norms and cultural patterns (modalities) in creating new structures, influencing power differences and shaping individual behavior into a sense of solidarity.

CONCLUSION

We have defined community development by its intention to build solidarity and agency (capacity building). There are three classical theories that are essential for community development practice. They include the macro theories of structural functionalism, conflict theory that relates to capacity building, and symbolic interactionism that is associated with solidarity building. We have provided some case studies that illustrate the importance of these theories to community development practice.

We have focused on Anthony Giddens' structuration theory because Giddens links macro and micro theories through his concept of modalities that represent the level where social solidarity is established. Modalities are symbolic norms and patterns that can be found in community cultures and traditions. Modalities are shaped by structures and power differences. However, they can also be transformed to influence structure and address power differences. For example, a community can transform its belief about the common good to build a stronger sense of unity and to take appropriate action steps rather than feel powerless. Our discussion of modalities is interspersed with examples from Appalachia and Poland.

This article is about reaching across the conceptual divide between theory and action. It is about stimulating dialogue and further discussion about essential theory for community development practice. We believe that Giddens and other synthesizers have reenergized interests in classical theory by linking theoretical camps in a novel way.

NOTES

1. There are several exceptions such as the text, *Community Economics* by Ron E. Shaffer (1989). It is theoretically driven. However, it focuses on one aspect of community development, namely economic development.

2. We argue that structuration theory represents an improvement over conventional micro theories (i.e., symbolic interactionists) which also visualizes behavior on two levels, the "me" and the "I." The 'me' is reminiscent of Giddens' modalities but the micro theorists miss the significance of the social structure and its divisions, which Giddens treats as the analytical third level.

3. Talcott Parsons original 1937 formulation of his theory was cast at a similar level, with the dimension of "culture" representing a bridge between personality and the social system, but subsequently it got lost as the social system swallowed up the micro dimension in Parsons' theorizing (Collins, 1988).

REFERENCES

Bhattacharyya, J. 1995. Solidarity and agency: Rethinking community development. *Human Organization* 54(1): 60-68.

Biddle, W., with L. Biddle. 1965. *The Community Development Process*. New York: Holt Rhinehardt and Winston.

Blumer, H. 1969. *Symbolic Interactionism: Perspective and Method*. New York: Prentice-Hall.

Chaskin, R. J., P. Brown, S. Venkatesh, & A.Vidal. 2001. *Building Community Capacity*. Hawthorne, NY: Aldine De Gruyter.

Christenson, J., & J. Robinson (eds). 1989. *Community Development in Perspective*. Iowa City: University of Iowa Press.

Collins, R. 1988. *Theoretical Sociology*. New York: Harcourt Brace Jovanovich, Publishers.

Coser, L. 1956. *The Functions of Social Conflict*. New York: The Free Press.

Dahl, R. A. 1971. *Polyarchy: Participation and Opposition*. New Haven, CT: Yale University Press.

Dahrendolf, R. 1959. *Class and Class Conflict in Industrial Society*. Stanford, CA: Stanford University Press.

Ejigiri, D. 1996. The value of local knowledge and the importance of shifting beliefs in the process of social change. *Community Development Journal* 31(1): 44-53.

Flora, C. B., J. L. Flora, & R. J. Tapp. 2000. Meat, meth and Mexicans: Community responses to increasing ethnic diversity. *Journal of the Community Development Society* 31(2): 277-299.

Foucault, M. 1965. *Madness and Civilization: A History of Insanity in the Age of Reason.* New York: Vintage.

Foucault, M. 1975. *The Birth of the Clinic: An Archeology of Medical Perception.* New York: Vintage.

Foucault, M. 1979. *Discipline and Punish: The Birth of Prison.* New York: Vintage.

Foucault, M. 1980. *The History of Sexuality, Volume 1, An Introduction.* New York: Vintage.

Foucault, M. 1985. *The Use of Pleasure. The History of Sexuality, Volume 2.* New York: Panthenon.

Galbraith, J. K. 1971. *The New Industrial State.* Boston, Houghton Mifflin.

Gaventa, J. L. 1980. *Power and Politics: Quiescence and Rebellion in an Appalachian Valley.* Urbana: University of Illinois Press.

Giddens, A. 1984. *The Constitution of Society.* Berkley: University of California Press..

Giddens, A. 1989. A reply to my critics. Pp. 249-301 in D. Held & J.B. Thompson (eds.), *Social Theory of Modern Societies: Anthony Giddens and His Critics.* Cambridge, UK: Cambridge University.

Goffman, E. 1959. *The Presentation of Self in Everyday Life.* Garden City, NY: Anchor.

Goffman, E. 1986. *Frame Anlaysis: An Essay on the Organization of Experience.* Boston: Northeastern University Press.

Horton, H. D. 1992. A sociological approach to black community development: presentation of the black organizational autonomy model. *Journal of the Community Development Society* 23(1): 1-19.

Jeffries, A. 2000. Promoting participation: A conceptual framework for strategic practice, with case studies from Plymouth, UK and Ottawa, Canada. *The Scottish Journal of Community Work and Development,* Special Issue, 6(Autumn): 5-14.

Mead, G. H. 1982. *The Individual and the Social Self: Unpublished Work of George Herbert Mead.* Chicago: University of Chicago Press.

Merton, R. K. 1968. *Social Theory and Social* Structure. Rev. ed. New York: The Free Press.

Nash, K. 2000. *Contemporary Political Sociology: Globalization, Politics, and Power.* Malden, Massachusetts: Blackwell Publishers Inc.

Parsons, T. (ed.). 1960. Some reflections on the institutional framework of economic development. In *Structure and Process in Modern Societies.* Glencoe, IL: Free Press.

Parsons, T., & E. A. Shils (eds.). 1951. *Toward a General Theory of Action.* New York: Harper & Row.

Perkins, D. D. 1995. Speaking truth to power: Empowerment ideology as social intervention and policy. *American Journal of Community Psychology* 23(5): 569-579.

Ritzer, G. 1996. *Sociological Theory*. 4th ed. New York: McGraw-Hill.

Rothman, J. & L. M. Gant. 1987. Approaches and models of community intervention. Pp. 35-44 in D. E. Johnson, L. R. Meiller, L. C. Miller & G. F. Summers (eds.), *Needs Assessment: Theory and Methods*. Ames, Iowa: Iowa State University Press.

Schellenberg, J. A. 1996. *Conflict Resolution: Theory, Research and Practice*. Albany, NY: State University of New York.

Shaffer, R. E. 1989. *Community Economics: Economic Structure and Change in Smaller Communities*. Ames, IA: Iowa State University Press.

Staniszkis, J. 1984. *Poland's Self-Limiting Revolution*. Princeton, NJ: Princeton University Press.

Turner, J. H. 1998. *The Structure of Sociological Theory*. 6th ed. Belmont, CA: Wadsworth Publishing Company.

Wallerstein, I. 1984. The development of the concept of development. *Sociological Theory* 2: 102-116.

Weber, M. 1947. *The Theory of Social and Economic Organization*. A.M. Henderson & T. Parsons (Trans.). New York: Oxford University Press.

THEORIZING COMMUNITY DEVELOPMENT

By Jnanabrata Bhattacharyya

ABSTRACT

This paper attempts a parsimonious definition of community development. It proposes that the purpose of community development is the pursuit of solidarity and agency by adhering to the principles of self-help, felt needs and participation. The erosion of solidarity and agency has been a historic process, connected particularly to the rise of industrial capitalism, the nation-state, and instrumental reason. Examples of community development practice as a positive response to the erosion are given from the fields of public health, violence, micro-economic development, and food. It also argues that "place" as a proxy for community has become conceptually as well as practically inadequate, and that effective community development calls for micro-macro coordination.

INTRODUCTION

This paper submits a theoretical framework for the practice of community development, intended to help to distinguish the field from other related endeavors. It perhaps goes without saying that it should be read as one person's idea of community development, although its debt to numerous authors should be evident throughout the paper. In an earlier exercise (Bhattacharyya, 1995) I had proposed that community development is different from other endeavors in that it aims at building solidarity and agency by adhering to three practice principles, namely, self-help, felt needs, and participation. That paper has been received in community development and related fields with interest. Among other reactions, it was utilized as a springboard for discussions at the 2003 Community Development Theory Retreat at the Taughannock Farm Inn in Trumansburg, New York. This paper reflects my response to some of the feedback I received at the Retreat, as well as my continuing engagement with the subject while iterating the earlier proposition.[1] I discuss some of the definitions of community development of the last forty years to show the continuing need for a more rigorous definition. I have suggested that the purpose of community development should be seen as different both from its methods and the techniques to implement the methods. I have argued that place or locality often used in community development literature as a proxy for community has become or is

Jnanabrata Bhattacharyya, Emeritus Associate Professor, Department of Political Science, and Director (1984-1994), Department of Community Development at Southern Illinois University at Carbondale. Email: jnan_bhattacharyya@yahoo.com becoming analytically irrelevant and practically inadequate. Finally, I have put forward the notion that in centralized states community development practice at the micro level increasingly calls for macro level intervention as well. I begin with a discussion of the problem of bounding the field of community development.

The Problem of Defining Community Development

A theory of community development will define the concept and delineate the characteristics of its practice. It will demarcate the field from other endeavors in clear and unambiguous terms. But in community development literature such a theory is generally not available. What precisely is community development? Why is engaging in it important? And where does it stand in relation to other practical as well as academic endeavors? These are questions that have been rarely posed and discussed. There has been, historically, a reluctance to define the concept. "[F]or the present, all approaches which claim to be Community Development be accepted as legitimate contributions," thus recommended William Biddle in 1966 (p. 12). Four years later, Lee J. Cary (1970) warned against""premature closure." Nearly a quarter century after that, Christenson and Robinson (1989, p. 14) said much the same thing: "[D]efinitions of community development are not clear-cut, how one interprets community development affects one's orientation when initiating a development program." Denise and Harris (1990, p. 7) expressed similar sentiments: "This concept [community development] is as varied in definition as those who profess to practice it." Many who call themselves community developers can perhaps do so because the field is unfenced; if it became fenced, they would be obliged to go their separate ways, or retrain.

The risk of exclusivity is probably real, but if the adherents themselves do not define the field, others will (as they have) and not necessarily to their advantage. For instance, a widely held belief in the U.S. and elsewhere is that community development is the same as "community organization" (CO), a specialty in Social Work, or only a part of this specialty. Especially since the 1968 publication of Jack Rothman's "*Three Models of Community Organization Practice*," community development has been viewed by many as Locality Development, which is one of the three models. Rothman's article exerted a profound influence on the definition of community development, in part because its publication coincided with the establishment of community development graduate programs in the United States, and it came in handy.

Without much reflection, community development practitioners interpreted CO or only Locality Development as community development. Rothman's article and, later, Social Work textbooks on CO (e.g., Kramer & Specht, 1969; Cox et al., 1974) were also the textbooks for introductory courses in community development graduate programs. The field was thus allowed to be defined by Social Workers. By adopting these textbooks, academic community developers legitimized the locality development definition while never ceasing to protest that in some inarticulate way community development was different from CO and Social Work. Lee Cary, the founding president of the Community Development Society, reinforced this definition. In his keynote address to the 1982 meeting of the Illinois State Chapter of the Community Development Society, he had observed in reference to Rothman's article that "the first model of practice is identified as *locality development,* what we would refer to as community development."

Certainly, community development is not lacking in "definitions." Indeed a surfeit of statements purporting to be definitions have been published each slightly differently worded in an idiosyncratic frenzy with no explanation as to why the particular terms were chosen. (For a comprehensive list of such definitions, see *The Handbook of Community Development,* compiled by the Department of Community Development, University of Missouri-Columbia, n.d.). Two observations need to be made about most of these definitions: first, they are conceptually vague, and, second, they have a tendency to conflate place with community. Just to illustrate the point, let us scrutinize the definition in *Community Development in Perspective* edited by Christenson and Robinson (1989). It was published with the endorsement of the Community Development Society, and it has been fairly influential. Under "Major Concepts" (pp. 5ff.), the editors observe: "Community development encompasses a loosely tied group of concepts based on the experiences of community development practitioners." (p.5) That is, community development is what community developers do. But how do we identify a community development practitioner? This is a circular definition.

Problems Defining Community

The editors then offer clarifications of the meaning of community, development, social change, community development, and related concepts (pp. 6ff.). They note that today:

> Places of work, of commerce, of recreation, and of sleep are often miles apart, perhaps communities apart. Yet no matter how complex communities have become, the need to understand and to be able define community is still of critical importance to community developers. Most of our meaningful interactions take place in *a defined spatial area.* Most of us live; work; attend church; send our children to school; drive on the same roads; complain about the same traffic problems; and buy groceries, gas, and clothing in a *general locality, neighborhood* or *community.* (p. 6, emphasis added).

Reading the first sentence closely, they state that places of work, recreation, residence, etc. are far from one another. Then, they confuse the issue by saying that most of our meaningful interactions take place in a "defined spatial area... a general locality, neighborhood or community." We can ask, what is this *defined spatial area,* especially since places of work, commerce, recreation, and sleep are far from one another? What principle or criterion defines it?

In the next paragraph, the editors use the expression *community or neighborhood* introducing new ambiguities:

> In short, a community or neighborhood can exist with close linkage to the larger society and still retain its identity and viability because it provides a basis for the *local* population to engage in *community* actions." (emphasis added).

Here again we need to ask, what is local? Leaving aside the substantive point of this paragraph which is highly debatable (Janowitz, 1978; Bellah et al., 1985), it appears that the authors attempt to slide from *general locality* through *neighborhood* into *community*. This paragraph is devoted to considering the relevance of place or territory to the concept of community. The editors point out disagreements among writers on this issue. But instead of confronting the disagreements with one another in order to reconcile or synthesize them or even to side with one of them, they peremptorily declare:

> The editors of this book think that spatial boundaries are an integral part of community and that most social interactions take place within defined and proximate spatial limits. Consequently, place or territory is considered a second component of our definition.(p. 14).

What are "defined spatial limits"? What is proximate in the days of fast transport?

Another example of circular reasoning – and imprecision – is in their discussion of the "fourth element" of community (pp. 7-8):

> The fourth element of community is the idea of common attachment of or psychological *identification* with a community. Most people are able to give you the name of the community in which they live. People become dependent on a particular *locality* for the purchase of goods and services, for recreation, for employment, and for socializing. This locality is what most people identify with as community.

Instead of defining community, the statement presupposes it and specifies one of its features (attachment, identification). The difficulty continues with "People become dependent on a particular community…" This thoroughly contradicts the prior observation (p. 6) that "Places of work, of commerce, of recreation, and of sleep are often miles apart, perhaps communities apart." Now people are dependent on "a particular community." And, in the next sentence, locality becomes community, with no explanation.

Confusion about the Definition of Community Development

A similar criticism can be made of their treatment of the definition of community development (pp. 11-14). After listing a number of definitions of community development they propose one of their own (p. 14): "a group of people in a locality initiating a social action process (i.e., planned intervention) to change their economic, social, cultural, and/or environmental situation." It may be recalled that the term locality and its relation to neighborhood, place, or community were left in a state of confusion; now in this definition it occupies a vital place. Also, why is political left out from the series? This definition no more and no less than the others they have cited is vague and arbitrary. There is no particular impetus for choosing one set of terms over another. But all this discussion of community development definition is rendered pointless by the conclusion of this section (p. 14), which I have already signaled: "In short, definitions of community development are not clear-cut, and how one interprets community development affects one's orientation when initiating a development program." So anything goes? It is another way of saying that, according to them, community development is not definable.

Much the same can be said about the work of Denise and Harris (1989). They write in the Introduction (p. 7), "This concept [community development] is as varied in definition as those who profess to practice it." As evidence, they note that the 22 authors in Christenson and Robinson (1989) each had defined the term differently. They then add one of their own. Thus, a community is "a collectivity of people, who can be identified geographically, who have something in common which unites them in action.... Such a definition includes micro communities (special interest groups, neighborhoods, subdivisions, villages, towns, etc.) as well as macro communities (cities, megalopolises, areas, regions, states, nations, international alliances, and global humanity)." Like Christenson and Robinson, Denise and Harris conclude:

> We believe that community development should be so defined as to encompass the wide spectrum of beliefs of those who practice it. Therefore, to the editors, the "field of community development" contains numerous approaches to community development with differing values, beliefs, goals, purposes, and methods – all of which are concerned with improvement of the communities (p. 7).

What is not an approach to community development, then? Every socially approved occupation exists because it is thought to contribute to community improvement. If community development is to be recognized as a distinct academic/professional field, then an all-encompassing concept is not going to accomplish it; not everything that contributes to community improvement can be claimed as community development. To define, after all, is to set limits.

A concept of community development must satisfy two conditions. First, it must be distinctive in its purpose and in its methodology. Second, it must be universal in scope: it must be applicable to all types of social formations, urban as well as rural, post-industrial as well as pre-industrial, to sedentary as well as nomadic populations. Our task therefore is to construct an unambiguous reference point to guide community development activities and to determine if certain activities fall within the orbit of community development. Such an attempt is made in the next section.

A Theory of Community Development

It is necessary at the outset to explain what I mean by theory. There is a widespread misconception that only explanations can be theories. In hard sciences, theories or laws are indeed explanations; they claim to explain how a phenomenon occurs and make predictions on the basis of that. But theories can also be teleological – charters for action towards a goal, such as theories of democracy, freedom, equality, etc. where the purpose or the end reflexively enters the causal stream, urging, when necessary, modification of our action. The purpose of building a rocket, for instance, cannot do that; it cannot alter the laws of physics. Democratic theories are not like the laws of physics. They are not explanations but they elaborate a vision of a kind of social order. A theory of community development is of this kind. It advocates a particular kind of social order and a particular methodology for getting there. How children learn is a matter of explanation, but "No Child Left Behind" is not a matter of explanation but a goal to be attained, which calls for changes in the way we manage our school education.

We assess the quality of a teleological theory by the reasonableness (to us) of its assumptions or value premises (e.g., We hold these truths to be self-evident that all men are created equal) and the logical coherence between the assumptions, the methods, and the goal. The assumptions or value premises are political choices, unlike the axioms of physics. Accordingly, a theory of community development will specify its purpose (goal, rationale), its premises, and its methods.

One important point needs to be made beforehand. A purpose is different from the methods that may be utilized to achieve it, and both of these in turn are different from the techniques or tools that may be utilized to implement the methods. We have a purpose to fulfill, we try to do that by following certain methods, and we implement the methods by means of certain techniques. A method refers to the logic of the actions to achieve the purpose. It is a more general description of what needs to be done than the techniques or tools. Suppose we want to revitalize our main street (the purpose). We choose to encourage various specialty stores to locate downtown (the method), and how we encourage them (tax incentives, pedestrian malls, antique streetlights, etc.) are the techniques. The asset-based community development (ABCD) approach (Kretzmann & McKnight, 1993), community development corporations (CDC) (Ferguson & Dickens, 1999), social planning, social action, locality development, etc. are techniques or tools, not to be conflated with either the purpose or the methods of community development. For community development to be a distinct field, its purpose and its methods must be specific to it. As regards tools, they need not be specific to community development at all; we could access the entire range of human knowledge as potential tools for the implementation of its methods.

I propose, as I had done earlier (Bhattacharyya, 1995), that we conceptualize the purpose of community development as the promotion of solidarity and agency. Although this formulation may appear to be yet another arbitrary definition of community development, I will argue that solidarity is the essential characteristic of community, and, there is an important view that the purpose of development is to promote agency (see, for example, Berger, 1974; Giddens, 1987; Sen, 1999). Moreover, I think these are the qualities that most community development writers intend to convey in their definitions of the term.

Community as Solidarity

For community development to be a universally relevant field, we have to extract the essence of the term community and not be limited by its common usage in the social sciences and community development literature. Durkheim's (1964[1893]) mechanical solidarity and Tonnies's (1957[1887]) Gemeinschaft referred to pre-industrial social formations – villages or tribes. Similarly, the community development definitions produced by the United Nations, the Ashridge Conference, the Cambridge Conference, the International Cooperation Administration (the precursor to the U.S. Agency for International Development) meant pre-industrial social configurations. So did most anthropologists and other social scientists that were concerned with development (Bendix 1964; Biddle & Biddle 1965; Brokensha & Hodge 1969; Dobyns, Doughty, & Lasswell 1971; Dube, 1963; Erasmus, 1961; G. Foster, 1973; Goodenough, 1963). With a few exceptions (e.g., Bradshaw & Blakely, 1979; Clinard ,1966; Ferguson & Dickens, 1999; Kretzmann & McKnight, 1993; Popple & Quinney, 2002; Spiegel & Mittenthal, 1968) most self-identified community development writers brought to their work a classical concept of community – as a village or at least a rural agricultural settlement or a small town (Batten, 1957; du Sautoy, 1958; Flora, 1998; Knowles, 1960; Sanders, 1958a, 1958b; Summers, 1986; Wileden, 1970).

From the very inception of the field, rural or agricultural settlements or small towns have stood as a proxy for community. Even in the exceptional cases signaled above, place or space (e.g., urban neighborhoods) has remained an integral constituent of community. It can thus be said that place, whether rural, urban or whatever, has been an invariant element of the concept of community, and, as I argue below, it must be transcended to reach a theory of community development.

Three observations need to be made on this connection of place with community. First, this mode of usage takes the meaning of community as self-evident. A neighborhood, a small town, or a village is automatically assumed to be a community, regardless of the absence of any cohesion in it.

Second, it obscures another understanding of the term that transcends all connections with place, such as Durkheim's organic solidarity and Tonnies's Gesellschaft, a solidarity based upon shared interests or circumstances. It is this quality that is invoked for such bodies as the Jewish community, the Christian community, the community of Islam (the Umma), the Black community, the medical community, and, at an earlier time, trades union. In this sense of community place is incidental, not integral to its definition.

Finally, it fails to take into account the radical social change brought about by modernity in the social significance of place. Modernity, very briefly, is the complex of transformations ushered in by industrialization. Wherever industry has become the dominant mode of production, it has had the effect of dissolving or at least weakening place-centered communities. We recognize place-centered communities better by an earlier term for it, namely, face-to-face communities (Gemeinschaft, mechanical solidarity, folk community). Place or locality was significant in such societies because most social activities took place within its confines and among people who were familiar with one another and who shared a common culture. Modernity divests place of this significance as most social activities can no longer remain confined in the "place" but must be oriented to unknown people in unknown places, to abstract institutions, and within rules that are different from the community norms (Berger, 1973; Giddens, 1990). It can even be said that the solidarity movements in the last century and a half arose in reaction to the decay of place-centered communities. Thus, a focus on place in the definition of community distracts from a theory of community development. A broader concept of community would not prevent us from seeing or developing community where place retains its significance, while freeing us to focus on the widest range of communities. Developing community in this sense has acquired an increasing urgency in recent decades in post-industrial as well as newly industrializing countries (for a useful summary of the concerns about community in the West, see Bellah et al., 1985; Fowler, 1991; Plant ,1974; Polanyi, 1944; Putnam, 1995; Wolin, 1990).

What is this quality that unites these two different understandings of community? The classic answer is solidarity (Durkheim), meaning a shared identity (derived from place, ideology, or interest) and a code for conduct or norms, both deep enough that a rupture affects the members emotionally and other ways. The decade old social capital movement conveys the same meaning: networks, trust, and mutual obligations enabling people to take collective measures to address shared problems (Putnam, 1995), as does the quality of life ideals listed by Ferguson and Dickens in their vision for community development (1999, p. 2). It is the weakening of this solidarity that has been in one way or another the point of departure for social criticism for over two centuries (e.g., Bellah et al., 1985; Fowler, 1991; Nisbet, 1962; Putnam, 1995; 1993; Wolin, 1990; Zagarella, 1988).

Understanding community as solidarity (shared identity and norms) serves to define the concept in a distinctive and intrinsic manner, making it possible to distinguish a community from all other types of social relations. We can say that any social configuration that possesses shared identity and norms is a community. The term is thus freed of the incidental baggage of territoriality, ethnicity or level of industrialization of the economy.

Development as Agency

The ultimate goal of development should be human autonomy or agency – the capacity of people to order their world, the capacity to create, reproduce, change, and live according to their own meaning systems, to have the powers to define themselves as opposed to being defined by others (de Certeau, 1986;

Giddens, 1984). Giddens (1984, p. 14) puts it succinctly as "to be able to 'act otherwise'," that is, "to be able to intervene in the world, or to refrain from such intervention, with the effect of influencing a specific process or state of affairs." Others have called it freedom (Sen, 1999). It is apparent that empowerment, capacity building, and similar "buzz words" are not ends in themselves but means for the higher end of agency.

Agency is a modern concept, and it is linked with the concept of choice, which in turn is the product of the pattern of social change called modernity (Apter, 1971). In pre-modern societies, neither the concept nor the problem of agency could arise because choice was either conceptually absent or very limited. It is only with the onset of modernity that we could think of choosing our occupation, our domicile, our attire, our diet, and even our religion. But, as will be discussed in slightly greater detail later, modernity even as it created unprecedented opportunities for choice and agency also unleashed forces to annul them. To foster agency is what sets part of the agenda for community development.[2]

There was a time when development was indistinguishable from economic development, or, more narrowly, growth in the value of gross domestic product (GDP). That still seems to be the meaning in ordinary language. Most people understand development as economic development. In the field of development studies, the focus on simple economic growth was replaced first by the idea of modernization (better technology and associated cultural change), and eventually by the idea of "human development" and freedom (Blomstrom & Hettne, 1984; Sen, 1999). The *Human Development Report* published by the United Nations Development Program since 1990 utilizes a Human Development Index to measure development. The index is a composite of life expectancy at birth, literacy rate, mean years of schooling, and GDP per capita in real terms. Human development is defined as the creation and promotion of people's choices and capabilities, that is, agency, which is the unifying concern of the social sciences and humanities today.

Wittingly or unwittingly, many governmental as well as private social service organizations create chronic dependency in the "clients," establishing a relationship as between givers and abject recipients, the latter rarely gaining the capability to break out of the relationship. They are service *providers*. In community development parlance, such projects are set up *for* the clients not *with* them. Examples abound in the social history of most welfare societies of the providers strongly discouraging the "clients" from developing a sense of entitlement to the services that they could *demand as* a matter of civic right. On the contrary, the clients, poor and ill educated, frequently the targets of social ridicule and contempt, are scarcely allowed to develop what Freire (1973) called the critical consciousness. Briefly put, *critical consciousness* means not accepting an undesirable condition as fate or unchangeable, understanding the structure of causes that brought it about, and then evolving strategies to mitigate them. Community development in order to promote agency aims at generating critical consciousness, addressing problems that the affected people "own" and define, and take active measures to solve.

Defining development as agency-promoting activity has the advantage of parsimony: it captures the goals typically enumerated in community development definitions (economic and social change, improvement of quality of life, etc.), and, besides, it specifies the ultimate goal of development.

We can thus say that for any activity (economic development, organizing migrant farm workers, mobilizing for minority rights, elderly care, the environment, cultural rights, or better schools) to be called community development, the activity must be animated by the pursuit of solidarity and agency. Defining community development this way – the fostering of social relations that are increasingly characterized by solidarity and agency – also aligns community development with the mainstream intellectual concerns in the humanities and the social sciences today, adding to the field's academic respectability. Furthermore, it opens up a vast field for action and research on the process of erosion of solidarity and agency and the means for reconstructing them.

The Context of Community Development

Community development is a positive response to the historic process of erosion of solidarity and agency. Its premise is that people have an inalienable right to agency and that solidarity is a necessity for a satisfying life. Community development is a part of the democracy project. At the core of democracy is the vision of solidarity ("fraternity") and emancipation from authoritarianism or "unnecessary domination" (M. Weber) (agency). At the highest level, solidarity demands that we feel a concern for every person in the nation and the world as a whole (the solidarity of the species), extending solidarity to people we do not know. This is also the argument for the public good. More practically, it implies a willingness to engage in collective effort to create and sustain a caring society.

Freedom from authoritarianism or agency means the opportunity for the affirmation of the human will. Authoritarianism means the exercise of power by persons or institutions demanding obedience: it permits no dialogue, no freedom to inquire, only compliance. It does not permit 'acting otherwise'. Agency means freedom from unnecessary restraints (negative freedoms) and access to resources that makes affirmation of the human will possible (positive freedoms). More practically, it means respect for different preferences, different cultures, and different ways of life.

Since I have said that community development is positive response to the process of erosion of solidarity and agency, it is necessary to trace the history of this process.

The Erosion of Solidarity and Agency

The erosion of solidarity and agency is a modern affair. In the evolution of human society, we see transformations of solidarity. For example, the domestication of plants and animals and the rise of agriculture dissolved the solidarity type of nomadic or hunting-gathering society, but they generated new ones of the type found in farming villages. Similarly, the invention of printing coupled with the spread of literacy vastly enlarged the private space at the cost of public entertainment (such as public poetry recitation) and of the leisure time spent in the company of friends and neighbors (see McLuhan, 1962; Febvre & Martin, 1976). But these also enabled the formation of new forms of solidarity based on more widely shared meanings, attitudes, and sentiments.

What we are confronted with today is erosion rather than transformation of solidarity at both micro and macro levels. The very titles of some works of the second half of the 20th century, *Bowling Alone* by Robert Putnam (1995), *The Lonely Crowd* by David Riesman (1950), *The Pursuit of Loneliness* by Philip Slater (1970) convey a sense of the state of solidarity today. In the case of the United States, Putnam (1995) noted the steep decline in a number of dimensions of solidarity (social capital) – in civic participation, church going, membership in social clubs, trade unions, in time spent with family and neighbors. During the last third of 20th century, they fell by 25 to 50 percent at both macro and micro levels. According to the 35 country World Values Survey, civic participation and social trust levels are worse in most other countries in the Survey than in the United States (Putnam, 1995), and the process of solidarity erosion, notes Meranze (2001, pp. 110-111),

> is visible all around us: in the closing of health facilities, the widespread stigmatization of some recipients of governmental assistance, the transfer of fiscal resources from schools to prisons, long-term attacks on labor unions and labor rights, the contraction of social commitments to shared basic rights, the tightening of "social borders."

It is impossible in this short essay even to outline the complex history of the erosion of solidarity and agency. I will therefore focus on several related factors of modernity that have played a decisive role in it, industrial capitalism, the rise of the nation state, and instrumental reason. It should be noted at the outset that social change, at least its modern variants, is almost always ambiguous; it ushers in changes that enhance life while at the same time making it less meaningful. This is true of these factors as well.

Industrial Capitalism

Beginning in the late 18th century in countries where it has become the common mode of production industrial capitalism has created unprecedented prosperity, numerous amenities, and freedom from famine. It has expanded literacy, increased life expectancy at birth, and has vastly enlarged opportunities for choice. In many cases, it has brought about a democratization of society.

However, the erosion or even destruction of solidarity has also been an integral feature of the process of industrialization, with its attendant ideology of the free market. This is a well traversed ground but bears a little recapitulation in view of the current euphoria in many quarters about globalization of free market economy that has tended to obscure the catastrophic effects of free market on human solidarity, since its beginning.

The dominant fact about industrial capitalism is the commodification of life and its consequences. This has been the verdict - and the warning - of social critics of diverse ideological persuasions from the 19th century to the present day. This is one point on which Marxists, non-Marxists, and even anti Marxists are in broad agreement (see, for example, Bellah et al., 1985; Berger, 1973, 1974; Marx & Engels, 1847; Nisbet, 1953; Polanyi, 1944).

A commodity, by definition, is an object produced for sale on the market, and a market is the intersection of demand for and supply of a commodity. There has to be a market for every ingredient of the economy, including labor, land, and money. But labor, land, and money are not commodities. Sixty years ago, Polanyi (1944, pp. 72-73), the distinguished economic historian, wrote:

> "Labor is only another name for a human activity which goes with life itself, which in its turn is not produced for sale but for entirely different reasons, nor can that activity be detached from the rest of life, be stored or mobilized; land is only another name for nature, which is not produced by man; actual money, finally, is merely a token of purchasing power which, as a rule, is not produced at all, but comes into being through the mechanism of banking or state finance. The commodity description of labor, land, and money is entirely fictitious."

But it is this "commodity fiction," Polanyi (1944, p. 73) continues, that is utilized as a

> vital organizing principle in regard to the whole of society affecting all its institutions in the most varied way, namely, the principle according to which no arrangement or behavior should be allowed to exist that might prevent the functioning of the market mechanism on the lines of the commodity fiction.

A free market would eventually ruin society. This is how Polanyi (1944, p. 73) deduced it:

> [T]he alleged commodity "labor power" cannot be shoved about, used indiscriminately, or even left unused, without affecting also the human individual who happens to be the bearer of this peculiar commodity. In disposing of a man's labor power the system would, incidentally, dispose of the physical, psychological, and moral entity "man" attached to that tag. Robbed of the protective covering of cultural institutions, human beings would perish from the effects of social exposure; they would die as victims of acute social dislocation through vice, perversion, crime, and starvation. Nature would be reduced to its elements, neighborhoods and landscapes defiled, rivers polluted, military safety jeopardized, the power to produce food and raw materials destroyed. Finally, the market administration of purchasing power would periodically liquidate business enterprise, for shortages and surfeits of money would prove as disastrous to business as floods and droughts in primitive society.

Polanyi pronounced these dire warnings sixty years ago. Their aptness is amply demonstrated today by the current state of the world: the acute social dislocations, crime, perversions and starvation, global warming and the despoliation of nature, and economic crises. The warnings that may not seem to have come to pass (such as food production) might yet do so; but the predicted ruination of society has been averted not by the mechanisms of the free market system but by its regulation by the state. The Great Depression in the United States, for example, did not come to an end because the market had corrected itself. It was overcome, and the society saved, by state intervention (the New Deal) to regulate the free market.

The implication for community development of the arrival of industrial capitalism and the free market ideology derives from the extraordinary fact that for the first time in human history, at the end of the 18th century, society became an accessory of the market. Until then the economic system was an accessory of the society controlled and subordinated by social authority. With industrial capitalism society came to be regarded as an aggregation of individuals as opposed to a complex web of relationships; and a new ideology emerged, anchored in the new science of economics, that defined the human being as an individual bent on optimizing individual utilities. This was reflected as methodological individualism in philosophy, economics, and the social sciences. Solidarity and the entire culture complex (meaning systems, sentiments, religion, language) were regarded as externalities: often hostile, dysfunctional, and in need of radical reform if they impeded the utility optimizing behavior, as pre-industrial solidarity and culture patterns almost always did (Foster, G., 1973; McCleland, 1961). The value of human beings came to rest on their market price. It is this historic reversal that provides the context for community development, the predominance of the market, the dis-embedding of economic activities from society, and the rise of the isolated individual that has structured the erosion of solidarity in modern and modernizing societies.

Market economies today are highly, though imperfectly, regulated by the state or other agencies (e.g., in the United States, the Federal Reserve Bank, and the Departments of Treasury, of Health and Human Services, of Labor, and the Securities and Exchange Commission). But the process of objectification, the underlying individualistic ideology, and its preoccupation with negative freedoms persist. There is mounting pressure in the United States (and elsewhere such as Britain, Germany, India) to drastically cut back state regulation of the market, and to reduce the role of public policy generally. In the United States, examples of the absence or erosion of solidarity at the macro level are large-scale poverty and illiteracy, the reluctance to increase minimum wage, millions of children who are not immunized, and OSHA regulations that are being weakened (Iceland, 2003).

The erosion of solidarity does not remain confined to the macro level but is mirrored in every social space (Bellah et al., 1985; Berger, 1973; Putnam, 1995). The logic of industrial capitalism with its attendant characteristics of commodification of life and radical individualism permeates every aspect of life and has a global reach. The implication for community development is that weak solidarity and meager social capital diminish the potential for collective action.

The Ascent of the Nation-State

Benedict Anderson (1983) has called the modern nation-state the imagined community. In the nation-state, we feel a kinship with fellow citizens by virtue of common nationality although we really do not know most of them. Beginning in the 19th century the nation-state, in tandem with industrialism has triumphed as the common and the dominant form of social organization. It has indeed become almost interchangeable with nation or even society. As with industrialization, the story of the nation-state is also ambiguous. It created the opportunity for broader communication and solidarity than earlier modes of social organization often encompassing multitudes of ethnic, linguistic and religious groups. The concomitant centralization of political, administrative, and fiscal powers often subdued the bigotry of ethnic and religious groups.

By the same token, the nation-state has ruined earlier solidarities based on cultural identity. Communities lost their relevance as economic and political powers were centralized and national social and ethical norms came to dominate community norms. The republican communitarian tradition in the United States, for instance, that had impressed de Tocqueville, was effectively brought to an end in the second half of the 20th century. The tradition of American federalism with strong regional cultures was disrupted by the rise of a strong center with a unitary national culture committed to individualism (Shain, 1994).[3]

The impetus to forge a single national identity led most frequently to the enthronement of one language as the national or official language to the exclusion and sometimes brutal suppression of all others. Turkey, for example, did not even acknowledge the very existence of Kurdish, the language of some 20 percent of the population, until August 2002 (Kurkcu, 2003). But this has happened in almost every nation, in the U.S., in Canada, all over Europe and Russia (Seton-Watson, 1977), in China, and the Philippines. In California, Hispanic children were punished for speaking in Spanish while at school (Hakuta, 1986), and it was the same with Native Americans in Canada. In post-Revolution France, all non-French languages were *abolished* by law (Weber, 1976). Anglicization in the U.K., Russification in the Russian Empire, and Sinicization in China, most prominently in Tibet (Dalai Lama, 1990) are examples of the same policy of cultural domination that almost always accompanies nation building. In numerous countries today communities submerged in the nation-state are striving for measures of autonomy or outright secession.

The challenge before community development is to find ways to resist the homogenizing impulse of the nation-state and to defend cultural pluralism.

Reason

Reason has numerous versions. Instrumental or technical reason is the reason of calculation and efficiency. Rational choice theory in sociology and political science is a loan from economics where rationality is defined as the capacity to choose the most efficient means to attain an end, and consistency in choice. It is concerned strictly with the means, and indifferent about what we choose for the goal that we should be efficient about. This reason pervading every modern institution obscures the goal from reasonable scrutiny and becomes an end in itself. Reason as efficiency is measured by market-price computation of benefit-cost ratios. The human or environmental benefits or costs figure in the computation only if and when they affect efficiency. This reason becomes the only kind of reason. It subverts community by expropriating the authority to judge and validate traditions, worldviews, and the entire range of human subjectivity (e.g., attachment to place and people). Modern societies are rationalized societies where every aspect of life has come under the purview of instrumental reason (Berger, 1973; Braverman, 1974; Weber, M., 1978).

As conceived in 18th century Western Enlightenment, reason is a mental faculty – absolute, eternal, and universal. It challenged and even supplanted the authority of the church and god. It is reason that is in charge of the universe, not god. It is the reason of science and technology, and of historicism. With its application, we can discover the laws of the universe and of human history and manufacture objects. These laws are independent of what we may think or feel. They are ineluctable as the laws of thermodynamics.

A third version views reason as context-bound, inter-subjective, dialogical, or communitarian. Reason means "the willingness to talk things over"; to be reasonable is "to be conversable" (Rorty, 2001). There is not just one, singular reason, absolute and universal. It is not a free and spontaneous activity, but contexted and historical. Modern rationality is merely a historical condition, and is therefore susceptible to change. Because reason is context-bound, there may be as many reasons as contexts. The purpose of rational inquiry is not to apprehend objective truth or reality, which is assumed to be already there, to be *discovered*. The truth or reality is that which results at the end of the investigation. Objectivity does not mean correspondence to a pre-given reality, but inter-subjective or communitarian agreement on the definition of the reality (see the debate in Brown, 1984; Rorty, 2001, Sahlins, 1976).

We can call the first two versions of reason positivist and the third version subject-centered or inter-subjective or communitarian. The positivist version was dominant in the social and behavioral sciences until the 1960s – the purpose was to discover laws of human behavior as scientific as those of the hard sciences (Giddens, 1987). Auguste Comte, the co-parent of sociology with Saint Simon, looked for sociological laws of human affairs (*prevoir pour pouvoir*). Karl Marx following the historicist tradition formulated his laws of economic determinism; Ernst Cassirer sought a "positive," "exact," political science. (The positivist version has returned in the social sciences as rational choice theory.)

The communitarians find support in Darwin: evolutionary progress is tychistic – it occurs through "accidental congruence of genetic modification with environmental niches" (Rorty, 2001, pp. 29-30). There is no systematic law in human affairs, which are full of uncertainties and randomness. Communitarian reason thus sought to debunk historicism and positivism as it applied to human societies: you cannot extrapolate from the past to the future. Human culture is an act of *bricolage*, tinkering: we fashion things out of what we have available around us. Positivist reason may explain natural and social phenomena. It can help us in determining benefit/cost ratios or evaluating the rationality of a course of action for a *given* end. But it cannot furnish the ends – the gods or demons we pursue are beyond the scope of instrumental reason (Bernstein, 1985).

The implication for community development is that positivism disregards our subjectivity – our will, our spontaneity, our meanings, and our capacity to order things. Positivism confronts us with seemingly ineluctable laws that we must obey. The ground is thus prepared for domination sponsored by the state, the party, religious bodies, teachers, parents, or the local planner, all of whom claim to uphold truth in compliance with objective facts and reason. Laws and decisions based on reason thus can be presented as apolitical, uncontaminated by particular preferences.

Reason liberated us from religious and political tyranny but harnessed to industrial capitalism has itself become tyrannical as instrumental reason. Cultures that do not obey the market logic of capital are labeled as irrational. In order to explain why poor countries remain poor, the resistance to or the slow pace of modernization, western social scientists and their Third World emulators in the 1950s and 1960s branded whole cultures as suffering from various syndromes which by their absence explain the "success" of the West. Thus, the Mexicans suffered from the *encogido syndrome* (Erasmus, 1961), some from the image of the limited good (G. Foster, 1973), or lacked the achievement motivation (McCleland, 1961). Southern Italians had amoral familism (Banfield, 1958), and now it seems all Italy does (Ginsborg, 2003). Such characterizations of cultures become meaningful only from the perspective of instrumental reason. Family, community, tradition, and place that made life meaningful are often viewed as an irrational drag on the march of rational choice. Where this reason takes hold, cultures lose their vitality; solidarity disintegrates into an aggregation of individuals bowling alone.

The same reason is at play when developers objectify people. Development research, for example, is frequently what Chambers (1983) calls extractive. The researchers extract information from people who act merely as passive reservoirs of information with no role in designing the research agenda or in the research process. People's cognitive participation (Berger, 1974) – their perception and knowledge of the problems are dismissed as irrational (Chambers, 1983). Thus, the agency-generating powers of defining the problems, explaining their causes, and proposing remedies are denied to the respondents. There is no dialogue; the ownership of the problem slips away from the people to the developer.

Industrial capitalism, the nation-state, and reason have shaped the modern world. They have made possible the production of great wealth, longer life, uncountable amenities, and freedoms from ancient tyrannies. Above everything else, they have given us the opportunity for choice, perhaps the defining characteristic of modernity. But they have exacted a price in human solidarity and agency.

As a field, community development is more concerned with the cost of positivist reason even as it acknowledges the benefits. Just as it should resist the homogenizing impulse of the nation-state, it should resist the tyranny of positivist reason by affirming that reasons can be as varied as cultures. So, how should we practice community development?

Self Help, Felt Needs, and Participation

Since the goal of community development is solidarity and agency, the practice of community development must be guided by this goal. Communism and capitalist modernization, the two grand movements of modern history, promise human emancipation but as the end product. Despite fundamental differences, both objectify people during the process (Berger, 1974; Freire, 1973). Agents of both know what is best for the people regardless of what the people think. This is development imposed from above. Communism has been debunked and development practices today show a greater recognition of the need for people's participation than before. But across the globe, the participatory rhetoric notwithstanding, development practices generally remain conventional, imposed from above. By contrast, echoing Freire (1973), community development practice must regard people as agents (subjects) from the beginning. And it is this that sets community development apart from other development practices. In this sense, community development proposes an alternative politics, a truly democratic politics – non-impositional, non-manipulative, and respectful of the will of the people.

Three overlapping principles – self-help, felt needs, and participation – are the appropriate methods for the practice of community development. The choice of these methods is not arbitrary. As I elaborate on them later in the paper, they seem to be appropriate and consistent with the goal of solidarity and agency. Self-help builds and utilizes agency, mobilizes people's cultural and material assets (e.g., indigenous technical knowledge, tools, and labor), and most importantly, avoids dependency. Felt needs (or demand) affirms human variation and thus resists developmental imposition from above. Both of these principles facilitate effective participation leading to agency and solidarity. Thus, more than being pragmatically efficacious, they are also intrinsically important for the growth of agency and solidarity, i.e., they ought to be practiced in their own right. Secondly, as a formulation of method, the three principles are parsimonious. They address the core concerns about agency and solidarity leaving open the choice of techniques.

Thirdly, they have the backing of tradition. From its inception as a named movement more than half a century ago these were the guiding principles adopted by the U.S. International Cooperation Administration, the United Nations, the Ashridge Conference, the Cambridge Conference, and numerous other organizations and individuals (for a near exhaustive record of the concept's formulations see the University of Missouri's *Handbook of Community Development*)." To be sure, neither the wordings nor the rationales used by these entities are identical, but the principles as stated here, I believe, correctly represent them.

Self-Help

Self-help is the opposite of helpless dependency. It does not mean the denial of inter-dependence or mutuality that is the very basis of social existence. The principle rests on a concept of human beings that when healthy they are willing and able to take care of themselves, to reciprocate, to be productive, more predisposed to give than receive, are active rather than passive, and creative rather than consuming (Fried, 1971). Human beings are *homo faber*, by nature they like to be productive. They are agents. But there are people who by a variety of causes have been rendered incapable of self-help. In some instances, the causes are rooted in individual pathology. But when the loss of agency afflicts large numbers of people or particular groups of people or is chronic, the causes are located outside of the individuals, in public policy, in the structure of economic and cultural opportunities (see Mills, 1959). The practice of self-help includes collective effort to alter these debilitating structures in order to restore agency.

Freire (1973) distinguishes problem solving from problematizing. Problem solving is the approach of conventional development practice. The problem to be solved is defined by outsiders (the state, the development organization, for example). The people whom the problem presumably affects have little role in defining it. They may have a role in implementing the solution (by sweat equity or matching funds, for example). By contrast, problematizing requires the people to determine what the problem is, so that they "own" the problem, which is the first necessary step for them to exert themselves for the solution. Problematizing is agency-generating whereas problem solving reinforces the agency-less passivity.

As a method, self-help is similar to the educational philosophy of Dewey, Piaget (1973), and Freire (1973) among many others. Proper education is agency-giving. It teaches the methods of learning, with which the pupils can launch ahead in the journey of creativity, as opposed to rote memorization or dependency-generating knowledge -consumption, which is analogous to the problem solving approach of conventional development practice.

Felt Needs

This principle, a complement to the principle of self-help, implies that development projects should respond to people's needs as they see them; they should be demand-based. It ensures project relevance. It is agency-generating because it recognizes and fosters people's capacities to define and prioritize their problems. Much conventional development work involves manipulating the people to buy what the developer intends to sell. Responding to felt needs can be an entry point for selling. But manipulation is inherently anti-agency –

making people do what they would not willingly do. Since the project may not "take," it can also lead to resource waste with high opportunity costs. The principle of felt needs is grounded on the premise that, given the knowledge and other resources available to a people, all their cultural practices including needs are rational (Vayda, 1983). The attempt to change a practice therefore should begin with changing the material/knowledge resource base, changing felt needs, and the experienced reality.

Participation

Participation is the most recognized of the three principles of community development practice. Understood properly, it encompasses the principles of self-help and felt needs. But commonly it is used in a narrow sense as in electoral participation. Like self-help and felt needs, it is also used as an empty formula or a device to promote people's acceptance of goals already decided by the development organization. This was the case, just to cite one example, with the rhetoric of participation in the Great Society program during the Johnson administration (Janowitz, 1978, Moynihan, 1969).

In its broadest sense, participation means taking part in the *production* of collective meanings. People can be excluded from it in many ways, by silencing a language, for example, or by overwhelming or de-legitimizing a culture, or by instrumental reason. Language is the heart of a culture, the vital medium for the production of collective meanings (Fishman, 1972), and its suppression has been one of the most common characteristics in the formation of nation-states (Anderson, 1983; Seton-Watson, 1977; Weber, 1976). In modern societies, the production of culture – history, ideas, literature, music, technology, and commodities of all sorts – is exclusionary (Braverman, 1974; Freire, 1973; Ranajit Guha, 1983; Johnson et. al., 1982; Lamont & Fournier, 1992[4]). Civilizations, in the sense of Great Traditions (Redfield, 1955), such as Christianity or Islam, have often de-legitimized cultures or Little Traditions (Niebuhr, 1951).

Similarly, positivist reason, pervasively embedded in the modern, bureaucratized, society undermines cultural or practical reason. The public-private distinction tends to disappear. The deep penetration of instrumental reason opens up to conscious scrutiny what are culturally settled practices and makes them contingent upon re-validation by instrumental reason. Every aspect of life becomes public, exposed to control and manipulation by the state and the market. This undermining of culture (meanings) finds its legitimation in the material abundance produced by the application of positivist reason (Bernstein, 1985; Foucault & Gordon, 1980; McCarthy, 1978; see also Baker & Reill (eds.), 2001).

Thus the principle of participation means inclusion, not merely in the electoral process or endorsing decisions but in deciding the agenda for debate and decision; it means inclusion in the processes of defining the problems to be solved and how to solve them. At a more important level, it means countering the domination and repression of positivist reason in its various manifestations be it the state, the scientized politics, the industrial production process, or the culture industry.

Together these three principles provide the necessary guidance for the practice of community development. The people must have the opportunity to own the problem by feeling and defining it, and also to apply their knowledge/material resources for solving it. By acting as agents from the beginning, people can regain or reaffirm their solidarity and their agency.

Community Development in Practice

Community development is being practiced by countless organizations, in numerous countries with diverse political traditions, addressing a truly astonishing variety of issues. Some of the organizations are small, stand-alone, neighborhood groups. Some are affiliated to umbrella organizations (e.g., the Industrial Areas Foundation, the Grameen Bank) that provide training in community organizing, routine administration, sometimes loans and/or grants, and a larger voice in regional and national politics. They are active in democratic countries (e.g., the United States, the U.K., India), in transitional democracies (e.g., countries of the old Soviet Union), and even in authoritarian countries (e.g., China).

Instead of describing exemplary cases of community development, which it is impossible to do in such a brief space,[5] I will point to some significant shifts in thinking about various social problems. What has become obvious is that "local" action, centered in neighborhoods and villages, is not adequate to the task of finding enduring solutions to social problems. The local problems are local manifestations of problems whose sources lie farther upstream. Community development thus calls for simultaneous action at both micro and macro levels. This is a tall order, but, as I illustrate below, such simultaneous actions are indeed happening.

Public Health

Perhaps the greatest change in thinking has been taking place in the field of public health, what has been called a 'paradigm drift' (Campbell, 2000, p. 185) away from the clinical epidemiological approach to the community development approach. Instead of focusing on modifying individual behavior, the new method focuses on the community and macro factors (Davis, Cohen, Baxi, & Cook, 2003). The typical approach to epidemics, such as HIV/AIDS, poliomyelitis, obesity, or infantile pneumonia, is clinical epidemiological. It attacks the clinical cause of the disease (the virus, the bacterium). Health care personnel administer medicines or preventive inoculation. The health education component – radio and television broadcasts, billboards, posters, group sessions, and school curriculum – follows traditional teaching format, experts giving out information to a passive audience. Such, for instance is the approach of the current WHO programs against the resurgence of polio in certain countries, notably India. It has also been the approach to HIV/AIDS in which case, in addition to medicines, people were urged to practice safe sex and abstinence.

The new thinking that is taking place has two related parts. One, there is increasing recognition that the health status of a population depends not so much on medical care as on the socioeconomic environment in which people live and work. In the United States, health disparities are determined by macro factors such as polluted residential area, poverty, lack of access to nutritious food, safe streets or playgrounds, and the absence of community norms that support healthful behavior (Acharya et al., 2003). To improve health, therefore, requires strategies to alter the environment.

The second part, 'the paradigm drift,' calls for participation and representation of local people in health programs (Campbell, 2000, pp. 182-196). The 'drift' was initiated by the World Health Organization and endorsed by a number of international declarations – the Alma-Ata Declaration of 1978, the Ottawa Charter of 1986, and the Jakarta Declaration of 1997 (Campbell, 2000). The most effective tool against HIV/AIDS, for instance, has proved to be community norms revitalized by community-based organizations (social antibodies) (Epstein, 2003; Hansen, 2003; Singer et al., 1991; Bhattacharyya, K. & J. Murray, 2000; Blum, H. L.; 1981, Frieden & Garfield, 1987; Madan, 1987; Nichter, 1984, 1989; Rifkin, 1981; Rifkin & Walt, 1986; Stone, 1992).

In each of these cases, the standard bureaucratic method of individual-targeted healthcare was shunned for a community approach. The people were not treated merely as carriers of disease, actual or potential. The diseases were understood in their relation with broader socioeconomic contexts. The people participated cognitively by understanding the disease and its causes, and, armed with the understanding, in developing community norms and implementing the programs. The successful programs have been those where micro and macro level organizations have worked in tandem.

Violence

As in the case of health, the standard bureaucratic posture to violence targets individuals, regarding it as a police, military, or behavior modification problem. The preventive measures, therefore, have generally been reactive rather than proactive – harsher punishment, more policing and more prisons, counseling. The relatively few proactive programs, such as the federal Safe School/Healthy Students program that was initiated in response to the Columbine School tragedy, have relied on greater vigilance (e.g., metal detectors), more rigorous monitoring of truancy, and more counseling (anger management, mediation). School personnel (counselors, social workers) make home visits more frequently to discuss children's problem behaviors with parents or other care providers. But even such programs have shown little readiness to formulate strategies to deal with the underlying socioeconomic causes of violent behavior although such causes - the cumulative effect of low SES, residential segregation by race, residential instability - have been known for nearly a century (Acharya et al., 2003; Sampson, 2004).

After studying 343 neighborhoods in Chicago, Sampson (2004) has shown how specifically those factors are related to neighborhood violence. The immediate cause, he concludes, is the absence of neighborhood solidarity (informal social controls or collective efficacy, not police and courts), "the capacity of a group to regulate its members according to desired principles – to realize collective as opposed to forced, goals."

The implication of this finding for community development is far reaching. Such solidarity is hard to achieve simply by neighborhood organizing. Solidarity grows out of face-to-face relations and trust over time and that becomes available with residential stability. Residential instability as well as the concentration of disadvantages is linked to macro political economy, not easily amenable to neighborhood solutions. Neighborhood organizing is necessary but without some level of micro-macro coordination, it alone is unlikely to be sufficient. For neighborhood solidarity to be achieved one needs to influence the policies of the city, the state, and the nation on employment, housing, pollution, education, police protection, and so on, as in the case of health.

Economic Development

The modernization movement over the last half-century or more has followed the growth model: growth in gross national product. This model relies on top-down decision-making, large scale enterprise by the state or the private sector, and increased labor productivity. The result has been the creation of a permanent underclass – unemployed, underemployed, or unemployable, ill educated and ill nourished. An approach that is gaining the attention of policy makers is the micro economic development model. The Ford Foundation has been an early supporter, and in 1996, the World Bank sponsored a global micro credit summit, and has since created a micro credit fund exceeding $50 million. The model is built on the recognition that job growth is unlikely to keep up with the growth in the number of underclass jobseekers. Its remarkable popularity amply demonstrates that it has tapped into a huge reservoir of felt needs for economic security and very poor people's capacity of enterprise.

This model consists of innovative lending and entrepreneurship development programs for people who are too poor to qualify for conventional bank loans. The problem of poverty is not caused by the lack of effort or cultural preference, as many believe, but by the unavailability of financial and psychological capital and technical knowledge, and by macro social, political and economic policies (sexism, racism, red-lining, urban bias). The micro credit organizations furnish the capital, sometimes as little as $100, and, given the characteristics of the population (chronic economic and social marginalization), literacy and health education, skills training (such as bookkeeping), and other support to generate self-help.

Prospective borrowers vouching for the initial borrower take care of the problem of attachable collateral. Perhaps the best known example of this model is the Grameen Bank. The model's effectiveness is best evidenced by the fact that it has been adopted in numerous countries with very different political economic systems, from China to the United States. (Ford Foundation, 1992). But there are a hundred other organizations practicing a similar community development approach to economic development: the Self Employed Women's Association (SEWA) in India, the Foundation for International Community Assistance (FINCA), The Trickle Up Program (TUP), the Women's World Bank, the ACCION International, the Working Capital, and numerous others (Ford Foundation, 1992; Aburdene & Naisbitt, 1992). They have created not only hundreds of thousands of self employed people, but some degrees of power and solidarity among historically marginalized people.[6]

Food

An interesting development in the United States in the last two decades is the Community -Supported Agriculture (CSA), a concept that is a step up from the farmers' market. In the CSA, consumers commit to buy a share of the harvest. According to Roosevelt (2003), the CSA movement began in Japan 30 years ago and spread to Europe and the United States. From one CSA in Massachusetts in 1986, the movement has grown to 1,200 farms with 1,000 families as members. The impetus for CSA is only partly the desire for fresh food. (Currently, U.S. grown produce travels 1500 miles and is 4-7 days old before reaching the supermarket.) Partly it is the desire for food that has not been genetically engineered and is free of pesticides and hormones.

But it is also a movement to create communities to recover the meaning of food. According to Nestle (2002), the U.S. population buys nearly half its meals prepared elsewhere, and is consuming more processed food, rather than locally grown "whole" foods. Among those who cook at home, few do so from scratch. There is a growing sense that large numbers of people have little control over what and how they eat. Just ten corporations dominate the global food market. Since 1960, the number of farms in the United States has declined from 3.2 million to 1.9 million. Such consolidation under giant corporations has raised productivity by 82 percent, but the corporations produce fewer crops, leading many varieties to virtual extinction (Nabhan, 2002).[7] People's control over food is also compromised by powerful marketing techniques of the food industry. In 1998, for instance, the ten leading manufacturers of *packaged food products* spent $8,228.5 million in advertising. Food and food service companies spend more than $11 billion annually on *direct media advertising*. In 1999, McDonald's spent $627.2 million, Burger King $403.6 million, and Taco Bell $206.5 million on direct media advertising (Nestle, 2002; Schlosser, 2002). Nearly 70 percent of food advertising is for promoting the most highly processed, elaborately packaged, and fast foods (Nestle, 2002).

The CSA movement along with farmers' markets and local food coops is an attempt to regain some control over food. It is restoring variety by bringing back heritage seeds and poultry. By practicing organic farming, it is producing wholesome food while protecting the environment. But it is more than that. "Even beyond economics, community-supported agriculture is about something deeper: a sense of common good uniting those who plant and those who eat." (Roosevelt, 2003, p. 61).

An interesting example of micro-macro linkage is the emergence last April of the National Cooperative Grocers Association consolidating the resources of 94 independent natural food co-ops with 111 retail locations. It has 400,000 member owners, millions of consumers, and an annual sales volume of $626 million. This is an excellent example of networking among food coops and independent organic growers. Their national clout was evidenced by, among other development, when the US Department of Agriculture last September finally issued the organic certification procedure.

Similar examples could be provided from almost every area of social life. But the few examples sketched above perhaps suffice to give a sense of how community development is being practiced and the changes it is causing in dealing with social problems.

Concluding Remarks

I have tried to present in these pages my vision of community development – the pursuit of solidarity and agency. For context – the reason for community development – I have focused on the corrosive effects of historical forces of industrial capitalism, the nation-state, and positivist–reason as applied to human affairs. None of these causes are likely to be transcended any time soon. They are inter-active, and deeply entrenched in national and global political economy, and in our habits of thought. Community development has to function – and it is functioning – within this environment. Thus, community development practitioners must address macro factors while working in microenvironments. Local problems today are likely to be only local manifestations of larger problems. This calls for political action, and networking among community organizations to gain political clout.

I have maintained that we need to distinguish among goals, methods, and techniques or tools. The various models of community development (conflict, community self-study, locality development, social planning, etc.) deal with techniques, as do community asset building programs. Techniques are the front end, the most immediately relevant and crucially significant aspect of community development. But they cannot – and should not – be ends in themselves. They are tools to implement certain methods (such as, self-help, felt needs, and participation), and as such, they must cohere and be consistent with the methods. The methods in turn are significant only to the extent they help to create and sustain a satisfying life, which I have defined as the acquisition of solidarity and agency.

The purpose of this paper was to bound community development as a distinct field. That distinction can be achieved, I have suggested, by adhering to the goals of solidarity and agency together with certain methods that are consistent with the goals which I have argued are self-help, felt needs, and participation.

NOTES

1. I am indebted to Drs. Karabi Acharya, Sumita Bhattacharyya and Susan Maher, and to Kakali Bhattacharya and Uttiyo Raychaudhuri, for help with different aspects of the paper. I thank Dr. Ted Bradshaw, Dr. Ron Hustedde, Noemi Danao and other members of the Taughannock Farms Inn Retreat for comments on an earlier incarnation of this paper and for the encouragement to write this one. I also thank Marilu Carter for her assistance.

2. There is no single work that deals with the problem of agency in such diverse fields as anthropology, history, literature, philosophy, political science, psychology, and sociology, and it will take too much space to cite even the major works in each field. An overly simplified introduction to some of the authors is W. Foster (1986). More scholarly sources are Lemert (1979), Giddens (1984), and Wolin (1990). None of these works deals with literature, especially post-modernist criticism, and on this there is no generally accessible overview; the interested reader may consult Berman (1988) and Kellner (1989)

3. The disruption of regional cultures was also a blessing as it abolished slavery and extended civil rights, once again illustrating the ambiguity of history.

4. See especially the articles in Part Two: High Culture and Exclusion, in Lamont and Fournier (1992).

5. See the excellent collection of recent cases in Putnam and Feldstein (2003). The annual *Report* and the quarterly Letter of the Ford Foundation commonly publish accounts of community development from across the world.

6. For a critical assessment of the movement see Jonathan Morduch (1999).

7. The large industrial farms have made inroads in the fast growing organic food market shipping organic produce to the U.S. from as far away as China and New Zealand (Roosevelt, 2003). The federal organic certification procedure released in September 2003 is too cumbersome and time consuming for truck farmers that had initiated and sustained the organic movement. The new label for locally grown organic foods is ecological.

REFERENCES

Aburdene, P., & J. Naisbitt. 1992. *Megatrends for Women*. New York: Villard Books.

Acharya, K., R. Davis, T. Gantz, & P. Leuna. 2003. *Salinas Safe Schools/Healthy Students Local Evaluation Report: Toward a Community of Caring*. Oakland, CA: The Prevention Institute.

Anderson, B. 1983. *The Imagined Communities: Reflections on the Origin and Spread of Nationalism*. London: Verso.

Apter, D. E. 1971. *Choice and the Politics of Allocation: A Developmental Theory*. New Haven,CT: Yale University Press.

Baker, K. M., & P. H. Reill, (eds). 2001. *What's left of Enlightenment?: A postmodern question*. Stanford, CA: Stanford University Press.

Banfield, E. 1958. *The Moral Basis of a Backward Society*. New York: The Free Press.

Batten, T. R. 1957. *Communities and Their Development*. London: Oxford University Press.

Bellah, R. N., R. Madsen, W. M. Sullivan, A. Swidler, & S. M. Tipton. 1985. *Habits of the Heart: Individualism and Commitment in American Life*. Berkeley: University of California Press.

Bendix, R. 1964. *Nation-Building and Citizenship*. New York: John Wiley & Sons.

Berger, P. L 1974. *Pyramids of Sacrifice: Political Ethics and Social Change*. New York: Basic Books.

Berger, P. L. 1973. *The Homeless Mind*. (With B. Berger and H. Kellner). New York: Vintage.

Berman, A.. 1988. *From the New Criticism to Deconstruction: The Reception of Structuralism and Post -Structuralism*. Urbana and Chicago: University of Illinois Press.

Bernstein, R. J. 1985. *Habermas and Modernity*. 1ˢᵗ MIT Press edition. Cambridge, MA: MIT Press.

Bhattacharyya, J. 1995. Solidarity and agency: Rethinking community development. *Human Organization* 54(1): 60-69.

Bhattacharyya, K. 1993. *Understanding Acute Respiratory Infection: Culture and Method*. Sc.D. dissertation, Johns Hopkins University.

Bhattacharyya, K. & J. Murray. 2000. Community assessment and planning for maternal and child health program: A participatory approach in Ethiopia. *Human Organization* 59(2): 255-266.

Biddle, W. 1966. The "fuzziness" of definition of community development. *Community Development Journal* 1: 5-12.

Biddle, W., with L. Biddle. 1965. *The Community Development Process*. New York: Holt, Rinehart & Winston.

Blomstrom, M., & B. Hettne. 1984. *Development Theory in Transition: The Dependency Debate and Beyond: Third World Responses*. London: Zed Books.

Blum, H. L. 1981. *Planning for Health: Generics for the Eighties*. New York: Human Sciences Press.

Bradshaw, T. K., & E. J. Blakely. 1979. *Rural Communities in Advanced Industrial Society: Development and Developers*. New York: Praeger.

Braverman, H., 1974. *Labor and Monopoly Capital: The Degradation of Labor in the Twentieth Century*. New York: St. Martin's Press.

Brokensha, D., & P. Hodge. 1969. *Community Development: An Interpretation*. San Francisco: Chandler Publishing Co.

Brown, S. C. (ed.). 1984. *Objectivity and Cultural Divergence. Supplement to Philosophy*. Cambridge: Cambridge University Press.

Campbell, C. 2000. Social capital and health: Contextualizing health promotion within local community networks. Pp. 82-196 in S. Baron, J. Field, & T. Schuller (eds.), *Social Capital: Critical Perspectives*. Oxford: Oxford University Press.

Carry, L. J., (ed.). 1970. *Community Development as a Process*. Columbia: University of Missouri Press.

Chambers, R. 1983. *Rural Development: Putting the Last First*. New York: John Wiley.

Christenson, J. A., & J. W. Robinson (eds.). 1989. *Community Development in Perspective*. Iowa City, IA: Iowa State University Press.

Clinard, M. B. 1966. *Slums and Community Development*. New York: Free Press.

Cox, F., J. Ehrlich, J. Rothman, & J. Tropman (eds.). 1974. *Strategies of Community Organization: A Book of Readings*. Itasca, IL: Peacock Publishers.

Dalai Lama. 1990. *Freedom in Exile: The Autobiography of the Dalai Lama of Tibet*. London: Hodder & Stoughton.

Davis, R., L. Cohen, S. Baxi, & D. Cook. 2003. *A Community Approach to Address Health Disparities*. Working Draft. Oakland, CA: THRIVE, Environmental Scan, The Prevention Institute.

De Certeau, M. 1986. *Heterologies: Discourse on the Other*, B. Massoumi (trans.). Minneapolis: University of Minnesota Press.

Denise, P. S., & I. Harris (eds.). 1990. *Experiential Education for Community Development*. New York: Greenwood Press.

Dobyns, H. F., P. L. Doughty, & H. D. Lasswell (eds.). 1971. *Peasants, Power, and Applied Social Change: Vicos as a Model*. Beverly Hills: Sage

Du Sautoy, P. 1958. *Community Development in Ghana*. London: Oxford University Press.

Dube, S. C. 1963. *India's Changing Villages*. London: Routledge & Kegan Paul.

Durkheim, E. 1964 [1893]. *The Division of Labor in Society*, G. Simpson (trans.). New York: The Free Press.

Epstein, H. 2003. AIDS in South Africa: The invisible cure. Pp.44-49 in *New York Review of Books*, July 17.

Erasmus, C. J. 1961. *Man Takes Control: Cultural Development and American Aid*. Minneapolis: University of Minnesota Press.

Febvre, L., & H. J. Martin. 1976. *The Coming of the Book: The Impact of Printing, 1450-1800*. London: New Left Books.

Ferguson, R. F. & W. T. Dickens (eds.). 1999. *Urban Problems and Community Development*. Washington, D.C.: Brookings Institution Press.

Fishman, J. 1972. The sociology of language. Pp.45-58 in Paolo Giglioli (ed.), *Language and Social Context*. Pier Harmondsworth, England: Penguin Books.

Flora, J.L. 1998. Social capital and communities of place. *Rural Sociology* 63: 481-506.

Ford Foundation. 1992. *The Report*. Washington, DC: The Ford Foundation.

Foster, G. M. 1973. *Traditional Societies and Technological Change*, 2nd ed. New York: Harper & Row.

Foster, W. 1986. *Paradigms and Promises: New Approaches to Educational Administration*. Buffalo, NY: Prometheus Books.

Foucault, M., & C. Gordon. 1980. *Power/Knowledge: Selected Interviews and Other Writings, 1972-1977*. New York: Pantheon Books.

Fowler, R. B. 1991. *The Dance with Community: The Contemporary Debate in American Political Thought*. Lawrence: University of Kansas Press.

Freire, P. 1973. *Education for Critical Consciousness*. New York: Seabury Press.

Fried, E. 1971. *Active, Passive: The Crucial Psychological Dimension*. New York: Harper Colophon Books.

Frieden, T., & R. Garfield. 1987. Popular participation in health in Nicaragua. *Health Policy and Planning* 2: 162-170.

Giddens, A. 1990. *The Consequences of Modernity*. Stanford, CA: Stanford University Press.

Giddens, A. 1987. *Sociology: A Brief but Critical Introduction*, 2nd ed. San Diego: Harcourt Brace Jovanovich.

Giddens, A. 1984. *The Constitution of Society*. Berkeley: University of California Press.

Ginsborg, P. 2003. The patrimonial ambitions of Silvio B. *New Left Review* 21(May/June): 21.

Goodenough, W. H. 1963. *Cooperation in Change*. New York: Russell Sage.

Guha, R. (ed.). 1983. *Subaltern Studies*. Oxford: Oxford University Press.

Hakuta, K. 1986. *Mirror of Language: The Debate on Bilingualism.* New York: Basic Books.

Hansen, K. 2003. Letter in *New York Review of Books* (November 20): 57.

Iceland, John. 2003. *Poverty in America: A Handbook.* Berkeley: University of California Press.

Janowitz, M. 1978. *The Last Half-Century: Societal Change and Politics in America.* University of Chicago Press.

Johnson, R., G. McLennan, B. Schwarz, & D. Sutton. 1982. *Making Histories: Studies in History, Writing and Politics.* London: Hutchinson in association with the Centre for Contemporary Cultural Studies, University of Birmingham.

Kellner, D. (ed.). 1989. *Post-Modernism: Jameson Critique.* Washington, DC: Maisonneuve Press.

Knowles, M. S. (ed.). 1960. *Handbook of Adult Education in the United States.* Chicago: Adult Education Association of the USA.

Kramer, R. M. & H. Specht. 1969. *Readings in Community Organization Practice.* Englewood Cliffs, N.J: Prentice-Hall.

Kretzmann, J. P., & J. L. McKnight. 1993. *Building Communities from the Inside Out: A Path Toward Finding and Mobilizing a Community's Assets.* Chicago: ACTA.

Kurkcu, E., 2003. Leyla Zana: Defiance under fire. *Amnesty Now* 29(3): 22-25.

Lamont, M. & M. Fournier (eds.). 1992. *Cultivating Differences: Symbolic Boundaries and the Making of Inequality.* Chicago: The University of Chicago Press.

Lemert, C. C. 1979. *Sociology and the Twilight of Man: Homocentrism and Discourse in Sociological Theory.* Carbondale: Southern Illinois University Press.

Madan, T. N. 1987. Community involvement in health policy: Socio-structural and dynamic aspects of health beliefs. *Social Science and Medicine* 25: 615-620.

Marx, K. & F. Engels. 1847. The communist manifesto. In *Selected Works, Vol. I, 1962.* Moscow: Progress Publishers.

McCarthy, T. 1978. *The Critical Theory of Jurgen Habermas.* Cambridge, MA: The MIT Press.

McCleland, D. C. 1961. *The Achieving Society.* New York: Free Press.

McLuhan, M. 1962. *The Gutenberg Galaxy: The Making of Typographic Man.* Toronto: University of Toronto Press.

Meranze, M. 2001. Critique and government: Michel Foucault and the question 'What is Enlightenment?'. In K. M. Baker & P. H. Reill (eds.), *What's Left of Enlightenment? A Postmodern Question.* Stanford, CA: Stanford University Press.

Mills, C. W. 1959. *The Sociological Imagination.* New York, Oxford University Press.

Morduch, J. 1999. The microfinance promise. *Journal of Economic Literature.* 37(December): 1569-1614.

Moynihan, D. P. 1969. *Maximum Feasible Misunderstanding: Community Action in the War on Poverty.* New York: Free Press.

Nabhan, G. P. 2002. *Coming Home to Eat: The Pleasures and Politics of Local Foods,* 1st ed. New York : W.W. Norton.

Nestle, M. 2002. *Food politics: How the Food Industry Influences Nutrition and Health.* Berkeley: University of California Press.

Nichter, M. 1989. *Anthropology and International Health.* Boston: Kluwer.

Nichter, M. 1984. Project community diagnosis: Participatory research as a first step toward community involvement in primary health care. *Social Science and Medicine* 19(3): 237-252.

Niebuhr, H. R. 1951. *Christ and Culture.* New York: Harper and Brothers.

Nisbet, R. A. 1962. *Community and Power.* New York: Oxford University Press.

Piaget, J. 1973. *To Understand is to Invent:The Future of Education.* New York: Grossman Publishers.

Plant, R. 1974. *Community and Ideology: An Essay in Applied Social Philosophy.* London: Routledge & K. Paul.

Polanyi, K. 1944. *The Great Transformation.* New York: Rinehart.

Popple, K., & A. Quinney. 2002. Theory and practice of community development: A case study from the United Kingdom. *Journal of Community Development Society* 33(1): 71-85.

Putnam, R. 1995. Bowling alone: America's declining social capital. *Journal of Democracy.* January: 65-78.

Putnam, R., R. D. Butler, & L. M. Feldstein (with D. Cohen). 2003. *Better Together: Restoring the American Community.* New York: Simon &Schuster.

Redfield, R. 1955. *The Little Community: Viewpoints for the Study of a Human Whole.* Chicago: University of Chicago Press.

Riesman, D., in collaboration with R. Denney & N. Glazer. 1950. *The Lonely Crowd: A Study of the Changing American Character.* New Haven: Yale University Press.

Rifkin, S. B., & G. Walt. 1986. Why health improves: Defining the issues concerning 'comprehensive health care' and 'selective primary health care.' *Social Science and Medicine* 23 (6): 559-566.

Roosevelt, M. 2003. "Fresh off the farm:" Community-supported agriculture. *Time.* Nov. 3, Vol. 162, issue 18, pp. 60-61.

Rorty, R. 2001. The continuity between the Enlightenment and 'Postmodernism'". Pp. 19-36 in K. M. Baker & P. Hans Reill (eds.), *What's Left of Enlightenment? A Postmodern Question.* Stanford, CA: Stanford University Press.

Rothman, J. 1968. Three models of community organization practice. *Social Work Practice 1968.* National Conference on Social Welfare. New York: Columbia University Press.

Sahlins, M. 1976. *Culture and Practical Reason.* Chicago: University of Chicago Press.

Sampson, R. J. 2004. Neighborhood and community: Collective efficacy and community safety. *New Economy* 1: 106-113.

Sanders, I. T. 1958b. Theories of community development. *Rural Sociology* 23: 1-12.

Sanders, I. T. 1958a. *Community Development and National Change.* Washington, DC: US International Cooperation Administration.

Schlosser, E. 2002. *The Fast Food Nation: The Dark Side of the All-American Meal.* New York: Perennial Press.

Sen, A.   1999.   *Development as Freedom*. New York: Knopf.

Seton-Watson, H.   1977.   *Nations and States: An Enquiry into the Origins of Nations and the Politics of Nationalism.* Boulder, CO: Westview Press.

Shain, B. A.   1994.   *The Myth of American Individualism: the Protestant Origins of American Political Thought.* Princeton, NJ: Princeton University Press.

Singer, M., C. Flores, L. Davison, G. Burke, & Z. Castillo.   1991.   Puerto Rican community mobilizing in response to the aids crisis. *Human Organization* 50: 73-81.

Slater, P. E.   1970.   *The Pursuit of Loneliness: American Culture at the Breaking Point.* Boston: Beacon Press.

Spiegel, H. B. C., & S Mittenthal.   1968. *Neighborhood Power and Control: Implications for Urban Planning. A Report Prepared for the Department of Housing and Urban Development.* New York: Institute of Urban Environment, School of Architecture, Columbia University.

Stone, L.   1992.   Cultural influences in community participation in health. *Social Science and Medicine* 35: 409-417.

Summers, G.   1986.   Rural Community Development. Pp. 333-340 in *New Dimensions in Rural Policy: Building Upon Our Heritage.* Studies prepared for the use of the Subcommittee on Agriculture and Transportation of the Joint Economic Committee, Congress of the United States. Washington,DC: US Government Printing.

Tonnies, F.   1957[1887].   In C. P. Loomis (trans. and ed.), *Community and Society*. New York: Harper Torchbooks.

University of Missouri at Columbia.   n.d.   *The Handbook of Community Development.* Columbia, MO: Department of Community Development.

Vayda, A. P.   1983.   Progressive contextualization: Methods for research in human ecology. *Human Ecology* 11: 265-281.

Weber, E.   1976.   *Peasant into Frenchman: The Modernization of Rural France, 1870-1914.* Stanford, CA: Stanford University Press.

Weber, M.   1978.   In G. Roth & C. Wittich (eds.), and E. Fischoff et al. (trans.), *Economy and Society: An Outline of Interpretive Sociology*. Berkeley: University of California Press.

Wileden, A. F.   1970.   *Community Development*. Totowa, NJ: Bedminster Press.

Wolin, S.   1990.   Democracy in the discourse of Postmodernism. *Social Research* 57: 5-30.

Zagarella, S. A.   1988.   Narrative of community: The identification of a genre. *Signs* 13: 498-527.

The Power of Community

M.A. Brennan and Glenn D. Israel

While formally and informally recognized as being central to community action, the research and theoretical literature provide little insight into the processes behind the emergence of community power. When power is explored, it is usually presented in a macro context where a culmination of numerous efforts results in a critical stage leading to a more equitable distribution of power. Far less often is the micro level considered. At the latter level, power is often given only a passing reference as an expected outcome of local empowerment, civic engagement, and capacity-building activities. Generally, it is implied that power naturally emerges from the presence of the latter conditions. An explanation of the processes, mechanisms, and conditions in which community power emerges or fails to emerge remains unstated. To facilitate such an understanding, we seeks to: (1) Explore the ways in which power is conceptualized at the micro level as a component of community development and social change; and (2) provide a theoretical framework, based on a field theoretical perspective, for understanding the processes by which local citizens gain entrée to power, as well as interact with elites that might otherwise limit the emergence of local capacity. Implications for future theoretical development are then offered.

Despite its central role in community, regional, and national life, the concept of power remains underdeveloped in the community theory literature (Domhoff, 2007; Fisher & Sonn, 2007; Gaventa, 1980; Stone, 1986; Waste, 1986). While formally and informally recognized as important, an exploration of the process by which power emerges, evolves, and is managed within the confines of the community remains scant in the research and theoretical literature (Beaver & Cohen, 2004; Fisher & Sonn, 2007; Gaventa, 1980). This is in part due to a lack of uniformity in conceptualization, as well as the complex mingling of history, culture, and local capacities which shape power structures. A need therefore exists for a more complete understanding of this important social entity and the complex processes through which it shapes local well-being.

Power, in its most simple definition, reflects the ability to act or influence the ability of others to either act or choose a path of inaction (Beaver & Cohen, 2004; Fisher & Sonn,

M.A. Brennan: 3002 McCarty Hall, PO Box 110310, Department of Family, Youth, and Community Sciences, The University of Florida, Gainesville, FL 32611-0310, BrennanM@ufl.edu, Telephone: (352) 392-1778 x229, Fax: (352) 392-8196. Glenn D. Israel: Department of Agricultural Education and Communications, The University of Florida. Acknowledgments: The authors wish to thank Jeffrey Bridger, John Allen, A. E. Luloff, Sebastian Galindo, Nikolay Kazakov, and the anonymous reviewers for their constructive critiques, suggestions, and contributions to the development of this manuscript. Their assistance was much appreciated.

2007). However, power is far more complex in its types, dimensions, and applications. In academic and program settings, it is all too often glossed over as being a simple condition resulting from economic, social, or political position. Anecdotally, local power structures are often viewed as insurmountable, entrenched, and a tool used to achieve domination by ruling elites. As well, power has been conceptualized as the consequence of coordinated collective actions of diverse local residents. Regardless of setting, the mechanisms and processes by which power emerges and exists in the community remain largely unexplored.

Contemporary theoretical perspectives pay little attention to the role of power in the emergence of community and community development. When power is explored, it is usually portrayed in a macro context, often in the settings of social movements, where a culmination of efforts results in a critical stage where sufficient media, social, economic, and political leverage has been obtained by the powerless. Far less often is the micro level considered. When explored at this level, power is typically tied to the condition which emerges as a result of local empowerment, civic engagement, and/or capacity-building activities (Beaver & Cohen, 2004; Fisher & Sonn, 2007; Gaventa, 1980). However, it is simply assumed or implied that power naturally emerges from these conditions and is successfully exercised. We believe such arguments lack the theoretical foundations and conceptual frameworks necessary to support such assumptions.

It is true that in many instances, building local capacity through collective action leads directly to the accumulation of power. Similarly, the power accumulated by citizen mobilization is often seen as providing the ability of local groups to liaise with power-holding elites. On the other hand, community action may emerge but fail to lead to the establishment of power among local residents. It may also be the case that in some settings, capacity building might inadvertently or by manipulation reinforce existing power structures by aligning new constituencies with local power-holding elites.

The failure of power to consistently emerge from collective mobilization suggests that the underlying process is not a universal occurrence, and may only take place under the right conditions. What remains unexplored is the process by which local action manages to exist and not be eliminated, dismissed, or exploited by local power elites. In short, little attention has been given to mechanisms and processes through which local residents successfully develop the capacity to address important local issues as they interact with various power structures.

To facilitate a more complete understanding of community power, we seek to: *(1) Explore the ways in which power is conceptualized at the micro level as a component of community development and social change; and (2) Provide a theoretical framework, based on a field theoretical perspective, for understanding the process by which local citizens amass power, as well as interact with elites that might otherwise limit or facilitate the emergence of local capacity.*

Understanding and Conceptualizing Power

In its broadest context, the exercise of power can be seen as falling into two general camps: pluralism and elitism (Dahl, 1961; Domhoff, 1986; Hunter, 1953; Israel & Beaulieu, 1990; Moffett & Freund, 2004; Waste, 1986). The former is the basis on which our grassroots, democratic, and locally based civic engagement strategies are founded. From this perspective, the collective capacities of diverse local residents form the basis of power and locally driven social change (Armstrong, 2006; Brennan & Luloff, 2007; Reed & McIlveen, 2006; Waste, 1986; Wilkinson, 1991; Varley & Curtin, 2006). Here, power is dispersed across a wide range of often competing local interests. However, such power is diluted because of its fragmented holdings (Gaventa, 1980; Groarke, 2004; Reed and

McIlveen, 2006; Waste, 1986). Community power, in this context, is tied to efforts aimed at coordinating and harnessing such collective capacity on a consistent and long-term basis (Armstrong, 2006; Brennan, 2007; Wilkinson, 1991; Varley and Curtin, 2006;). At the same time, the inherent and underlying assumptions of this viewpoint remain questionable. Indeed, it is often the case that those most in need of civic engagement and participation in the democratic process are often the ones lacking the capacity to do so (usually in terms of educational attainment, financial stability, and limited social networks).

In contrast, elitism is often seen as the basis for the perceived insurmountable local power holdings of local and extralocal dominants (Beaver & Cohen, 2004; Domhoff, 1986; Domhoff, 2007; Hunter, 1953; Mills, 1956; Moffett & Freund, 2004). In such cases, a small number of individuals, based on their social, political, or economic positions, control the community and its decisions. Here, power is distributed hierarchically through the local social structure, with those in visible or hidden positions of authority, prestige, and wealth disproportionately holding power (Arcidiacono et al., 2007; Beaver & Cohen, 2004; Domhoff, 1986; Gallardo & Stein, 2007; Mills, 1956). The ability to obtain and hold power is therefore seen as being outside of the realm of the average citizen. To better understand pluralist and elitist holdings of power, we must first examine its manifestations in the context of the conflict and consensus within our communities.

Conflict and Consensus

At its most basic level, community power and decision-making are the result of either conflict or consensus situations. These conditions are often portrayed as the "two faces of society" (Bachrach & Baratz, 1970; Dahrendorf, 1959). While both are used as ideal types, they are not necessarily mutually exclusive and can exist at the same time in the same settings. The concepts of conflict and consensus are deeply rooted in social and philosophical thought that attempts to explain how local decisions are made and power structures emerge (Ebenstein, 1991; Hobbes, 1960; Rousseau, 1978). Conflict models see the decision-making process largely from an elitist perspective, represented by constraint, monopolization of power, dominance, and manipulation (Dahrendorf, 1959; Hyman et al., 2001).

Alternatively, the more pluralist consensus models emphasize decision making and resulting social change as the result of shared values, needs, wants, and agreement among community members (Armstrong, 2006; Dahrendorf, 1959; Hyman et al., 2001; Reed & McIlveen, 2006). Generally, those following a populist approach emphasize an integrative model which reflects society as being relatively stable as it meets the common needs of its members. Social interaction is central to this process of consensus and represents the communal efforts of people within a locality (Wilkinson, 1991). However, consensus does not necessarily mean an open acceptance of ideas and decisions. More often, it represents a process where community members reach agreement and compliance with needs and wants reflective of the broader community (Brennan & Luloff, 2007; Israel & Beaulieu, 1990; Luloff & Bridger, 2003; Reed & McIlveen, 2006; Wilkinson, 1991; Varley & Curtin, 2006).

In addition to the traditional focus on conflict and consensus, there is an emerging literature on community conflict that argues that power and local decision-making are contextual and not necessarily just the result of conflict or consensus (Daniels and Walker, 2001). This perspective argues that effective local decision making emerges from collaborative efforts representing a wide range of local interests. In contrast to consensus, such an approach brings together a wide range of diverse local interests to effectively plan and maximize the use of local resources. Understanding how community power is concentrated and decisions are made is essential for understanding the forms power may take and how it is wielded. We turn to this discussion next.

Faces and Dimensions of Power

Five contexts of power relationships are often identified: threat, authority, influence, manipulation, and force (Bachrach & Baratz, 1970). Threat power is a rational concept based on the relationship between two or more parties. It is based on compliance with requests or orders by one group as a result of pressure and deprivations by another. This concept is based on reason in that the second party must perceive the threats presented to them and view them as valid considerations. While threat power may work for a short period of time, it tends to arouse resentment and consequently less success, so that long-term implications for sustaining this type of power are limited.

Authority can be similar to threat power, when it is based not on the immediate threat to deprive individuals of something, but on the perceived ability to do so. Authority is found in a belief that those in power maintain legitimacy and a right to that power (Coser & Howe, 1977; Weber, 1947). This authority can take many forms. Some forms rest on a belief in the legitimacy and legality of laws, rules, and the rights of those in power to issue commands. More traditional authority is based on an established belief in the tradition, sanctity, and legitimacy of those exercising authority under them. Similarly, some people are charismatic and their authority centers on a devotion to the specific and extraordinary characteristics of an individual person, and of the orders given by this person. Finally, authority can rest on an attachment to a set of values or belief systems that is the object of intense commitment.

Influence is a third form of power and involves a belief that a person making a request deserves to, or needs to be, obeyed. Lukes (1974) saw this as the cornerstone of power structures. The ability to influence behavior sets the stage for agenda setting and quiescence (Dahl, 1961; Gaventa, 1980; Lukes, 1974). Obedience and influence may result from who the person is in the community (reputation or respect) or from agreement with the request itself (as a result of discussion and debate). In this setting, one person has influence over others to the extent that the first causes the second to change their course of action.

Manipulation is an invisible power characterized by doing what another wants without being aware of it. In this situation there is a conflict of values, in that one person would not take the action without being manipulated. Lukes (1974) and Gaventa (1980) stress the ability of this form of power in shaping agendas and public perceptions of power holders. These abilities allow local elites to dictate local decision making without needing to resort to a final form of power.

Finally, *force* is obvious power. Force involves the application of severe sanctions threatened in a power relationship. In this setting, action is taken against a person's will. The key to the power relationships is who chooses the ultimate action.

Building on these contexts, Boulding (1989) distinguishes four forms of power. *Destructive power* refers to the capacity to destroy something or someone. It can sometimes be used constructively, but is most often used to enforce some kind of threat or sanction that has been ignored. It includes killing, injury and the destruction of property often by using weapons. *Productive (or sometimes called economic) power* reflects the ability to obtain something wanted by means of exchange. Following this reasoning, the more an individual has to give in exchange (money, tangible items, labor, knowledge, etc.), the more power they have. Economic power can be acquired temporarily by taking things away from others, but ultimately individuals need to be able to produce more funds or resources to sustain their power. *Knowledge power* (Hyman et al., 2001) represents a special form of productive power and it can play an important role in local action. Given the effects of globalization and the development of a knowledge economy, developing or acquiring this power may become an increasingly important focus of community agency. Knowledge power is based in the accumulation of information, skills, and experiences that provide people a competitive advantage in taking a course of action. *Integrative power* refers to the capacity to get people to act out of respect, care, affinity, or love. The role of integrative power in maintaining a social structure is both its most important and least recognized or understood element (Boulding, 1989; Hyman et al., 2001).

With all of these forms of power, the issue of access to various resources and their exploitation becomes central. Those with access to such resources, or those with the capacity to mobilize dispersed resources, accumulate power. With these resources, power is exhibited in destructive, productive, or integrative ways.

Theoretical Perspectives on Power

The concept of power and its role in broad social change has often been at the core of macro-level classic and contemporary theory. Most often cited in this context is the work of Marx, where the holders of power controlled all major aspects of society at the expense of the powerless (Coser & Howe, 1977; Marx, 1994). So absolute was their monopolization of resources that revolution and violent social change was the only likely means of redistributing power among the masses. Gramsci (1971) expands the work of Marx to include the ideas of ideological hegemony as a controlling tool of the elite. Regardless of how powerful and omnipresent, ruling elites can not sustain themselves through force and threats alone. To achieve long-term sustainable power, the popular support of the powerless must be obtained to legitimize the regime and maintain stability (Boggs, 1976; Entwistle, 1979; Gramsci, 1971; Scott, 1990). Such support allows power holders and their associates to become integrated into the social structure, so that their presence is seen as a natural condition. This sets the stage for long-term monopolization of power.

C. Wright Mills, in *The Power Elite* (1956), explains power as being monopolized at all levels by coalitions of social and economic elites. Such individuals represent business leaders, government officials, and prestigious families who dictate local life and control access to opportunities by the wider population. Such individuals bond together in an attempt to retain and expand their power holdings. These power holders are also linked by a stratified system in which they bond through common groups, classes, organizations, schools, institutions, and social circles. As a result, a more tightly defined structure is evident than would be found in a more diverse pluralist setting. Here, power does not need to be explicitly evident in political or other settings. Instead, it can remain masked and/or hidden at a level where non-decision characterizes local resident life and potentials for social change (Domhoff, 1986; Domhoff, 2007; Gallardo & Stein, 2007; Mills, 1956). Elite power is also characterized in the ability to dictate who runs for political offices, is appointed to decision-making roles, or has a chance to bring issues forward for public discussion (Beaver & Cohen, 2004; Gaventa, 1980; Mills, 1956). Similarly, in the works of Parsons (1977) and other functionalists, power is seen as an integral part of a bureaucracy designed to maintain structure and expected behaviors. Social change, particularly the redistribution of power relations and ruling elites, is unwanted and undesirable.

The above perspectives tend to focus at the macro level. While important, they fail to explore the origins, mechanism, and processes of power at the micro, or community level. More contemporary theoretical perspectives, such as interactional theory and social capital perspectives, have acknowledged power at this level, but like their predecessors have often viewed power as a given or the natural outcome of individual efficacy or collective action. While addressing broader processes leading to the emergence of community, attention to the nuances of the power dynamics have been limited. An exception has been the work of

Gaventa (1980), which explored the detailed workings of power at the community level.

Power and Powerlessness

Perhaps one of the best and most thorough explorations of community power can be found in Gaventa's *Power and powerlessness: Quiescence and rebellion in an Appalachian Valley* (1980). The author argues community power is far more complex than previous research and theory would suggest. Common explanations, such as poverty, social status, and traditional expectations, are not sufficient explanations for powerlessness. Gaventa suggests power be viewed as a multidimensional process, which results in a variety of outcomes and relationships.

The first dimension of power is characterized by the ability of one group to prevail over another in bargaining over the resolution of key issues. Those with more social, political, and economic resources generally have more bargaining power. In this setting, grievances and challenges raised by the powerless are quickly defeated in traditional political or legal systems.

Building on these conditions, the second dimension is found. This dimension is characterized by a set of values, beliefs, institutions, rituals, and procedures fostered by elites which place them in a position of advantage at the expense of others. This level allows elites to control the actual emergence of issues or their ability to be addressed in any formal setting. Through force, threat, precedents, or formal and informal pressures, the issues of the powerless fail to emerge in the legal or political systems. The exercising of threat, force, and other drastic means is, however, sufficient to hold power only in the short term (Boggs, 1976; Entwistle, 1979; Scott, 1990). To facilitate long-term control by ruling elites, power must take on another dimension.

Gaventa's third dimension represents the social construction of meanings that foster a sense of powerlessness among certain groups. It is this level of control which is most unique, and in the long term most commanding. Shaped by social, political, and historical conditions, quiescence emerges when the powerless provide elites with near-mythic abilities and adopt the ideologies dictated by them. In this setting, the powerless are manipulated into reconstructing their worldview in accordance with that of the ruling elites. Force, coercion, or threat is unnecessary, as the powerless have taken on the ideas and beliefs which serve to justify the interests, behaviors, and actions of local elites.

This condition is similar to the ideological hegemony described by Scott (1990) and Gramsci (1971). By establishing an ideological bond between the powerful and powerless, the actions of elites are legitimized and seen as characteristic of normal life. While the powerless may not be entirely content, they view conditions as normal, not the dominating actions of controlling elites. Scott (1990) further delineates two types of hegemony: thin and thick. The former is indicative of an environment where local residents, while potentially harboring resentments, accept local order and power structures as inevitable. Coversely, thick hegemony reflects an environment where the powerless are manipulated to believe that local conditions are as good as they possibly could get, and therefore just and fair.

Gaventa stresses that these dimensions do not act alone. They are interdependent and reinforce each other based on the context and social reactions of community members. According to Gaventa (1980: 168):

> Once having prevailed in the decision-making of the organization (first dimension),
> the leaders develop barriers for the exclusion of certain participants and issues
> (second dimension), having a further effect upon their consciousness of their own
> power (third dimension).

While Gaventa provides needed insights into the emergence of power structures, and

and answers the question of how and why power structures are propagated, his work does not clearly identify the mechanisms for inserting local residents into this process. Neither does he present an explanation of how local-level actions by the powerless are sustained. We suggest an interactional perspective of community helps clarify this process. Wilkinson (1991, pp. 24-25) began a discussion of how and why community can confront quiescence:

> The argument that territoriality is class hegemony posing as community, while no doubt true in some cases (Bridger, 1988; Massey, 1980), generally underestimates the tendency for quiescence to become conflict (Gaventa, 1980) and the potential for conflict to encourage community development (Robinson, 1989). Quiescence changes into conflict when conditions permit a challenge to inequality. The reason this occurs is not because people are forced to give up a treasured state of peaceful subservience but because community - a powerful natural bond - demands that inequality be challenged.

Community is obviously key to challenging quiescence. However, Wilkinson appears to suggest an inevitable process, which the evidence does not always show to be true. We believe the role of interactional capacities or community agency is central to starting the process whereby quiescence is challenged, prevailing doctrines questioned, and local residents empowered. Yet this capacity brings with it the choice to act or not act. An understanding of the interplay between agency and choice is therefore essential. Agency facilitates the emergence of collective capacity and community itself (Wilkinson, 1991; Luloff, 1990; Luloff & Bridger, 2003; Brennan, 2007; Brennan & Luloff, 2007).

A Field Theoretical Approach to Community Power

To understand the emergence of power, we view the community from a field theoretical perspective which emphasizes the roles of local interaction and community agency as the basis for the emergence of community. Community field theory views locality as a place where people live and meet their daily needs together (Brennan, 2007; Luloff & Bridger, 2003; Theodori, 2005; Wilkinson, 1991). In this framework, a local society is seen as a comprehensive network of associations that meet common needs and express common interests. Such associations and the realization of common interests occur around, and are made possible through, social interaction. Interaction is therefore the essential element of community.

All local societies have distinct and diverse social fields or groups where residents act to achieve various self-interests and goals (Wilkinson, 1991). How these individual fields are organized and interact with each other has a great deal to do with how power is distributed within a local society. The community field emerges through the process of coordinating the individual social fields and it reflects purposive community-wide efforts. It cuts across class lines, organized groups, and other entities within a local population by focusing on the general and common needs of all residents. This encompassing field is similar to other individual social fields, but differs in that it pursues the general interests and needs of the entire community (Brennan et al., 2005; Brennan & Luloff, 2007; Bridger & Luloff, 1999; Luloff & Bridger, 2003; Wilkinson, 1991).

The emergence of the community field is affected by the context of local life, but more directly is facilitated by purposive interaction among the diverse residents of a locality. The exercise of power in relation to the emergence of the community field is therefore a fundamental concern. Power can be used to facilitate social interaction or to suppress it. As Wilkinson (1991, p. 17) notes, "community implies all types of relations that are natural among people, and if interaction is suppressed, community is limited."

To this extent, as interaction is limited, disaffection as a result of fragmentation, anomie, and alienation occur, hindering community from emerging (Arcidiacono et al., 2007; Luloff & Swanson, 1995).

Such a focus on interaction does not imply that structural or system-level characteristics are unimportant. Nor does it presuppose a romantic or utopian view of community that is devoid of conflict and self-interest. Indeed, the local economy, sociodemographics, organizations, natural resources, and institutions are vital to the makeup of the community and its residents (Brennan et al., 2005; Brennan, 2007; Luloff & Bridger, 2003). However, they serve only as the backdrop for local participation and reveal little about the motivations and ability of local people to come together to address common needs. Such collective capacity may occur in varying degrees and often in uninspiring, yet essential forms (Luloff & Swanson, 1995).

As residents and groups interact over issues important to all of them, what has come to be known as community agency, or the capacity for local action and resiliency, emerges (Wilkinson, 1991; Luloff & Bridger, 2003; Brennan & Luloff, 2007). Agency reflects the building of local relationships that increase the adaptive capacity of local people within a common territory. Agency can therefore be seen as the capacity of people to manage, utilize, and enhance those resources available to them in addressing locality wide issues (Brennan, 2007; Bridger and Luloff, 1999; Luloff and Bridger, 2003; Luloff and Swanson, 1995; Wilkinson, 1991). This is the basis for the development of the community field. As Luloff and Swanson (1995, p. 2) note:

> The collective capacity of volition and choice, however narrowed by structural conditions, makes the notion of community agency important in understanding community well-being. Just like the individuals that compose them, communities make choices and act on them. But communities are much more than the simple sum of their individuals. How they make these choices, how their perceptions of local issues are constructed, and the ability of the members of the community to find and process information are important factors in the utilization of their economic and social resources.

The key component to this process is the creation and maintenance of linkages and channels of interaction among local social fields that otherwise are directed toward more limited interests (Brennan et al., 2005; Brennan & Luloff, 2007; Luloff & Bridger, 2003; Theodori, 2005; Varley & Curtin, 2006). Such actions connect social fields and represent the development of the community field. Through interaction, common needs that cut across individual fields and the means to address them are identified. As a result, local people are linked more inclusively and are able to focus on a wider range of community issues. The culmination of this process is the emergence of community. These community interactions, in turn, shape the power capacity of local residents (Brennan et al., 2005; Luloff & Bridger, 2003; Wilkinson, 1991).

The emergence of agency is not always an easy process and is difficult in the face of established opposition from elites. Often, communities are characterized by elites who formally or secretly discourage collective mobilization leading to agency. Under conditions of disaffection and acquiescence, local citizens may believe they are incapable or acting or choose not to act. In this light, Luloff and Swanson (1995, p. 4) state:

> Central obstacles for community development include overcoming both the under-utilization of local capacities for effective community agency and the institutionalization of undemocratic and elitist local development decision-making processes. We argue that when community agency is limited to the interests of the

local elite, regardless how paternalistic, it is inherently restricted.

While the emergence of agency may encounter obstacles, it is far from impossible to achieve. Indeed, exploitation and resulting grievances may serve as the catalyst for local citizens to band together. Collective actions in the form of protests, boycotts, rebellions, challenges to prevailing ideologies, and other activities may emerge. Such actions are relatively uncommon, but emerge when the ability exists for local residents to interact and reach agreements over general needs, and have the potential to mobilize and establish local and extralocal alliances.

Community agency can be seen as a cornerstone of local power, where the ability to mobilize a broad range of local interests is essential to meeting general needs and an equitable utilization of resources. This can be seen in the work of Wilkinson (1991) and others (Brennan, 2007; Brennan & Luloff, 2007; Luloff & Bridger, 2003) where distributive justice is a central element in community well-being. Wilkinson (1991, p. 73) stresses the importance of this equity:

> Equity in a broader sense than equity-in-exchange refers to human recognition and endorsement of the ultimate *fact* of human equality, a fact underlying even the most uneven systems of distribution of access to such goods as material resources, life chances, and prestige. People are equally human, and recognition of this simple fact, along with the incorporation of this recognition into purposive actions, removes inequalities, would facilitate communication and encourage affirmative, accurate interpersonal responses.

The implications of local capacity building, community agency, and distributive justice are significant. Such conditions set the stage for understanding local responses to power elites and the emergence of grassroots power. Using this field theoretical perspective, we present a theoretical model of understanding how these conditions shape choices, consequences, and the emergence of community power.

A Theoretical Model for the Emergence of Community Power

The building of local capacity and implementation of collective action strategies can create power (Brennan, 2007; Luloff, 1990; Luloff & Swanson, 1995; Wilkinson, 1991). However, without continued support for the processes of community development and the linkage of social fields, local efforts will be limited in their ability to amass and maintain power (Bridger & Luloff, 1999; Luloff, 1990; Summers, 1986). We suggest power, local capacity, and community action can be better understood within a set of choice-and-consequence scenarios. Choice can be seen as the decision to pursue action or remain inactive, while consequences reflect the positive and negative impacts of both action and inaction. Power exists in all of these scenarios, yet is wielded by different interests in distinctly different ways. It is also the case that different social fields have different opportunities, agendas, and access to resources which might shape choice. Linking social fields is therefore essential. We present four scenarios to explore the conditions which explain local power (Table 1). Using these, we can identify the power characteristics, outcomes of the use of power, and who benefits from such use.

No Choice-Negative Consequence –Ritualized Agency

In this first scenario, local citizen action is suppressed, citizens choose not to act, or simply lack this capacity altogether. In this environment, decision-making is controlled by local and/or extralocal elites, with minimal or no contribution from local citizens. Similarly, interaction among diverse social fields is limited or in extreme cases strictly and human resources, leading to an overall negative community quality of life (Gallardo & Stein, 2007; Gaventa, 1980; Hunter, 1953).

Table 1. The Choice and Consequences of Power

		Choice Setting	
		No Choice	**Choice**
Consequence	**Negative**	*Characteristics*: Minimal agency or collective capacity to act; quiescence; disaffection among local residents; unconnected social fields; oppression at the hands of the elite; abandonment of hope by locals for overcoming power obstacles. *Outcomes*: Negative life environment with little concern for the masses. Fragmentation of powerless groups. *Benefits*: Private *Example*: Exploited labor in a company town; disenfranchised racial or ethnic minorities.	*Characteristics*: Presence of agency or collective capacity, yet failure to achieve goals. Interacting, but not fully connected, social fields. Development 'in' community where locals interact with elites to enhance segments of the locality but not the entire community. *Outcomes*: Action seen as a one-off occurrence or as successful goal attainment. Action focused on select segments of the community. Failure signals end of local empowerment. *Benefits*: Primarily Private and limited Public *Example*: Growth Machine and the 'great Buffalo hunt'; Building industrial parks that lay empty
	Positive	*Characteristics*: Minimal agency or collective capacity to act; quiescence; minimally connected social fields; hidden oppression at the hands of the elite; belief by populace that action is not needed, as the elites will take care of them. *Outcomes*: Good/tolerable life based on the arbitrary positive treatment by elites. *Benefits*: Private and Public *Example*: 'Town fathers' that take care of the community; the "free rider" problem of apathetic, uninvolved, or acquiescent residents.	*Characteristics*: Agency, empowerment, and collective capacity. Strongly connected social fields. Development 'of' community. Communities achieve goals, negotiating a place at the decision-making table, mobilizing to facilitate change, fail to achieve goals, yet mobilizing to continue their efforts. *Outcomes*: Episodic action seen as one in the scope of many. Community and development seen in the actions of individuals, not goal attainment. Enhanced social well-being. *Benefits*: Public *Example*: Community unites to defeat unwanted extralocal development attempts; restoration of significant local historical site and development of cultural center

Benefits from such a power arrangement go to private interests, and rarely benefit the general public. Such conditions mirror Gaventa's (1980) description of parts of Appalachia and highlight his three dimensions of power. There, extralocal control over resources and economies left communities at the mercy of power-holding elites and their industries. This control, and the choice or inability of local residents to act, is often the result of overt force and threat. In the end, quiescence emerges, where the worldview of the powerless social fields are transformed to support and comply with local elites. In the short term, power holders are perceived by local residents as being too big, omnipresent, politically connected, and economically advantaged to be overcome. More importantly, in the long term, they may also be seen as the legitimate controllers of local life, economies, and services, who need not be questioned.

Yet, this form of oppressive control is difficult to maintain, leading to power being a fleeting condition in some settings. Such oppression in parts of Appalachia, for example, led to revolt and protest which eventually diminished the strict control of extralocal power holders (Gaventa, 1980). However, this ability for such change was often part of a wider social environment. In this example, the natural resource base which fed power structures became more unstable as markets for resources diminished. With this loss, the ability of extralocals to strictly control all aspects of local life also declined. These market conditions coincided with wider social, economic, and political change where regulations, unions, and legal rights (brought on by other coordinated communities under less despotic control) signaled an end to the domination previously seen. Yet in other communities, quiescence by the powerless was firmly entrenched and the prevailing ideology still remains today.

It may also be the case that a form of suppressed or ritualized agency can be seen. In this context of controlled agendas, limited agency might emerge during proscribed community events. Venues of interaction organized, sponsored, and most importantly sanctioned by elites can set the stage for a minimal local capacity. Through formal community and corporate events such as old home days, 4th of July celebrations, and other events endorsed by elites, the potential for social fields to interaction and agency to emerge are present, albeit in a controlled setting.

In such settings, the question of how disaffection and quiescence can be overcome to achieve a more equitable environment remains. As a beginning point, social fields that otherwise are not interacting and communicating must be encouraged to do so. This is the basis for capacity building, and more importantly, a beginning for the powerless to break or challenge the ideological bond that exists between the power holders and their subservient population. In this scenario in particular, structural change and ideological change need to be seen as part of the same concerted effort.

To do this, the powerless must be able to conceive action, mobilize citizens, create awareness, establish partnerships, and foster sustainable action plans that counter the prevailing environment of the powerful (Gaventa, 1980; Pigg, 1999; Wilkinson, 1991). The powerless also need to establish coalitions, partnerships, and alliances with other powerless groups inside, and possibly external to, the community (Pigg, 1999). In this scenario, the environment for significant capacity building is likely insufficient to immediately challenge local elites, but may be sufficient to establish connections and partnerships with similarly disenfranchised extralocal groups, elites, and organizations (Gallardo & Stein, 2007). Based on these conditions, the powerless need to develop capacities, issues, and actions if social change is to emerge. They must act when the powerful are weakened or create conditions which can lead to their being weakened such as the establishment of alliances with extralocal forces. For example, in recent years Appalachia has seen significant local action and extralocal alliances in the face of mountaintop removal and other coal extraction activities. Such alliances and connections to larger environmental protection efforts have empowered and brought together local social fields to challenge power holders in their communities. Through such partnerships, awareness is spread, coalitions established, and actions coordinated to facilitate local and more widespread social change. It may also be the case that the ability of local citizens to obtain knowledge power can help facilitate the emergence of community agency. This knowledge, in a variety of forms (such as legal, skills, information, education), may prove essential in advancing grassroots power and establishing alliances outside the community. Through such structure-building, the powerless are empowered to confront the local barriers to power and become part of the decision-making process (Arcidiacono et al., 2007; Bridger & Luloff, 1999; Luloff & Swanson, 1995; Gallardo & Stein, 2007;

Wilkinson, 1991).

No Choice-Positive Consequence - Abandoned Agency

In contrast to the despotic picture painted above is a gentler, but nonetheless still controlled scenario. Here, local life is pleasant, yet power remains private, benefiting elites (Beaver & Cohen, 2004; Duncan, 1999). Social fields remain, at best, minimally connected. The inaction of local citizens is rewarded with social, economic, and other support from powerful elites. Such conditions reflect the firmly entrenched quiescence outlined by Gaventa (1980) and the ideological hegemony presented by Scott (1990). As a result of manipulation and control by elites, the powerless have clearly altered their worldview to openly accept and support the elites without question. Under this benevolent framework, local citizens are provided for much like a parent looks after a child. Examples of this condition can be found in many communities where the often beloved 'town fathers' hold enormous sway in the decisions affecting local life. Such conditions mask an inactive community, where interactive capacities remain controlled. A tolerable life for citizens comes at the price of their capacity to act. In effect, this scenario, while pleasant on the surface, may be direr to local communities than the previous repressive environment.

This citizen response to power is different in theory and practice to the previous scenario which was based on force, threat, and direct domination. While these tools of domination remain hidden in the background in the event that power holders need them, in this scenario, acquiescing to power and complacency comes more in terms of allegiance, love, honor, and respect for those making decisions (Beaver & Cohen, 2004; Duncan, 1999; Pateman, 1970). It is assumed that power holders are legitimate and act in the best interest of the populace. Additionally, citizens often believe they are not capable of acting at the same standards as local power elites, and therefore leave action to those they perceive will act on their behalf (Beaver & Cohen, 2004). Pateman (1970) sees this as reflective of authoritative structures in institutions (schools, family, and workplace) where people spend most of their lives. Such environments are often designed to deliberately prevent local people from acting. As a result, these conditions undermine the socialization process, reduce interaction and cooperation, and hinder the involvement of diverse local residents in the collective decision-making process. This acts to concentrate, retain, and reinforce the power of local elites (Luloff & Swanson, 1995).

In this scenario, the potential for citizens joining together in collective action most likely is not seen as a threat or concern to power elites, as community mobilization against elites would likely be seen by the powerless themselves as a betrayal. While in a different context than the previous scenario, the failure to act remains an abandonment of citizen capacity for action. The potential for agency may exist, but citizens (while aware of their ability to act) are convinced that there is no utility in doing so. As local residents become convinced elites are acting in their best interests, their ability to act or rebel becomes even more diminished. The long-term result is that the powerless may not be able to overcome the inertia of inaction, even in the face of desperate need, and thus rely on local elites.

In this setting, community agency would have the potential to emerge and contribute to social change. However, a significant challenge to the ideological hegemony that exists is first needed. Gramsci (1971) called for counter-hegemony to be cultivated to challenge the prevailing conditions propagated by ruling elites. Change must be sought not only to the structures of the local community, but equally important, to the prevailing ideology. To counter existing ideologies, the powerless need to be made aware of agenda setting and the visible or hidden ideologies of the powerful. They must also be exposed to other groups which can reinforce the belief that their treatment at the hands of the elite is not normal, but distinctly controlled and different from other communities. Before local citizens can act, they need to be able to question and challenge the rights of the elite to rule.

To foster community agency, capacity-building activities that include purposive and focused interaction among social fields are essential. Such interaction and conscious efforts to recruit/involve citizens from all segments of the community would develop connections and ties across social fields, thereby providing a basis for action. It is important that an initial project be selected on the basis of the likelihood for achieving success, because this can become the basis for challenging the ideology that elites can best run the community. In addition, the establishment of explicit processes for hearing all local voices and reconciling differences (but not necessarily reaching consensus) among social fields would lead to a more informed and united community that could challenge prevailing ideologies.

Local citizens groups can also tap external allies in an effort to change the local power equation within their communities. Such alliances would indicate the limited and inherent capacities of local elites to effectively meet local needs, by highlighting their weaknesses and vulnerabilities. Ultimately, in both 'no choice' scenarios, the lack of local interaction among social fields, limited collective capacity, propagation of elite ideologies, and lack of community itself allow an environment to flourish where existing power structures and elites operate unrestricted. In response, networks, interaction, and connections among social fields must first be established and maintained. From these, challenges to prevailing ideologies and power structures can then be made.

Choice-Negative Consequence – Incomplete Agency

In this scenario, a more complete form of agency emerges but fails to achieve desired goals or broader community well-being. Benefits from such a setting are designed for the general needs of the community, but remain largely in the private realm. Social fields interact, but fail to exhibit strong channels of communication and purposive interaction. Examples of this scenario include locally based efforts to establish an industrial park coupled to the failure to recruit industry or related businesses, or action that fosters economic growth for some industries and inhibits growth for others. Local capacity may lead to a concerted effort for development, yet this effort may be incomplete, resulting in ineffective actions. In part, this may reflect a narrow focus on specific needs of some community segments (infrastructure and the economy) at the expense of the larger community context (Immergluck, 2005; Israel & Beaulieu, 1990).

While usually presented in a positive light, collective action need not always have this result. The choice to act is not easy or without negative repercussions. Collective action can threaten local power holders and result in obstacles, conflict, and retribution. Similarly, a minimal, unrepresentative, or incomplete organizing of local residents may inadvertently reinforce existing power structures. Ill-prepared groups might be easily manipulated or convinced to align themselves with local-power holding elites. Negative impacts can also be seen in the failure of local mobilizations to achieve goals. Their failure may result in more negative outcomes, such as a loss of confidence among members in their abilities to facilitate change or decreased status associated with being on the losing side. In either situation, without purposive and controlled plans for continued action, local efforts can falter.

From a community development perspective, the building of collective capacity may result in less than positive conditions if the community development process is not maintained. The mobilization and organization of residents leading to the emergence of agency and community takes time, effort, and most importantly commitment. Under situations of extreme threat, this process may naturally emerge, such as when communities face severe economic, health, or natural resource threats. All are clear indications of a common general community need, capable of drawing a wide range of citizens into action. Such action is often characterized as a "one-off" situation, where the success or failure of the action signals the end of collective capacity building and efforts to link social fields (Immergluck, 2005). In the end, these responses may do little to contribute to local well-being, long-term capacity building, and/or the emergence of community. Indeed, such limited activities might detract from community building by setting a negative tone in circumstances of defeat and also by highlighting the differences/disagreements that may initially emerge as disparate groups come together to achieve common ground (Immergluck, 2005; Varley & O'Cearbhaill, 1999). In this setting, the collective action process may actually end with these disagreements, fostering disaffection, and further fragmenting the powerless (Luloff & Swanson, 1995).

Similarly, community building activities may be too narrowly focused toward select segments of the locality (economy, health care, schools, etc.). This represents what Summers (1986) referred to as development 'in' community and usually involve a group of homogenous local individuals and groups who liaise with power holders internal and external to the community. This is seen as distinctly different from the development 'of' community characterized by broad-based citizen contributions to decision making and the building of diverse local capacities for long-term sustainable development.

This scenario also reflects the 'growth machine' presented by Molotch (1976), where competition among power holders over high-value land drives growth, sprawl, and urban development. Such activities, while important, do little to develop broad-based citizen action. Agency can emerge in these settings, but the focus on select social fields may inhibit wider social development. Failure may also result from the lack of resources rather than disagreement.

To advance development, local capacity building might better facilitate access of additional local or extralocal resources. Such mobilization would also help reconcile differences of opinion among diverse local residents, which in turn would lead to the identification of more clearly defined general community needs that all groups could work toward. Without broad-based local capacity building, future development efforts may remain unsuccessful, as well as opening the door for manipulation by elites and potentially the emergence of quiescence among those with little power.

Choice-Positive Consequence – Authentic Agency

The fourth scenario, albeit uncommon among contemporary communities, focuses on the positive face of action which is most often presented to highlight the potentials of community action, civic engagement, and grassroots social change. This setting includes the ability of local citizens to access and manage resources, prevent domination by elites, link various social fields/interest groups, and establish a foundation for current and future action (Brennan, 2007; Brennan & Luloff, 2007; Duncan, 1999; Wilkinson, 1991). Benefits of action are clearly focused on the public and designed to meet the general needs of the community. Social fields interact in a consistent and substantive manner. In this scenario, active communities experience a variety of conditions, including goal achievement, negotiating a place at the decision-making table, mobilizing to facilitate change, and failing to achieve their goals, yet mobilizing to continue in their efforts.

Coalitions of residents are broad-based and representative of the diversity of communities. Community and its development are seen in the continuous actions of individuals, not goal attainment (Brennan, 2007; Duncan, 1999; Luloff & Bridger, 2003; Wilkinson, 1991). Here in its purest sense, interaction, collective mobilization of local residents, and local capacity building lead to the emergence of agency and community.

residents, and local capacity building lead to the emergence of agency and community. This allows for the dispersed power of diverse local residents to be harnessed, overcoming the control of elites (Brennan, 2007; Gaventa, 1980; Varley & Curtin, 2006).

This scenario represents what Summers (1986) describes as the development 'of' community. The bringing together of diverse local groups to develop plans for sustainable long-term action is the basis for the development of community (Brennan et al., 2005; Brennan, 2007; Varley & Curtin, 2006). Efforts to establish channels of communication, interaction, and capacity building are essential, and represent an entity greater than the sum of its parts. This collective entity is a force that enables local citizens to obtain power and navigate the nebulous local and extralocal channels of power. Equally important, it creates an environment where quiescence and the ill intentions of elites do not emerge to dominate local life.

Conclusion

This article has explored and conceptualized community power. This often nebulous concept is essential to local community life and the relationships that take place within it. Drawing from the work of Gaventa and others, we have examined the complexity of power, its processes, and context. Building on previous theory and research, we portray local power in a choice/consequence model interpreted through a field theoretical perspective.

In all of the power scenarios discussed, community capacity and agency are central to the empowerment of local citizens. The first step involves identifying the various social fields that make up the community, their roles in decision-making, and the linkages that do or should exist between them. Such an assessment provides a description of both the community power structure and the community field. The key to developing the latter is the articulation and creation of linkages among the diverse individual social fields. Through this process the potential exists for common ground to be reached and the dispersed power of local residents to be consolidated. Such activities are a starting point for strengthening the community field and the development of community. Equally important, this process is essential in allowing the powerless to remain cognizant of their ability to act and to the emergence of quiescence.

In the end, understanding power does not serve our ability to monopolize or manipulate its hold on local communities, but more correctly to facilitate social change. In an age of devolution, declining service budgets, globalization, and increasingly fragmented communities, our ability to coordinate resources, agendas, and actions to meet general community needs may in many ways signal survival for our communities. The establishment of channels of communication/interaction among those with and without power should not be seen as a threat to local power or agendas nor an abandonment of their self-interests, but as a key to their long-term success and well-being.

References

Arcidiacono, C., Procentese, F., & DiNapoli, I. (2007). Youth, community belonging, planning and power. *Journal of Community and Applied Social Psychology, 17*(4): 280-295.

Armstrong, C. L. (2006). Revisiting structural pluralism: A two-dimensional conception of community power. *Mass Communication and Society, 9*(3): 287-300.

Bachrach, P., & Baratz, M. S. (1970). *Power and poverty: Theory and practice.* New York: Oxford University Press.

Beaver, W., & Cohen, E. (2004). Power in a rural county. *Sociological Spectrum, 24*(6): 629-650.

Boggs, C. (1976) *Gramsci's Marxism.* London: Pluto Press.

Boulding, K. E. (1989). *Three Faces of Power.* Newbury Park, CA: Sage Publications.

Brennan, M.A. (2007). The development of community in the west of Ireland: A return to Killala twenty years on. *Community Development Journal.* 42(3): 330-374.

Brennan, M.A.,& Luloff, A.E. (2007). Exploring rural community agency differences in Ireland and

Pennsylvania." *Journal of Rural Studies* 23: 52-61.

Brennan, M.A., Luloff, A.E., & Finley, J.C. (2005). Building sustainable communities in forested regions. *Society and Natural Resources,* 18(9): 1-11.

Bridger, J., & Luloff, A.E. (1999). Toward an interactional approach to sustainable community development. *Journal of Rural Studies,* 15: 377-387.

Coser, L. A., & Howe, I. (1977). *The new conservatives: a critique from the left.* New York: New American Library.

Dahl, R. A. (1961). *Who governs? Democracy and power in an American city.* Yale studies in political science, 4. New Haven: Yale University Press.

Dahrendorf, R. (1959). *Class and class conflict in industrial society.* Stanford, CA: Stanford University Press.

Daniels, S. E., & Walker, G. B. (2001). *Working through environmental conflict: The collaborative learning approach.* Westport, CT: Praeger.

Domhoff, G. (1986). *The power elite and the state: How policy is made in America.* New York: A. de Gruyter.

Domhoff, G. W. (2007). Commentary: C. Wright Mills, Power structure research, and the failures of mainstream political science. *New Political Science, 29*(1): 97-114.

Duncan, C. (1999). *Worlds apart: Why poverty persists in rural America.* New Haven, CT: Yale University Press.

Ebenstein, W. (1991). *Great political thinkers.* New York: Holt, Rinehart and Winston.

Entwistle, H. (1979). *Antonio Gramsci: Conservative schooling for radical politics.* London: Routledge.

Fisher, A. T., & Sonn, C. C. (2007). Power in community psychology research and practice. *Journal of Community and Applied Social Psychology, 17*(4): 255-257.

Gallardo, J., & Stein, T. (2007). Participation, power and racial representation: Negotiating nature-based and heritage tourism development in the rural south. *Society and Natural Resources, 20*(7): 597-611.

Gaventa, J. (1980). *Power and powerlessness: Quiescence and rebellion in an Appalachian Valley.* Urbana, IL: University of Illinois Press.

Gramsci, A. (1971). *Selections from the Prison Notebooks.* London: Lawrence and Wishart.

Groarke, M. (2004). Using community power against targets beyond the neighborhood. *New Political Science, 26*(2): 171-188.

Hobbes, T. (1960). *Leviathan.* Oxford, UK: Basil-Blackwell.

Hunter, F. (1953). *Community power structure: A study of decision makers.* Chapel Hill: University of North Carolina Press.

Hyman, D., McKnight, J. & Higdon, F., (2001). *Doing democracy: Conflict and consensus strategies for citizens, organizations, and communities.* NY: Erudition Press.

Immergluck, D. (2005). Building power, losing power: The rise and fall of a prominent community economic development coalition. *Economic Development Quarterly, 19*(3): 211-224.

Israel, G. D., & Beaulieu, L. J. (1990). Community leadership. In A. E. Luloff and L. A. Swanson (Eds.), *American rural communities.* Boulder, CO: Westview Press.

Lukes, S. (1974). *Power: A radical view.* London, UK: MacMillan.

Luloff, A.E. (1990). Community and social change: How do small communities act? In A.E. Luloff and L.A. Swanson (Eds.), *American rural communities.* Boulder, CO: Westview Press.

Luloff, A.E., & Bridger, J. (2003). Community agency and local development. In D. Brown and L. Swanson (Eds.), *Challenges for rural America in the twenty-first century,* University Park, PA: Pennsylvania State University Press.

Luloff, A. E., & Swanson, L. A. (1995). Community agency and disaffection: Enhancing collective resources. In L. Beaulieu and D. Mulkey (Eds.), *Investing in people: The human capital needs of rural America,* Boulder, CO: Westview Press.

Marx, K. (1994). *Selected writings.* Indianapolis, IN: Hackett Publishing.

Mills, C. W. (1956). *The power elite.* New York: Oxford University Press.

Moffett, S., & Freund, B. (2004). Elite formation and elite bonding: Social structure and development in Durban. *Urban Forum 15*(2): 134-161.

Molotch, H. (1976). The city as a growth machine. *The American Journal of Sociology* 82(2): 309-332.

Pateman, C. (1970). *Participation and democratic theory*. Cambridge, UK: Cambridge University Press.

Parsons, T. (1977). *Social systems and the evolution of action theory*. New York: Free Press.

Pigg, K. (1999). Community leadership and community theory: A practical synthesis. *Journal of the Community Development Society, 30*(2): 196-212.

Reed, M. & McIlveen, K. (2006). Towards a pluralistic civic science?: Assessing community forestry. *Society & Natural Resources*. 19:591-607

Rousseau, J. (1978). *On the social contract*. New York: St Martins Press.

Scott, J. (1990). *Domination and the arts of resistance: Hidden transcripts*. New Haven, CT: Yale University Press.

Stone, C. (1986). Power and social complexity. In D. Waste (Ed.), *Community power: Directions for future research*, pp. 77-113. Thousand Oaks, CA: Sage.

Summers, G. (1986). Rural community development. *Annual Review of Sociology, 12*: 341-371.

Theodori, G. (2005). Community and community development in resource-based areas:

Operational definitions rooted in an interactional perspective. *Society and Natural Resources, 18*(7): 661-669.

Varley, T., & Curtin, C. (2006). The politics of empowerment: Power, populism and partnership in rural Ireland. *Economic and Social Review, 37*(3): 423-446.

Varley, T. & O'Cearbhaill, D. (1999). Empowering communities through community action in rural Ireland: The case of Muintir na T're. In R. Byron and J. Hutson (Eds.), *Local enterprise on the North Atlantic Margin: Selected contributions to the fourteenth international seminar on Marginal regions*. London: Ashgate.

Waste, D. (1996) *Community power: Directions for future research*. Thousand Oaks, CA: Sage.

Weber, M. (1947). *The theory of social and economic organization*. Glencoe, IL: Free Press.

Wilkinson, K. P. (1991). *The community in rural America*. Westport, CT: Greenwood Press.

Theories of Poverty and Anti-Poverty Programs in Community Development

Ted K. Bradshaw

In this paper I explore how five competing theories of poverty shape anti-poverty strategies. Since most rural community development efforts aim to relieve causes or symptoms of poverty, it makes a difference which theory of poverty is believed to be responsible for the problem being addressed. In this paper five theories of poverty are distilled from the literature. It will be shown that these theories of poverty place its origin from (1) individual deficiencies, (2) cultural belief systems that support subcultures in poverty, (3) political-economic distortions, (4) geographical disparities, or (5) cumulative and circumstantial origins. Then, I show how each theory of poverty finds expression in common policy discussion and community development programs aimed to address the causes of poverty. Building a full understanding of each of these competing theories of poverty shows how they shape different community development approaches. Although no one theory explains all instances of poverty, this paper aims to show how community development practices that address the complex and overlapping sources of poverty more effectively reduce poverty compared to programs that address a single theory.

> Which view of poverty we ultimately embrace will have a
> direct bearing on the public policies we pursue.
> —Schiller 1989, p. 4

Community development has a variety of strategies available to meet the needs of those persons and groups who are less advantaged, usually in poverty. Community developers help all communities, but their passion lies disproportionately with people who do not have adequate personal resources to meet their needs or with communities with large populations of people who need assistance. These people and communities receiving attention from community developers are extensively varied in most respects other than being poor—the poor are both rural and urban, they are ethnically minority

Ted K. Bradshaw (October 28, 1942—August 5, 2006) was professor, chair, and research sociologist in the Human and Community Development Department at the University of California, Davis. Since 2002, he was Editor of *COMMUNITY DEVELOPMENT: Journal of the Community Development*. In 1974, he received his Ph.D. in Sociology at the University of California, Berkeley. With co-author Woodrow W. Clark II, Bradshaw published *Agile Energy Systems: Global Lessons from the California Energy Crisis* in 2004. Ted Bradshaw died suddenly while running near his home in Oakland, California. This article represents a revision of papers presented at the meetings of the Community Development Society (2001) and the Rural Sociology Society (2003). Research assistance from students, Vlade Stasuc and Christine McReynolds, is greatly appreciated.

or not, they live in places with weak and strong economies, and they have been helped for decades or neglected for as long. In short, fixing poverty is a dominant theme within community development, but we have infrequently examined the theories that underlie the dominant practices addressing poverty.

The thesis of this paper is that community anti-poverty programs are designed, selected, and implemented in response to different theories about the cause of poverty that "justify" the community development interventions. The definition of poverty and theories that explain it are deeply rooted in strongly held research traditions and political values, reinforced by encompassing social, political, and economic institutions that have a stake in the issue. Thus, a purely objective explanation of poverty is displaced by a proliferation of socially defined issues and concerns from both liberal and conservative perspectives. Moreover, no one theory of poverty has emerged that either subsumes or invalidates the others (Blank, 1997). Explaining poverty remains a lucrative field for academics, policy makers, book publishers, and ideologues, and as a consequence the range of explanations has proliferated.

A sampling of community-based poverty programs shows how varied community level anti-poverty efforts can be.

1. A county directed its schools to identify children not attending school more than ten days per school-year without medical excuses, and then if the family received Temporary Assistance for Needy Families (TANF) benefits, the child's portion of the family welfare payments were withheld to enforce school attendance and assure that welfare kids not get left behind for another generation.
2. Pre-school programs are advocated in order to help poor kids gain skills and internalize the value of learning that will help them succeed in school, and after-school programs are designed to keep children away from negative influences of unsupervised street cultures.
3. Public programs (such as equal opportunity) help remove social and economic barriers to housing, good jobs, health care, and political processes, based on the premise that otherwise qualified people are commonly excluded from poverty reducing opportunities by race, class, gender, or other factors not relevant to ability to perform.
4. Communities utilize a range of local economic development tools such as redevelopment, business attraction, or enterprise zones to stimulate development of poor and disadvantaged areas hurt by regional isolation, economic backwardness, blight, and disinvestment.
5. Non-profits and community development corporations (CDCs) develop comprehensive approaches to poverty based on a multifaceted approach including employment development, education, housing, access to health care and social services, as well as personal networks and participation in community programs that increase social capital.

The first example is based on theories that poverty is perpetuated by individual or family irresponsibility, which should be stopped by stiff penalties; the second example addresses subcultures of poverty and tries to acculturate poor children into mainstream values; the third sees poverty not as an individual problem but a social one that needs to be addressed politically and structurally; the fourth addresses regional or geographic concentrations of poverty through spatially targeted benefits; and the final addresses poverty in a comprehensive and cumulative way. Each example reflects a different theory of what causes poverty and how to address it.

I consider a theory an explanation that links several concepts; in this case theories explain poverty (as defined below) by linking different factors thought to cause or perpetuate poverty through distinctive social processes. Interventions that reduce a cause of poverty should reduce poverty as a consequence. The emphasis here is on poverty in developed countries such as the USA. The purpose of this paper is to expand our understanding of five different theories of poverty that underlie the common toolbox of programs, which community developers apply to address the problem of poverty in their community. In contrast to the typical focus that limits theoretical review to only two or three contrasting perspectives (Ropers, 1991; Egendorf, 1999; Epstein, 1997), this paper suggests that there are five major theoretical explanations for poverty.[1] Poverty, it is argued, is a very complex social problem with many variants and different roots, all of which have validity depending on the situation (Blank, 2003; Shaw, 1996, p. 28).

Definitions of Poverty

Poverty in its most general sense is the lack of necessities. Basic food, shelter, medical care, and safety are generally thought necessary based on shared values of human dignity. However, what is a necessity to one person is not uniformly a necessity to others. Needs may be relative to what is possible and are based on social definition and past experience (Sen, 1999). Valentine (1968) says that "the essence of poverty is inequality. In slightly different words, the basic meaning of poverty is relative deprivation." A social (relative) definition of poverty allows community flexibility in addressing pressing local concerns, although objective definitions allow tracking progress and comparing one area to another.

The most common "objective" definition of poverty is the statistical measure established by the federal government as the annual income needed for a family to survive. The "poverty line" was initially created in 1963 by Mollie Orshansky at the U.S. Department of Agriculture based on three times her estimate of what a family would have to spend for an adequate but far from lavish diet. According to Michael Darby (1996, p. 4), the very definition of poverty was political, aimed to benchmark the progress of poverty programs for the War on Poverty. Adjusted for inflation, the poverty line for a family of four was $17,050 income in 2000 according to the U.S. Census. Most poverty scholars identify many problems with this definition related to concepts of family, cash income, treatment of taxes, special work-related expenses, or regional differences in the cost of living (Blank, 1997, p. 10; Quigley, 2003).

Regardless of how we look at the "science" of poverty, or what O'Connor calls the "knowledge of poverty," it is essential to retain focus on the fact that the definition of poverty and the policies addressing it are all shaped by political biases and values.

> It is this disparity of status and interest that make poverty research an inescapably political act: it is an exercise of power, in this case of an educated elite to categorize, stigmatize, but above all to neutralize the poor and disadvantaged through analysis that obscures the political nature of social and economic inequality (O'Connor, 2001, p. 12).

In this sense, political agenda are the overriding factors in poverty that not only influence the choice of theory of poverty but also the very definition of poverty to be explained by each theory. Powerful interests manage how poverty is discussed and what is being done about it; unfortunately this paper can only identify the politicization of theories of poverty rather than separate them out for analysis.

Sources and Approach

The approach in this paper is to review strategically selected programs and approaches used by communities to address poverty in the United States. The approach starts by examining some of the most significant recent books and articles (and several classics) that discuss poverty in America,[2] and then it distills from them the theoretical perspectives most central to their analysis. The task here is not to do a complete review of all the literature on poverty, as that includes thousands of items and is beyond the scope of this paper. Nor is the task to distill all the recent abundance of information on poverty, especially the empirical evidence of who the poor are and what their condition is.

I approach poverty programs from the community development perspective, addressing the range of programs available to a typical community. Since this portfolio of programs changes rapidly over time and from community to community, I attempt to generalize and build grounded theory that captures the range, even if it blurs some details. I was guided in this task by the recent books on poverty policy such as Sar Levitan's colleagues whose inventory of "Programs in Aid of the Poor" (Levitan et al., 2003) catalogued many federal programs available to local areas. In addition, I base my analysis on those programs I have known over years of community-based work. Simply put, the task of this paper is to look in the literature for theoretical explanations of poverty that link up with the practices at the core of community development.

For each of the five theories that make up the bulk of the poverty literature, I identify the set of variables most significantly associated with causing poverty according to that theory, the mechanisms by these variables cause poverty, the potential strategies that can be addressed in response to poverty, and finally community-based examples of how anti-poverty programs based on that particular theory are implemented. These five theories are summarized in Figure 1.

Figure 1. Five Theories of Poverty and Community Anti-Poverty Programs

Theory	What causes Poverty?	How does it work?	Potential Community Development responses	Community examples to reduce poverty
1. Individual	Individual laziness, bad choice, incompetence, inherent disabilities	Competition rewards winners and punishes those who do not work hard and make bad choices	Avoid and counter efforts to individualize poverty, provide assistance and safety net	Drug rehabilitation, second chance programs, making safety net easier to access, use training and counseling to help poor individuals overcome problems
2. Cultural	Subculture adopts values that are non-productive and are contrary to norms of success	Use community to the advantage of the poor; value diverse cultures, acculturation, and community building; alternative socialization through forming new peer groups	Head Start, after school, leadership development within subcultures, asset-based community development	Head Start, after-school leadership development within subcultures, asset-based community development

Figure 1. Cont'd.

Theory	What causes Poverty?	How does it work?	Potential Community Development responses	Community examples to reduce poverty
3. Political-economic structure	Systematic barriers prevent poor from access and accomplishment in key social institutions including jobs, education, housing, health care, safety, political representation, etc.	Selection criteria directly or indirectly exclude some groups of persons based on inappropriate criteria	Community organizing and advocacy to gain political and economic power to achieve change; create alternative organizations	Policies to force inclusion and enforcement
4. Geographic	Social advantages and disadvantages concentrate in separate areas	Agglomeration, distance, economies of scale, and resource distributions reinforce differences	National redistributions, concentration of development on local assets	Redevelopment areas, downtowns, rural networking, urban revitalization
5. Cumulative and cyclical	Spirals of poverty, problems for individuals (earnings, housing, health, education, self confidence) are interdependent and strongly linked to community deficiencies (loss of business and jobs, inadequate schools, inability to provide social services), etc.	Factors interact in complex ways. Community level crises lead to Individual crises and vice versa, and each cumulate to cause spirals of poverty	Breaking the spiral of poverty with a spiral of success through a comprehensive program that addresses both individual and community issues	Comprehensive CDC programs that build self-sufficiency in a community reinforced environment, programs that link individuals and community organizations, asset-based approaches

FIVE THEORIES OF POVERTY IN CONTEMPORARY LITERATURE

Recent literature on poverty uniformly acknowledges different theories of poverty, but the literature has classified these theories in multiple ways (e.g., compare Blank, 2003; Goldsmith & Blakely, 1992; Jennings & Kushnick, 1999; Rodgers, 2000; Schiller, 1989; Shaw, 1996). Virtually all authors distinguish between theories that root the cause of poverty in individual deficiencies (conservative) and theories that lay the cause on broader social phenomena (liberal or progressive). Ryan (1976) addresses this dichotomy in terms of "blaming the victim." Goldsmith and Blakely, for example, distinguish "poverty as pathology" from "poverty as incident or accident" and "poverty as structure." Schiller (1989, pp. 2-3) explains it in terms of "flawed characters, restricted opportunity, and Big Brother." Jennings

(1999) reviews variants on these individual vs. society conceptions, giving emphasis to racial and political dynamics. Rank is very clear: "The focus on individual attributes as the cause of poverty is misplaced and misdirected." Structural failings of the economic, political, and social system are causes instead (Rank, 2004, p. 50). The various theories are divergent, and each results in a different type of community development intervention strategy.

1. Poverty Caused by Individual Deficiencies

This first theory of poverty consists of a large and multifaceted set of explanations that focus on the individual as responsible for his or her poverty situation. Typically, politically conservative theoreticians blame individuals in poverty for creating their own problems and argue that with harder work and better choices, the poor could have avoided (and now can remedy) their problems. Other variations of the individual theory of poverty ascribe poverty to lack of genetic qualities such as intelligence that are not so easily reversed.

The belief that poverty stems from individual deficiencies is old. Religious doctrine that equated wealth with the favor of God was central to the Protestant reformation (Weber, 2001) and blind, crippled, or deformed people were believed to be punished by God for either their or their parents' sins. With the emergence of the concept of inherited intelligence in the nineteenth century, the eugenics movement went so far as to rationalize poverty and even sterilization for those who appeared to have limited abilities. Books like Herrnstein and Murray's *The Bell Curve* (1994) are modern uses of this explanation. Rainwater (1970, p. 16) critically discusses individualistic theories of poverty as a "moralizing perspective" and notes that the poor are "afflicted with the mark of Cain. They are meant to suffer, indeed must suffer, because of their moral failings. They live in a deserved hell on earth." Rainwater goes on to say that it is difficult to overestimate the extent to which this perspective (incorrectly) under-girds our visions of poverty, including the perspective of the disinherited themselves.

Ironically, neoclassical economics reinforces individualistic sources of poverty. The core premise of this dominant paradigm for the study of the conditions leading to poverty is that individuals seek to maximize their own well being by making choices and investments, and that (assuming that they have perfect information) they seek to maximize their well being. When some people choose short-term and low pay-off returns, economic theory holds the individual largely responsible for their individual choices—for example to forego college education or other training that will lead to better paying jobs in the future.

The economic theory that the poor lack incentives for improving their own conditions is a recurrent theme in articles that blame the welfare system's generosity on the perpetuation of poverty. In a *Cato Journal* article, economists Gwartney and McCaleb argue that the years of the war on poverty actually increased poverty (adjusted for non-cash transfers) among working age adults in spite of unprecedented increases in welfare expenditures. They conclude that "the application of simple economic theory" suggests that the problem lies in the war on poverty programs:

> They [welfare programs] have introduced a perverse incentive structure, one that penalizes self-improvement and protects individuals against the consequences of their own bad choices. (1985, p. 7)

This and similar arguments that cast the poor as a "moral hazard" also hold that "the problem of poverty continues to fester not because we are failing to do enough, but because we are doing too much that is counterproductive" (Gwartney & McCaleb, 1985, p. 15). Their economic model would solve poverty by assuring that the penalty of poverty was great enough that none would choose it (and welfare would be restricted to the truly disabled or otherwise unable to work).

A less widely critiqued version of the individualistic theory of poverty comes from American values of individualism—the Horatio Alger myth that any individual can succeed by skills and hard work, and that motivation and persistence are all that are required to achieve success (see Asen, 2002, pp. 29-34). Self-help literature reinforces the belief that individuals fail because they do not try hard enough. Frank Bettger (1977, pp. 187-188), in the Dale Carnegie tradition, tells how he got a list of self-improvement goals on which to focus and became one of the most successful and highly paid salesmen in America. He goes on to say that anyone can succeed by an easy formula—focused goals and hard work. This is the message of hundreds of self-help books, articles, and sermons. By extension, this literature implies that those who do not succeed must face the fact that they themselves are responsible for their failure.

Although scientifically it is routine to dismiss the individual deficiency theory as an apology for social inequality (Fischer, et al., 1996), it is easy to see how it is embraced in anti-poverty policy that suggests that penalties and incentives can change behavior.

Anti-Poverty Programs from the Perspective of an Individual Theory of Poverty

Community development practice, embedded in decades of welfare and social policy, frequently deals with programs aiming to remedy poverty based on individual deficiency theories. Explicitly or implicitly, individual deficiencies represent an easy policy approach not always carefully explored as it gets implemented. The key initiatives today are to push the poor into work as a primary goal, what Maskovsky calls the "workist consensus." Indeed this move is accompanied by an increasing emphasis on "self help" strategies for the poor to pull themselves from poverty, strategies encouraged by the elimination of other forms of assistance (Maskovsky, 2001, pp. 472-473). Earned income tax credits are one aspect of the strategy to assure that the poor work even at below living-wage jobs.

However, from a community development perspective, addressing poverty by focusing on individual characteristics and bad choices raise fundamental conflicts in philosophy and in what is known to succeed. The compassion of community development shies away from blaming the individual, and individual level programs are usually embedded in community efforts by the very nature of community development. Thus, anti-poverty programs in community development tend to oppose strategies that punish or try to change individuals as a solution to poverty, though working with individual needs and abilities is a constant objective. This tension runs through all anti-poverty programs.

However, many contemporary anti-poverty programs are not designed with compassion in mind; they use punishment and the threat of punishment in order to change behavior and get people off public assistance (see O'Connor, 2001; Quigley, 2003). The best example of this response to poverty is to limit the number of years people can be on family assistance and to require participation in work activities after two years on welfare (see Levitan et al., 2003, pp. 59-72), a core part of the politically conservative (and ironically named) Personal Responsibility and Work Opportunity Reconciliation Act (PRWORA). The threat of a cut-off in assistance is believed to change behavior since a person will loose assistance after five years. Another program I have been studying (MERCAP) reduces assistance payments to families if their children fail to attend school; it is hoped that children will eventually graduate from high school and will not become another generation of welfare recipients. This study found that the punishment did little to change behavior, although attention from teachers and school administrators helped identify more complex reasons for poor school attendance (Campbell & Wright, 2005). The punitive approach of individual theories of poverty justifies policies that restrict public assistance to services and goods instead of cash because there is a lack of trust in the discretion of poor people. Providing food for children at school and offering homeless people shelters rather than offering cash to pay for housing are examples.

Individual level anti-poverty efforts have a social component, however. First a reliable safety-net that can help people who are otherwise unable to help themselves is really a civic responsibility. The disabled, elderly, children, and even the unlucky are part of every community, and without blame, their individual needs can be met by collective action. A safety net, without pejorative connotations, is a key to civility. Making the safety net work and available is broadly accepted.

In sum, to the extent that policy makers or program leaders hold the individual theory of poverty, it is increasingly unlikely that they will pursue a community development approach to solving poverty. Thus, despite the widespread societal view that individuals are responsible for their own poverty, community developers look to other theories of poverty for more positive approaches.

2. Poverty Caused by Cultural Belief Systems that Support Subcultures of Poverty

The second theory of poverty roots its cause in the "Culture of Poverty." This theory is sometimes linked with the individual theory of poverty or other theories to be introduced below, but recently it has become so widely discussed that its special features should not be minimized. This theory suggests that poverty is created by the transmission over generations of a set of beliefs, values, and skills that are socially generated but individually held. Individuals are not necessarily to blame because they are victims of their dysfunctional subculture or culture.

American sociology has long been fascinated by subcultures of immigrants and ghetto residents as well as the wealthy and powerful. Culture is socially generated and perpetuated, reflecting the interaction of individual and community. This social interaction makes the "culture of poverty" theory different from the "individual" theories that link poverty explicitly to individual abilities and motivation. Technically, the culture of poverty is a subculture of poor people in ghettos, poor regions, or social contexts in which they develop a shared set of beliefs, values, and norms for behavior that is separate from but embedded in the culture of the main society.

Oscar Lewis was one of the main writers to define the culture of poverty as a set of beliefs and values passed from generation to generation. He writes,

> Once the culture of poverty has come into existence it tends to perpetuate itself. By the time slum children are six or seven they have usually absorbed the basic attitudes and values of their subculture. Thereafter they are psychologically unready to take full advantage of changing conditions or improving opportunities that may develop in their lifetime. (*Scientific American*, October 1966, quoted in Ryan, 1976, p. 120).

Cultures are socialized and learned, and one of the tenants of learning theory is that rewards follow to those who learn what is intended. The culture of poverty theory explains how government anti-poverty programs reward people who manipulate the policy to stay on welfare. The underlying argument of conservatives such as Charles Murray in *Losing Ground* (1984) is that government welfare perpetuated poverty by permitting a cycle of "welfare dependency" in which poor families develop and pass on to others the skills needed to work the system rather than to gain paying employment. The net result of this theory of poverty is summed by Asen's (2002, p. 48) perceptive phrase, "from the war on poverty to the war on welfare."

This theory of poverty based on perpetuation of cultural values is fraught with controversy. No one disputes that poor people have subcultures or that the subcultures of the poor are distinctive and perhaps detrimental. The concern is over what causes and constitutes the subculture of poverty. Daniel Patrick Moynihan found the concept particularly applicable to his study of Black poverty in the early 1960s and linked Black poverty to the largely "dysfunctional" African American family found in central cities. Valentine (1968, p. 20) criticizes E. Franklin Frazier, who with Daniel Patrick Moynihan (1965) portrayed the culture of the Negro poor as an "immoral chaos brought about by the disintegration of the black folk culture under the impact of urbanization."

In other subcultural situations the cultural portrayal of the poor is more sympathetic. For example, many liberal scholars understand the cultural problems that Native Americans face trying to assimilate middle class value systems. Ironically, after a number of generations we recall the "heroic" efforts of Irish or Italian immigrant groups and their willingness to accept hard work and to suffer for long-term socioeconomic gains; we forget the cultural discrimination they faced for not fitting in during the first generations after they arrived. Today, the subcultural values for higher education and entrepreneurship among Asian and Indian immigrant groups are prized as an example of how subcultures can work in the favor of groups trying to escape poverty.

Anti-Poverty Programs from a Culture of Poverty Perspective

From a community development perspective, if the theoretical reason for poverty lies in values and beliefs, transmitted and reinforced in subcultures of disadvantaged persons, then local anti-poverty efforts need to intervene to help change the culture. This is socialization as policy, which may work in three ways based on Valentine's (1968) suggestion of different models of cultural theories of poverty.

1. If one thinks of the culture of the poor as a dysfunctional system of beliefs and knowledge, the approach will be to replace that culture with a more functional culture that supports rather than undermines productive work, investment, and social responsibility. Innovative prisoner release programs, for example, may try to relocate prisoners from the environment where they got in trouble and assure that they adopt new values appropriate for work. Some experiments were tried with mixed results, relocating the poor from ghetto housing projects to suburbs with the hope that the new culture will help the family emerge from poverty (Goetz, 2003; Goering, Feins, & Richardson, 2003).

2. On the other hand, if one thinks of the culture of poverty as an opportunistic and non-productive subculture that is perpetuated over generations, then the focus will shift to youth to stop the re-creation of the detrimental culture. Head Start and many educational programs according to Zigler and Styfco (1996) are successful at providing an alternative socialization for the next generation to reduce poverty, though the programs need more coherence and quality. Similarly, community developers are often involved in helping establish after-school programs for teens where their peer culture is monitored and positive social values are established, while keeping youth away from gangs and detrimental behavior. These programs are a policy favorite (Levitan et al., 2003) because they are believed to change the culture of youth while their values and norms are still malleable.

3. A third approach to the culture of poverty is to try to work within the culture to redefine culturally-appropriate strategies to improve the group's well being. For example, community developers can enhance and build upon cultural values with the subcultures of the poor that can become assets for economic development. Local crafts cooperatives are examples, as are programs that tap the traditions of small business and entrepreneurship found in subcultures as different as urban gangs and middle class single mothers. Institutions by which ethnic groups or clans assist each other in creating and financing businesses are well documented in the literature. Although programs

promising micro-enterprise as a path from poverty are often oversold (Goldstein, 2001), the mystique of Grameen Bank-type programs as a road out of poverty offers culturally compatible strategies that build on a group's strengths.

3. Poverty Caused by Economic, Political, and Social Distortions or Discrimination

Whereas the first "individualistic" theory of poverty is advocated by conservative thinkers and the second is a culturally liberal approach, the third to which we now turn is a progressive social theory. Theorists in this tradition look not to the individual as a source of poverty but to the economic, political, and social system that causes people to have limited opportunities and resources with which to achieve income and well-being. Research and theories in this tradition attempt to redress the problem noted by Rank, Yoon, and Hirschl: "Poverty researchers have in effect focused on who loses out at the economic game, rather than addressing the fact that the game produces losers in the first place" (2003, p. 5).

The nineteenth century social intellectuals developed a full attack on the individual theory of poverty by exploring how social and economic systems overrode and created individual poverty situations. For example, Marx showed how the economic system of capitalism created the "reserve army of the unemployed" as a conscious strategy to keep wages low. Later Durkheim showed that even the most personal of actions (suicide) was in fact mediated by social systems. Discrimination was separated from skill in one after another area, defining opportunity as socially mediated. Taken to an extreme, radical thinkers argued that the system was flawed and should be radically transformed.

Much of the literature on poverty now suggests that the economic system is structured in such as way that poor people fall behind regardless of how competent they may be. Partly the problem is the fact that minimum wages do not allow single mothers or their families to be economically self sufficient (Jencks, 1996, p. 72). The problem of the working poor is increasingly seen as a wage problem linked to structural barriers preventing poor families from getting better jobs, complicated by limited numbers of jobs near workers and lack of growth in sectors supporting lower skilled jobs (Tobin, 1994). Interestingly research is showing that the availability of jobs to low income people is about the same as it has been, but wages that workers can expect from these jobs have fallen. In addition, fringe benefits including health care and promotions became scarce for low-skilled workers. These and related economic changes documented by Blank (1997) and Quigley (2003) show the way the system creates increasingly difficult problems for those who want to work.

Elimination of structural barriers to better jobs through education and training was the focus of extensive manpower training and other programs, generating substantial successes but also perceived failures. However, despite perceived importance of education, funding per student in less advantaged areas lags behind that which is spent on richer students, teachers are less adequately trained, books are often out of date or in limited supply, amenities are few, and the culture of learning is under siege. This systemic failure of the schools is thus thought to be the reason poor people have low achievement, poor rates of graduation, and few who pursue higher education (Chubb & Moe, 1996).

A parallel barrier exists with the political system in which the interests and participation of the poor is either impossible or is deceptive. Recent research confirms the linkage between wealth and power, and shows how poor people are less involved in political discussions, their interests are more vulnerable in the political process, and they are excluded at many levels. Coupled with racial discrimination, poor people lack influence in the political system that they might use to mobilize economic benefits and justice.

A final broad category of system flaws associated with poverty relates to groups of people being given a social stigma because of race, gender, disability, religion, or other groupings, leading them to have limited opportunities regardless of personal capabilities. No treatment of poverty can be complete without acknowledging that groups against which discrimination is practiced have limited opportunities regardless of legal protections. The process of gaining stronger rights for minorities in poverty is an ongoing one, for which legal initiatives and public policy reform must work with efforts to change public attitudes.

Anti-Poverty Programs from a Structure of Poverty Perspective

If the problem of poverty is in the system rather than in the poor themselves, a community development response must be to change the system. This is easy to say but hard to do, which may explain why so many policy programs revert to trying to change individual behavior. How can one get more jobs, improve schooling for the poor, equalize income distributions, remove discrimination bias from housing, banking, education, and employment, and assure equal political participation by poor persons? None of these tasks are easy and all require interventions into the systems that create the barriers that block poor persons from gaining the benefits of society.

Changing the system can take place at three levels. From a grassroots level, *social movements* can exert pressures on vulnerable parts of the system to force desired change. Although most studies show a decline in support for poor people's social action, Rank (2004, pp. 189-191) argues that change could be mobilized to support better jobs for the poor and a more effective system since as the subtitle of his book states, "American poverty affects us all." For example, public pressure including unionization can increase wages and gain employment for persons systematically excluded. Civil rights movements have had a strong impact on breaking down formal barriers, as has the woman's movement. Community organizing in the Alinsky (1945) tradition has helped reduce poverty across the country (Rank, 2004, p. 233).

A second strategy within community development for changing the system involves creating and developing alternative institutions that have access, openness, innovation, and a willingness to help the poor gain well being. This strategy is at the cornerstone of most community development corporations that aim to provide alternative businesses, housing, schooling, and programs. In addition, business strategies such as employee ownership or networks of minority or women's businesses function admirably. Community owned businesses such as community banks provide alternative structures.

Finally, change can occur through the policy process (Page & Simmons, 2000). The range of federal and social policies that can be adjusted to accomplish poverty reduction include providing jobs, raising wages, expanding the safety net, assuring effective access to medical care, and coordinating social insurance programs. In order to protect these programs in an era of governmental retrenchment, it is increasingly clear that the poor and their advocates need to be more politically mobilized. Legal changes to enforce civil rights of the poor and to protect minority groups are needed. For example, the Americans with Disabilities Act (ADA) established many gains for otherwise able persons who happen to be blind, deaf, or with limited mobility. One of the boldest policy moves is suggested by Quigley (2003) and others who advocate a constitutional amendment to guarantee a job to anyone who wants one and to guarantee that anyone working full time would be able to earn a living wage.

4. Poverty Caused by Geographical Disparities

Rural poverty, ghetto poverty, urban disinvestment, Southern poverty, third-world poverty, and other framings of the problem represent a spatial characterization of poverty that exists separate from other theories. Although this geographically-based theory of poverty builds on the other theories, this regional theory calls attention to the fact that people, institutions, and cultures in certain geographic areas lack the objective resources needed to generate well-being and income, and that they lack the power to claim redistribution. As Shaw (1996, p. 29) points out, "Space is not a backdrop for capitalism, but rather is restructured by it and contributes to the system's survival. The geography of poverty is a spatial expression of the capitalist system."

That poverty is most intense in certain areas is an old observation, and explanations abound in the development literature about why particular regions lack the economic base to compete. Recent explanations include disinvestment, proximity to natural resources, density, diffusion of innovation, and other factors (see Morrill & Wohlenberg, 1971, pp. 57-64). In a thorough review of the literature on rural poverty, Weber and Jensen (2004) note that most literature finds a "rural differential" in poverty, but the spatial effect is not as clearly isolated from individual effects as needed for confidence. Goldsmith and Blakely offer a comprehensive perspective on the link between development and poverty in urban contexts. In their book, *Separate Societies*, they argue that the joint processes of movement of households and jobs away from poor areas in central cities and rural regions creates a "separation of work, residence, and economic, social and political life" (1992, pp. 125). These processes, which we already discussed, are multiplied by racism and political indifference of the localities in which they flourish.

One theoretical perspective on spatial concentrations of poverty comes from economic agglomeration theory. Usually used to explain the emergence of strong industrial clusters (Bradshaw, King, & Wahlstrom, 1999) agglomeration shows how propinquity of similar firms attracts supportive services and markets, which further attracts more firms. In reverse, the propinquity of poverty and the conditions leading to poverty or the consequences of poverty (crime and inadequate social services) generate more poverty, while competitive areas attract business clusters, drawing away from impoverished communities. Low housing prices in such locations may attract more poor persons, for example, leading to housing disinvestment by building owners. In a world in which the criteria for investment is "location, location, location," it is not unreasonable to track investment going to neighborhoods, communities, and regions in which there is already substantial investment, while leaving less attractive areas.

A second theoretical insight is from central place theory and related "human ecology" examinations of urban growth that traces the flows of knowledge and capital (*Rural Sociological Society*, 1990, pp. 71-74). As Niles Hansen (1970) points out, rural areas are often the last stop of technologies, and low wages and competitive pricing dominate production. Infrastructure allows the development of human resources, but if it is lacking, economic activity is stifled that might use these resources. Places left behind (Lyson & Falk, 1992) experience the largest competition in restructuring of the economy because the jobs in these categories are most likely to move to less developed countries. An increasing body of literature holds that advantaged areas stand to grow more than disadvantaged areas even in periods of general economic growth and that there will be some "trickle-down" but not as equalizing as classical economists would have us believe (*Rural Sociological Society*, 1990, pp. 114-119).

A third perspective involves selective out-migration. One part of Wilson's book, *The Truly Disadvantaged* (1987), holds that the people with the highest levels of education, the greatest skills, widest world-view, and most extensive opportunities are those who migrate out from ghetto areas of central city locations to other places. In addition, he argues, these departing people are the community's best role models and are often civic leaders. Rural poverty is similarly attributable to selective out-migration. Population density (both low rural density and the negative impact of high density) is another part of a growing body of theory on spatial variables in social science using the tools of GIS to track spatial dynamics of opportunity and poverty (Bradshaw & Muller, 2003).

Anti-Poverty Programs from a Geography of Poverty Perspective

A geographical theory of poverty implies that responses need to be directed to solving the key dynamics that lead to decline in depressed areas while other areas are growing. Instead of focusing on individuals, businesses, governments, welfare systems, or cultural processes, the geographical theory directs community developers to look at places and the processes by which they can become self-sustaining. Interestingly, a few disadvantaged communities around the world are finding their way out of poverty and as such show that it can be done. However, as Morrill and Wohlenberg (1971, pp. 119-120) point out, it is hard.

Some who view regional poverty analyses made proposals in the 1970s to encourage out-migration under the premises that it would reduce poverty to have people in a place where there was a growing economy. Instead, the rural poor people moving to the city became urban poor, with much the same hopeless situation. It is said that much of urban poverty is actually displaced rural poverty.

No matter how badly buffeted by geographical forces, community development programs attempt to help communities identify their assets and address their condition. Many government and foundation programs assist in this effort, and progress can be demonstrated. Several approaches were taken to build stronger geographical areas; the following represent examples rather than an exhaustive list.

- Improved local industry competitiveness through cluster development (Blakely & Bradshaw, 2002) or development of creative communities (Florida, 2002)
- Enterprise zones, redevelopment, and other tax-based incentive programs to promote economic development and channel private investments
- Inclusionary zoning, affordable housing, and similar programs that place conditions on development
- Downtown revitalization and civic improvements that increase amenities and make areas more attractive to stimulate employment and tax revenues
- Investment in infrastructure, including interstate highways, parks, water, waste disposal, schools and other public facilities
- Community organizing
- National and regional reinvestment that shifts funds from one area to another, such as a commitment that helped the Southern United States grow after WW II

The community development approach through community visioning, planning, and especially community investment is central to efforts to turn around distressed areas and places where poverty is rampant. Because community developers understand community, their efforts often leverage community assets, integrate economic development in an area with housing and other spatially allocated factors, and hope that the changes will increase opportunities for residents.

5. Poverty Caused by Cumulative and Cyclical Interdependencies

The previous four theories demonstrate the complexity of the sources of poverty and the variety of strategies to address it. The final theory of poverty I will discuss is by far the most complex and to some degree builds on components of each of the other theories in that it looks at the individual and their community as caught in a spiral of opportunity and problems, and that once problems dominate they close other opportunities and create a cumulative set of problems that make any effective response nearly impossible (Bradshaw, 2000). The cyclical explanation explicitly looks at individual situations and community resources as mutually dependent, with a faltering economy, for example, creating individuals who lack resources to participate in the economy, which makes economic survival even harder for the community since people pay fewer taxes.

This theory has its origins in economics in the work of Myrdal (1957, p. 23) who developed a theory of "interlocking, circular, interdependence within a process of cumulative causation" that helps explain economic underdevelopment and development. Myrdal notes that personal and community well being are closely linked in a cascade of negative consequences, and that closure of a factory or other crisis can lead to a cascade of personal and community problems including migration of people from a community. Thus the interdependence of factors creating poverty actually accelerates once a cycle of decline is started.

One place where the cycle of poverty is clearly defined is in a book on rural education by Jonathan Sher (1977) in which a focus is on the cycle by which education and employment at the community and individual level interact to create a spiral of disinvestment and decline, while in advancing communities the same factors contribute to growth and well being. For example, at the community level, a lack of employment opportunities leads to out-migration, closing retail stores, and declining local tax revenues, which leads to deterioration of the schools, which leads to poorly trained workers, leading firms not to be able to utilize cutting edge technology and to the inability to recruit new firms to the area, which leads back to a greater lack of employment.

This cycle repeats itself at the individual level. The lack of employment leads to lack of consumption and spending because of inadequate incomes, and to inadequate savings, which means that individuals cannot invest in training, and individuals lack the ability to invest in businesses or to start their own businesses, which leads to lack of expansion, erosion of markets, and disinvestment, all of which contribute again to inadequate community opportunities. Health problems and the inability to afford preventive medicine, a good diet, and a healthy living environments become reasons the poor fall further behind. In addition, the cycle of poverty means that people who lack ample income fail to invest in their children's education. Their children do not learn as well in poor quality schools, they fall further behind when they seek employment, and they are vulnerable to illness and poor medical care.

A third level of the cycle of poverty is the perspective that individual lack of jobs and income leads to deteriorating self-confidence, weak motivation, and depression. The psychological problems of individuals are reinforced by association with other individuals, leading to a culture of despair, perhaps a culture of poverty under some circumstances. In rural communities this culture of despair affects leaders as well, generating a sense of hopelessness and fatalism among community leaders.

This brief description of the cycle of poverty incorporates many of the previous theories. It shows how people become disadvantaged in their social context, which then affects psychological abilities at the individual level. The various structural and political factors in the cyclical theory reinforce each other, with economic factors linked to community and to political and social variables. Perhaps its greatest value is that it more explicitly links economic factors at the individual level with structural factors that operate at a geographical level. As a theory of poverty, the cyclical theory shows how multiple problems cumulate, and it allows speculation that if one of the linkages in the spiral were broken, the cycle would not continue. The problem is that the linkages are hard to break because each is reinforced by other parts of the spiraling system.

Anti-Poverty Programs from a Cycle of Poverty Perspective

The complexity of the cycle of poverty means that solutions must be equally complex. Poverty has many aspects but our anti-poverty efforts seem to focus on only part of the solution. Community developers are specialists in appreciating the interdependence of different parts of the community, and their solution is to try to address issues like poverty from a multifaceted approach. Steps taken to break the cycle of poverty are necessarily complex. However, multi-pronged initiatives offer a better solution to poverty than most single approaches. Broad-based community development initiatives are embedded in some of the most successful anti-poverty programs such as community development corporations, local neighborhood revitalization projects, and other efforts linking grass roots problem-solving with diversified organizational management. The limitations to the first four theories of poverty lead us to want to look closely at the cyclical theory. On the whole, the cycle of poverty is rarely mentioned by poverty scholars, but its success in programs such as the Family Independence Initiative (FII) in Oakland gives hope. I highlight this program just as an example of the cycle-breaking efforts of many innovative community-based development organizations.

Helping poor people achieve "self-sufficiency" is an increasingly significant phase in poverty reduction. Although called by various names, the emphasis is on providing both "deep and wide" supports and services for people. A full step from poverty requires six interdependent elements of self-sufficiency that can be identified and tracked (Miller et al., 2004):

1. *Income and economic assets,*
2. Education and skills,
3. Housing and surroundings (safe, attractive),
4. Access to health care and other needed social services,
5. Close personal ties, as well as networks to others, and
6. Personal resourcefulness and leadership abilities.

An essential piece of this comprehensive approach towards helping individuals from poverty is that there is no way the public can do all of this for every person without first increasing social capital among communities or subcultures of the poor. Miller has a strong belief that strong interpersonal ties as in villages or organized groups can provide shared assistance that professionals can not. The key is helping groups of poor people build supportive communities with shared trust and mutuality. This program consciously seeks the benefits of building social capital (following Putnam, 2000) based on "affinity groups" in which people share common interests from their ethnicity, religion, family history, living area, or other sources of friendship. Building personal ties and leadership linking individual families to their community is perhaps the most challenging part of the FII model. Thus, this model is vital to see the interrelation between financial and material resources and ties to the community.

In facing the overwhelming task of helping both poor people and their poverty neighborhoods, there is no easy answer in breaking the cycle of poverty. Asset-mapping (Kretzmann & McKnight, 1993) offers a way to identify whatever strengths the community has and to use them to solve problems in the most effective way, rather than to spend time identifying problems for which there may be no adequate answers. Moreover, previously existing organizations with roots in the community are generally more effective in bridging the range of problems in a community facing poverty cycles than new single-purpose organizations.

Community development programs structure their efforts around three focal points for breaking the cycle of poverty. These program structures, like the cyclical theory itself, combine strategies and tools from response to the other theories of poverty.

1. Comprehensive Program. The first strategy in breaking the cycle of poverty is to develop comprehensive programs. Comprehensive programs are those that include a variety of services that try to bridge the individual and community needs.

2. Collaboration. The key to managing extensive programs without their becoming too uncontrolled is to collaborate among different organizations to provide complementary services that by the combination of efforts, the output is greater than what could be done by any alone. Collaboration involves networks among participants, though the coordination can vary from formal to informal.

3. Community Organizing. Finally, community organizing is a tool by which local people can participate to understand how their personal lives and the community well-being are intertwined. Breaking the cycle of poverty must include individuals to participate as a community in the reversal, just like individuals create the spiral downward when they and their community interact in a cycle of failure. For the poor, empowerment is central to this issue.

It is interesting that this approach to poverty is the least commonly described in the poverty literature, but community-based examples are brought out whenever successes are discussed. There are no comprehensive community-based self-sufficiency programs from the federal government or most states. The bulk of efforts remain experimental and rooted in programs from foundations. In our review of what works to build community and improve the lives of poor people, we recall examples such as the Dudley Street Neighborhood Initiative of Roxbury, Massachusetts (Medoth & Sklar, 1994)—quite the contrast to a welfare office scenario. The key to these successes is as Fung (2004) suggests, empowered participation.

IMPLICATIONS

This essay started with the premise that the theory or explanation of poverty that is held shapes the type of anti-poverty efforts that community developers pursue. The fact that poverty theory addresses individuals, their culture, the social system in which they are embedded, the place in which they live, and the interconnection among the different factors suggests that different theories of poverty look at community needs from quite different perspectives. The diversity and complexity of causes of poverty allow for these multiple points of view. Although none are "wrong" from a community development perspective, it is consequential which theories are applied to particular anti-poverty efforts. How one frames the question of community development determines who receives various types of services and who gets left out.

However, this essay also argues that the first four theories do not fully explore the relation between individuals and their community in the process of placing people in poverty, keeping them there, and potentially getting them out. The growing realization is that individuals are shaped by their community, and communities are as a consequence shaped by their individual members. The strength of the growing interest in social capital by social scientists following Putnam (2000) points to this interdependence in which individuals through association memberships create communities characterized by more trust and reciprocity; and in these communities with more social capital, thousands of small activities are possible that contribute to reversing the spiral of decent into poverty. It is no wonder that communities with strong social capital (or similarly entrepreneurial communities described by Flora and Flora) are shown to be more resilient to adversity—and thus they protect their residents from the spiral into poverty that less civic communities experience when facing similar challenges.

Similarly, community economic and political systems and institutions reflect community values and respond to the social capital that underlies these values. Although reforming social institutions is a policy response to poverty essential in poverty communities, Duncan (1999) concludes her book on rural poverty with the observation: communities that value equality and have narrow gaps of opportunity also have institutions reflecting these values and to a greater degree try to not leave anyone behind too far. She thinks that education is the most important local institution capable of reversing this dynamic in poor communities. In their book, *Separate Societies* (1992), Goldsmith and Blakely make the same type of argument. Policies that build community institutions help to close the gap between impoverished and rich communities; many policies that obstruct community institutions help to widen the gap.

Increasing the effectiveness of anti-poverty programs requires that those designing and implementing programs need not only to develop adequate theories of poverty to guide programs, but also to ensure that community development approaches are as comprehensive as possible.

NOTES

1 Several authors distinguish similar lists or theories. Blank (2003) covers six theories that are variations on my first and third theory. Morrill and Wohlenberg (1971) also offer a selection of six theories, though they differ slightly from the ones used here.

2 The perspective developed here is paralleled by discussions in Europe. See for example Alcock (1993).

REFERENCES

Alcock, P. (1993). *Understanding Poverty*. London: Macmillan.

Alinsky, S. D. (1945). *Reveille for Radicals*. Chicago: University of Chicago Press.

Asen, R. (2002). *Visions of Poverty: Welfare Policy and Political Imagination*. East Lansing: Michigan State University Press.

Bettinger, F. (1977). *How I Raised Myself from Failure to Success in Selling*. New York: Simon & Schuster.

Blakely, E. J., & Bradshaw, T. K. (2002). *Planning Local Economic Development*. Thousand Oaks: Sage.

Blank, R. M. (1997). *It Takes a Nation: A New Agenda for Fighting Poverty*. Princeton NJ: Princeton University Press.

Blank, R. M. (2003). Selecting Among Anti-Poverty Policies: Can an Economics Be both Critical and Caring? *Review of Social Economy*, 61(4), 447-471.

Bradshaw, T., & Muller, B. (2003). Shaping policy decisions with spatial analysis. In M. F. Goodchild & D. G. Janelle (Eds.), *Spatially integrated social science: Examples in best practice* (Chapter 17). New York: Oxford University Press.

Bradshaw, T. K. (2000). Complex Community Development Projects: Collaboration, Comprehensive Programs and Community Coalitions in Complex Society. *Community Development Journal*, 35(2), 133-145.

Bradshaw, T. K., King, J. R., & Wahlstrom, S. (1999). Catching on to Clusters. *Planning*, 65(6), 18-21.

Campbell, D., & Wright, J. (2005). Rethinking Welfare School Attendance Policies. *Social Service Review*, 79(1), 2-28.

Chubb, J. E., & Moe, T. M. (1996). Politics, markets, and equality in schools. In M. R. Darby (Ed.), *Reducing Poverty in America: Views and Approaches* (pp. 121-153). Thousand Oaks: Sage.

Darby, M. R. (1996). Facing and Reducing Poverty. In M. R. Darby (Ed.), *Reducing Poverty in America: Views and Approaches* (pp. 3-12). Thousand Oaks, California: Sage.

Duncan, C. M. (1999). *Worlds Apart: Why Poverty Persists in Rural America*. New Haven: Yale University Press.

Egendorf, L. K. Ed. (1999). *Poverty: Opposing Viewpoints*. San Diego: Greenhaven Press.

Epstein, W. M. (1997). *Welfare in America: How Social Science Fails the Poor*. Madison: University of Wisconsin Press.

Fischer, C. S., Hout, M., Jankowski, M. S., Lucas, S. R., Swidler, A., & Voss, K. (1996). *Inequality by Design: Cracking the Bell Curve Myth*. Princeton: Princeton University Press.

Florida, R. (2002). *The Rise of the Creative Class*. New York: Basic books.

Fung, A. (2004). *Empowered Participation: Reinventing Urban Democracy*. Princeton: Princeton University Press.

Goering, J., Jeins, J. D., & Richardson, T. M. (2003). What have we learned about housing mobility and poverty deconcentration. In J. Goering, & J. D. Feins (Eds.), *Choosing a Better Life? Evaluating the Moving to Opportunity Social Experiment* (pp. 3-36). Washington D.C.: Urban Institute Press.

Goetz, E. G. (2003). *Clearing the Way: Deconcentrating the Poor*. Washington, D.C.: Urban Institute Press.

Goldsmith, W. W., & Blakely, E. J. (1992). Separate Societies: Poverty and Inequality in American Cities. Philadelphia: Temple University Press.

Goldstein, D. M. (2001). Microenterprise training programs, neo-liberal common sense, and the discourses of self-esteem. In J. Goode, & J. Maskovsky (Eds.), *The New Poverty Studies* (pp. 236-272). New York: New York University Press.

Gwartney, J., & McCaleb, T. S. (1985). Have Anti-poverty Programs Increased Poverty. *Cato Journal*, 5(5), 1-16.

Handler, J. F., & Hasenfeld, Y. (1997). *We the Poor People*. New Haven: Yale University Press.

Hansen, N. (1970). *Poverty and the Urban Crisis*. Bloomington: Indiana State University.

Herrnstein, R. J., & Murray, C. (1994). *The Bell Curve*. New York: Free Press.

Jencks, C. (1996). Can we replace welfare with work? In M. R. Darby (Ed.), *Reducing Poverty in America* (pp. 69-81). Thousand Oaks: Sage.

Jennings, J. (1999). Persistent Poverty in the United States: Review of Theories and Explanations. In L. Kushnick, & J. Jennings (Eds.), *A New Introduction to Poverty: The Role of Race, Power, and Politics*. New York: New York University Press.

Jennings, J., & Kushnick, L. (1999). Introduction: Poverty as Race, Power, and Wealth. In L. Kushnick & J. Jennings (Eds.), *A New Introduction to Poverty: The Role of Race, Power, and Politics* (pp. 1-12). New York: New York University Press.

Kretzmann, J. P., & McKnight, J. L. (1993). *Building Communities from the Inside Out*. Chicago: ACTA Publications.

Landau, M. (1988). *Race, Poverty and the Cities*. Berkeley: Institute of Governmental Studies.

Levitan, S. A., Mangum, G. L., Mangum, S. L., & Sum, A. M. (2003). *Programs in Aid of the Poor*. Baltimore: Johns Hopkins University Press.

Lyson, T. A., & Falk, W. W. (1992). *Forgotten Places: Uneven Development and Underclass in Rural America*. Lawrence: University of Kansas Press.

Maskovsky, J. (2001). Afterword: Beyond the privatist consensus. In J. Goode, & J. Maskovsky (Eds.), *The New Poverty Studies*. New York: New York University Press.

Medoff, P., & Sklar, H. (1994). *Streets of Hope: The Fall and Rise of an Urban Neighborhood*. Cambridge: South End Press

Miller, M. L., Mastuera, M., Chao, M., & Sadowski, K. (2004). *Pathways Out of Poverty: Early Lessons of the Family Independence Initiative*. Oakland: Family Independence Initiative.

Morrill, R. L., & Wohlenberg, E. H. (1971). *The Geography of Poverty*. New York: McGraw Hill.

Moynihan, D. (1965). *The Negro Family*. Washington, D.C.: U.S. Department of Labor, Office of Policy Planning and Research.

Murray, C. (1984). *Losing Ground*. New York: Basic.

Myrdal, G. (1957). *Economic Theory and Underdeveloped Regions*. London: Gerald Duckworth and Co.

O'Connor, A. (2001). *Poverty Knowledge*. Princeton: Princeton University Press.

Page, B. I., & Simmons, J. R. (2000). *What Government Can Do: Dealing With Poverty and Inequality*. Chicago: University of Chicago Press.

Parisi, D., McLaughlin, D. K., Grice, S. M., Taquino, M., & Gill, D. A. (2003). TANF Participation Rates: Do Community Conditions Matter? Rural Sociology, 68(4), 491-512.

Putnam, R. D. (2000). *Bowling Alone*. New York: Simon Schuster.

Quigley, W. P. (2003). *Ending Poverty As We Know It*. Philadelphia: Temple University Press.

Rainwater, L. (1970). Neutralizing the Disinherited: Some Psychological Aspects of Understanding the Poor. In V. L. Allen (Ed.), *Psychological Factors in Poverty* (pp. 9-28). Chicago: Markham.

Rank, M. R. (2004). *One Nation, Underprivileged*. Oxford and New York: Oxford University Press.

Rank, M. R., Yoon, H.-S., & Hirschl, T. A. (2003). American Poverty as a Structural Failing: Evidence and Arguments. *Journal of Sociology & Social Welfare*, 30(4), 5.

Riessman, F. (1969). *Strategies against Poverty*. New York: Random House.

Rodgers, H. R., Jr. (2000). *American Poverty in a New Era of Reform*. Armonk, New York: M. E. Sharp.

Ropers, R. H. (1991). *Persistent Poverty: The American Dream Turned Nightmare*. New York: Plenum.

Rural Sociological Society Task Force on Persistent Poverty. (1990). *Persistent Poverty in Rural America*. Boulder: Westview Press.

Ryan, W. (1976). *Blaming the Victim*. New York: Vintage.

Schiller, B. R. (1989). *The Economics of Poverty and Discrimination*. Englewood Cliffs, NJ: Prentice Hall.

Sen, A. (1999). *Development as Freedom*. New York: Anchor.

Shaw, W. (1996). *The Geography of United States Poverty*. New York: Garland Publishing.

Sher, J. P. (1977). School Based Community Development Corporations: A New Strategy for Education and Development in Rural America. In J. P. Sher (Ed.), *Education in Rural America* (pp. 291-346). Boulder: Westview.

Tobin, J. (1994). Poverty in Relation to Macroeconomic Trends, Cycles, Policies. In S. H. Danzinger, G. D. Sandefur, & D. H. Weinberg (Eds.), *Confronting Poverty: Prescriptions for Change*. Cambridge: Harvard University Press.

Valentine, C. A. (1968). *Culture and Poverty*. Chicago: University of Chicago Press.

Weber, B., & Jensen, L. (2004). *Poverty and Place: A Critical Review of Rural Poverty Literature*. Oregon State University: Rural Poverty Research Center, Working Paper 2004-2003.

Weber, M. (2001). *Protestant Ethic and the Spirit of Capitalism*. New York: Routledge.

Wilson, W. J. (1987). *The Truly Disadvantaged: The Inner City, the Underclass and Public Policy*. Chicago: University of Chicago Press.

Zigler, E., & Styfco, S. J. (1996). Reshaping early childhood intervention to be a more effective weapon against poverty. In M. R. Darby (Ed.), *Reducing Poverty in America* (pp. 310-333). Thousand Oaks, CA: Sage.

The Community Capitals Framework: an empirical examination of internal relationships

Kenneth Pigg*, Stephen P. Gasteyer, Kenneth E. Martin, Kari Keating and Godwin P. Apaliyah

There is a small but growing amount of research on the use the Community Capitals Framework (CCF) as it relates to changes and development at the community level. There are conflicting arguments regarding how the community capitals are related to each other, but almost no empirical studies that actually investigate this relationship. Using the CCF, this article examines how the capitals may be related using data from a large sample of participants in community leadership development education programs where the framework was used to document the effects of these programs. Discussion examines how the empirical relationships among the capitals effect community development and how useful the CCF is in helping to understand this process. The findings suggest that elements of the CCF need some modification as the process appears to have a more complex relationship than proposed in prior research.

In a world where community development has become ever more complex, there is a need for tools that help us understand the dynamics of community change. The challenge of building community capacity for sustainable community development remains significant (Chaskin, Brown, Venkatesh, & Vidal, 2001; Kirk & Shutte, 2004). The need to improve community capacity has led to the creation of a number of tools and approaches for use by community development practitioners and researchers.

The Community Capitals Framework (CCF) (Flora & Flora, 2008; Green & Haines, 2002) provides a way of organizing information and ideas about how community development takes place as the result of community leadership development (CLD) efforts, as participants in these program efforts leverage the resources represented by the CCF among and against one another. The CCF has been proposed as a method for understanding the nature of and process(es) underlying community development. The elements of this framework are described as seven forms of "capital" existing in communities that can be used individually and in combination to produce community change: human, social, political, cultural, built, natural, and economic or financial.[1] While there is a growing literature on the community capitals by many of the

---

*Corresponding author. Email: PiggK@missouri.edu

proponents of this perspective, there is little empirical work published that details the interaction of the capitals as they may be deployed by community residents (an exception is Stofferahn, 2012). One of the questions we seek to answer is how these capitals may be related to one another and better used to achieve changes in the community.

We take the position that the CCF can be seen as an applied view of field theory in that the areas of interest represented by the capitals can be interpreted as representing the fields of community activity where interaction takes place (Bridger, Brennan, & Luloff, 2011). For example, financial capital might be represented by the organized interests in the areas of economic development in the community, such as industrial recruitment, new business, or tourism development. Material improvements in any of these areas may increase the level of financial capital in the community. Similarly, people interested in building new schools, parks, hospitals, or community centers might represent the development of community physical capital. As argued by Wilkinson (1991), pursuing these specific areas of interest does not represent community development, as the community field is not engaged. A question for this research is whether there may be evidence available to support the notion that the community capitals (and those individuals pursuing material changes in each of the areas represented by them) work together in some fashion that might be interpreted as representing the community field. Alternatively, perhaps, the CCF may lead to a more explicitly holistic and different heuristic view of how the community development process works.

Our analysis differs from others found in existing literature. For example, Sturtevant (2006) studied a specific two-county region engaged in issues related to natural resources and documented the effects of social capital on the process of issue resolution. Similarly, Macias and Nelson (2011) found that social capital among residents of three states, especially the diversity of their network (weak) ties, had an effect on the residents' level of environmental concern. A broader view is the idea presented by Emery and Flora (2006) that presents the relationships among all seven of the community capitals as a "spiraling up" of effects as the change in one type of capital may create changes in another type of capital. For example, they cite the example of investments in human capital produced increases in social and cultural capital in their study site. Stofferahn (2012) used the same idea in his study of a North Dakota community nearly destroyed by a tornado, finding multiple and reinforcing effects of changes in various capitals as a result of the large cultural capital asset possessed by the residents of the community. In contrast to these single community studies that may often be limited to examinations of effects between two types of community capital, we have collected data from 20 communities in five states represented by over 200 specific projects and activities. Our findings indicate a somewhat different relationship among the capitals that we feel is better captured by the ideas represented by field theory. That is, we argue for viewing the relationships among the capitals as more complex than the "spiraling up" notion would imply. The findings suggest that the capitals are more multiple in their dimensionality and more limited in their relationships, presenting opportunities for different kinds of interventions to affect development.

Research methods

This research focused on 20 sites in five states where there had been implemented at least one CLD program between 2002 and 2006.[2] We invited a small group of key community informants to share a list of projects and activities undertaken in their communities during the previous two to three years and to identify individuals who had served as leaders for these activities. We then matched the names of these individuals with the list of CLD participants provided by the program sponsors. The contact information for the persons involved was also acquired from the key informants. These CLD participants were contacted by phone and interviewed to gather details of each activity, what had taken place, who else may have been involved, goals to be achieved and obstacles faced, resources used, and their overall assessment of their CLD experience and its applicability to these activities.

For these 20 sites, we were able to identify 212 projects and activities for which former CLD participants had served as leaders, or approximately ten per site. We eliminated many that seemed to be incomplete or involved primarily institutional officials performing their duties rather than citizen activists. Some of these activities involved annual events such as holiday festivals. Some of the projects involved the construction of new community facilities or the improvement of existing facilities. Some involved remediation or protection of natural resources for the betterment of the community, and others involved projects to improve the health and/or safety of disadvantaged residents or youth. In short, the specific nature of these projects and activities was very diverse across the 20 sites studied. The number of individuals named as associated with these projects and activities was well over 400 individuals from the communities.

Each of these projects or activities was coded based on the judgment of the research team using the CCF. Each activity was assigned as many as four types of capital using the definitions provided by Flora and Flora (2008). The first type of capital assigned was used to identify what the respondents indicated as the primary goal or purpose of the activity. So, a project to create a shelter for abused children was categorized as a human capital project as it addressed the health and safety of at-risk residents. In addition, CCF categories were assigned based on the respondents' description of what was done and how the project was implemented. So, if the shelter project required raising money to purchase or build a facility, the category for financial capital was assigned to the project as a secondary capital represented. If the shelter project required some sort of agency support or local government approval, the category for political capital was also assigned. Finally, if the respondents described the process as involving people from other community sectors or counterparts from the CLD program, the category of social capital was assigned.

What we found in the analysis

The analysis shows that the community capitals appear to be organized into two clusters and do not, at least to us, represent the "spiraling up" analogy that has been used previously to describe the relationship among the capital categories. The analysis seems to point to a more discriminating analogy that appears to relate more to how community residents perceive the world to work when they tackle problems that need solutions.

Figure 1 shows the results of the coding of activities using the definitions of the individual community capitals as described above. As shown in Figure 1, for all cases studied, human capital projects were most frequently implemented, followed by financial capital and cultural capital. Especially, as it deals with the first two of these capital categories, it should be of little surprise given the needs often identified in small, rural communities for retaining young people and skilled workforces and for finding the necessary financial resources to support efforts to meet community needs. The second most frequently mentioned type of community capital employed in these projects and activities was social capital followed by financial capital and political capital. Clearly, to get things done in their communities, the CLD participants drew heavily on their network of like-minded residents

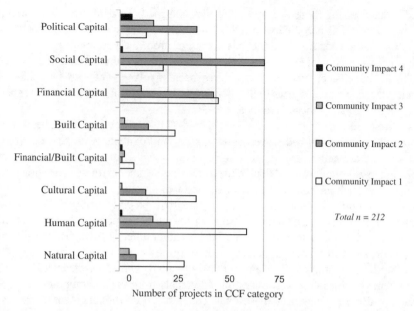

Figure 1. Type and frequency of community capitals reflected in community projects and activities.

and had to raise funds and get some sort of political support for their efforts in order to achieve their goals. Although this sort of interpretation is quite simplistic, it does give us a sense of the inter-relatedness of the community capitals for these 212 activities.

In addition, the research team developed a checklist of specific items that might have been present in each community related to each of the community capitals using ideas gleaned from various published sources (see, e.g. Flora & Flora, 2008; Stofferahn, 2012). As the researchers listened and took notes while the respondents described what happened in each activity, they also completed the checklist as pertinent items were named by respondents. These completed checklists were then entered in the database and summative indices were used to further measure the nature and "amount" of each capital utilized in each project or activity. As can be seen in Table 1, if a project or activity was considered to be primarily focused on a human capital outcome, the score on the human capital index used in the research was higher than for any other index. However, it is important to note the second and third highest index scores for each of the types of projects listed; these were often social, human, and/or political capital. This result again demonstrates the inter-relatedness of the community capitals.

This inter-relatedness appears to have some validity as the table below (Table 2) shows that a statistically significant relationship exists between the financial capital index and the CCF category assigned to each project or activity investigated in the 20 communities. The same sort of significant relationship was found for relationships between the social capital index and the project classifications as well as between the political capital index and the project classifications used.

Relationship of community impacts and CCF indices

As noted above, the research team collected information on recent community projects and activities from key informants in focus group interviews and follow-up interviews

Table 1.   Mean values of community capital for community projects by type of primary capital represented.

	SOCAP SUM	POLCAP SUM	HUCAP SUM	CULCAP SUM	FINCAP SUM	BILTCAP SUM	NATCAP SUM
Human capital projects	1.5472	1.6226	3.1887	.3770	1.0189	.3019	.0943
Financial capital projects	1.4634	.8049	1.4878	.4390	1.6829	.2683	.0732
Natural capital projects	2.4444	3.0741	1.8519	1.4074	.8148	.6667	3.3333
Cultural capital projects	2.2813	1.1563	1.2500	3.5938	.7813	.5000	.7813

Note: Cells lightly shaded represent mean index score for the highest scoring CCF index used; cells shaded more darkly represent the next highest mean scores for specific indices used. SOCAPSUM is the variable name assigned to the aggregate score for social capital; POLCAPSUM is the variable name for the aggregate score for political capital, and so forth.

with citizen leaders involved with each project or activity. Each of these projects was coded as to the community capitals represented (by interviewees) in each project. An effort was made to capture the primary capital represented by each project in addition to as many as three additional capitals that may have been involved in the project's success. For Table 3, each of the four possible classifications of the community capitals represented was considered such that, if one of the impacts was mentioned among the four, the score for that capital was a "1" and if it was not mentioned, the capital was given a "0." Logistic regression was then performed for each capital as the dependent variable.

The independent variables used in the regression represent the scores on the particular indicators used for each of the community capitals from the CCF checklist devised for this analysis. The number of indicators present according to the interviewees was summed for all the CCF capitals.

The results in Table 3 represent the odds ratio estimates for each of the community capitals represented in the various projects and activities and percent concordant measure for each index score from the SAS routine for logistic regression. Concordance is defined as a measure similar to a correlation. The concordance measure indicates the percentage of cases in which the independent variables accurately predicted the result represented by the dichotomous dependent variable.

As indicated in this table, the odds of a project being classified as addressing natural capital in some fashion was increased by a factor of 17 (17.24) through the use of the natural capital index used in the research. The same analysis shows that the odds of a project being classified as addressing natural capital was reduced by a factor of .49 through the inclusion of the cultural capital index score and by a factor of .35 by including the social capital index score. Another way to interpret this result is that the natural capital index is validating the classification of the project as having a natural capital component with cultural capital and social capital also involved although in a different fashion or, that the significant effects of cultural capital and social capital mean that the higher the value in these indexes the lower the odds that a project will be classified as natural capital holding the natural capital index constant. Almost 98% of all the projects are consistent with this result.

Table 2.   Community project category by financial capital index cross-tab analysis.

Statistical test	Value	df	Asymp. sig. (two-sided)
Pearson χ^2	58.867	40	.027
Cramer's V	.236		.027
n of valid cases = 212			

Similarly, the odds of a project being classified as having a human capital component is increased by a factor of 2.91 by the human capital index score and reduced by .61 by the inclusion of the natural capital index and by .40 by including the cultural capital index score. About 87% of the projects are consistent with this result.

Projects classified as having a cultural capital component have greater odds of being so classified when considering the score on the cultural capital index by a factor of nearly six. The odds of a project being so classified are also increased by the social capital index score in these cases by a factor of 1.65. The odds of being classified as a cultural capital project are reduced by the natural capital, human capital, and financial capital indices (by factors of .42, .39, and .37, respectively).

The results shown for the remaining community capital designations of projects are more complicated. For example, a project's likelihood of being classified as having a built capital component is reduced by about .25 by the human capital index. None of the other indices played a significant part in this logistic regression analysis, and only about 69% of the analyses are consistent with this result. It is possible that, since there are so few projects/activities designated as having a built capital component, this result does not really tell us very much about the relationship. The result for the financial capital classification of projects also omits the financial capital index as having any significant effect. Instead, the built capital index increases the odds of being classified as having a financial capital component by a factor of 7.73, while the human capital index decreases the odds of being so classified by nearly .50, and the cultural capital index decreases the odds by .60. In other words, knowing the score on the built capital index increases the odds of a project being classified as having a financial capital component and this relationship makes sense, because most building projects would require substantial financial capital to be completed. This analysis shows a 90% concordance rate.

Table 3.   Logistic regression analysis of community projects classified by CCF (odds ratio estimates).

	Community activities & projects						
CCF index	Natural capital	Human capital	Cultural capital	Built capital	Financial capital	Social capital	Political capital
Natural capital	17.236***	.612**	.415***				.700*
Human capital		2.906***	.394***	.248*	.481***		
Cultural capital	.494**	.396***	5.996***		.600*	.650***	
Built capital					7.733***		.525**
Financial capital			.369**			4.787***	
Social capital	.350***		1.652**				3.363***
Political capital							.741**
Percent concordant	97.7	86.8	93.0	69.0	90.1	82.2	82.7

***$p < .0001$, **$p < .001$, *$p < .01$.

The result for social capital as a component of a community project or activity is also complex. The odds of a project being classified as having social capital involved are increased by the financial capital index (over 4.79) and reduced by the cultural capital index (by .65). In other words, to know whether a project or activity would be classified as a social capital project, you are likely better off to examine the score on the financial capital index than you are to look at the actual score on the social capital index. Another way to look at this result, assuming the measurement was good, is that people involved in community activities see that even though social capital might be a reasonable substitute for financial capital, it is easier to raise the funds necessary to hire the work done than call in favors and ask for volunteers.

The odds of having a project classified as having a political capital component are increased by the social capital index (by over 3.36) but reduced by the natural capital, built capital, and political capital indices (.70, .52, and .74, respectively). This finding may reflect the likely close relationship between social and political capital (when viewed as the attribute of networks).

In summary, the indicators used for measuring the degree of natural, human, and cultural capital appear to be discriminating as intended while those for the other capitals are not. There may be some problem with the indicators used to separately identify built and financial capital and, indeed, some of the literature on community capitals does not separate these categories. In addition, the indicators used in the indices for social and political capital appear to be off target although there is some evidence in the literature of very close links between social and political capital. The fact that both social and political capital were very often included in interviewees' discussions of the various community projects would indicate that these components are generally recognized as present and separable conceptually.

Another element shown in this analysis is the dynamic nature of the relationship among the community capitals. Emery and Flora (2006) note this sort of relationship in their characterization of the "spiraling up" of the capitals. Although we may not agree with the specific imagery used by Emery and Flora, this analysis appears to demonstrate that different community capitals are often involved in different ways in community projects. Logically, this seems appropriate as the status of any of the community capitals at any given time differs within and among communities. How they may be employed may also differ according to local conditions and the nature of the collective actions and interactions involved among the project leaders. Sturtevant (2006) and Putnam (1993) both demonstrate how social capital supports collective civic action and is enhanced by such action. Crowe and Smith (2012) show how social, cultural, and human capital inter-act to support the establishment of alternative food systems in communities. Similar demonstrations could likely be developed for the other community capitals with suffi-cient research (Crowe, 2006, 2008). These dynamics are important elements of civic engagement and collective action for improving community well-being.

Cluster analysis of CCF elements

Given the findings discussed above, we wanted to further explore the relationships among the CCF elements. Using cluster analysis, we examined the categories assigned to the various projects/activities in which citizen leaders engaged after their learning experience.[3] This analysis included only the initial coding assigned to each project/activity in a community.

There were two components found in the analysis of the CCF elements. This analysis is a bit more reasonable than that outlined previously in that the financial, built, and natural capitals are clustered together and the social, political, and human capitals are clustered together. The one CCF component that seems a bit out of place is cultural capital for which there seems little logical explanation for linking it with the financial, built, and natural capitals and the association appears very week compared to the relationship among the other three capitals in this cluster. This structure of relationships is similar to that posited by Gutierrez-Montes, Emery, and Fernandez-Baca (2009) that placed the community capitals into two factors: human (including social, human, political, and cultural capital) and material (including natural, financial, and built capital). Although such a clustering seems reasonable, we find contradictory empirical evidence of this structure in our data using the combination of regression and the cluster analysis dendogram approach.

Further research is likely necessary to more fully understand the relationships among the capitals. For now, it would appear that there is some underlying linkage within the seven capitals in the framework in which one tends to be frequently deployed in community actions in a pattern of combination with several others. However, unlike the Emery and Flora's argument (see also: Stofferahn, 2012) which seems to argue that all of the capitals are linked together more or less the same and that their interaction represents a sort of "spiraling up" of relational intensity, this analysis suggests a more discriminating process is at work with people taking into account the actual nature of the task at hand, the situation in their community, and the resources necessary to getting things done.

For example, a project focused on natural capital – such as a waterway reconstruction project – will likely require mobilizing financial resources from many sources and getting access to construction supplies and expertise that often have to be hired and paid for with the financial resources. Other resources such as political capital in the form of agency permits may also be necessary, but these appear to be of lesser importance in the way people actually carry out such work in the community. This would mean that the participants in CLD programs have recognized the leveraging effect among the capitals and have learned to differentially mobilize multiple types of resources/assets in their attempts to make their communities better places in which to live.

Summary

The data collected and analyzed in this project show that people take on and complete a wide variety of projects and activities they feel will benefit the material lives of their community and employ a variety of community resources to achieve their goals. These activities appear to be "self-organizing" in that individuals who feel empowered are brought together through interactions that focus on a shared purpose or objective without much external intervention, encouragement, or approval by formal authorities in the local community. These citizens may take on problems that range from conserving natural resources and open spaces for environmental reasons or for leisure activities to raising money to support health objectives to creating spaces in which the arts can flourish to organizing community events that may bring new tourists to their community and supplement the local economy. Although there were undoubtedly obstacles presented to these citizen activists, these sorts of obstacles were not mentioned in any of our key informant interviews. The fact that our selection process included what we had defined as high and low viability communities (based on quantitative, time series data) may indicate that such external classifications are inaccurate and unwarranted. What matters are how local people feel about themselves and their neighbors, how they assess their personal and collective leadership efficacy, and their commitment to the places where they live. Add a bit of knowledge about how to get things done in their community and you have the basis for forms of action and interaction that can materially benefit all the residents of the community.

We attempted to understand the nature of the changes achieved by these residents using the CCF by examining the relationships among the seven capitals identified by others and posited as reflecting a way of analyzing community development efforts from a structural perspective (Emery & Flora, 2006). This research demonstrates support for this basic proposition. Citizen leaders exhibit an understanding of the variety of resources present in the community and how to mobilize and deploy these resources (in the form of "capitals") to produce desired change. Interesting is the fact that it did not appear that any of the citizen leaders interviewed had any direct knowledge of the CCF or the ideas about how to produce changes in the community based on the CCF rationale. Rather, the ideas related to this framework appear to be generally recognized and broadly understood by community leaders. What matters most is their willingness to become engaged in civic affairs and whether they feel they can be successful in what they want to achieve. This research has been able to demonstrate that the CCF elements are quite useful for understanding the nature and scope of community development efforts. The research has demonstrated that mostly all community development activities investigated exhibited the deployment of multiple capitals that appear to interact with each other in mutually beneficial ways. The term "leveraging" can be used to describe the way in which the deployment of one capital appears to influence the deployment of another form of capital.

However, the formulation of the CCF elements and their relationships in the case of these communities is not a "spiraling up" as Emery and Flora (2006) and Stofferahn (2012) argue. Rather, people who act as leaders in the projects studied here are discriminating in their assessment of which capitals will be of greatest use to them and produce the desired benefits. The community capitals tend to cluster and the clustering effect appears to be related to the nature of the desired primary effect. So, producing an improvement in the human capital of the community (as may be expressed in improved health and/or safety for example) may require leveraging social and political capital by emphasizing the underlying social cohesiveness of the community. At the same time, producing an improvement in the natural capital of the community may require leveraging political capital through the civic engagement of activists who can effectively engage local and external agencies in change efforts.

There is an alternative explanation of our results that may also be valid and relevant, although our data are not useful in this regard. We have not tried to gage the longer term effects of the community projects and activities undertaken by these residents. Sustaining this sort of civic action over a longer period of time can be difficult, as most experienced community developers know. Had the citizen activists involved in the projects about which they were interviewed been engaged in educational exercises to apply the CCF ideas early on, it is possible that the "spiraling up" process may have been better understood and thus, more likely to have been acknowledged by those individuals interviewed for this study. It would be reasonable to assume that this sort of added experience would have further increased participants' sense of personal efficacy and community knowledge (human capital) as well as encouraged the formation of even stronger and more extensive networks (bridging social capital) among the participants as well as others in the community. These effects could then easily support greater leveraging of the other forms of community capital and lead to greater cumulative effects as proposed by Emery and Flora (2006). This alternative cannot be evaluated in this study but certainly deserves greater attention by researchers and those involved in developing greater community building capacity among local people.

Notes

1. We recognize that not all community change results in material benefits or improvements of some sort and that the community capitals can be deployed for maintaining status quo as easily and effectively as for change. This research was funded in part by a grant from the US Department of Agriculture, National Research Initiative under Grant No. 2006-35401-17560.
2. The complete methodology is discussed in Pigg, Gasteyer, Martin, Keating, and Apaliyah (in press).
3. This clustering technique produces what is known as a dendogram, and it is used to represent the hierarchical nature of the relationships among variables so the underlying statistical procedures used are somewhat different than for a principal components analysis. This hierarchical clustering technique relies on measures of the proximity between each case or the distance between the empirical values for each case (see Rencher, 2002). Discussion of the cluster analysis results is included in the text. Actual figures may be obtained from the corresponding author.

References

Bridger, J. C., Brennan, M. A., & Luloff, A. E. (2011). The interactional approach to community. In J. W. Robinson Jr & G. P. Green (Eds.), *Introduction to community development: Theory, practice, and service-learning* (pp. 85–100). Los Angeles, CA: Sage.

Chaskin, R. J., Brown, P., Venkatesh, S., & Vidal, A. (2001). *Building community capacity.* New York, NY: Aldine De Gruyter.

Crowe, J. (2006). Community economic development strategies in rural Washington: Toward a synthesis of natural and social capital. *Rural Sociology, 71*, 573–596.

Crowe, J. (2008). Economic development in the nonmetropolitan west: The influence of physical, natural, and social capital. *Community Development: Journal of the Community Development Society, 39*, 51–70.

Crowe, J., & Smith, J. (2012). The influence of community capital toward a community's capacity to respond to food insecurity. *Community Development: Journal of the Community Development Society, 43*, 169–186.

Emery, M., & Flora, C. (2006). Spiraling up: Mapping community transformation with Community Capitals Framework. *Community Development: Journal of the Community Development Society, 37*, 19–35.

Flora, C. B., & Flora, J. (2008). *Rural communities: Legacy and change* (3rd ed.). San Francisco, CA: Westview Press.

Green, G. P., & Haines, A. (2002). *Asset building and community development.* Thousand Oaks, CA: Sage.

Gutierrez-Montes, I., Emery, M., & Fernandez-Baca, E. (2009). The sustainable livelihoods approach and the Community Capitals Framework: The importance of system-level approaches to community change efforts. *Community Development: Journal of the Community Development Society, 40*, 106–113.

Kirk, P., & Shutte, A. M. (2004). Community leadership development. *Community Development Journal, 39*, 324–351.

Macias, T., & Nelson, T. (2011). A social capital basis for environmental concern: Evidence from Northern New England. *Rural Sociology, 76*, 562–581.

Pigg, K., Gasteyer, S. G., Martin, K. E., Keating, K., & Apaliyah, G. (in press). *Community effects of leadership development: Citizen empowerment for civic engagement.* Morgantown: West Virginia Press. Rural Studies Series.

Putnam, R. (1993). *Making democracy work: Civic traditions in modern Italy.* Princeton, NJ: Princeton University Press.

Rencher, A. C. (2002). *Methods of multivariate analysis.* New York, NY: John Wiley & Sons.

Stofferahn, C. W. (2012). Community capitals and disaster recovery: Northwood ND recovers from an EF 4 tornado. *Community Development: Journal of the Community Development Society, 43,* 581–598.

Sturtevant, V. (2006). Reciprocity of social capital and collective action. *Community Development: Journal of the Community Development Society, 31,* 52–64.

Wilkinson, K. P. (1991). *The community in rural America.* New York, NY: Greenwood Press.

SOCIAL WELL-BEING AND COMMUNITY
By Kenneth P. Wilkinson

ABSTRACT

An interactionist perspective is used to show the influence of community in the well-being of people. Well-being is discussed in terms of the humanist concept of self-actualization. The thesis is developed that sustenance adequacy and community are social conditions which encourage emergence of the self-actualization motive. Hypotheses are presented concerning the contributions of various community types to social well-being. Community development is defined in interactional terms, and strategies of community development to encourage social well-being are suggested.

INTRODUCTION

Community development, as a purposive activity, is justified by the assumption that community is a factor in the well-being of people. This assumption has generated many community development efforts and continuing interests of social scientists in the phenomenon of community. Scientific research on the effects of community and community development, however, has been meager and has tended to focus not upon community as such, but upon programs and conditions in a community context. As a consequence, the goals of community development have been based less on systematic theory and evidence concerning the effects of community change than on unsupported value biases [Warren, 1970; Speight, 1973]. A conceptual framework is needed to organize research on the fundamental relationship of social well-being to community and to guide efforts in community development.

The purpose of this paper is to present a conceptual framework, from the perspective of interactionist theory, for examining the relationship of social well-being to community and for focusing community development upon malleable aspects of that relationship. Social well-being and community are defined in interactional terms, and hypotheses concerning their interrelationship are presented and discussed in the light of evidence from previous research. Implications of the framework for community development are described in a concluding section.

Kenneth P. Wilkinson is a professor of rural sociology in the Department of Agricultural Economics and Rural Sociology, The Pennsylvania State University, University Park, Pennsylvania.

SOCIAL WELL-BEING

Concepts of social well-being and social improvement have been discussed from many perspectives. Any systematic treatment of development must begin with delineation of desired goals, outcomes, or direction of change. Values frequently enter such delineations. One approach to dealing with the problem of value-bias is to select goals on which there is widespread consensus. An example is emphasis on "felt needs" of indigenous participants. Another example is emphasis on goals expressing the ethos of the larger society. Problems of this approach have to do with the limited perspectives of those who are "developing" and with power differentials within the community and between the community and the larger society. A second approach is to take a structural perspective which assumes that values are epiphenomenal to the system of norms through which necessary social functions are performed. A problem with this approach with respect to social well-being is that the dependent variable of development is the adaptive capacity of the system rather than realization of the potentials of people. A system might adapt to its environment through mechanisms such as rigid social stratification which restrict the well-being of some of the people.

The interactionist perspective, which is used in this paper, deals explicitly with interpersonal processes [Mead, 1934]. The mental life of the individual, which produces statements of felt needs, can be understood from this perspective in terms of the social processes of which the individual is part. Thus, social well-being is to be located in interpersonal dynamics. This approach differs from that of structural-functionalism in that the focus is upon human behavior in social processes rather than upon the system of norms set up to regulate those processes. Alfred McClung Lee expresses this point in introducing a discussion of "humanist sociology" with the title "Man is not a Tool; Society is not a System" [1973, p. 1].

Human potential. The humanist emphasis in interactionist theory is the key to defining social well-being from this perspective. Values and felt needs are of secondary importance to the potential of people for achieving well-being in social relationships. The dialectical materialism of Marxian theory, for example, contains a concept of social well-being as an outcome of an evolutionary process through which opposing values reflecting interests of social classes are finally reconciled in a form of society which expresses the full human capacity for community [Ollman, 1971].

Human potential for social well-being is also a central concept in humanist psychology as developed by Gordon Allport, Abram Maslow, Carl Rogers, and others. The term, self-actualization, suggested by Kurt Goldstein and elaborated by Maslow [1954], refers to a growth motive of the individual which emerges when motives for survival, security, and esteem are satisfied. Self-actualization is the search for new experience and the expansion of independent competency in a socially responsible fashion. Similar ideas are expressed by such terms as self-regarding sentiment (McDougall), self-realization (Horney), propriate striving (Allport) and mature love (Fromm). The self-actualizing person is open and revealing of feelings in intimate relationships; trust and respect for others grow out of trust and respect for self. Self-actualization is assumed to be a natural tendency in people but one which can be suppressed either by deficits in meeting primary needs, such as for food and shelter, or by sociocultural patterns which discourage its expression.

Social well-being refers to social conditions which foster self-actualization of individuals. Two broad categories of social conditions are suggested by Gordon Allport's distinction between tension-reduction and growth motives [1955]. These may be referred to as sustenance and community, respectively. The former consists of social arrangements for meeting primary needs for food, safety, gratification, and the like. These are needs which if unmet become preemptive of human energy and attention. Community refers to certain social relationships in the life space of the person, which, it is argued, serve both as a means of achieving social well-being and as a definition, or end, of its realization.

Sustenance. The first requirement of social well-being is that sustenance organization be adequate to meet primary needs and thus free human energy and attention from tension-reduction motives. This is a social condition in that the human organism cannot survive in isolation from others during infancy and rarely does so in other life stages. For example, caloric inputs must be secured to assure homeostatic functioning of physiologic systems in relation to the environment. Then, if self-actualization is to emerge as a motive, arrangements must be made to minimize the proportion of human caloric output required for securing the necessary energy inputs. Technology and division of labor contribute to this. Human energy and attention can be thus liberated for other uses, such as for development of more efficient technology and of social organization for maintaining and improving the flow of energy through the sustenance system.

How much freedom from want, as this might be expressed, is required for emergence of the self-actualization motive? Experimental evidence can be used to describe thresholds for individuals [Maslow, 1954]. How much is required for a community or society to move to a second stage toward social well-being is partly affected by how access to resources for meeting primary needs is distributed within the population. Social stratification entails differential access to resources for meeting primary human needs.

Another question is, how much is too much? Emile Durkheim [1951] identified unlimited aspirations for material acquisition as a factor in anomic suicide. The economic-technological revolution which has increased material standards of living of the industrialized nations has also contributed to alienation and anxiety among individuals and to concern about exponential consumption rates of finite resources. The sustenance requirement for social well-being occurs in an optimum range, as yet undefined, below which human energy is bound up in the meeting of primary needs and beyond which energy is diverted into maladaptive activities such as obsessive hoarding and overconsumption.

Community. Community is an important factor in social well-being for a number of reasons. As René König has noted, the community is the setting for the individual's empirical contact with the abstraction, society, and it is global (i.e., complete) in an institutional sense [1968, pp. 4–5]. It is the primary realm, beyond the family, of social experience of the individual; and it is the most comprehensive social structure with which one can have direct contact. Community is also a significant aspect of the self-concept of the individual. Self is an interactional phenomenon consisting of identities of the person with specific others and with the "generalized other" or community [Mead, 1934]. Community is an arena for immediate expression of the fundamental human disposition toward association. Further, the argument has been presented that community relationships of a particular type and quality foster an attitude of responsibility among people concerning protection of the natural environment [Wilkinson, 1973].

While the term has been used in many ways, all social scientific definitions of community refer to one or another type of common bond among people. The community is a territorial unit, and in most sociological treatments it is a local society. Differences in definition beyond these common elements express differences in level of analysis and perspective among observers. The community is a place where people live together. It is also a system of roles and institutions through which a common life is organized and a field of collective action through which people express common interests and deal with local problems. These meanings of the term, expressing respectively the ecological, social systems, and interactionist perspectives, relate to different levels of the same phenomenon. In each case the distinguishing feature of community is the local network, whether it is expressed as ecology, system, or field.

The interactionist approach focuses upon the dynamic processes of community action as the central elements of community. A community field consists of the interconnections among actions which express the common interests of the local population (see Wilkinson, 1972, which draws upon field theories in several scientific disciplines). The essential, distinctive process of the community field is generalization across interest lines. This is manifested in generalizing roles of individuals and organizations which contribute to the accomplishment of action goals by linking interest groups. The generalizing process of the community field is of particular importance for identifying a distinct role for community in modern societies in which many areas of local life are oriented toward the structure and symbols of the larger society. Generalization of social action at the local level is the process by which the local aspects of a society are integrated into a community.

Numerous trends in modern society have altered the role of community in the lives of people. Roland Warren [1978] has described a "Great Change" in modern civilization resulting from the technological revolution, which has shifted importance at the local level from the horizontal (i.e., local) axis to the vertical (i.e., extralocal) axis. Studies of leadership have discovered a "bifurcation" which occurs as economic power moves from local to extralocal agencies, leaving local leaders to deal with political and expressive domains [Schulze, 1961]. The institutional involvements of local residents have been found to be spread over larger geographic areas than formerly [Clemente, Rojek, and Beck, 1974]. A question can be raised as to whether the term "community" has a referent in modern, mass society. If community, as an integrated local network through which people express collective needs and form social identities, is accepted as a requisite for social well-being, these trends denote a crisis for humankind and a challenge for community development. Yet, it seems clear that modern sustenance needs and demands of people cannot be met fully through local interaction [Warren, 1970], and that behavior and identities of people will be oriented to action fields beyond their immediate existential experience.

The facts remain, however, that social life is experienced on site and self-actualization depends upon concrete encounters with people. Therein lies the significance of the community field for social well-being. Local interaction is a given. The degree to which that local interaction is vested in a community field is indicative of a social condition supportive of self-actualization. The community as an ecological unit and as a social system has had decreasing significance in modern societies; but as an interactional phenomenon, community has continuing significance for social well-being.

The immediacy of social experience of the individual in the community is one reason for considering community as a factor in social well-being. The community field contributes to self-actualization in several ways. One is in providing a channel for expression of associational needs and a process through which the individual can develop independent competency and social responsibility. Community action is a dynamic process to which the individual can contribute. Opportunities for creative behavior and new experience are essential for self-actualization. The range of concerns expressed through a community field reflects a variety of interests of people; participation in actions concerning a range of interests also provides a range of contacts and experiences for broadening individual competencies in social interaction. Participation in the community field allows people to take an active part in developing the social structures in which their lives are existentially rooted.

There are other factors in social well-being and in self-actualization relating to specific aspects of the person and to unique experiences. Community, as the concept is used here, is assumed to be one important social condition for self-actualization.

Social relationships similar to community but lacking some of its characteristics might contribute in a more limited way to self-actualization and to social well-being. For example, a pattern of intimacy and face-to-face interaction often prevails in rural villages which are geographically and economically isolated. Relationships among people tend to be close in such settings as a means of coping with economic and environmental necessity. This intimacy contributes to social well-being, but in a way which might restrict opportunities for self-actualization. Individuals in such patterns are in symbiotic bondage to one another and to the whole. Their lives might be orderly and peaceful, but their potentials for self-actualization are stifled. A modern challenge for community development is to create situations in which both freedom and discipline can be realized.

A second example of human organization similar to community but lacking its full contribution to social well-being is dominance of the local society by an economic or political elite. Several studies have suggested that the concentration of community power in a few hands contributes to accomplishment of goals (e.g., Hawley, 1963). Warren [1970] has referred to such findings to support the proposition that two common goals of community development, widespread participation and efficiency in problem solving, are in tension. This relates to a broad issue of the tension between task accomplishment and structure maintenance which has not been addressed directly in comparative community research, but has been considered in studies of small groups and complex organizations. Task accomplishment can be enhanced in the short run by authoritarian practices which over the long run undermine the structure of the group or organization [Lippitt and White, 1943; Morse and Reimer, 1956]. Evidence that dominance and stratification can contribute to short-term goal attainment is not surprising, particularly when the goals are more clearly associated with the interests of the elite than with those of the community as a whole. The contribution of the community field to social well-being is assumed to be restricted by stratification, power concentration, or any other structural cleavage which results in differential participation in community action. Community, as the term is used here in an idealized sense, is a comprehensive field of action from which no local groupings are excluded. While this ideal is seldom realized, one goal of community development is to pursue it.

A third example of organization similar to community but lacking in its central characteristics is seen in the associations of people whose relationships cover only a few of their interests. Hillery [1968], for example, has shown how life in total institutions, such as prisons and asylums, cannot be regarded as communal because of the absence of the family. Absence of other important institutions in local life in urban neighborhoods raises a question as to whether these should be viewed as communities. What is lacking in these settings, and in many "New Towns" and suburban and satellite areas, is comprehensiveness of institutional structures. This is the case to some degree in many small towns and rural areas in modern societies. People depend upon and participate in a larger field than that of their immediate residence for meeting many needs. While interaction among people regarding some of their interests can contribute to a sense of community among them, the contribution of community to social well-being is lessened by the restrictions.

HYPOTHESES

The relationship of social well-being to the community field can be examined in terms of a variety of community field characteristics such as the scope of interests represented in coordinated actions, the extent of coordination achieved, the extent of participation of local organizations and individuals in community action, and the outcomes of actions which are undertaken. The effects of a number of characteristics can be examined at once through formulation of a series of ideal types of community fields based on theoretical models and descriptive reports in the research literature. Four types can be abstracted from this literature.

One type is suggested by Norton Long's [1958] description of the community as an "ecology of games." "The real estate game," the "local government game," "the health services game," and others operate more or less independently in the local society. Patterns of coexistence and accommodation are worked out on a symbiotic basis, but with little coordination among the games. Decision organizations within each social field seek autonomy and specialized extralocal linkages so as to maximize goal attainment. Actors in one game might use those in another to further their own ends. The "civic" and "social" games provide a vague sense of order but result in little coordination.

A second type of community field is one in which interest fields are in opposition. Groups compete with one another for scarce resources and commitments. Unlike the autonomous situation of an ecology of games, social fields in opposition maintain an active interrelationship. Behaviors in one field are viewed by actors in other fields as directly opposed to their own ends. Cross-cutting and overlapping cleavages create a situation of dissention.

A third type of community field is one based on functional interdependency, as in the division of labor. Interest groups cooperate so as to secure needed resources from one another. People promoting industrial growth, for example, might find an advantage in pursuing their goal in cooperation with another group working on increasing the employment skills of poor people.

A fourth type of community field is one in which social fields are linked through a sense of communal identity among participants [Vogt and O'Dea, 1953]. Local residents identify various problems as parts of a collective concern and undertake concerted action that is generalized because of the shared sentiment.

Using the social well-being concepts and propositions discussed above, three general hypotheses can be stated concerning these four ideal types. The first of these hypotheses is a restatement of the proposition developed in the previous section, namely that connections among social fields contribute to social well-being. The flow of information and resources among fields, by whatever means, is assumed to increase community effectiveness in its overall pattern of problem solving and in providing social opportunities for self-actualization. The existence of autonomous fields, such as those indicated by the "ecology of games" concept, might contribute to a high level of achievement in some of the special interest organizations, but the overall pattern of the accomplishment of community action goals is related to the degree of linkage among organizations [Aiken, 1970, p. 516]. The autonomous style of community action would be expected to contribute less to social well-being than would the styles represented by the other three types discussed above. Opposition among fields implies an interactive relationship, as do functional interdependency and communal identity.

A second hypothesis is that cooperative linkages among fields are more supportive of social well-being than are relationships of opposition and isolation. Opposition might intensify action and serve to check attempts of one interest group to dominate others. Introduction of new demands and influence into community decision making through location of a new firm or agency in the community can increase equity through confrontation of the existing power structure [Walton, 1967]. But the effects of opposition in "opening" a system are short ranged, and reintegration on a new basis must follow if fragmentation is to be avoided. Bates and Bacon [1972] have described "interstitial" mechanisms through which accommodations are made among opposing interests, thus making possible the continuation of community as a unified phenomenon. Both cooperation and opposition contribute to self-actualization of the individual; but, as Erich Fromm [1956] has shown, the role of opposition is in freeing the individual from passive dependency so that independent competency can emerge and a "reunion" with others can occur on a mature basis. Community, in the long run, depends upon cooperation. Thus, cooperative relationships such as those indicated in community fields based on functional interdependency and communal identity are more supportive of social well-being than are relationships of opposition and autonomy.

A third hypothesis is that a community field based upon a shared commitment to comprehensiveness and cooperativeness is more facilitative of social well-being than is a field in which such commitment is lacking. Comprehensiveness of linkage might be achieved through opposition or functional interdependency, while cooperativeness might also arise from the latter. Psychological involvement in the process of linkage gives added strength to the relationship of linkage to social well-being. Self-actualization involves creative expression of will and conscious commitment to union. Purposive action by people who share an identity can contribute to the creation of community. Leadership effectiveness in complex organizations and small groups is related to the degree to which an individual participates consciously in the creation of social structures. A community field based on communal identity is one in which shared sentiment guides action. While such sentiment might be encouraged by other forces, such as functional interdependency and common territory, its effects are assumed to be independent of its sources. Communal identity is the type of community field which would be expected to be most facilitative of social well-being.

These types of community fields are, of course, monothetic in that they are idealized abstractions. The linking mechanisms indicated by them would probably be found in combination in most empirical cases. Likewise, the hypotheses concerning them are stated in abstract form so that they could not be tested directly. As propositions, however, they illustrate the thesis of this paper concerning the relationship of social well-being to community and suggest aspects of community interaction which can be dealt with in community development.

COMMUNITY DEVELOPMENT

Most programs of development are concerned with economic growth, reflecting the fact that most of the people of the world have unmet primary needs. Economic growth and related developments, such as in technology and in specialized service delivery systems, should be seen as means rather than ends of social well-being. Community development is a broader process than economic development, being both a means and an end of social well-being. Economic development can contribute to the emergence of community, but it is not a sufficient condition for community. Economic development without community development can increase the gap between social classes and reduce the expression of natural human tendencies toward interpersonal warmth, cooperativeness, tolerance, and respect [Wilkinson, 1973]. Community development as a purposive activity is needed to realize the potential social well-being benefits of economic development.

Community development, from the interactionist perspective, refers to attempts by people to strengthen a community field. It consists of acts by people that open and maintain channels of communication and cooperation among local groups. Thus, it is a process of action that is concerned with structure. This process is purposive, meaning that people intend to strengthen relationships, and it is positive in that the intentions have to do with a shared concept of improvement. It does not follow that community development is always successful. Many other factors are involved in structural change at the community level, and a community is never finally "developed." The essence of community development is in the attempt. It is action undertaken with positive purpose in regard to the structure of the community field [Wilkinson, 1972, p. 46]. Community development is a local process, but one in which outside actors and agencies are involved to the extent that they participate in community action.

How can community development be encouraged? Scientific research has not produced a complete answer to this question, but has suggested a number of important leads. The concept of community used in this paper is based on the assumption that community development is a natural inclination of humankind, one which expresses the essence of human potential. We also assume that community development can be suppressed and, thus, that human potential for social well-being can fail to be realized. But what actions should we undertake to stimulate it or to remove barriers to its emergence?

Economic development must be given high priority in many communities, as must improved delivery of social services, but in perspective of the idea that the social well-being benefits of these activities decline beyond some optimum range of accomplishment. Equitable distribution of access to resources is also a pressing need, and can be addressed through programs to increase the participation of less advantaged groupings in public decision-making. Outside agencies committed to community development as a goal can adopt a "collaborative" strategy to replace the tendency toward "intervention" which has been seen in many programs. A collaborative strategy would consist of participating with community members in pursuit of common goals. The frequent practice of channeling outside resources through highly specialized local organizations could be altered by the policy of requiring that local sponsorship of state and federal programs be vested in a multi-interest network at the local level. Training and education programs aimed at increasing the level and skill of participation of local citizens in public affairs decision making should be expanded and modified in light of the findings of evaluation research, which in recent years has used much more sophisticated methods than formerly. Equally important are educational programs in process skills, which have recently been systematized [Robinson and Clifford, 1972]. Findings of recent studies [Voth, 1975; Howell and Weir, 1978] show clearly that community development and leadership education programs can have significant impacts on community action.

Given the significance of the larger society in trends which affect local interaction, a crucial factor in community development for the future will be the degree to which national policy is informed by an understanding of the significance of community in the well-being of people. Programs which ignore community in favor of economic efficiency and increased levels of material consumption run the risk of undercutting the essential social structures through which well-being is encouraged. An appropriate national policy would be based upon a concept of economic growth and improved services as a means and the development of community as an end. Social well-being requires both sustenance and community.

REFERENCES

Aiken, M. "The distribution of community power: Structural bases and social corre-
1970   lates." In M. Aiken and P. Mott (eds.), *The Structure of Community Power*. New York: Random House, pp. 487–525.

Allport, G. W. *Becoming*. New Haven, Connecticut: Yale University Press.
1955

Bates, F. L. and Bacon, L. "The community as a social system." *Social Forces*
1972   50(March):371–379.

Clemente, F., Rojek, D., and Beck, E. M. "Trade patterns and community identity:
1974   Five years later." *Rural Sociology* 39(Spring):92–95.

Durkheim, E. *Suicide*. Trans. by J. A. Spaulding and G. Simpson. Glencoe, Illinois:
1951   The Free Press.

Fromm, E. *The Art of Loving*. New York: Bantam.
1956

Hawley, A. H. "Community power and urban renewal success." *American Journal*
1963   *of Sociology*   68(January):422–431.

Hillery, G. A., Jr. *Communal Organizations: A Study of Local Societies.* Chicago:
1968   University of Chicago Press.

Howell, R. E. and Weir, I. L. "An assessment of changes in affiliations in public
1978   affairs organizations among graduates of four intensive leadership development programs." Paper presented at the annual meeting of the
Rural Sociological Society, San Francisco (August).

König, R. *The Community.* Trans. by E. Fitzgerald. New York: Schocken.
1968

Lee, A. M. *Toward Humanist Sociology.* Englewood Cliffs, New Jersey: Prentice-
1973   Hall.

Lippitt, R. and White, R. K. "The 'social climate' of children's groups." In R. G.
1943   Barker, J. Kounin, and H. Wright (eds.), *Child Behavior and Development.* New York: McGraw-Hill, pp. 485–508.

Long, N. "The local community as an ecology of games." *American Journal of*
1958   *Sociology*   64(November):251–261.

Maslow, A. H. *Motivation and Personality.* New York: Harper.
1954

Mead, G. H. *Mind, Self, and Society: From the Standpoint of a Social Behaviorist.*
1934   Ed. by C. W. Morris. Chicago: University of Chicago Press.

Morse, N. and Reimer, E. "The experimental change of a major organizational
1956   variable." *Journal of Abnormal and Social Psychology*   52:120–129.

Ollman, B. *Alienation: Marx's Conception of Man in Capitalist Society.* New York:
1971   Cambridge University Press.

Robinson, J. W., Jr. and Clifford, R. A. *Process Skills in Community Organizations.*
1972   Urbana, Illinois: Cooperative Extension Service, University of Illinois.

Schulze, R. O. "The bifurcation of power in a satellite city." in M. Janowitz (ed.),
1961   *Community Political Systems.* Glencoe, Illinois: The Free Press.

Speight, J. E. "Community development theory and practice: A Machiavellian per-
1973   spective." *Rural Sociology*   38(Winter):477–490.

Vogt, E. Z. and O'Dea, T. F. "A comparative study of the role of values in social
1953   action in two southwestern communities." *American Sociological Review*   18(December):645–654.

Voth, D. E. "An evaluation of community development programs in Illinois."
1975   *Social Forces*   53(June):635–646.

Walton, J. "The vertical axis of community organization and the structure of
1967   power." *Social Science Quarterly*   48(December):353–368.

Warren, R. L. "Toward a non-utopian normative model of community." *American*
1970   *Sociological Review*   35(April):219–228.

Warren, R. L. *The Community in America.* Third edition. Chicago: Rand McNally.
1978

Wilkinson, K. P. "A field-theory perspective for community development research."
1972   *Rural Sociology*   37(March):43–52.

Wilkinson, K. P. "Sociological concepts of social well-being: Frameworks for evalu-
1973   ation of water resources projects." In W. H. Andrews, et al. (eds.),
*The Social Well-Being and Quality of Life Dimension in Water Re-
sources Planning and Development.* Logan, Utah: Utah State University.

Perspective in Retrospect: Community Development During the Sixties

Otto G. Hoiberg

As one plans for the future, it is helpful to study the past for perspective. Much has transpired during the sixties in the broad field of community development and the task of identifying major trends is difficult. It seems, however, that the following developments would be among those worthy of mention. Briefly, the last decade has seen:

1. A Growing Emphasis on Community Development at Colleges and Universities throughout the Nation. The Community Development Division of NUEA came into existence in 1955 and has experienced substantial growth. The trend goes on, as witness the recent inter-departmental workshop at the University of Nevada/Reno, where attention was given to defining the future role of that institution in relation to continuing education, including community development.

"Urban Studies" and "Urban Affairs" centers are appearing on campuses all over the country.

Community colleges are entering the field of community development. The National Council on Community Services for Community and Junior Colleges has just emerged as a product of the Community Services Project of the American Association of Junior Colleges. Its orientation is clearly reflected in the following passages from a recent AAJC publication (1): "It is in this period (the 1960's) that community services has (sic) emerged as an identifiable component of the community college. Problems relating to technology, race, poverty, and urbanization have mandated a broadening of the college mission to provide a more viable base for the development of human resources in the community;" and "it now appears that community services is (sic) erupting as the major thrust in program development for the 1970's."

Also, it is noteworthy that the Cooperative Extension Service has a concerted program expansion in mind along community de-

This paper was delivered by Dr. Hoiberg at the Community Development Division meeting during the annual conference of the National University Extension Association in Kansas City, Mo. May 2, 1970. Dr. Hoiberg is the Head, Community Development, University Extension Division, University of Nebraska. He is past chairman of NUEA's Community Development Division.

velopment lines. Their newly-published bulletin, "A People and a Spirit," leaves no doubt on this point.

2. Proliferation and Diversification of Community Development Agencies. In addition to the trends just noted in colleges and universities, *a major thrust* along CD lines has occurred (a) in the Federal Government through the Peace Corps, Vista, the Community Action Program of O.E.O., and Title I; (b) in private enterprise where both *action* programs (e.g., the community development program of Northern Natural Gas Company) and *supportive* programs (The Sears-Roebuck Foundation, the Kellogg Foundation, etc.) are in evidence; and (c) in state departments of planning and economic development. In Nebraska, to illustrate the latter, our State Department of Economic Development earlier devoted all its efforts to enticing industry into the State; but today such effort is undergirded by the work of several planners and community development specialists who operate in the broader field of community development.

3. Greater Effort toward Liaison, Coordination and Integration between Major Elements of the National CD Pattern within Each Element. Illustrative of this trend are: (a) The establishment of the Community Development Society in 1969, with a stated goal of providing interagency liaison between the CD efforts of universities, government, private enterprise, and voluntary associations; (b) the formation of a CD Division within the National University Extension Association to foster cooperative effort among universities; (c) the merger of Cooperative Extension and general Extension programs in the State of Missouri and elsewhere; and (d) a variety of programs involving joint CD action on the part of universities, private enterprise, and government agencies.

We still have a long way to go in regard to interagency communication and coordination, but substantial progress was made during the sixties.

4. Professionalization of the CD Field. One of the unmistakable signs of a growing professionalism is the effort to conceptualize. In the case of community development, conceptualization is admittedly a major undertaking. A wide variety of definitions and concepts of community development is apparent, even to the casual observer. Such heterogeneity is wholesome, particularly in the initial stages of an emerging, vigorous discipline; but men are now needed who endeavor to visualize central purposes, underlying concepts, and major currents. Examples of such effort are found in the theoretical contributions of Roland Warren; in Saul Alinsky's concept concerning the role of power in social action; in the Brokensha and Hedge volume on *Community Development, An Interpretation;* and in the recently published NUEA/CD Position Paper.

These budding efforts at conceptualization are creating an image of CD that is beginning to command respect on university campuses. Community Development is gaining status as a discipline within the academic family. Also, the relation between CD and other disciplines is being visualized somewhat more clearly now, but this requires further attention. Not long ago, I heard CD referred to as a threat to city planning. In reality, of course, CD is an essential support for city planning rather than a threat. Many comprehensive plans today lie shelved in a non-functional coma for the very reason that no attention was paid to the fundamentals of the CD process in their development.

A second evidence of professionalization is found in the growth of academic advanced degree programs in community development at several major universities and in a broad range of non-credit training programs. Examples of the latter are found in the Peace Corps and CAP; in workshops for university community development personnel; and in human relations and sensitivity training laboratories.

Further evidences of professionalization are found in the scholárly journal now being published by the Community Development Society and in the growing body of research data on community development—research being done in regular academic departments as well as in specialized "urban studies" centers, with increasing attention being given to interdisciplinary investigations. A noteworthy current emphasis on community development research is found in the Rural Sociological Society.

5. *Increased Attention to Problems of Urbanization and the Inner City.* We admittedly have insufficient progress to boast about in this respect; but, on the other hand, we do have a Dr. Moynihan on the national government scene and a growing functional concern on university campuses with the problems of the ghetto and urban blight.

Concurrently, by the way, there has been an increasing stress on community development in rural areas. To a considerable degree, rural and urban problems actually represent the two sides of a single coin. One can hardly analyze urban congestion intelligently without also considering rural out-migration. The two are very closely related . . . "Can smaller cities be developed to provide adequate education, more jobs at decent wages, cultural and recreational opportunities, and sufficient amenities, in general, to attract a substantial portion of the 100 million persons who allegedly will be added to the U.S. population by the year 2000?" This question has generated a renewed interest in rural community development, symbolized by the work of the President's Advisory Commission on Rural Poverty

(1967), the President's Task Force on Rural Development (1969), and establishment of the national Council for Rural Affairs (1969).

6. *Growing Emphasis on CD as It Relates to Area (Regional) Planning and Development.* This trend is relevant to both urban and rural areas.

A veritable maze of multi-county and inter-community groupings of many kinds is now taking shape across the land: Councils of government (COG's), metropolitan area planning agencies, comprehensive health planning areas, regional telecommunications systems, watershed development projects, educational service units, rural water districts, and on and on.

These larger groupings are evolving in response to obvious needs. Rural communities can, through joint endeavor, gain or improve essential services which have been lacking through independent action. Metropolitan problems that transcend traditional political boundary lines can be more effectively resolved through an area-wide approach.

The role of community development is vital in connection with this trend. It is inherent in the oft-disregarded maxim that a new organization, no matter how perfectly structured, can easily come to naught if the motivation, understanding, and skills to make it functional are lacking.

7. *A Shifting Emphasis from THINGS to PEOPLE.* I may be a bit optimistic here; but it seems to me that community development personnel are today placing relatively less stress on physical/material developments (though these necessarily still remain very important), and relatively more on race relations, the problems of youth and old age, culture and the performing arts, job opportunities, and the like.

8. *Finally, the CD Approach Has Gained Considerable Ground within the University Institution, Itself* during the past decade. A university community comprises a student body, a faculty, an administration, and a legislative/governing body of some kind (e.g., a board of regents). Much work has been done in recent years to arrive at a decision-making process within the university family that will give appropriate voice to all of these elements on an integrated basis.

Somehow it is a good feeling to know that the principles of involvement and meaningful participation that for years we have promoted as essential in communities around the country are also now beginning to take root more firmly on our own campuses. There is need for further judicious effort along this line.

REFERENCE

1. Myran, Gundar A., Community Services in the Community College," AAJC, Washington, D.C., 1969, p. 4.

SAUL D. ALINSKY'S CONTRIBUTION TO COMMUNITY DEVELOPMENT

By Donald C. Reitzes and Dietrich C. Reitzes

ABSTRACT

The works of Saul D. Alinsky are widely known but not systematically treated in the social sciences. The present research interprets Alinsky's contribution to community development from the perspective of three underlying themes: community as the unit of analysis and community cohesiveness as one of the goals of community organization; political participation and goal of broadening community participation in city-wide decision making; and the use of non-violent conflict as a means of unifying diverse local interests and effectively bargaining with extra-community agents. Analysis reveals that Alinsky's understanding of the task of community organization complement existing community development perspectives and provides a basis for assessing his strategies.

The work of Saul D. Alinsky deserves serious and systematic treatment in the field of community development. Through words and deeds Alinsky demonstrated a remarkable ability to generate interest in the promise and possibility of community organization. Yet there has been only superficial treatment of Alinsky's work in the social sciences. Reitzes and Reitzes (1980) reviewed over one hundred citations to Alinsky and found that most were short references to either catchy phrases such as his description of the War on Poverty as political pornography or brief references to specific tactics. The few extended treatments of Alinsky's work tend to include: descriptive accounts of individual Alinsky community organizations; assessments of his use of conflict strategies; or the only belated recognition that while Alinsky used a radical vocabulary his political orientation stressed democratic citizen participation.

The absence of systematic analysis and assessment of Alinsky's contribution to community development may stem from four sources. First, Alinsky was clearly impatient with theoretical discussions of community and criticized sociologists for their failure to direct their attention to the task of community building. "Asking a sociologist to solve a problem is like prescribing an enema for diarrhea" (Alinsky, 1972:64). Second, during the period of the 1950s and early 1960s, when Alinsky was gaining

Donald C. Reitzes is assistant professor in the Department of Sociology at Georgia State University, Atlanta, Georgia. Dietrich C. Reitzes is in the Department of Sociology at Roosevelt University, Chicago, Illinois.

popular recognition through his publications and community organizations activities, the social sciences were ideologically dominated by conservative structural-functional theories and a methodological concern for quantitative or at least behaviorally-oriented research (Walton, 1976). Alinsky's interest in conflict strategies and community action must have seemed out of step with the times. Third, Alinsky directly antagonized some sociologists by attacking the University of Chicago Sociology Department in the early stages of his organizing in neighboring Woodlawn. Finally, both his flamboyant personal style and rhetorical, discursive writing style were directed more towards a popular, rather than academic audience. Thus, he tended to underplay the importance of sociological concepts to the formulation of his community organization principles. However, the past pattern of minimal recognition of Alinsky does not excuse the neglect of his contribution to community development.

The purpose of the present inquiry is to review the sociological foundations of Alinsky community organization and to present an integrated treatment of his underlying theoretical orientation. A thoroughly sociological perspective was contained in Alinsky's writings and implied in his community activities. Community served as the unit of analysis and a unified, cohesive community was one of the goals of his organizations. Local community political participation was consistent with his recognition of the connection between local community and larger units of social structure and with his political commitment to pluralist democracy. Nonviolent conflict served as the means to heighten interest and participation in the local community as well as to broaden influence in extra-community decision-making. Thus, Alinsky's theoretical orientation aids in understanding his contribution to community development theory and practice.

COMMUNITY

Meenagan (1972:354) noted, "Alinsky's effort is primarily one of creating a sense of community; not delineating one." Alinsky's emphasis on community action masked two sociological insights which integrated his community organization activities. Alinsky argued that local communities were not autonomous, self-sufficient units of social structure but reflected the social problems and processes of an urban society. The position departed from earlier models of community as a complete local social system (Effrat, 1974). Thus, an early Alinsky (1941:797) criticism of traditional community organizations was that they tended "to view the community as a social, political, and economic entity which is more or less insulated from the general social scene." In contrast, one of the goals of community organization for Alinsky was to make local residents aware of the functional relationship between the community and larger units of social structure (Alinsky, 1969:167). Indeed, Alinsky (1969: 169) noted with pride, "Today Back of the Yards (his first community organization) leaders not only know more about governmental procedures than most professors of civics, they are also completely cognizant of the place of their community in the general mosaic of communities which make up this nation." While not new, Alinsky's position is consistent with Hunter's (1979:269) description of neighborhood as "a uniquely linked unit of social/spatial organization between the forces and institutions of the larger society and the localized routines of individuals in their daily lives."

Alinsky's view of community also had direct implications for community development. The recognition of the relationship between local community and the larger society suggested a broad scope and range of community activities. Alinsky (1941:798) encouraged community organizations to direct their attention to "those larger socioeconomic issues which converge upon local communities." Alinsky organizations became active in such issues as public housing, urban renewal, unemployment, and public school education. Further, the link between local community and the larger society suggested that one of the tasks of a community organization was to generate municipal and national support for local programs. In Back of the Yards, the Alinsky organization sought funds from private social service agencies for social welfare, job training programs from private industry, higher state and federal standards for unemployment relief payments, and a federally funded school lunch program (Alinsky, 1941).

A second Alinsky theme was that community was neither the only, nor necessarily the most important, unit of local participation and identification. Alinsky (1969:776–788) noted that community social structure in poor, inner-city neighborhoods was often quite complex. Typically these communities contained a diverse set of groups which competed for the time, money, and commitment of local residents and encouraged hostilities among segments of the local community. Alinsky (1971) called the result of these multiple, fragmented ties "organized apathy," a pattern of interaction which encouraged intra-community conflict and a reluctance to participate in cooperative community action.

The task of the organizer was to combat organized apathy and heighten community-wide ties. Central to Alinsky's strategy of community organization was the realignment of community interest toward issues and problems which were shared concerns of local residents.

The purpose of the [community-wide] organization should be interpreted as proposing to deal with those major issues which no single agency [or group] is — or can be — big enough or strong enough to gram; but all are being banded together to achieve sufficient strength to cope with issues that are so vast and deep that no one or two community agencies would ever consider tackling alone (Alinsky, 1969:87).

Further, many such issues would attract a broader cross-section of local residents and local groups.

[Community-wide] organizations must be based on many issues. . . . It is impossible to maintain constant action on a single issue. A single issue is a fatal strait jacket that will stifle the life of an organization. Furthermore, a single issue drastically limits your appeal, where multiple issues would draw in the many potential members essential to the building of a broad, mass-based organization. . . . Communities are not economic organizations like unions, with specific economic issues, they are as complex as life itself (Alinsky, 1971:120).

Alinsky's emphasis on the purposive social construction of community was in substantial agreement with the more explicitly stated propositions of a community field perspective. Wilkinson (1972:47) stated, "community development is purposive action which is oriented in a positive way toward the structure of a community field." Alinsky and Wilkinson recognized that community development required purposive action based on shared interests and directed toward the establishment of structural ties and linkages among local residents. Further, Alinsky's understanding of the complexity of local community social structure highlighted the difficult but possible task of community development.

COMMUNITY POWER AND ORGANIZATION

Alinsky (1972:50) defined power as the ability to act and community power as a community's successful participation in local and extra-community decision-making. The importance Alinsky placed on power reflected both his understanding of community as connected to larger units of social structure and his belief in purposive action as the basis for community development. Alinsky (1969) and Long (1958) were critical of static and rigid descriptions of social structure produced by functional necessity. They presented instead a picture of social structure as a dynamic pattern of interaction produced by sets of players (social groups) competing to achieve their own particular goals and striving to win in their particular games (institutional domains or fields). Yet, Alinsky disagreed with Long's assumption that coordination among groups could best be achieved by symbiotic relations. The problem for Alinsky was that not all the players or teams were represented in the major games. Alinsky (1965) argued that the urban poor, lacking the financial resources and

interest group affiliations of middle class groups were systematically under represented in city-wide decision-making.

> With the urban society's development of vertical city-wide organiza-
> tions and agencies, the disappearance of an articulate and active
> mass base has in effect insulated the heads of these organizations
> from their bodies. . . . I do not believe that democracy can survive
> except as a formality if the ordinary citizen's role is limited to voting,
> and if he is incapable of initiative or all possibility of influencing
> the political, social, and economic structures that surround him
> (Alinsky, 1969:217–218).

Thus, Alinsky feared that an unintended consequence of the concentration and centralization of power and authority was a general restriction
of the scope of citizen participation.

The role of the local community for Alinsky was to actively represent
local interests in the extra-community arenas where policies and programs
were formulated which directly influenced the interests of the local community. "The democratic process cannot function lacking the essential
prime mix of legitimate, bona fide representatives to meet accredited
representatives of other sectors of society in the pushing, hauling, dealing,
and temporary compromises before the process begins to repeat in the
perpetual process of pressure of the democratic way" (Alinsky, 1968:
293). The emphasis Alinsky placed on the role of the local community
as a spokesman for local interests compliments Bates and Bacon (1972)
analyses of the limited community as interstitial groups, and Jacobs'
(1970) description of the role of the district (local community) "to mediate between the indispensable but inherently politically powerless, street
neighborhoods, and the inherently powerful city as a whole."

One of Alinsky's special contributions to community development was
his attempt to create community organizations which incorporated democratic participation in the organization with representations of local interests in city-wide affairs. Using Back of the Yards as a model, Alinsky
(1969) proposed that bona fide legitimate community organization required a political structure based on indigenous leadership and citizen
participation; an economic structure which ensured financial independence; and a social commitment to rigorously defend local interests while
avoiding issues which would fragment and divide local support.

CONFLICT

Alinsky's analysis of local community social structure and power stressed
that effective community development required: (1) the establishment
of community-wide ties; and (2) the active, purposive representation of

local interests in extra-community affairs where policies and programs are initiated which directly influence the local community. The brilliance of Alinsky's organizational strategy was his use of non-violent conflict with extra-community organizations and institutions to pursue the development of a community organization capable of both achieving community cohesion and participation in city-wide affairs.

Alinsky typically began by using conflict to generate community-wide identification and participation in community-wide organization. He (1969) noted that local residents were often distrustful of outsiders and that established local groups, often resisted attempts to organize on a community-wide level. In the face of such obstacles, Alinsky (1971:116) suggested the strategy of "rubbing raw the resentments of the people of the community." For example, upon arrival in Rochester, New York, where he had been invited by white church leaders to organize the black community, Alinsky publicly attacked a major company, newspaper and university: "...as far as I know, the only thing Eastman Kodak has done on the race issue in America has been to introduce color film" (Alinsky, 1971:137). He maintained that his purpose was to provoke a negative response from city leaders which aided in winning local black acceptance for him as an organizer and for a locally based community organization. Alinsky argued (1969) that the task of the organizer was to use conflict with external antagonists to demonstrate to local residents that their private discontents were shared social problems requiring a cooperative and organized community response. Thus, conflict was initially used to create a situation more conducive to positive community development.

Alinsky also advocated non-violent conflict later in the development of the community organization. He insisted upon formal invitation to organize in order to gain acceptance by the community. Alinsky (1969) suggested that the task of the organizer was to learn local customs and traditions, identify indigenous leaders, and to record issues which were of importance to local residents. Upon completion of his community study, Alinsky typically called for a constitutional convention to establish an umbrella community organization composed of existing local organizations and diverse segments of the local population. The purpose of the convention was to ratify the by-laws of the organization, specify its goals, and elect officers.

Once the representative and locally led organization was formed, Alinsky returned to conflict strategies to solidify local support and generate local commitment for the organization. Alinsky (1971) carefully selected issues which could both be easily won and were of concern to local residents. The purpose of these conflicts were to demonstrate to local residents that organized community-wide action could be successful in delivering local services and improving the everyday lives of residents. Furthermore, repeated conflicts aided in maintaining local interest in community affairs and fostering a community-wide identification while providing an opportunity to train leaders in the effective uses of conflict strategies and conflict resolution. Only after community building and community organization training was Alinsky ready to engage in conflict with extra-community antagonists over such major issues as employment, housing, or improved public school education. Borrowing strategies from labor union organization, Alinsky (1971) suggested the principles of picking and freezing a target, and personalizing and polarizing an issue. Thus, Alinsky preferred a single, representative target, one store among many downtown commercial establishments, or one office or agency in a complex line of decision-making, such as a city planning agency when the issue was urban renewal. The personalization and polarization of the issue represented Alinsky's willingness to simplify complex issues to a single issue and/or demonic personality. The purpose was to define the issue in a manner which was easy to understand and present the position of the community organization in the most favorable light. Thus, Alinsky reduced the complex issue of urban public education to the single issue of an arrogant, self-serving, and racist school superintendent preventing children from receiving equal educational opportunities (Alinsky, 1971). The purpose of the tactics was to minimize the expense of maintaining the conflict for the community organization while maximizing the costs of prolonged conflict to antagonists.

The importance that Alinsky places on compromise highlights his special use of non-violent conflict as a community development strategy. Alinsky noted that as important as the issues were, the goal of conflict was to confirm the legitimate right of the local community decision-making. Thus, he called his proxy battle with Kodak a success when a compromise was reached and the community organization was officially recognized by the company as the voice of the community (Alinsky, 1972). Similarly, Alinsky stated that he was ready to leave Woodlawn when the community organization proved itself as a potent political and economic force and he noted:

> We didn't solve all their problems overnight, but we showed them that those problems *could* be solved through their own dedication and their own indigenous black leadership...When we entered Woodlawn, it was a decaying, hopeless ghetto, when we left, it was a fighting, united community (Alinsky, 1972:170).

Alinsky felt his task was complete when the community organization had won enough conflicts that it could risk losing a few battles and still not jeopardize either local cohesiveness or their place as legitimate power in city-wide affairs.

Alinsky's use of non-violent conflict with extra-community antagonists appears at odds with alternative approaches, such as field theory, which emphasizes consensus and cooperative strategies for community development. A comparison of Alinsky's discussion of conflict and Wilkinson's (1979) discussion of community well-being suggests that Alinsky differs from Wilkinson more in the implementation of community development strategies than in the underlying goals for community development. Wilkinson identified three dimensions of community well-being: scope of interests, extent of coordinated action, and extent of participation of local organizations and individuals in community action. Similarly, Alinsky's discussion of effective community organization stressed the creation of a broad based, multiple issue community-wide organization capable of generating community cohesiveness and participation in city-wide affairs. Wilkinson (1979) proposed, and Alinsky's discussion of power supports, the evaluation of that symbiotic social ties, similar to Long's ecology of games, contributes less to the establishment of broad based, multi-purpose community activities than purposive, interactive relationships among community groups. Further, Wilkinson proposed, and Alinsky's comments appear to support, that relationships based on a communal identity are most effective in generating local commitment. However, the question for Alinsky was how to establish a community identification when existing local groups are competitive and hostile. His position suggests that communal ties are not antithetical with conflict strategies but produce shared interests.

Similarly, the importance he placed on unified community action supports Wilkinson's proposition that cooperative relationships may best be achieved through ties based on functional interdependence and a communal identity. Alinsky's strategy of conflict represented the means to achieve cooperative ties both within the local community and between the local community and larger units of urban social structure. Alinsky (1972:170) responded to the charge that his conflict approach may have impeded community objectives by noting: "How do you ever arrive at consensus *before* you have conflict? In fact, of course, conflict is the vital core of an open society; if you were going to express democracy in a musical score, your major theme would be the harmony of dissonance. ..." Thus, while Wilkinson created the four ideal types of autonomous, conflictual, functionally interdependent, and communal interactional patterns to explore community well-being, Alinsky emphasized that conflict with extracommunity antagonists generated cooperative and communal ties.

DISCUSSION AND ASSESSMENT

One of the contributions of an integrated treatment of Alinsky's theoretical orientation is that the three themes of community, power, and conflict provide a basis for an assessment of Alinsky community organization and its impact on community development theory and practice. Alinsky's understanding that part of the task of community development was to establish community-wide ties remains sparsely treated in the social science literature. Meenagan (1972) and Glab and Sardell (1974) noted the importance of the goal of community cohesiveness for interpreting Alinsky's community organization strategies. In addition, Silberman (1964) and Fish (1973) both argued that one of the contributions of the Alinsky organization in Woodlawn was the development of a strong local constituency and an increased sense of dignity and pride in the local community.

Two case studies are especially helpful in outlining conditions which may aid in developing community cohesiveness. Irvine (1967) noted that the Alinsky organization in Chelsea, a community in New York City, failed to develop a unified and cohesive local community. Unlike the example of Back of the Yards, the Alinsky organization in Chelsea was never able to locate a set of issues or external antagonists which could bridge local differences in ethnicity, social class, religion, or length of residence.

Bailey (1972), in his study of the Alinsky organization in Austin (Chicago) contrasts residents who actively participated in the organization with a random sample of community residents. The findings may be used to identify conditions which contribute to successful community organization and the goal of creating active community-wide participation. Bailey found that while there appeared to be general value consensus among Austin residents, activists were more committed than other residents to achieving community values. The finding suggests that the more residents are committed to the improvement of the local community the more likely they will be to participate in community-wide activities. A second finding was that activists were more committed than other residents to community attachments, were more socially involved in local voluntary associations and tended to place more salience on the local community as a geopolitical unit than other community residents. The finding suggests that the establishment of community cohesiveness may be more likely to succeed when local residents are involved and committed to the local community. Further, Bailey found that activists tended to perceive greater dissatisfaction with local governmental services and particular local government programs than other residents. One possible motivation for community participation may be dissatisfaction when actual levels of public service fall below expectations. Finally, Bailey found that activists tended to be better educated and have higher incomes than other community residents. Bailey (1972) offered the explanation that the social skills necessary for effective participation in formal voluntary associations are often associated with higher education. A relatively higher income may also increase one's financial stake in the community as well as providing the financial resources necessary for the commitment of time and energy for community service.

A comparison of the Chelsea and Austin cases aids in specifying some of the contextual conditions which facilitate the creation and maintenance of community-wide ties. In Austin, the Alinsky organization began after a period of intense racial tension and after the initial transition from a predominantly white working-class to a predominantly black community. A core of the remaining whites and middle-class blacks shared a basic set of community values, a commitment to the local community, and dissatisfaction with existing social and political services. Thus, in Austin, at least some residents were initially receptive to community-wide organization and cooperative action directed toward shared common social problems. In Chelsea, on the other hand, the transition had just begun, residents shared fewer concerns and the control of the local community was still being contested by numerous competing groups. On one hand, Alinsky may be accused of over-selling the capability of a community organizer to create multiple common interests and for failing to specify the conditions which facilitate the creation and maintenance of community-wide participation. On the other hand, it is to Alinsky's credit that he did recognize the difficulty of establishing community-wide ties in the face of multiple, fragmented, and competitive local groups.

There has also been substantial praise for Alinsky's attempts to establish broader local political participation and community organizations capable of participation in city-wide affairs. Riessman (1965) noted that one of Alinsky's contributions to community organization was to disprove the myth that the poor are apathetic, without indigenous leadership, and incapable of concentrated political participation. Warren (1977) noted that Alinsky's principles of independent power and an adversary relation to established organizations provided a prototype of citizen action and heightened the importance of political participation among the powerless. Similarly, Bailey (1972) argued that while only one of the four Alinsky organizations in Chicago were in the city's poorest communities, Alinsky community organizations demonstrated success in increasing local political participation and the political influence of the local community.

A lingering problem with some assessments of Alinsky's political objectives has been an apparent willingness to accept Alinsky's self-proclaimed radicalism. Despite the use of a radical vocabulary, Alinsky's underlying political goal was not revolutionary upheaval but broad, grass-roots political participation. Alinsky may be more accurately described as a social reformer and a social democrat than as a radical or revolutionary. Similar to de Tocqueville, Alinsky was strongly committed to local voluntary associations as protection against attempts to exclude local communities from participation in democratic decision-making.

Alinsky perceived that his sociological understanding of the connection between the local community and with the larger society complemented his political goal of establishing autonomous, but effective community organizations. He further argued that multiple independent community organizations would eventually serve as a base for a national coalition of community organizations engaged in pursuing shared interests on a national level. While Alinsky may have been successful in gaining increased political participation for his community organizations in Back of the Yards, Rochester, Woodlawn, and Austin there is little evidence that he either succeeded or even seriously attempted to establish a national coalition of community organizations. Lancourt (1977) argued that Alinsky's emphasis on local independent community organizations made it unlikely that his organizations would exchange their local autonomy for participation in a centralized national movement. In fact, Lancourt (1977) noted Alinsky community organizations did not act jointly even when several existed in the same city. Alinsky never seriously considered that the particular interests of one community could directly conflict with the interests of another community. Thus, a major weakness of Alinsky's organizational strategy was that local political autonomy may have limited his goal of maximum local political effectiveness.

The most controversial aspect of Alinsky community organization was his advocacy of conflict strategies. Past discussions may have misconstrued and overemphasized Alinsky's reliance on conflict strategies. Throughout his career, Alinsky reflected on the use of violence. He noted (Alinsky, 1972) that communities with his organization did not engage in self destructive rioting or violence. Bailey (1972:136) argued that "the existing literature so overemphasizes the protest tactics taught by organizers that the teaching of skills such as parliamentary procedures, and the reinforcement of democratic norms such as voting, go almost unnoticed." Indeed while Alinsky apparently preferred to highlight many of his imaginative protest and non-violent conflict strategies, Bailey

(1972) found that Alinsky organizers in Austin used a variety of strategies to establish the community organization as a mediator between the local community and extra-community organizations and institutions. Thus, in addition to boycotts, picketing, and rent strikes, Alinsky organizers also used traditional strategies such as demanding the full enforcement of city housing regulations, participation at public hearings, and lawsuits to upgrade the delivery of social and protective services. Further, Bailey (1972) noted that at least occasionally a special reciprocal relationship developed between the community organization and city bureaucrats. The repeated accurate reporting of housing code violations led a chief building investor to come to trust and respect the Alinsky organization and promptly pursue their requests. Similarly, the Alinsky organization in Austin was able to coexist with many local politicians by not contesting local elections or running challenge candidates. The result has been a working relationship which has often provided political allies for the community organization.

Nevertheless, caution is required in assessing Alinsky's strategies, particularly their ability to provide tangible improvements in the local community. On one hand, Alinsky (1941) noted that his Back of the Yards organization succeeded in improving the community by initiating a number of programs including: an infant welfare station, a recreation center, a public housing project for low income residents, a community-owned dental clinic, and the conversion of several vacant lots into usable parks. Bailey (1971) lists among the tangible accomplishments of the Alinsky organization in Austin: a state funded day care center, an employment counselor, a community housing referral service, successful pressure on the school board to construct new schools, and some success in pressuring realtors to repair slum apartment units. Yet an Alinsky supporter noted that "it is difficult to discover indices that reveal that the quality of life in Woodlawn has improved ... physical structures are continuing to deteriorate ... welfare, unemployment, crime, and school drop-out rates remain high (Fish, 1973). Bailey concluded:

> It is difficult to assess the overall impact of the OBA [Alinsky organization in Austin]. On balance, I think the community is safer, cleaner, more liveable place because of the organization. However, many of the social processes that gradually turn old urban neighborhoods into slums are beyond OBA's control. The organization can only mitigate and slow, not stop these processes.

It is clear that even an active Alinsky organization is not a complete solution to contemporary urban social problems. At best, Alinsky strategies aid in improving existing services or generating new services, but it is unrealistic to fault Alinsky organization for failing to comprehensively improve local communities.

Alinsky's conflict strategies may also be assessed on their ability to broaden local citizen participation. Hunter and Suttles (1972:63–64) note that Alinsky organizations were among the few community organizations in Chicago to "succeed in getting high administrators together with them at the bargaining table and to acknowledge the legitimacy of the organizations' representational role." They concluded that what was remarkable was not the limited success of Alinsky organization but the difficulty in establishing regularized contact between government, business, and community organization. A modest claim is that Alinsky organizations were, on occasion, able to win recognition for their right to participate in extra-community policy making.

In conclusion, Alinsky's work offers a promising source to further our understanding of community processes and to suggest strategies for the development of existing communities. Alinsky's contribution to community development includes his recognition that an active community organization is necessary to: (1) unify diverse local interests and to establish common community-wide ties; and (2) mobilize local resources to broaden community participation in city-wide decision making. An awareness of Alinsky's goals of community cohesion and political participation may aid in interpreting his imaginative tactics and in providing a realistic set of standards for the evaluation of community organizations. Alinsky succeeded in generating interest in local community organization. The next task is to incorporate his insights into the cumulative growth of community development theory and practice.

REFERENCES

Alinsky, S. D. "Community analysis and organization." *American Journal of*
1941   *Sociology* 46:797–808.

Alinsky, S. D. "The war on poverty — political pornography." *The Journal of*
1965   *Social Issues* 21:41–47.

Alinsky, S. D. "What is the role of community organization in bargaining with
1968   the establishment for health care services?" In John C. Norman,
          Medicine in the Ghetto. New York: Appleton-Century-Crofts.

Alinsky, S. D. *Reveille for Radicals.* Chicago: University of Chicago Press.
1969

Alinsky, S. D. *Rules for Radicals.* New York: Random House.
1971

Alinsky, S. D. "Interview with Saul Alinsky." *Playboy* (March):52–178.
1972

Bailey, R., Jr. *Radicals in Urban Politics.* Chicago: The University of Chicago
1972   Press.

Bates, F. L. and Bacon, L. "The community as a social system." *Social Forces*
1972   50:371–379.

Effrat, M.   "Approaches to community: conflicts and complementarities." In
1974   M. Effrat (ed.), *The Community: Approaches and Applications*. New
           York: The Free Press.

Fish, J. H. *Black Power/White Control*. Princeton, New Jersey: Princeton Uni-
1973   versity Press.

Gleb, J. and Sardell, A. "Strategies for the powerless." *American Behavioral Scien-
1974   tist*   17:507–530.

Hunter, A. and Suttles, G. "The expanding community of limited liability." In
1972   Gerald Suttles (ed.), *The Social Construction of Communities*. Chi-
           cago: The University of Chicago Press, pp. 44–81.

Irvine, B. K. "Saul Alinsky: a history of the Chelsea Community Council, 1956–
1967   1960." Master's Thesis, Columbia University, 1967.

Jacobs, J. "The uses of city neighborhoods." In R. Gutman and D. Popenoe (eds.),
1970   *Neighborhood, City, and Metropolis: An Integrated Reader in Urban
           Sociology*. New York: Random House, pp. 819–837.

Lancourt, J. "Evaluation and analysis of goals, tactics and results of citizen action
1977   organizations: the Alinsky model." Ph.D. Dissertation, Brandeis Uni-
           versity, June, 1977.

Long, Norton E. "The local community as an ecology of games." *American Jour-
1958   nal of Sociology*   44:251–261.

Meenagan, T. M. "Community delineation: alternative methods and problems."
1972   *Sociology and Social Research*   56:345–355.

Reitzes, D. C. and Reitzes, D. C. "Saul D. Alinsky: a neglect source but promising
1980   resource." Paper presented at annual meetings of the American So-
           ciological Association, New York.

Reissman, F. "Self-help among the poor: new styles of social action." *Transaction*
1965   2:32–37.

Silberman, C. E. *Crisis in Black and White*. New York: Random House.
1964

Walton, J. "Community power and the retreat from politics: full circle after
1976   twenty years." *Social Problems*   23:292–303.

Warren, R. L. *Social Change and Human Purpose: Toward Understanding and
1977   Action*. Chicago: Rand McNally College.

Wilkinson, K. P. "A field-theory perspective for community development re-
1972   search." *Rural Sociology*   37:43–52.

Wilkinson, K. P. "Social well-being and community." *Journal of the Community
1979   Development Society*   10:5–16.

Section 2
Planning and Policy Development
Introduction

Community development does not happen by itself, it requires strenuous and time-consuming efforts by community residents. The complicated process of community development necessitates the participation of many community-based entities, including but not limited to local government agencies, area development corporations, neighborhood associations, business organizations, and a variety of youth and citizen groups.

While involving residents in the development process seems like a necessity, it is not an easy undertaking as "residents often are more concerned with daily tasks than thinking about, and coming up with, a vision of their community's future" (Green & Haines, p. 78). Because of the involvement of a wide range of participants with varying view points and perspectives, and the complexity and technical dimensions of the process, private consultants, university faculty, or other specialists will often help facilitate the planning and development of community development programs. This section includes seminal articles on planning and policy development published in *Community Development*.

Communities, naturally, widely differ in social, economic, geographic, and other demographic factors. No single approach to planning for the development of diverse communities exists so each community must formulate a unique set of development strategies. These strategies should be carefully crafted, reflect area assets and needs, be supported by local resources, and, in most cases, be implemented by the locality.

Community development policies and strategies are operationalized in many ways. They can be part of city government's comprehensive plan, a business organization's programmatic outreach, part of the programs of various community-based organizations, or contained in a stand-alone document.

Successful community development strategies face numerous challenges and obstacles before they are completed. Unfortunately, not all community development strategies succeed in reaching their goals and objectives. Identifying successful and workable strategies, policies, and programs, and describing their formulation are critical to community development. From its early beginnings, then, contributors to *Community Development* examined and researched the development of community strategies, programs, and policies. The authors provided guidance to practitioners, based on applied research methods, and careful analysis and observation, on the planning and development of community improvement strategies.

The following section in this volume shows that contributions to the thinking on planning and policy development in *Community Development* have a long history. These contributions began in the early years of the journal and continued well into the 21st century. Clearly, the planning and development of strategies and policies have been important contributions to the field.

While many articles in the following section address the planning and development of strategies and policies from a rural perspective, the processes, methods, frameworks, and concepts also apply to urban areas. Concepts like Smart Growth, place-based development, sustainability, entrepreneurship, community capitals, collaboratives, and measurement, which the authors discuss in detail, can be used in development efforts regardless of urban or rural setting, or in different size places. Likewise, they are easily adapted to independent self-contained cities, suburbs, or urban neighborhoods.

Many articles in this section rely on case study methodologies as their research approach when discussing rural development planning and policy. While the application of the findings from this approach to other research may seem limited, the authors make strong cases for broad-based applicability to planning and development issues. Taken as a whole, the accumulation of these case studies in *Community Development* provides a solid foundation for advancing the understanding of the planning and policy development process which is a major contribution.

Several themes emerge in the following articles. Arguably, the most important theme is that a range of development strategies is possible in most communities. Community developers have choices in adopting specific strategies which make them more diverse. The articles explain how engaging residents in the planning process can identify specific development strategies.

The Community Capitals Framework (CCF), as discussed in the opening article by Emery and Flora, is often recognized as the theoretical foundation for diversification of development strategies. They used the CCF to track community transformation in a holistic perspective that resulted from a specific state program. A goal of community developers is to assist in transforming communities in a positive manner that reflects the vision of residents.

Ayres, Leistritz, and Stone continue this theme of community strategy diversification by arguing for and demonstrating how developers can employ a retail development approach. They suggest several ways that a community can implement a retail development tactic to complement its strategic portfolio. Their recommendations include providing technical and financial assistance to local business owners, and the development of processes for the future transfer of business ownership. This article informed community developers of the emerging local strategy of retaining and expanding of existing business in a community.

In another article that addresses the need to diversify local development strategies, Goudy and Tait demonstrated how a community survey can be employed in new ways. While attitude surveys have been used in many community development efforts, Goudy and Tait demonstrated how it would be used to uncover new and innovative strategies. Their field research resulted in recreation improvement and housing development, which were little used action initiatives for the time (1979).

The Lichtenstein, Lyons, and Kutzhanova article also shed light on ways that community developers can diversify their local strategies. In particular, they focused on the increasingly important and popular strategy of facilitating local entrepreneurship. They provided guidance on the creation and enhancing of entrepreneurial communities, which possess the ability to foster new business, and help expand emerging local businesses. Entrepreneurial development is accepted as a critical local strategy.

Community engagement surfaced as a second cross-cutting theme in the planning and policy development articles. In addition to the authors noted above, others in this section discuss this theme as a critical component in the community development process. As early as 1972, Anderson and Catalano noted a "need for vastly more involvement of non-traditional planners" ...[and] "productive interaction" among regional development agencies and organizations (p. 83). Pulver also elaborated on the importance of engagement by discussing how community volunteers, working with a community development professional, can assess development needs and community assets to identify and implement unique local strategies.

Organizational collaboration appeared as a third theme in the articles on planning and policy development. In addition to the Anderson and Catalano article discussed above, which explored interaction among development entities, Zeuli, Freshwater, Markley, and Barkley provide an analytical framework for examining the role of regional and local organizational collaboration in community development. The nature of this relationship continues to be studied by researchers, as it is an important part of the entire community development process, especially in rural areas. Understanding the nature and structure of organizational collaborations among communities and area entities also interests public administration and local government management scholars (Blair & Janousek, 2013.)

Honadle, in her examination of a failed USDA program, shows that organizational collaboration does not come easily and is complicated by federalism. In particular, she examined legislation passed in Washington, DC: USDA's Rural Collaborative Investment Program. This program did not recognize the complexity of rural communities and failed to provide localities with the ability to plan holistic community development strategies. Honadle argues that communities should have the flexibility to design collaborative relationships that reflect local needs and structures and rural development policies and programs, should not be housed exclusively in the USDA.

The final theme in articles in this section can be labeled as innovations in planning and policy development. These authors highlight emerging issues and promote creative approaches to community development. For instance, while sustainability now constitutes a widely accepted "critical feature in the community development process" (Green & Haines, p. 57.), that was not always the case.

In 1995, Shaffer, in a lead article in the journal, offered a framework for sustainable economic development in communities. He argued for a "reframing of issues... as a method to create new options" (Shaffer, p. 145). In later editions, other articles on innovative approaches to community development were published. Daniels in 2001 connected an emerging planning concept designed to manage urban sprawl, Smart Growth, to broader community development practice. In general, Smart Growth employs a comprehensive and collaborative approach to community development that focuses on infrastructure development and sustainable practices.

Bridger and Alter (2008) challenged traditional community development efforts and offered an innovative approach that integrates economic, environmental, and social factors. Using interactional techniques, Bridger and Alter argue, gives rural communities the ability to develop strategies that strengthen regional competitiveness. The authors note that global factors are transforming rural America, and in uncertain times, this mandates the employment of creative strategies to community development.

Continuing in the theme of innovation in community development, a more recent article (2013) by Blanke and Walzer describes the need for program evaluation and measurement. Closely related to concepts of sustainability, they argue that in an environment with limited resources and the need for accountability, community developers need to be able to demonstrate the impact of programs. Their article provides community developers with tools to develop an evaluation and measurement program.

As the articles in this section show, the planning and development of community policy continues to evolve. *Community Development* in the past 50 years has taken a leadership role in publishing cutting-edge articles in this important dimension of community development, and will continue to fulfill that mission. The themes that emerged from this section – engaging residents in the formulation of community strategies, formulating diverse approaches to community improvement, facilitating collaboration among local and regional development organizations, and employing innovation in development efforts – are commonly used in the practice of public administration, the planning field, and the policy development and implementation process. It is clear that as an interdisciplinary journal, *Community Development* has made significant contributions.

REFERENCES

Anderson, M. & Catalano A. 1972. An effective process for rural planning. *Journal of the Community Development Society* 3(2).

Blair, R. & Janousek, C. 2013. Collaborative mechanisms in interlocal cooperation: A longitudinal examination. *State and Local Government Review* 45(4): 268–282.

Green, G. & Haines, A. 2016. *Asset Building and Community Development*. Fourth Edition. Thousand Oaks, CA: Sage.

Shaffer, R. 1995. Achieving sustainable economic development in communities. *Journal of the Community Development Society* 26(2): 145–154.

Spiraling-Up: Mapping Community Transformation with Community Capitals Framework

Mary Emery and Cornelia Flora

This paper uses the Community Capitals Framework (CCF) to look at community change from a systems perspective. We find that social capital—both bonding and bridging—is the critical resource that reversed the downward spiral of loss to an upward spiral of hope—a process we call "spiraling-up." Focusing on the example of a change process implemented in Nebraska, HomeTown Competitiveness, we delineate the assets invested, created, and expanded by the project. We also apply the CCF to understanding the flow among the capitals and the impact of this flow on community capacity to initiate and sustain a process of change, particularly in building social capital.

Social capital is a critical community characteristic. It can influence, as well as be influenced by, the stock and flows of other capitals. By examining the interaction among community capitals, as well as the investment from the outside in different capitals, we can better understand the critical role of social capital. By analyzing one case of such investments in the context of creating a new system of positive community change, we illustrate how identifying community capitals and strategically increasing capitals stocks resulted in a spiraling up of those capitals as they begin building on one another. We apply the Community Capitals Framework (CCF) to analyze a comprehensive community development effort, the HomeTown Competitiveness program. Using field data and interviews, we follow how capital investments were made and with what results.

In July 2001, the National Rural Funders Collaborative (NRFC) widely distributed a call for collaborative strategic proposals to "reverse patterns of neglect and disinvestments in rural America." The NRFC asked for collaborations of regional funders and at least two organizations or agencies to develop place-based strategies (as opposed to an individually-oriented program) to reduce poverty in a specific rural region.

The possibility of garnering $750,000 over a three-year period, coupled with increased concern for declines in rural population on the part of the state of Nebraska, brought together three Nebraska-based not-for-profits to initiate formally HomeTown Competitiveness (HTC). Members of HTC focused on an integrated strategic approach to reverse the population and per-capita income decline in rural communities on the Great Plains. Thus, they combined the strengths of the three groups: leadership development (Heartland

Mary Emery is the Associate Director of the North Central Regional Center for Rural Development. She can be reached at 107 Curtiss Hall, Iowa State University, Ames, IA 50011. Phone: (515) 294-2878, E-mail: memery@ iastate.edu. Cornelia Butler Flora is a Charles F. Curtiss Distinguished Professor of Agriculture and Sociology and the Director of the North Central Regional Center for Rural Development. She can be reached at 108 Curtiss Hall, Iowa State University, Ames, IA 50011. Phone: (515) 294-1329, E-mail: cflora@iastate.edu. The authors would like to thank the Editors for their help with this manuscript.

Center for Community Leadership Development), entrepreneurship development (RUPRI Center for Rural Entrepreneurship), and community foundations (Nebraska Community Foundation). Their focus on stemming youth out-migration meant that they looked for ways to include youth in each of these groups.

The three organizations had already created place-based strategies, and the leaders of all three groups had roots in rural Nebraska. The leaders of the organizations had worked together informally and formally in different capacities for many years, and the mission statements of the three organizations were compatible. They were well connected in the state and the nation, having achieved individual reputations for effectiveness and integrity. The newly formed HTC thus had high levels of both bonding and bridging social capital as they began to implement the integrated strategy (Emery, 2003).

HTC was one of five collaboratives awarded a $50,000 learning partner grant in 2002, which was renewed for another year at $50,000 in 2003. The second grant allowed HTC to devote time and resources to support collaborative development and to integrate its separate strands: philanthropy to support entrepreneurship through strong local leadership. HTC formalized its four-part strategy: (1) to increase philanthropy by directing rural wealth transfers to community foundations; (2) to retain youth in the community by including them in leadership, philanthropy, and entrepreneurship; (3) to increase leadership capacity through inclusive leadership development; and (4) to strengthen local economies by identifying and building on local assets, particularly through intergeneration business continuity and innovative business opportunities.

The NRFC used the Community Capitals Framework (CCF) as an analytical tool to determine the effectiveness of its investments in addressing structural conditions of rural poverty via capacity-building, leading to increased assets for rural families and communities, the transformation of rural leadership through expanded and inclusive leadership pools, and increased opportunities for families to attain self sufficiency. The NRFC used the CCF to analyze how community capitals were used in the transformative strategy.

We looked at HTC's approach by using the CCF to document how the strategy in one community reversed the spiral of decline that has gripped many rural communities. Decline in financial capital may trigger the downward spiral. The loss of an industry or various firms in a particular region makes it more difficult to mobilize political capital, which stimulates additional losses in human and social capitals in a vicious cycle of despair. The HTC approach sought to reverse this spiral through a series of public and private interventions we call "spiraling-up." In this paper, we analyze one of the first communities, Valley County, Nebraska, in which HTC officially worked to show the degree to which HTC's integrated, collaborative strategy effectively and systematically increased all the community capitals in a mutually-reinforcing spiral of community development. Through this spiraling up process, we identify critical investments in social capital as the entry point for community change.

Community Capitals Framework

The Community Capitals Framework (CCF) offers a way to analyze community and economic development efforts from a systems perspective by identifying the assets in each capital (stock), the types of capital invested (flow), the interaction among the capitals, and the resulting impacts across capitals. The NRFC analysis includes indicators of seven different components of community capital: natural, cultural, human, social, political, financial, and built capitals. The NRFC chose this approach because of its emphasis on assets (rather than needs or deficits) and its focus on investments (see Figure 1).

    1. Natural capital refers to those assets that abide in a particular location, including weather, geographic isolation, natural resources, amenities, and natural beauty.

Natural capital shapes the cultural capital connected to place (Pretty, 1998; Constanza, et al., 1997).

2. Cultural capital reflects the way people "know the world" and how they act within it, as well as their traditions and language. Cultural capital influences what voices are heard and listened to, which voices have influence in what areas, and how creativity, innovation, and influence emerge and are nurtured. Hegemony privileges the cultural capital of dominant groups (Bourdieu, 1986; Flora et al., 2004; Bebbington, 1999).

3. Human capital is understood to include the skills and abilities of people to develop and enhance their resources and to access outside resources and bodies of knowledge in order to increase their understanding, identify promising practices, and to access data for community-building. Human capital addresses the leadership's ability to "lead across differences," to focus on assets, to be inclusive and participatory, and to act proactively in shaping the future of the community or group (Becker, 1964; Flora et al., 2004).

4. Social capital reflects the connections among people and organizations or the social "glue" to make things, positive or negative, happen. Bonding social capital refers to those close redundant ties that build community cohesion. Bridging social capital involves loose ties that bridge among organizations and communities (Narayan, 1999; Granovetter, 1973 & 1985). A specific configuration of social capital—entrepreneurial social capital (ESI)—is related to community economic development (Flora & Flora, 1993; Flora et al., 1997). ESI includes inclusive internal and external networks, local mobilization of resources, and willingness to consider alternative ways of reaching goals.

5. Political capital reflects access to power, organizations, connection to resources and power brokers (Flora et al., 2004). Political capital also refers to the ability of people to find their own voice and to engage in actions that contribute to the well being of their community (Aigner et al., 2001).

6. Financial capital refers to the financial resources available to invest in community capacity-building, to underwrite the development of businesses, to support civic and social entrepreneurship, and to accumulate wealth for future community development (Lorenz, 1999).

7. Built capital, finally, includes the infrastructure supporting these activities (Flora et al., 2004).

Figure 1. Community Capitals

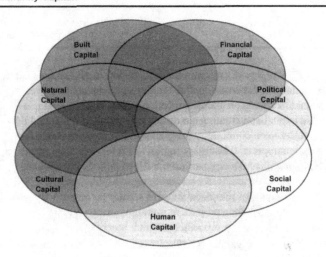

In applying the CCF to HTC, we thought to demonstrate increased capacity by showing that a project's strategies invested assets from vital areas (human, social, and financial capital) resulting in increased assets among those capitals as well as others. Others using the CCF had determined that the increase in specific assets, while helpful to the community, might not have an impact on overall capacity. Guiterrez-Montez (2005) found that the flow of assets across capitals—that is, human capital invested in a project leading to increases in the stock of assets in financial, political, cultural, and social capital—can initiate an ongoing process of assets building on assets, leading to the effect of an upward spiral. Or, as many have observed, "success builds on success." Our study of HTC in Valley County provides additional support for the notion that capacity cannot be measured merely by increases in stocks of assets within the specific capitals, but requires an increase in the flow of assets that build stock in additional capitals. As we mapped the strategies connected to HTC, we observed examples of processes and strategies that led to increases in assets across the capitals (see Figure 2).

Figure 2. The Spiraling of Capital Assets

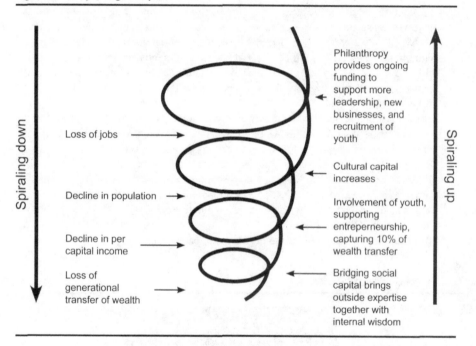

In the spiral-down period, the community declined in all capitals, resulting in a loss of hope and direction. Both human capital and financial capital decreased, as fewer people were able to make a living on increasingly large farms. Young people left the county, decreasing social capital and creating a culture of despair and resignation. Political capital was reduced to reliance on commodity programs and lobbying through farm organizations for increased price supports. The infrastructure deteriorated. This situation corresponds to the theory of *cumulative causation*. Gunnar Myrdal (1957) formulated this theory that states: "The place that loses assets, for whatever reason, will continue to lose them through system effects." Additionally, the place that, for whatever reason, gains assets will attract other assets, which helps explain why there is an increasing inequality that is place-based.

"Spiraling-up" represents a process by which assets gained increase the likelihood that other assets will also be gained (Gutierrez, 2005). In our model using community capitals, as one capital is increased, it is easier for increases, instead of declines, in the other community capitals to occur. However, the usual rural development strategy of beginning with infusions of financial capital or built capital is often not cumulative. Spiraling-up reverses declines in assets through a similar *cumulative causation* process in which asset growth becomes a self-reinforcing cycle of increasing opportunity and community well being. Our research looked at the spiraling-up period, and how cumulative causation helped to explain how increase in one capital can lead to increases in the others. Our contention is that the best entry point to spiraling-up is social capital.

METHODOLOGY

We collected data to analyze community capitals based on interviews with community leaders in 2003 and 2004, with HTC partners in 2003 and 2004, from project partner Websites and reports, and from participant observations in July 2003. In addition, project partners reviewed an earlier version of this paper and provided feedback.

In 2000, Valley County, Nebraska, had a population of 4,647, a 10% decline since 1990. Ord, the county seat and commercial center, had a 2000 population of 2,269. Typical of rural counties in the Great Plains, the population was aging rapidly, with high out-migration of young people.

Valley County's labor force of 2,440, according to 2002 state employment reports, experienced only a 2.6% unemployment rate, masking a serious problem of underemployment. The county, however, was also home to high number of self-employed people and small business owners, including ranchers, farmers, and shopkeepers. Manufacturing was limited, and government, both medical and educational, was—and continues to be—among the largest employers.

In the late 1990s, the County Commission passed a resolution to fund the Valley County Economic Development Council (VCEDC) and to hire a professional staff person to manage its efforts and to staff the Chamber. Determination, good intentions, and money, however, were not enough to turn around decades of decline. The leadership of Valley County realized they needed help to identify how best to use their limited resources for the most strategic outcomes. When offered the invitation to join the Collaborative funded by the National Rural Funders Collaborative (NRFC) and to implement HTC's integrated strategy, they welcomed the opportunity. Since 2002, the newly-created collaborative of community and economic development practitioners and leaders in Valley County (HTC team) has worked together proactively to shape a future that not only mitigates the effects of their current economic situation, but also reaches out to reshape a "landscape of loss" (Nothdruft, 2002) into one of "opportunity" compatible with the region's assets.

Implementing HTC in Valley County, Nebraska

The HTC approach began with an assessment process developed in cooperation with community leaders. Recognizing the dearth of local resources available to rural communities, the collaborative worked with community leaders to identify specifically targeted strategies that emerged from the assessment process related to leadership development, entrepreneurship, youth, and wealth transfer. When undertaken in unison, the strategies created a an upward spiral of growing assets across capitals that reversed the downward spiral of declining assets found in many distressed rural community. This approach required commitment to an intentional and focused use of scarce resources that became strategic in the force, depth, and breadth of their impact as indicated by changes in the various capitals. The place-based focus of the approach allowed each community to choose the strategies that best utilized their strengths (investing their assets) in addressing opportunities to transform their landscape into opportunity.

Community leaders focused on the flight of young people, agreeing that it was not just the call of the city that compelled them to migrate; it is also the lack of opportunity that drove them away. The Center for Rural Entrepreneurship developed a formula that advocates how small towns can design efforts to halt this trend. Using existing data on population change, Valley County calculated that it needed to retain or encourage the return of three high school graduates per year to stop the overall population decline, a realistic target for action (Emery et al., 2004).

Based on this assessment, community leaders decided on several strategies. To mobilize community members to work for a new future, they began a leadership development program that included students from the high school and created task forces around each of the main strategies. Although Valley County had a small group of dedicated residents committed to "making a difference," all agreed that leadership development was their greatest challenge. Two years into the project, interviews with important leaders indicated that they still identified leadership as the most critical element for success (Emery, 2003). Working to increase the number of people committed to building a new future for Valley County, as well as their skills to do so effectively, was the cornerstone upon which other strategies depended.

Each of the three strategies used in Valley County included a "youth" component. The local HTC leadership team looked for opportunities to include young people; the local HTC entrepreneurship team found ways to help young people gain experience as entrepreneurs and to see entrepreneurship as a viable choice for a career; and the local HTC wealth transfer team recruited youth volunteers. Local leaders, however, saw a further need to develop a youth team to coordinate the youth-related activities and to launch a "youth initiative." This team worked on strategies to attract young professionals to the community to work in expanding businesses or to take over firms whose owners were ready to retire.

Using data developed on the wealth transfer predicted in Valley County, the Nebraska Community Foundation developed a reasonable target for capturing 5% of this transferred wealth, or $6,470,000 between 2002 and 2010, into a community foundation capable of funding future community and economic development efforts (Nebraska Community Foundation, 2004).

Finally, many rural communities invested resources in economic development, but lacked a strategic plan for investing those resources to create viable employment opportunities and to develop businesses. Using strategies developed by the Center for Rural Entrepreneurship[1] and the results of a business survey, the VCEDC directed its energies to support two specific groups: (1) the inter-generational transfer of small businesses, particularly those on Main Street and (2) companies with the potential to "break-through" to a broader product line or a larger market and to grow new jobs rapidly. Prior to this intervention, the VCEDC had a strategic plan detailing over 20 specific economic development goals, but it lacked a method to determine the value of its investment in any one goal.

Together, these strategies provided VCEDC with specific attainable goals allowing it to target its scarce resources for maximum effect. Its leaders felt that together, these strategies addressed the root causes of rural decline and offered the community a way to work toward a healthy and sustainable future.

Implementing HTC in Valley County: Strategy Implementation and Results

The HTC strategy had found fertile ground in Valley County. Previously, Valley County had passed a local option tax that committed resources and personnel to create new jobs and protect existing businesses. Earlier, the Nebraska Community Foundation had begun work in the area by forming the Valley County Foundation Fund. These efforts, together with the following readiness factors (Emery, 2003), created an environment ready for change. Leaders knew things had to change. Outside agencies coached local advocates on the threats and possibilities. Participants worked to set up "wealth capture" options and to identify internal resources to aid in that change

Community Capitals Stocks and Flows

In her study of the effect of forest fires on community assets, Gutierrez-Montes (2005) found that the downward spiral of decreasing assets within the community had an accumulative effect. The fire destroyed the environment, which led to decreased employment, which led to poverty and health problems, which began the destruction of cultural and social capital within the community, which led to a decline in maintaining roads and other infrastructure, etc. The downward spiral was reversed when the local people and outside consultants came together as equals to combine their knowledge and change the direction of the spiral. The resultant actions led to an upward spiral of increasing assets across the capitals. Social capital played a similar role in the HTC project—bridging social capital facilitated mobilizing resources that increased the stocks of other capitals.

We analyzed how each of the three HTC projects, which consisted of flows of capital through holistic community capacity-building, contributed to increased stocks of community capitals in Valley County. The changes in community capital that we measured qualitatively and quantitatively were systematically sorted into the appropriate community capital, and we found that each of the three projects contributed to the spiraling up of community assets, and that the three projects not only stimulated the other projects, but also reinforced them as well.

Leadership and capacity building

Using a common process for community leadership development, the local HTC team set up an eight-month program. Sixteen people, including four high school students, reserved one day each month to participate in a program to increase skills, create awareness of leadership opportunities, and expand their understanding of the County.

A second and third class was also well attended and generated similar evaluation results. The local leadership team worked to coordinate activities and information among community groups and to recognize the role of volunteers and local leaders (Emery, 2004b).

We found that community leaders invested their assets in social capital, both bonding and bridging to recruit students and access human capital resources for instruction. They invested local and partner assets in human and financial capital to offer the course. These investments led not only to increases in the capitals invested, but also to other capitals, thus contributing to the spiraling-up process. Of particular importance, we saw changes in cultural capital regarding community norms and values about participating in the community and supporting local leaders. We observed the beginning of new assets in political capital as interviewees reported that people outside the traditional leadership structure were finding a voice in community affairs.

Leadership development and capacity-building undergirded the integrated HTC strategy. Without changes in the traditional leadership structure and actors, the community could not have mobilized citizens to support changes. The collaborative partners provided technical assistance and coaching that encouraged 35 people to graduate from two leadership classes. Buoyed by this success, the leadership team promised to offer the class each year. They will increase the value of the program each year as they learn from their experiences. The team was dedicated to long-term development of community human capital. The involvement and support of youth was particularly important to the team's sense of accomplishment. The leadership team reported that more people increased their involvement in community groups, and the leadership core expanded somewhat to include new voices.

The impacts these leaders hoped to see in the future included developing a supportive culture in which leaders no longer risk their businesses by running for office and in which many people from different walks of life participate in leadership roles. The leaders are working with the Nebraska Community Foundation to look at ways the Foundation can support diversified leadership development through scholarships. Already, the community supported the involvement of more youth and adult-to-youth interaction. Leaders have also increased their ability to interact with state and local government agencies, as well as with other agencies connected to their issues.

The experience in Valley County has changed the behaviors of some institutions whose management saw how local leaders succeeded in turning around long-term decline. For example, officials of the utility companies now provide financial resources to support the HTC program in Valley County and in other locations as well. The leadership team saw an emerging outcome of the project in that more community members understand that each person can make a difference and a contribution to positive community change. By building on their own history, the team hoped to nurture a culture of working together for the good of the whole community. Indeed, the local leaders realized that the community was working to overcome historical conflicts that prevented successful community capacity-building in the past.

Local leaders recognized that more people were willing to run for office and participate as leaders in the community. In the 2004 election, all offices had at least two candidates running, in contrast to previous elections when recruiting just one candidate to run for office was difficult. The experience in Valley County changed how people think about its leaders, what they do, and how they do it. The leaders are making progress in including all groups in the community, so all have a voice. A big success for them was the willingness of a woman to run for county office. Finally, the ultimate success of this effort will be evident in the long-term ability of local teams to generate and encourage o the recruitment of new leaders and increase participation within the community leadership over the next decade.

Capturing funds from the transfer of wealth

HTC organized training for financial managers and attorneys to help people understand the options available for estate planning. In addition, collaborating agencies coached the community on revitalizing the community foundation, recruiting volunteers beginning a massive effort to promote community awareness. They attained their 5% goal in 2004, and set a goal of capturing 10% of calculated transfer of wealth by 2010.

The primary inputs to the strategy to capture 5% of the wealth transfer involved increasing the human capital of financial planners, attorneys, and real estate professionals to develop and to enhance skills in charitable giving. In addition, the human capital of the local foundation increased when members received training and coaching on how to ask for gifts and how to make giving back to the community an important part of everyday life in Valley County. In addition, however, foundation members worked hard to make philanthropy a community norm as measured by the percent of the population participating in giving.

Consequentially, the Foundation learned techniques from other organizations and groups on how to focus on giving strategically. That is, projects must be selected to build local assets to achieve a sustainable future instead of selecting "band-aid" and "feel-good" projects. The leaders recognized the limitations of investing in projects like community parks when, without a change in direction, there would be few children to enjoy the parks. Developing indicators to measure the consequence of their investment was critical to success. Recently, the foundation assisted twenty young professionals in moving to the community (Stier, 2005).

Finally, Valley County leaders are working on developing an umbrella foundation to organize giving campaigns and to share management expenses, thus formalizing the emerging social capital focused on community giving. Under the umbrella foundation, community participation will be a strong indicator of how well the community has matured beyond previous conflict and generated value-added capacity for working together in creating a sustainable and healthy community that will, in turn, increase stock in cultural, human, and social capital.

The HTC team set a new goal of capturing 10% of the wealth transfer. Again, the role of bridging social capital is important in blending the outside expertise on wealth transfer with the local leaders and their knowledge of place. The investment of social capital, human capital, and financial capital to support the launch of this strategy created an upward spiral across the capitals, in particular changes in cultural capital that encourage people to give back to the community. Both human and social capitals expanded as more people became involved in the work either as volunteers or as donors. Long-term investment of local assets in achieving their wealth transfer goal will provide financial capital to support self-development in perpetuity. Used wisely to support the community's vision of the future, financial and cultural capitals can sustain the upward spiral well into the future.

Economic development and entrepreneurship

HTC worked with the VCEDC to prioritize several essential strategies, thus enabling the staff to focus on those most likely to make a difference in the near future. Training local team members to conduct interviews with local businesses helped the team to identify several strong firms with skills that they were willing to share with others to build their business development assets, thus expanding the human and social capital of the local team. These interviews aided the local team in identifying those businesses with high job growth potential and determining how the team might best assist them in their growth. In the process of interviewing businesses and collecting data on other businesses, the team uncovered a pool of 25 businesses with some potential for fast growth or generational transfer. Targeting several businesses with the potential for inter-generational transfer not only helped the retiring generation preserve the assets they worked hard to develop, but also assisted with capital needs of the younger generation, related or otherwise, enabling the business to continue successfully as an asset for the community. The team looked at the profile of business ownership in Valley County to determine the best strategy for creating good jobs. By offering hands-on technical assistance to these businesses, the VCEDC experienced an immediate return on its investment while increasing the visibility and importance of their efforts.

To date, the local entrepreneurship team can show some outcomes with several businesses in terms of job creation and work toward successful business successions. The team worked to revive a local investment club to use its capital to support local business development. Finally, the team identified ways to encourage young people to see entrepreneurship as positive career choice with growth potential in Valley County. A local person was hired as an entrepreneurship coach to benefit young people and existing businesses. In spring 2005, the HTC entrepreneurship coach worked with high school and middle school youth to develop business ventures that culminated in a business fair that netted thirty young entrepreneurs over $4,000 in sales (Rural Electric Nebraskan, July 2005: 15).

The HTC team hopes that the long-term impact of their work will result in a community that is supportive of entrepreneurial efforts and small but growing businesses. Additionally, HTC worked with the VCEDC to understand the notion of regional competitiveness better.[2]

The entrepreneurial coach's portfolio of active business clients grew to over 100 businesses. The excitement in the community about future opportunities helped it win a major investment by an ethanol plant from an outside business (Stier, 2005). The community's success in business development and support are reflected in the growth of local businesses and jobs and an increase in per capita income. To reach its goals, the community eventually wants to work on a regional economic development approach that supports the development of business clusters and successful global marketing.

Previously, local leaders sought to generate jobs through "industrial attraction" alone with little or no return on this investment after the initial success with the call center. , Bridging social capital brought outside entrepreneurship development expertise, together with local volunteers and businesses, offering a new vision of the community's potential. The processes continued to generate new bonding and bridging social capital as additional entrepreneurs and volunteers joined in. Furthermore, all partners expanded their knowledge of what interaction worked to create good jobs in rural America.

HTC provided local leaders and the local entrepreneurship team with technical assistance and coaching on how to work with local businesses thus increasing human capital. The interviews with local business owners generated new social capital. Success led to increased cultural capital as the community became more supportive of entrepreneurial efforts and local businesses. The growth in businesses and jobs expanded financial capital with implications for expanding human capital as incomes increase and families have additional options. Changes in cultural capital provided impetus to continue an upward spiral of asset creation as community members found reasons to support local business and received support to follow their own ideas. Their efforts have influenced institutions outside the community, such as utility companies, rural development programs, and state economic development agencies to value investing resources in entrepreneurial economic development strategies.

Spiraling-Up

The spiraling-up caused by building on existing assets included expanding human capital not only in skills and knowledge but also in the way local people now see themselves as part of the community. The project increased social capital assets by creating opportunities for youth and adults to work together and by bringing more people into the leadership arena. Finally, the project modified cultural capital to foster an increased acceptance of youth and other non-traditional leaders as important actors within the community.

This particular change process is still very recent in Valley County. The increase in community capitals was very promising and demonstrated the strategic nature of the intervention. While inputs and activities focused on investing primarily in human, financial, and social capitals, these investments showed immediate increases in the stock of most of the capitals (see Table 1). Clearly, by carefully targeting resources and inputs in a few areas, primarily in building human capital and encouraging the development of social capital through leadership development and foundation development, the limited resources systemically influenced five capitals. Eventually VCEDC and the local teams will have the capacity to influence all seven capitals as they work to build a healthy, sustainable future for Valley County.

Both leadership (human capital) and social capital develop in relation to specific goals rather than as broadly framed capacity development activities. Thus, HTC built leadership and community capacity to achieve wealth capture goals, expand entrepreneurial activities, and attract youth. In this way, leadership training was explicitly tied to community capacity development rather than focused on developing the human capital of individuals. By incorporating the components of the three areas simultaneously, the synergistic design of the project led to changes in all areas, eventually offering the potential to create system change.

The community's mobilization of social and then financial capital were vital first steps in reversing the spiral of decline. First, leaders came together (using existing bonding social capital) to commit to change and to find ways of financing that at change. Investing

Table 1. Changes in community capitals as a result of HTC

Capital	Change in capital
Human	35 graduates of leadership classes report increased skills
	Increase in volunteer hours
	Increased knowledge of entrepreneurship
	Financial planners, attorneys, real estate professional develop/enhance skills to facilitate charitable giving.
	New professionals move to community
Social	New opportunities for youth and adults to work together in projects through the youth development team, leadership training, and entrepreneurship training
	Community overcomes historical conflicts
	Community works together more as evidenced in participation on teams and in increased volunteer hours
	Community accepts change more readily
	More organizations and groups are linked together through the participation of members in teams
	Community foundation leadership becomes an effective team as indicated by the increase in the number of people volunteering, the number giving, and the dollars donated
	Community Foundation connects to other organizations within Nebraska
	Community networks support youth entrepreneurship and generational transfer as indicated in the work with several businesses to plan for succession
	Local businesses linked to multiple agencies for technical support
	Valley County connects to other entrepreneurial communities through participation in HTC field days
Political	Leadership diversified, more women and young people run for office.
	Local elections have at least two candidates running.
	Leaders increase connections to and relationships with state and local government
	Regional economic development planning underway
	State policy more supportive of entrepreneurship as indicated by financial support for HTC in Valley County
	Business owners participate more in state and local government

Table 1 cont'd. Changes in community capitals as a result of HTC

Financial	Increased donations to community groups
	Board of the community foundation is strengthened
	Scholarships created to support leadership training for youth and other unheard voices
	Local Foundation has access to additional funders, state agencies, and the Nebraska Community Foundation.
	Foundation exceeds its target in bequests and gifts
	An increase in the number of community members giving to the Foundation
	Local investment club revived
	Ten businesses change hands (rather than close)
	Formation of business clusters
	Local businesses increase links to global market
	Retail sales increase 20% compared to state's 16.2%
	Personal income increases 11.8% compared to 4.6% for the state
	Per capital income increases 13.9% compared to 3.8% for the state
	25 entrepreneurs increase assets/cash flow
	Investment club invests in local business development
Natural	Leaders act to enhance green space
	Community foundations supports sustainable economic development
Cultural	Community more pro-youth
	Increased confidence in attracting new residents
	"Giving back" both in dollars and time becomes a dominant value theme
	Community people believe in their ability to shape their future
Built	Local businesses increase their use of technology
	Local pharmaceutical manufacturer expands capacity
	Younger generation builds assets in transfer of ownership
	Ethanol plant construction planned

in financial capital indicated that the community leaders viewed the future as something they must take control over. The leaders soon realized, however, that they needed to do more than just provide financial and human capital resources. They also had to mobilize bridging social capital to link themselves to technical assistance and to those outside the community willing to invest in the community's future. Sometimes referred to as linking social capital (Schneider, 2004), relationships that create access to resources, particularly financial resources and political influence, play a critical role in sustaining the effort. Finally, we observed the importance of the new social capital links that created the opportunity to join outside expertise with the internal knowledge and understanding of place. Thus, in Valley County, mobilizing social capital created the conditions for the five mechanisms in which social capital effected outcomes as described by Narrayan and Pritchett (1997):

- improving the ability to monitor the performance of government which in Valley County began with passing the bond and attending to performance,
- increasing possibilities of co-operative action as demonstrated by the work of HTC implementation teams,
- facilitating the diffusion of innovation that allowed new ideas about economic development and entrepreneurship to surface and be implemented,
- reducing information imperfections to decrease transition costs and facilitate "deal-making" that led to new business strategies and opportunities for leadership development, and
- increasing informal assurances that allowed households and individuals to engage in risky activities such as engaging in entrepreneurship or running for office knowing the community supports these efforts (Hobbes, 2000).

In the long-term, the greatest challenge in Valley County lies in its ability to mobilize social capital in ways that cut across groups, so that all voices participate and visualize the possibility of prosperity (Varshney, 1998).

The analysis of the project using the CCF led to two significant impacts. First, the HTC process facilitated the growth of social capital as it engaged the community and external partners in learning together about strategies that could transform landscapes of loss to those of prosperity. Falk and Kilpatrick (1999) found that quality learning environments can increase the accumulation of social capital. A second observation that emerged from applying the CCF was the importance of transforming community cultural capital into a "pro-change" asset. For example, a leadership training program alone would have limited impact on human and social capital. A leadership development program designed to include youth and people from various locations within the county using local expertise impacts cultural capital as people socially reconstructed the structure of leadership. Young persons became leaders, local people, experts, and community leaders,, collaborators as new relationships were developed outside the previous vision of possible relationships.

This interaction across capitals spurred the momentum to provide more opportunities to more kinds of people, leading to increased human, social, and cultural capitals. Because' people began to imagine their community and themselves differently, crucial changes in political capital occurred. These changes led to more support for local businesses and efforts that influenced financial capital. To build the synergy necessary for the spiraling-up effect to kick in, the attitudes, norms, and approaches to working together for change in the community had to be reformed to foster a sense of agency within the community, to reduce long-term conflict, and to appreciate assets and invest them wisely. In Figure 3, we see how the initial investments in social capitals led to both increases in the stock and flow of other capitals causing critically important changes in cultural capital. These changes provided the foundation for additional growth in the stock and flow of capitals assets leading to increasing capacity within the community.

Figure 3. Mapping the Loss of Capital Assets in Landscapes of Loss and Growth of Assets Connected to HTC

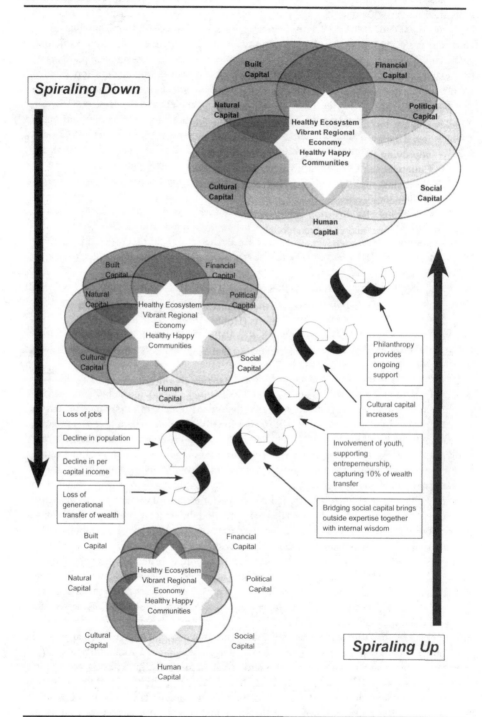

Sustainability of the HTC approach

HTC clearly increased stocks across the capitals in Valley County by addressing significant capital flows in that community. At the community level, HTC developed a clear strategy for using efforts of "wealth capture" to provide ongoing financial capital that supported the spiraling-up effect. But is HTC itself a sustainable organization capable of catalyzing change in numerous communities? By applying its entrepreneurial strategy to itself, HTC brought in two private telephone companies, an RC&D, and CDBG funds to support the implementation of the approach in various locations. In addition, the regional economic development districts, community colleges, and USDA Rural Development have become partners. The Main Street program played an essential role in several locations. The HTC approach to rural entrepreneurship garnered a two million dollar grant from the Kellogg Foundation to promote rural entrepreneurship, and other funders are contributing to expand the approach. In addition, they are exploring several possibilities for endowment development. They developed a business plan that includes fee-for services, so they can continue to offer the program to communities interested in reversing decades of decline.

SUMMARY

The Community Capitals Framework offers us a new viewpoint from which to analyze holistic community changes. The framework encourages us to think systemically about strategies and projects, thus offering insights into additional indicators of success as well as potential areas of support. Discussion of the capitals framework provided a broader understanding of the strategic nature of HTC, particularly among its partners. Using the framework to think systemically about the project helped the members of the collaborative to identify indicators in all the capitals beyond those related to the specific activity as they strive to evaluate the project's impact and learn from that experience.

CCF can offer a mechanism for systemic evaluation, an evaluation process that looks at impact beyond to the project's specific goals, to the community or system as a whole. Applying the framework allowed us to map outcomes by capitals and to identify indicators that can measure the degree of system change. In the case of HTC, the CCF illustrated the project's impact in creating a flow of assets that led to increased stock in multiple capitals. As funders and community developers alike require better ways of understanding impacts and outcomes, the CCF provided an effective way of mapping the investment of capital stocks, strategies that influence the flow of assets across capitals, and results indicated by the increase of capital stocks. The CCF allowed us to study the interaction among capitals that can result in "success leading to success." Such an approach will be useful when we look at two similar communities facing very different futures. We see from the flow of capitals the significance of cultural capital in driving the ongoing flow of capital assets toward an upward spiral that allowed synergetic capitals to grow and continually build on themselves.

In our use of the CCF to study the process of building capacity in community, we found the increases in both the stocks and flows of social capital were the initiating factors in the spiraling up process. As we use this understanding in our work with communities, we will continue to expand out learning of how the interaction among the capitals contributes to the spiraling-up process. We see the need to learn more about the quality of the social capital interaction between outsiders and local leaders. Clearly, given the parameters of the new economy and the need for individual communities to find their niche and succeed, the joint learning involved in bridging local wisdom with outside expertise played a critical role in initiating an upward spiraling process.

NOTES

1 Retrieved January 2006 from http://www.ruraleship.org/index_html?page=content/tools.htm
2 Personal correspondence with Don Macke, Heartland Center for Leadership Development Co-Director.

REFERENCES

Aigner, S. M., Flora, C. B., & Hernandez, J. M. (2001, Fall). The Premise and Promise of Citizenship and Civil Society for Renewing Democracies and Empowering Sustainable Communities. *Sociological Inquiry*, 71: 493-507.

Bebbington, A. (1999). Capitals and Capabilities: A Framework for Analyzing Peasant Viability, Rural Livelihoods and Poverty. *World Development*, 27: 2021-2044.

Becker, G. (1964). *Human Capital: A Theoretical and Empirical Analysis with Special Reference to Education.* New York: Columbia University Press.

Bourdieu, P. (1986). The forms of capital. In J. G. Richardson (Ed.), *The Handbook of Theory: Research for the Sociology of Education* (chapter 9, pp. 241-258). New York: Greenwood Press.

Coleman, J. S. (1990). *Foundations of Social Theory.* Cambridge, MA: Harvard University Press.

Costanza, R., d'Arge, R., de Groot, R., Farber, S., Grasso, M., Hanson, B., Limburg, K., Naeem, S., O'Neil, R. V., Parvelo, J., Raskin, R. G., Sutton, P., & van den Belt, M. (1997). The Value of the World's Ecosystem Services and Natural Capital. *Nature*, 387: 253-260.

Emery, M., Carlson, R., & Schroeder, C. (2004.) A formula for community builders: how to retain youth and attract families. *Vanguard*, 36: 3.

Emery, M. (2004). Mid-term evaluation report. Unpublished report to the HomeTown Competitiveness collaborative. Lincoln, NE.

Emery, M. (2003). Interim report to the collaborative. Lincoln: Heartland Center for Leadership Development.

Falk, I., & Kilpatrick, S. (1999). *What is Social Capital? A Study of Interaction in a Rural Community.* Australia: University of Tasmania.

Flora, C. B., & Flora, J. (1993, September). Entrepreneurial social infrastructure: a necessary ingredient. *Annual of the American Academy of Political and Social Science,* 529 :48-58.

Flora, C., Flora, J., & Fey, S. (2004). *Rural Communities: Legacy and Change* (2nd ed.). Boulder, CO: Westview Press.

Flora, C. B., Fey, S, Bregandahl, C., Chen, L., & Friel, J. (2004). *Rural community and economic development case study resources: A summary report.* North Central Regional Center for Rural Development, Ames, IA.

Flora, J. L., Sharp, J. S., Flora, C. B., & Newlon, B. (1997). Entrepreneurial social infrastructure and locally-initiated economic development. *Sociological Quarterly*, 38(4): 623-645.

Granovetter, M. S. (1973). The strength of weak ties. *American Journal of Sociology*, 78(6): 1360-1380.

Granovetter, M. S. (1985). Economic action, social structure and embeddedness. *American Journal of Sociology*, 91: 481-510.

Gutierrez-Montes, Isabel. 2005. *Healthy Communities Equals Healthy Ecosystems? Evolution (and Breakdown) of a Participatory Ecological Research Project Towards a Community Natural Resource Management Process, San Miguel Chimalapa (Mexico).* PhD Dissertation, Iowa State University, Ames, IA

Havens, J. J., & Schervish, P. G. (2003). Millionaires and the Millennium: New Estimates of the Forthcoming Wealth Transfer and the Prospects for a Golden Age of Philanthropy by the Social Welfare Research. *The Journal of Gift Planning* 7(1) January: 11-15, 47-50.

Hobbes, G. (2000). What is social capital? A brief literature overview. Retrieved October 2005 from http://www.caledonia.org.uk/soc_cap.htm

Lochner, K., Kawachi, I., Kennedy, B. P. (1999). Social capital: a guide to its measurement. *Health and Place* 5: 259-270.

Lorenz, E. (1999). Trust, Contract and Economic Cooperation. *Cambridge Journal of Economics* 23: 301-15.

Macke, D. (2005). Personal correspondence to Mary Emery.

Myrdal, G. (1957). *Economic Theory and Underdeveloped Regions.* London: Duckworth.

Narayan, D. (1999). *Bonds and Bridges: Social Capital and Poverty.* Washington: World Bank, Report no. 2167.

Narayan, D. & Prichett, L. (1997). *Cents and Sociability: Household Income and Social Capital in Rural Tanzania.* Washington, D.C.: World Bank.

Nebraska Community Foundation. (2004). Retrieved January 21, 2006 from http://www. nebcommfound.org/wealthanalyses.htm

Nebraska Community Foundation. (2005a). Retrieved January 21, 2006 from http://nebcommfound.org/ HTC.htm

Nebraska Community Foundation. (2005b). Retrieved January 21, 2006 from http://www.htcnebraska. org/about?PHPSESSID=21d9535caab341972e3be3eb94206e1f

Nothdurft, W. (2002). *Across the Great Divide: People, Places, and Poverty in Northwest Area Foundations' Region.* St. Paul: Northwest Area Foundation. Retrieved June 20, 2003 from http://www.nwaf.org/pubs/Nothdruft.pdf

Pretty, J. N. (1998). *The Living Land: Agriculture, Food and Community Regeneration in Rural Europe.* London: Earthscan Publications Ltd.

Rural Electric Nebraskan. (2005). Hometown Competitiveness: A Unique Approach to Rural Community Enhancement. 59(7): 14-15.

Schneider, J. (2004). *The Role of Social Capital in Building Healthy Communities.* Casey Foundation. Retrieved January 2005 from http://www.aecf.org/initiatives/mc/readingroom/documents/ Social.Capital04.pdf

Stier, K. (2005, November 14). Rural America: in Ord, Neb., the latest success is 20 new residents. *New York Times.* Retrieved January 22, 2006 from http://www.htcnebraska.org/vcordsuccess.

Varshney, A. (1998). *Ethnic Conflict and the Structure of Civic Life.* Paper presented at the annual meeting of the American Political Association, Boston Science.

RURAL RETAIL BUSINESS SURVIVAL: IMPLICATIONS FOR COMMUNITY DEVELOPERS

By Janet Ayres, Larry Leistritz, and Kenneth Stone

ABSTRACT

The loss of retail businesses and sales in rural areas has been accelerating for many years. This study was conducted in 37 rural communities in Indiana, Iowa, and North Dakota that appeared to have better-than-average retail sales. The purpose of the study was to identify strategies, if any, that were employed by communities and individual businesses which contributed to viable retail districts.

This study suggests several possible actions for community development practitioners involved in efforts to improve and sustain rural retail business communities. These actions include: the need to assist rural communities build a more diversified economic base, provide business management training and technical assistance, establish mechanisms to transfer established business operations to new owners, develop financing mechanisms for new or aspiring businesses, and assist rural communities to deal with change and plan for their futures.

INTRODUCTION

Small towns in the Midwest have been losing retail trade for many years (Stone, 1988; Leistritz et al., 1990; Johnson & Young, 1987). For example, in North Dakota taxable sales adjusted for inflation decreased 17.9 percent from 1980 to 1987. The share of total sales captured by towns with less than 10,000 population fell from 36.4 percent in 1980 to 29.8 percent in 1987 (Leistritz et al., 1989a). However, some small towns have been able to maintain a more viable retail sector than others. This study examined 37 of the more "successful" towns in three midwestern states to identify common char-

Janet Ayres is an Associate Professor, Department of Agricultural Economics, Purdue University; Larry Leistritz is a Professor, Department of Agricultural Economics, North Dakota State University; and Kenneth Stone is a Professor, Department of Economics, Iowa State University. This research was funded in part by the North Central Regional Center for Rural Development at Iowa State University. A copy of the full report titled "Revitalizing the Retail Trade Sector in Rural Communities: Lessons from Midwestern States" can be obtained from NCRCRD, Iowa State University, 216 East Hall, Ames, IA 50011.

acteristics that contribute to a viable business district. These towns were identified as those that had better-than-average retail sales, had a relatively stable business occupancy rate, and were perceived by the community leaders as "doing well." The results of this study provide insights into strategies which community development practitioners can initiate to help maintain rural retail communities.

The relative decline of the rural retail sector can be traced back several decades. For example, in a study conducted for the White House Conference on Small Business, Stone (1980) found that rural counties in Iowa, Kansas, Missouri, and Nebraska experienced a retail "leakage" (the loss of retail dollars out of a community) of about 5 percent during the 1950s, 10 percent in the 1960s, and 15 percent in the 1970s. The leakage in the 1980s averaged well over 20 percent for rural counties in Iowa.

A number of factors have contributed to the decline of the smaller rural trade centers, beginning with improvements in rural roads and highways. School consolidation led to decreased traffic to the towns that lost their schools. Television sets in almost every rural home increased consumers' exposure to new products and urban shopping centers. More recently, the expansion of urban and suburban malls, shopping centers, and discount stores are increasingly luring customers out of the rural areas (Leistritz et al., 1987, 1989b).

Whatever the causes, the effects of declining retail sales volume can be devastating to small towns. In Iowa, during the period 1980–1988, towns with 500 to 1,000 residents had an average decrease in deflated taxable sales of 51.9 percent, and towns of 1,500 to 2,500 had a decrease of 32.9 percent, compared to a statewide decrease of 13.7 percent. The continual loss of retail sales in small towns translates into loss of businesses. For example, Iowa has experienced a net loss of 605 grocery stores (33 percent) in the last 10 years—most in towns of less than 1,000 population. The loss of a key business, such as a grocery store, can be a severe blow to a small town because residents may be forced to travel more frequently to larger towns to shop, and sales of the surviving local stores may suffer. Business closures also eliminate jobs for local residents and reduce the tax base of local governments. Declining employment opportunities may lead to out-migration of local residents, which further erodes the clientele base for main street businesses. Thus, the whole process can become a vicious cycle with economic, demographic, and public sector decline reinforcing each other (Ekstrom & Leistritz, 1988).

This study was conducted to better understand the dynamics of retailing in the rural Midwest and to determine whether it is possible to develop strategies for successful small town retailing. The overall goal of the effort was to provide information to enhance rural retail businesses. Specific objectives included determining the recent changes and current status of rural retail communities in Iowa, North Dakota, and Indiana, communities which represent the diversity of the rural Midwest; identifying successful community organizational techniques; identifying innovative and effective business funding techniques; determining the extent and success of new business recruiting techniques; identifying successful promotional campaigns based on local resources or factors; and determining the most critical needs common to business communities.

METHODS

The study was aimed at identifying successful strategies employed by communities and individual businesses in rural communities. A three-step approach was used to gather the data.

The first step was to identify communities that had been relatively successful in maintaining or expanding their retail sector. Two major data sources were used in this first phase. One source was secondary data collection from state sales tax records, the *Survey of Buying Power*, and the 1982 and 1987 Censuses of Retail Trade. State sales tax records (available in Iowa and North Dakota) offer a means of gauging overall changes in retail sales volume for rural communities. In North Dakota, taxable sales were examined for communities in three different population size groups (500–999, 1,000–2,500, 2,500–5,000). Within each group, the communities' taxable retail sales for 1980 and 1987 and the change in sales from 1980 to 1987 were calculated. "Successful" communities all had above average sales per capita and an above average percent change in sales, relative to the group average. A similar procedure was used in Indiana using the 1982 and 1987 Retail Census data on a county basis. Sales tax data are not available in Indiana.

The second data source used to identify communities was a survey of town clerks in all towns between 500 and 5,000 population in Iowa and Indiana. In North Dakota, the mayors and Chamber of Commerce presidents were surveyed instead of town clerks. Because of the size of communities in North Dakota, communities in the 300–500 population range were also included in the study. Participants completed a questionnaire about the number of vacant stores, the number of business losses, the dominant stores, and a number of other questions relating to the community's retail business sector. The response to the survey ranged from 71 percent in Indiana to 92 percent in North Dakota.

After analyzing the secondary data and the survey results, 12 towns in Indiana (of 221 total communities), 12 towns in Iowa (of 380 communities) and 13 towns in North Dakota (of 72 communities) were chosen as among the more "successful" small retail communities; that is, having "better than average" retail sales, a relative stable business occupancy rate, and perceived by community leaders as being "successful." Twelve communities were between 500–999 population size; 15 were between 1,000–2,499 population; and 10 were between 2,500–5,000 population.

The third phase was an in-depth study in the 37 communities. In Indiana and North Dakota, county extension agents were asked to identify appropriate persons to interview. The town clerks in Iowa were asked to suggest key people who should be interviewed in each selected Iowa community. In general, local elected officials, bankers, retail business people, and local civic leaders were suggested with an average of 10 interviews in each town.

A questionnaire was developed for the interviews. The questionnaire was based on previously conducted retail surveys (Ayres, 1979, 1981) and adapted to focus on the objectives of the survey. The same questionnaires were used in the three states. The interviews were conducted May–August 1988 in North Dakota; September–November 1988 in Indiana; and winter 1988–1989 in Iowa.

FINDINGS

Characteristics of the Study Communities

There was great diversity among the small towns included in the survey. In Indiana all of the communities were located on a federal highway and all but one community were within 30 miles of an urban area of 50,000 or more population. In contrast, one community in North Dakota was 113 miles from a city of over 10,000 population and 25 miles from a federal highway. Communities highly dependent upon the energy industry and considered "atypical" were not included in the North Dakota sample. The communities were geographically distributed across each of the states and represented a variety of economic bases. Communities in Indiana were more dependent on manufacturing industries as a source of employment and income, while Iowa and North Dakota communities were more dependent on agriculture.

Fifteen of the 37 communities were county seat towns and derived some benefit from this additional traffic. Some of the communities had special tourist attractions such as the Grotto, a religious shrine in West Bend, Iowa, and Amish Acres, an educational Amish farm in Nappanee, Indiana.

General Findings

Three general findings resulted from the study. First, constant change is occurring in small rural communities. While small communities may appear as if little change is occurring, the research found a great deal of turnover and change. From the time the initial mail questionnaire was sent to the communities until the in-depth interviews were conducted, some retail businesses closed while other new businesses opened. Rural communities are dynamic. One of the struggles for local leaders is dealing with this constant change.

A second discovery was that there is no "ideal" community. While better-than-average retail communities were chosen for this study, they still confront many problems. Some communities had a relatively strong retail sector yet were struggling to diversify the economic base or were threatened with the loss of their elementary schools. Even within the retail sector, while some businesses were doing well, others were near the point of closing. Some communities had an active business organization, but did not have available financing for new businesses. No communities exhibited outstanding efforts in all aspects of the community. Most were struggling to do the best they could with available resources. This reality of small town life reflects the constant change in the community, the dependency on volunteer leadership to deal with the change, and the limited availability of human and financial resources to assist in community efforts.

The third general finding was the similarity of the issues. The researchers were expecting to find different issues regarding the retail community due to the differences in economic base and degree of urbanization in the three states. However, the concerns and issues expressed in the communities were almost identical. These findings are discussed below.

Common Issues

Community Organizational Techniques. All of the successful retail towns had some type of organization devoted to furthering the good of the retail sector. The smaller towns usually had a business group without any paid employees. Most of these groups had officers and/or a board of directors. The larger towns and a few of the intermediate size towns had a Chamber of Commerce. An active Chamber of Commerce was the point of community promotion activities. Twelve of the 37 communities hired a part-time or full-time person to coordinate Chamber and economic development activities. The presence of a Chamber executive or development coordinator seemed to be a key factor contributing to the community's success. The employment of a development coordinator appeared to be a definite trend among the larger towns (2,500–5,000 population). Several comments indicated that a part-time or full-time person was instrumental in bringing the business community together, keeping people informed, developing promotions, and in recruiting needed business to town. It is difficult for volunteers to spend the necessary time to carry out these activities in addition to their full-time businesses.

In the "successful" communities interviewed, the organizations worked together in a spirit of cooperation and strong commitment. For example, in Sunman, Indiana, 95 percent of the businesses belonged to the Chamber of Commerce and were active in it. There appeared to be strong ties between city and county governments, the Chamber of Commerce, and other community groups such as the Jaycees and the Kiwanis. There were close communication linkages between the organizations.

Several communities demonstrated examples of cooperation between county and city governments which appears to offer opportunities for the future. The county and city combine their resources to hire a full-time development coordinator. One city and county in North Dakota had joined with two other counties and several other cities to fund a tri-county development office. These efforts made possible the position for a full-time person who could assist in business recruitment, community promotion, and marketing. Although such cooperation is ideal, especially in more remote rural areas, there is concern that the larger, more dominant towns will receive the most benefits and that the smaller towns will lose out. County officials were sometimes reluctant to help fund such development efforts because of possible inequities. This research discovered the beginning phases of multi-community collaboration efforts. Although it holds promise for pooling scarce resources in rural communities, it is too early to determine its success. The possibility exists that as some of these multi-community units develop, they could raise funds through public and private sources to offer low-cost loans to retail businesses.

Business Financing. The availability of adequate financing is often seen as the key to rural economic development (Daniels & Crockett, 1988). Substantial evidence was found in all three states that "successful" established business people had little or no problem financing the business with operating capital. However, arranging long-term debt and equity capital as well as operating capital for new or aspiring business people was identified as a problem. Respondents from the financial institutions were more precise in defining the problem. The financiers indicated that most of the new or aspiring business people were undercapitalized, and many had little or no experience in running a business. Apparently remembering their experiences from the farm debt crisis in the early 1980s, most bankers viewed loans to undercapitalized, inexperienced business people as risky and imprudent. Some financiers indicated that they sometimes made these types of loans when Small Business Administration loan guarantees could be secured.

Respondents from several towns indicated that the town had sought state or federal grants or financial help on behalf of businesses in the community. However, at both the state and federal levels, grant programs have been significantly reduced from their 1980 levels, or have been eliminated altogether. At the state level, loans and grants are being awarded very judiciously because of the inability to resolve problems of equity connected with such programs.

In some communities, limited partnerships have been used to provide capital for an entrepreneur with the ability, but without the capital. "Silent partners" provide a share of the capital in return for a pro-rated share of the returns. A few communities have established a revolving loan fund earmarked for new businesses. In at least one case in Iowa, the initial loan pool was obtained through a grant from the federal government.

There were several cases of long-time businesses being sold through owner financing. This method of buying "on contract" can be beneficial to both the seller and the buyer in certain cases. However, in cases where the seller is selling a "run down" store and the buyer is too inexperienced to realize it, the result can be disastrous.

Business Recruitment. Officials from nearly all of the more successful towns directed some effort toward recruiting new business and industry. More emphasis was placed on attracting industries, however, than retail businesses. The leaders in the community worked together to develop a strategy, to promote the community, and to actively recruit businesses or to assist local businesses in expanding. Several of the communities had some successes. For example, Guthrie Center, Iowa, attracted Illinois Tool Works and Rose Acres, a large egg production facility. Other towns benefited from successful "home grown" businesses, such as Agri-drain Company in Adair, Iowa.

Industry and jobs, however, do not guarantee the success of the retail sector. There are many examples in all three states where towns have strong industrial sectors, but the retail sector is so weak that most of the money earned in the towns is spent somewhere else.

Consumers have choices in where to shop. The type of retail businesses in the community, the selection and cost of merchandise, and
service offered by the merchants affect where people shop (Ayres,
1979, 1981). This situation negates one of the supposed benefits of
having industry, the multiplier effect.

Theoretically, money earned in a community could turn over five
or six times in the community thereby approximately doubling the
original economic activity. But, when wage earners in a town spend
their money elsewhere, this benefit is lost. Keeping the money at
home was a struggle for nearly all of the communities, even the more
successful communities.

Most of the respondents in the successful communities recognized
that their town was in need of additional retail businesses and varying
degrees of recruiting activity were cited. In the simplest case, officials
encouraged local people to buy stores that were going out of business.
In other cases, vigorous recruiting was aimed at bringing needed
businesses to town. One of the more successful efforts of this type
was accomplished by Bancroft, Iowa, after it lost its grocery store
several years ago. The leadership of the community banded together
to develop a strategy on how to recruit a grocery store to the community. After obtaining some cost/benefit analysis and other information from Iowa State University, they actively contacted a number
of grocery store chains. By offering an incentive of reduced rent for
a period of time, they were successful.

Promotional Campaigns. Nearly every successful town had some
type of promotional campaign. In the smaller towns, farmer appreciation days seemed to be popular and effective. Some towns had
annual events that attracted national audiences, such as Dyersville,
Iowa, with its National Farm Toy Show and Ida Grove, Iowa, with
its Aviation Expo. Still other towns capitalized on local attractions.
For example, West Bend, Iowa, attracts visitors with its Grotto, and
Nappanee, Indiana, has developed Amish Acres, a working Amish
farm.

Some towns sponsored events that combined a fun time with shopping promotions. Examples of these are Jesse James Days (Adair,
Iowa), Hog Wild Days, the Window Walk, and many other promotions
that were identified in all three states.

In North Dakota, most of the communities had a monthly or bi-
weekly advertising pamphlet with information from a number of local
businesses. A variation of this theme was found in Hettinger, North
Dakota, where advertising materials from a number of businesses
were distributed monthly in a plastic "mailbag."

The towns in Indiana had success with direct mailings to customers three to four times a year.

Several towns sponsored "shop locally" campaigns. These featured slogans that were promoted in newspapers, radio, and other media. Most respondents indicated some success with these efforts and felt that a home-owned newspaper is a major asset to a community.

IMPLICATIONS FOR COMMUNITY DEVELOPMENT

A number of critical needs were identified in the study which have implications for community development practitioners as they work to improve and sustain the rural retail community. They include:

Strong Economic Base

Most all of the communities in the three states were attempting to diversify and strengthen their economic base. This was viewed by the community leaders as being a critical component to a viable retail district. The communities that were successful in attracting new businesses had a long-term commitment to the effort and had established an effective coordinated effort among the community's business and civic leaders. The leaders of these communities were also aware of available outside resources and had pursued them. The presence of a paid development coordinator or Chamber executive seemed to be a critical factor in assuring continuity of community efforts. However, smaller towns may not be able to afford the services of such an individual. A county- or region-wide economic development office may be a partial solution in such cases.

Business Management Training

A second lesson learned was the importance of technical assistance for rural businesses. Both business proprietors and community leaders indicated a high level of interest in technical assistance. Areas frequently mentioned included financial management, developing business plans, merchandising, inventory management, personnel management, and customer relations. Many of these topics are currently offered as extension programs through colleges and universities. A surprise to the researchers was the general lack of knowledge about available programs. It was also learned that many of the businesses which are part of a national chain have access to technical information, while the locally owned stores do not have such assistance available. A practitioner can help identify the particular training needs in the community and either arrange for such classes in the community or connect the business people with other sources of training. Classes are often offered in the local school. At a minimum, written materials and video tapes could be obtained on specific topics from the Small Business Administration, Cooperative Extension Service or business schools.

Mechanisms to Transfer Business Operations

Many small town merchants are older people who have operated a store that has been in the family for many years. The study found that even in successful communities, the transfer of business operations is a problem. When business people approach retirement age, most have not made provisions for transferring the operation to someone else. Consequently, the business is closed and gone forever. A community development practitioner could work with business operators to develop creative mechanisms to transfer the operation of the business to capable new owners before the business closes.

Innovative Financing Mechanisms for
New or Aspiring Businesses

This study found a pervasive problem in obtaining both debt and equity financing for new ventures. Local lenders are reluctant to supply funds to new enterprises they perceive as high risk loans. Improved access to technical assistance in developing a business plan and making key financial management decisions could aid some potential entrepreneurs in gaining approval of their loans. Community development practitioners could help rural communities establish financial mechanisms such as revolving loan pools, cooperative financing, limited partnerships, and others.

Planning for the Future

Perhaps the most important single lesson from the interviews with community leaders is the need for both individual businesses and communities to adopt a strategic approach in planning their future. This approach anticipates the future and reflects a readiness to make the most of opportunities arising from change as well as acts to forestall potential threats. Assisting the community in a strategic planning process may be the most significant contribution a community development practitioner can make in small rural communities.

REFERENCES

Ayres, Janet S. *Consumers and Business People Speak Out About Downtown Washington.*
　1979　　West Lafayette, IN: Purdue Cooperative Extension Service, Paper No. 44.

Ayres, Janet S. *Consumer Attitudes Toward Shopping in Kentland, Indiana.* West Lafayette,
　1981　　IN: Purdue Cooperative Extension Service, Paper No. 74.

Daniels, Belden H. & Crockett, Catherine A. *Rural North Carolina Finance Action Place.*
　1988　　Boston, MA: Counsel for Community Development, Inc.

Ekstrom, B. L. & Leistritz, F. L. *Rural Community Decline and Revitalization: An Annotated*
　1988　　*Bibliography.* New York: Garland Publishing, Inc.

Johnson, B. & Young, J. *Trends in Retail Sales Activity Across Nebraska's Counties and*
　1987　　*Communities.* Lincoln, NE: University of Nebraska, Department of Agri-
　　　　cultural Economics.

Leistritz, F. Larry, Ekstrom, Brenda L. & Ureugdenhil, Harvey G. *Selected Characteristics*
　1987　　*of Business Operators in North Dakota Agricultural Trade Centers.* Agricultural
　　　　Economics Report No. 217. Fargo, ND: North Dakota State University,
　　　　Department of Agricultural Economics.

Leistritz, F. Larry, Mortensen, Timothy L., Bastow-Shoop, Holly, Braaten-Grabanski,
　1989a　　Joan, Schuler, Alan & Fedorenko, Julie. *Revitalizing the Retail and Trade*
　　　　Sector in Rural Communities: Experiences of 13 North Dakota Towns. Agricul-
　　　　tural Economics Report No. 250. Fargo, ND: North Dakota State Univer-
　　　　sity, Department of Agricultural Economics.

Leistritz, F. Larry, Bastow-Shoop, Holly E., Mortensen, Timothy L. & Ekstrom, Brenda
　1989b　　L. Why do people leave town to buy goods and services? *Small Town* 20(1):
　　　　20–27.

Leistritz, F. L., Wanzek, J. & Hamm, R. R. *North Dakota 1990: Patterns and Trends in*
　1990　　*Economic Activity and Population.* Agricultural Economics Statistical Series
　　　　Report No. 46. Fargo, ND: North Dakota State University, Department
　　　　of Agricultural Economics.

Survey of Buying Power. 1980, 1987. In *Sales and Marketing Management.* New York: Bill
　1980,　　Communications.
　1987

Stone, K. E. *A Guide to Using Sales Tax Data to Assess Business Risks in Community Devel-*
　1988　　*opment Extension Programs.* Ames, IA: Iowa State University, Department
　　　　of Economics.

Stone, K. E. & McConnon, J. M., Jr. *Retail Sales Migration in the Midwestern United States.*
　1980　　Ames, IA: Iowa State University, Department of Economics.

U.S. Bureau of the Census. *Census of Retail Trade, 1982 and 1987, Geographic Area*
　1984,　　*Series: Indiana, Iowa, North Dakota.* Washington, DC: U.S. Department of
　1989　　Commerce, Bureau of the Census.

INTEGRATING RESEARCH WITH LOCAL COMMUNITY-DEVELOPMENT PROGRAMS

By Willis J. Goudy and John L. Tait

ABSTRACT

Even though community attitude studies have long been conducted by development specialists, many researchers and practitioners fail to define research as an integral part of the community development process. This article presents a case study of a small rural Iowa community which integrated a community survey and a community development seminar into a total community effort. The results included the initiation of new action programs in recreation and housing, the involvement of more citizens in leadership roles, and the development of communication networks within the community.

Research that gathers the ideas and opinions of residents is frequently conducted as part of a community development effort. Yet, this information seldom is used adequately when it is available. This occurs because primary research has not been defined as an integral part of the community development process by many researchers and practitioners. In this paper, we discuss an integration of primary data collection with educational programs conducted in the local community by using one small town as an example. A description of the sessions held in the community before and after data collection are reported, and the research is described. Finally, actions taken and planned for the future in the study community are noted.

THE COMMUNITY SETTING

In 1976, Iowa State University's Cooperative Extension Service worked with a leadership core group in Sac City, Iowa, in planning and conduct-

The authors are, respectively, associate professor of sociology, and professor of sociology and extension sociologist in the Department of Sociology and Anthropology, Iowa State University, Ames, Iowa. This article is based upon a paper delivered at the 1978 meeting of the Community Development Society of America, Blacksburg, Virginia. The research reported here was supported in part by the Iowa Cooperative Extension Service and the Iowa Agriculture and Home Economics Experiment Station, Ames, Iowa. This is Journal Paper No. J-9249 of the Iowa Agriculture and Home Economics Experiment Station, Project No. 2079.

ing a community development workshop. One of the active participants in this educational program was the owner-editor of a weekly newspaper in the nearby town of Lake View. This rural town of approximately 1,300 people is located in west-central Iowa. The economic base of the community and the county in which it is located is predominantly agricultural.

As a result of her participation in the Sac City workshop, the owner-editor explored alternatives for a program in Lake View with the Lake View Community Betterment Council. The council was receptive to the idea and appointed a committee composed of representatives from a cross-section of the community's institutions. Members included a banker, a businessman and city council member, two ministers, the mayor, the vocational agriculture instructor at the high school, a school principal, and the owner-editor of the newspaper, who served as chairperson for the committee. The chairperson contacted the county extension director who enlisted the aid of university support staff.

At the first meeting between the committee and a member of the support staff, the committee requested information regarding community development educational programs and research that had been conducted with Iowa communities by university personnel. Two major topics were discussed.

The first was an educational program. As a part of the Extension Service's community resource development program, a number of development seminars had been conducted. These seminars provided community leaders and citizens with opportunities to improve their leadership skills to deal with community changes. In devising a seminar, a local planning committee with the support of extension personnel designed a series of meetings to explore local needs. In the past, seminar content had focused on areas such as local government, education, political socialization, adoption-diffusion, power structures, attitude change, communications, and social action. In addition to providing opportunities in these content areas, the participants applied the concepts and processes to solve actual problems in their communities.

The second topic was a summary of a research study of 27 rural Iowa communities. A goal of this study was to determine the perceptions and evaluations that local residents held about their towns. A questionnaire from the study, which asked residents about local services, opportunities, and social factors, was shared with the planning committee.

After discussing possible research projects and educational programs, the planning committee developed an interest in integrating research and education into a total community development effort. The committee felt an ideal program would be to conduct a community survey to identify and assess community factors and then to present the data as part of a seminar for interested citizens. Of course, the ultimate goal of the committee was to develop new action programs to enhance life in the community. Thus, research and education were to be combined, not unlike the efforts of many community development specialists. The strength of the links between the community attitude survey, the local seminars, and the resulting action programs reaffirmed the importance of both research and education to successful development.

RESEARCH: THE COMMUNITY SURVEY

After the committee had decided to gather ideas and opinions from local residents, the university support staff worked with them to determine what they wished to learn. The committee believed a general evaluation of community attributes was in order, research similar to that completed by the support staff in other communities. In addition, however, the committee had some specific areas that they decided also needed examination, including opinions on the role tourism played in the community and the possibility of obtaining an industry. A questionnaire was developed that incorporated the ideas of both the committee and the support staff.

The committee decided that four groups should be asked to respond to the questionnaire: in-town residents, residents of the rural area surrounding the incorporated city limits, high school students, and individuals who would be most likely to attend the educational seminars dealing with community development. For the first two groups, samples of all dwelling units were randomly selected for potential response. The questionnaires were hand delivered by volunteers recruited by the planning committee, together with a letter of introduction and instructions for determining which adult was to complete the questionnaire. Completed questionnaires were returned by 143 in-town and 33 rural residents. The response rates in these groups were over 90 percent, primarily because of announcements in the local newspaper and the personal delivery and pickup of questionnaires.

In addition to these groups, 32 senior high school students in a social studies class completed the instrument and 24 were filled out by potential seminar participants. This latter group included committee members responsible for generating interest and participation in the community development seminar as well as other persons whom these committee members thought would be interested in the seminar. Thus, the fourth group was not a sample of any specific organization, but it contained numerous community leaders.

The questionnaire contained 159 items. Questions on local services, opportunities, and social factors were included, as were items on general community satisfaction, personal quality of life, and sociodemographic characteristics. One section requested evaluations of services and opportunities such as "good police protection" and "good recreational opportunities" (Table 1). Five responses were listed for each: (1) definitely describes this community well, (2) describes this community, (3) may or may not describe this community, (4) does not describe this community, and (5) definitely does not describe this community at all. For presentations by the support staff at local meetings, mean scores were calculated. The coding was reversed and mean scores based on 100 were reported to facilitate interpretation. That is, the most positive response was given the highest score: $1 = 100$, $2 = 75$, $3 = 50$, $4 = 25$, $5 = 0$. In addition, respondents were asked to indicate the degree of improvement needed (1, none; 2, some; 3, much) in each item such as "police protection" and "recreational opportunities." Again, responses were placed on a 0 to 100 scale ($1 = 0$, $2 = 50$, $3 = 100$) and means calculated; greater improvement needed was indicated by higher scores.

The results of the survey clearly showed that the potential for development was greatest in the service areas of public transportation and housing (Table 1). Evaluations of these items were negative, and much improvement was suggested. These results hardly were surprising for a small town, of course. There was strong agreement among three of the four groups on questions about services; the fourth group, high school students, tended to provide less positive evaluations in most instances. In the area of opportunities, employment was of concern, as were programs and activities for youths and older residents.

In terms of social factors operating at the local level, again there was general agreement among the groups (Table 2). In this instance, respondents were asked about both Lake View and a desired community. This was not done with services and opportunities because it was assumed that the best possible levels were desired, such as good fire and police protection, excellent employment opportunities, and good recreational and educational facilities. But the same attitudes might not have existed about social factors. Residents may not want everyone to participate in community affairs, to know each other, or to be committed to the local community. Thus, it was necessary to establish the desired levels on the social factors and then compare Lake View with these desires.

Each item, such as "residents participate in community affairs," was listed twice, once for Lake View and once for an ideal community. In both instances, five responses were possible, from (1), definitely describes this (the ideal) community well, through (5), definitely does not describe this (the ideal) community at all. Codes were reversed and set equal to the 0 to 100 scale as described previously, making the most positive evaluations equal to the highest scores. In addition, the mean score for Lake View on each factor was subtracted from that of the ideal community to indicate the gap between the actual social factor and an ideal situation.[1] When these calculations were done, it was evident that power, social rank, and participation were major concerns (Table 2). In general, however, although improvement could bring Lake View closer to what residents desired in terms of social factors, the gaps were not very large.

EDUCATION: THE COMMUNITY DEVELOPMENT SEMINAR

During the research phase, the planning committee discussed the series of meetings that would be the community-development seminar. Questions that the committee examined included the timing of the seminar, the number of sessions, the objectives and program content, and the recruitment of participants.

In consultation with extension personnel, the committee established three goals for the seminar: to provide the participants with opportunities to become better informed about the community's challenges and needs; to explore ideas and develop skills for carrying out action programs; and to apply data in developing action programs in Lake View. The committee assessed the willingness of community leaders and citizens to attend a series of meetings over several weeks. While some Iowa communities had ten two-and-a-half-hour sessions over ten consecutive weeks, this committee believed that six sessions was the maximum that they could realistically expect residents to attend.

After considering several content areas, the planning committee selected six topics. They were: (1) What Is a Good Community, (2) The Problem-Solving Process and Establishing Priorities, (3) Recreational Development in Small Communities, (4) Industrial Development in Small Communities, (5) The Community Power Structure, and (6) The Social Action Process.

In recruiting the audience, the planning committee identified representatives of community organizations, leaders, potential leaders, and interested citizens whom they felt should be invited to participate in the seminar. After listing individuals, committee members personally invited them to be participants in the seminar. In addition, public announce-

---

[1] Less complicated tables than those included in this paper were provided for seminar participants; also, additional data, interpretation, and comparisons with information from other communities, which space precludes reporting in this article, were provided by the support staff.

Table 1
Evaluations of Local Services and Opportunities

Evaluation Items	Lake View Residents		Rural Lake View Residents		High School Students		Potential Seminar Participants	
	E^1	I^1	E	I	E	I	E	I
Services:								
Good fire protection	91	11	85	14	71	38	89	21
Good utilities	88	25	84	33	72	30	88	30
Good waste disposal and sewage system	88	12	78	27	65	33	87	21
Good local newspaper	86	17	98	11	59	48	90	19
Good street lighting and maintenance	81	28	80	34	56	48	80	31
Good shopping facilities for daily needs	80	30	74	38	58	36	72	38
Good health care	74	36	70	35	62	41	72	40
Good police protection	70	42	66	44	51	59	75	45
Good local government	69	46	74	45	56	45	79	41
Good welfare program for people in need	64	41	60	36	52	45	59	38
Adequate housing available to buy	55	52	45	64	49	50	49	58
Adequate housing (rent or buy) for older residents	39	65	35	63	46	57	34	71
Adequate housing available to rent	32	67	38	64	43	45	28	71
Public transportation available	11	70	12	65	27	35	11	79

Opportunities:

Good religious opportunities....................	88	13	87	7	73	25	87	19
Good educational opportunities.................	80	33	75	34	63	42	83	39
Variety of clubs and organizations to join......	72	24	67	38	49	32	76	28
Good opportunities for citizen involvement in local government..	63	48	63	45	50	45	68	57
Good recreational opportunities................	61	58	65	54	47	75	74	50
Good cultural opportunities....................	60	48	55	53	39	63	63	48
Good programs and activities for older residents..	59	49	49	56	40	62	61	46
Good employment opportunities.................	52	63	52	62	43	67	62	60
Good programs and activities for youth.........	51	66	39	76	30	78	57	58

[1] E = evaluation of the item (the higher the score the more the statement was thought to describe the community; potential range = 0 through 100).

[2] I = perception of improvement needed (the higher the score the more improvement thought to be necessary; potential range = 0 through 100).

Table 2
Evaluations of Social Factors in Lake View and a Desired Community

Social Factors	Lake View Residents			Rural Lake View Residents			High School Students			Potential Seminar Participants		
	A^1	D^1	d^2	A	D	d	A	D	d	A	D	d
Anyone who wants to is welcome to live in the community	87	87	0	78	79	—1	70	79	—9	86	89	—3
Residents have pride in the community	84	90	—6	91	93	—2	73	85	—12	87	96	—9
Residents know each other	78	79	—1	80	82	—2	76	81	—5	76	79	—3
Local residents control their own affairs	73	77	—4	68	77	—9	56	60	—4	68	61	+7
The community is effective in dealing with its problems	72	85	—13	69	83	—14	53	75	—22	70	86	—16
Residents see the community as the center of their lives	71	75	—4	67	76	—9	56	61	—5	72	68	+4
Events in this community are not run by people in one social group	68	81	—13	62	78	—16	53	72	—19	67	82	—15
The various social classes mix well in this community	67	84	—17	67	81	—14	53	73	—20	89	68	—21
Conflict usually doesn't take place between people or groups in the community	66	74	—8	61	74	—13	50	54	—4	66	67	—1
Residents participate in community affairs	66	81	—15	63	82	—19	59	77	—18	69	81	—12
Neighborhoods control their affairs	65	72	—7	61	76	—15	51	60	—9	63	57	+6
The community controls its present affairs	63	73	—10	58	71	—13	50	58	—8	57	67	—10
Residents are similar to each other	58	61	—3	60	62	—2	52	56	—4	63	56	+7
Power to make community decisions is shared by residents	57	75	—18	55	84	—29	50	81	—31	59	80	+7
Everyone is about the same in social rank in this community	46	58	—12	59	64	—5	41	55	—14	51	62	—11

¹ A = perceptions of Lake View and D = perceptions of a desired community (higher the score, the more the statement was thought to describe Lake View or the desired community, respectively; potential range = 0 through 100).

² d = difference between the two perceptions (potential range = —100 through +100; higher scores = greater discrepancies between Lake View and the desired community).

ments were made through the weekly newspaper, radio programs conducted by the county extension director, and other meetings conducted in the community. The seminar was open to any residents who wished to attend; there was no enrollment fee. Average attendance at the Lake View seminars was 25. Participants included the mayor, city council members, business persons, bankers, school board members, organizational representatives, younger potential leaders, and interested citizens. They included all age groups from high school students through senior citizens.

The first seminar topic provided the framework for presenting and interpreting the research findings to seminar participants. Data were gathered during the first week of January, 1977, coded, analyzed, and summarized during the next two weeks, and reported to seminar participants during the final week of the month. This relatively rapid turnaround was necessary to take advantage of the strong interest generated by articles in the newspaper, by the survey itself, and by the recruitment of seminar participants. Copies of selected tables and frequency distributions on each question were given to participants and they were urged to study these materials before the next meeting. Four-page summaries of responses also were provided on in-town residents, rural respondents, and high school students; these were made available to anyone else in the community who wanted copies.

The second seminar focused on the problem-solving process and establishing action program priorities. After learning a problem solving model, participants were involved in a workshop to identify community concerns they believed might be solved with local effort. Four major problem areas were identified. The first, dredging Black Hawk Lake (a lake bordering on the community), was supported by responses to questions asked about the role of tourism in the community. All sample groups strongly endorsed the importance of tourism and believed even more should be done to promote it. Also, responses to the items on recreational opportunities indicated problems which could be reduced by making the lake more useful.

The second problem identified was the lack of employment opportunities in the community. The magnitude of this problem was clear from the evaluations and degree of improvement needed on this item, overwhelming endorsement of a need to attract new industry, and responses, especially by the in-town residents, that few general opportunities were available for young adults wishing to stay in Lake View.

The third problem concerned local swimming facilities. Since the lake was not suitable, building an outdoor swimming pool was suggested. This was based on an item about the need for a pool, the relatively low ratings of programs and activities for youths and older residents, and the low evaluations high school students gave to local recreational opportunities.[2] In addition, a pool was listed more frequently than most other possible recreational items as needed for the community.

The final problem involved developing public housing projects for older residents and low-income families. Again, this was highlighted by the responses on the evaluation items, especially those on rental housing. Additional comments volunteered on the questionnaires frequently noted this concern.

Thus, seminar participants continually pointed to the survey data in assessing problem areas they wished to study. At the conclusion of the second session, the participants decided to create workshop groups on the four concerns. Each group was encouraged to develop a more specific problem statement, establish goals and means, and develop an action plan to resolve the problem. Each group was asked to present its plan at the final seminar session.

Because of concern for Black Hawk Lake and a recreational area operated by the Iowa Conservation Commission, the planning committee invited a member of that commission to present the third seminar. In particular, the representative was asked to provide information related to dredging the lake or making it more suitable for varied recreational uses. Given the high cost and relatively low priority of dredging the lake in comparison with other needs within the state, the commission representative was not encouraging.

The fourth seminar topic focused on industrial development. The planning group invited a representative of the Iowa Development Commission to discuss this topic. The representative presented a realistic appraisal of the potentials for industrial growth as well as an outline of how his agency might assist the Lake View community in expanding existing industry or locating new industry.

In the last two seminars participants were provided with procedures for bringing about social change. At the fifth one, information on power structures was presented while the final session focused on developing an overall strategy for implementing community action programs. A social action construct was presented to provide learning opportunities on

---

[2] It should be noted that the relatively negative ratings given by the students were not given the weight — higher or lower — that some participants thought necessary. Seminar participants did realize that student perceptions had to be dealt with, of course. Also, they knew that some evaluations by the potential seminar participants had to be discounted slightly to compensate for an acute attack of "boosterism" that hits some local leaders when asked to rate their community. This is especially true in response to questions asking whether the local community is a good place to live, is rated highly by residents of nearby communities, or is headed for a bright future.

strategies for action. In the second through the fifth sessions, workshop groups were given time to develop their action plans. In addition, these were presented to other seminar participants at the final meeting.

With the owner-editor of the newspaper serving as chairperson, the planning committee had access to news coverage in the local weekly paper. After the first seminar session, she published a front-page story disseminating the survey findings to the community. Following each of the remaining five meetings, front-page news stories provided information about the seminar content and the progress of the workshops.

ACTION: RESULTS IN LAKE VIEW

At the final meeting, concern was expressed by some participants that further action might not take place unless commitments were made at that time. Prospects for dredging Black Hawk Lake and obtaining new industry in the community did not seem promising, even though they were identified as high-priority problem areas in both the survey and the seminar. Although the participants were not optimistic regarding the dredging, they recommended that local elected officials continue to keep in touch with state officials about further planning and development for the lake recreational area. Obtaining new industries would likely involve a long-range solution. The seminar participants decided not to proceed further at this time regarding these two problem areas.

The participants were positive, however, about the possibilities for improving recreation and housing. These areas were identified as priority concerns in both the survey and the seminars. The seminar participants decided that the workshop groups on the swimming pool and housing should become ad hoc committees to continue planning and to implement action plans. Seminar participants who had participated in the industrial development and lake workshop groups were encouraged to join the other two groups. At the final seminar, decisions were made for additional meetings of both groups.

Since the survey-seminar, the ad hoc housing committee has initiated a number of steps toward achieving low-income housing. These included inviting an extension housing specialist who provided information about alternatives for meeting housing needs in rural communities. The committee also contacted the local Farmers Home Administration Director. At this stage the committee has located and purchased land for a public-housing development. The committee has also obtained a loan from the Farmers Home Administration for the construction of a public housing project with twelve units. Currently, the final plans for the project are being developed.

After study, the ad hoc swimming pool committee learned that the community would need to develop a recreational plan to be eligible for a federal grant. The committee has undertaken fund-raising projects to finance the development of a recreational plan and purchase land for the pool. Fund raising has included two "gong shows" and a softball game. Another goal of these fund raising projects has been to involve community residents and create awareness of the swimming pool project. The committee has raised $5,000 from these activities. Two major fund raising activities, a house-to-house canvass and a benefit dance, are planned. Currently, the committee is cooperating with the regional planning agency in developing a long-range community recreation plan. It also has located a site near the community high school for the swimming pool. At this location, the pool could be used by the school district as a part of its physical education program.

Plans in both housing and pool action areas were tempered by concerns raised by the evaluations of social factors in Lake View. Especially troublesome were the somewhat negative evaluations of questionnaire items dealing with social status and the control of local decisions. Seminar participants believed they had made progress in breaking some barriers in the community, but they knew that broad based leadership and support would be necessary for the success of any action program. Thus, they set out to build committees that include representatives from a cross-section of local groups. This aided some initial organizing efforts and continues to help in reaching local goals.

The survey data and seminar discussions have had community impacts beyond the housing and recreational areas. The mayor has indicated that the survey data and comments made by the seminar participants have provided valuable information for community decision-making. As an example, he cites the annexation of property on the north side of Black Hawk Lake into the city. Property owners in this area have been requesting that city services be provided to meet their needs.

One of the goals of the survey and seminar program was to involve more citizens in community leadership roles. The chairperson of the planning committee (the owner-editor of the newspaper) believes the program has resulted in younger citizens assuming new leadership roles in community affairs. As an example, she cites the chairperson of the ad hoc swimming pool committee. Before his involvement in the community survey and the seminar program, this man had only been involved in leadership roles in his church. Also, several senior citizens who were active at one time in the community have again assumed leadership roles, particularly in the efforts to obtain public housing.

Another impact of the research and educational program has been increased communication among citizens and organizations. Through developing the communication networks within the community, residents have developed a better understanding of community concerns and alternative ways of dealing with them.

CONCLUSIONS

A major effort was made in this project to integrate research and education into community development. We believe that the impact of this integration was greater than could have been achieved by either conducting a community survey or a community development seminar alone. Combining local data with development concepts and processes provided a more ideal learning situation than would otherwise have been possible. This conclusion supports the work of many community development pioneers, but it is neglected by some specialists forced into development roles because of changing emphases in federal and other agencies.

The involvement of local citizens, leaders, and organizations in planning and designing the survey helped to motivate them to be interested in the research findings. Because the planning committee had decided to integrate the survey and seminar ideas at the beginning of the project, the volunteers who delivered and collected questionnaires from those in the sample were able to create awareness of the follow-up seminar, at which time the data would be disseminated. Thus, the overall strategy of integrating research and education had a plan from the beginning for survey feedback to the community. Integrating the research findings and their interpretation into the kick-off meeting of the seminar was a positive strategy in recruiting the audience for the seminar. Through the survey and the publicity, the entire community had been made aware that the seminar program would include the survey results and involve the participants in further discussion of community concerns.

Since the seminar program continued over six weeks, it provided the opportunity for the participants to study, interpret, and explore possible alternatives for the creation of community action programs. Although the survey findings suggested that employment opportunities and the lake dredging were priority community concerns, the seminar program probed these problem areas in depth and explored alternative solutions. Given the complexities of these two problems and the long-range solutions to them, the participants decided against initiating immediate action in these areas. Instead, they initiated action programs in which they believed solutions could be obtained in the near future, namely, housing and recreation.

The authors have used this approach to integrating research and education to produce community-action programs in several communities. The success of these programs has varied with the degree of participation at the local level. This also determines whether action programs ever are implemented. Local participation cannot be overemphasized; the authors serve strictly as a support staff. The nature of the program is determined by community residents.

The case study presented here is a reaffirmation of but one strategy that can be used to integrate research and education into community development efforts. Alternative strategies should of course be considered in deciding what is best for a given situation, but development will probably be enhanced if the change agent develops strategies that integrate research and education into a total community development effort.

BUILDING ENTREPRENEURIAL COMMUNITIES: THE APPROPRIATE ROLE OF ENTERPRISE DEVELOPMENT ACTIVITIES

By Gregg A. Lichtenstein, Thomas S. Lyons, and Nailya Kutzhanova

ABSTRACT

This article examines the concept of building entrepreneurial communities as a strategy for community economic development. It begins by attempting to define what is meant by the term "entrepreneurial community" and to clarify how economic developers go about trying to create such places – using activities known as the "enterprise development" to help entrepreneurs grow new business. The article then analyzes the current approach to enterprise development and explains why it is incapable of producing entrepreneurial communities. The authors conclude by calling for a systemic and transformational approach to enterprise development that can truly yield community-wide economic development.

INTRODUCTION

Enterprise development is growing in popularity as an approach to community economic development. Its goals are to create wealth for owners and employees by helping entrepreneurs start and grow their businesses. Enterprise development is arguably more sustainable, more cost-effective and more attuned to community development than its sister economic development strategies of business attraction and business retention/expansion (Harrison & Kanter, 1978; Dabson, Rist, & Schweke, 1994; Lyons & Hamlin, 2001).

Gregg A. Lichtenstein, Ph.D., is President of Collaborative Strategies, a consulting firm that specializes in working with entrepreneurs, business incubation programs, and strategic alliances. Dr. Lichtenstein received his Ph.D. in entrepreneurship and social systems sciences from the Wharton School of the University of Pennsylvania. Gregg A. Lichtenstein, Ph.D., President, Collaborative Strategies, 411 N. Exeter Avenue, Margate, NJ 08402. P: (609) 487-8488. F: (609) 487-8889. Email: galichten@aol.com

Thomas S. Lyons, Ph.D. is the Fifth Third Bank Professor of Community Development in the School of Urban and Public Affairs and the Director of the Center for Research on Entrepreneurship and Enterprise Development (CREED) at the University of Louisville. Thomas S. Lyons, Ph.D., Fifth Third Bank Professor of Community Development, School of Urban and Public Affairs, University of Louisville and Director of the Center for Entrepreneurship and Enterprise Development, University of Louisville, 426 W. Bloom St. Louisville, KY 40208-5457. P: (502) 852-8256. F: (502) 852-4558. Email: tslyon01@louisville.edu.

Nailya Kutzhanova is a graduate research assistant and doctoral candidate in the School of Urban and Public Affairs at the University of Louisville. Nailya Kutzhanova, Graduate Research Assistant, School of Urban and Public Affairs, University of Louisville. Email: nrkutz01@louisville.edu.

Recently, the discussion about enterprise development has begun to shift from asking how communities can help entrepreneurs to raising a much broader and more inspiring question: "How can we build entrepreneurial communities?" This, of course, leads to a number of other questions: "What is an entrepreneurial community?" Can they be created and, if so, how? And why have our current approaches to enterprise development not been successful in producing such communities across the country?

This paper seeks to address these questions by first offering a definition of *entrepreneurial community.* We then examine the current major approaches to enterprise development in light of this definition, pointing out their limitations. Our conclusions are based on in-depth diagnoses conducted in dozens of different regional and community settings—urban, rural, high-tech, manufacturing-oriented, disadvantaged, etc.—throughout the world. Finally, we offer a set of guiding ideas, based on years of specific action research projects, as to how local communities might realistically organize themselves to become entrepreneurial communities (See Argyris, Putman, & Smith, 1985; Bourdieu, 1990; Bourdieu & Wacquant, 1992; Lewin, 1951; Schon, 1983; Schon, 1987; Whyte, 1986; and Whyte et al., 1991, regarding action research methods and their scientific foundations).

What is an "Entrepreneurial Community"?

In order to answer the question about what is an "entrepreneurial community," we must first define the term, "entrepreneur." Klein (1977, p. 9) characterizes an entrepreneur as someone who acts "as a marriage broker between what is desirable from an economic point of view and what is possible from a technological [i.e., operational] point of view." This definition highlights two important attributes of the entrepreneurial process: opportunity and innovation. To put these into perspective, "an entrepreneur's goal is to create or capitalize on new economic opportunities through innovation—by finding new solutions to existing problems, or by connecting existing solutions to unmet needs or new opportunities" (Lichtenstein & Lyons, 1996, p. 21). What is considered innovative will depend on the context in which the activity takes place (Lichtenstein & Lyons, 1996).

In our view, entrepreneurial communities are distinguished by certain kinds of behaviors or activities. First, they possess a critical mass of entrepreneurs who are actively engaged in capturing new market opportunities. Their contribution must be sufficient to continually replace any decline in economic activity from existing businesses within the community.

Second, there is a group of entrepreneurs that constitute a distinct and recognizable community within the community. This group, characterized by a network of relationships through which support, resources, know-how and business pass, provides its peers with the conditions necessary to grow their firms. The observation that it takes a village to raise a child applies here as well; it takes a community to develop an entrepreneur and his or her venture (Lyons, 2002).

Third, the community as a whole is entrepreneurial, not just some of its parts. The community is open to change and invests in the conditions necessary to encourage entrepreneurship. Referred to sometimes as entrepreneurial spirit or entrepreneurial culture (labels which tend to obfuscate or mystify what is going on), this characteristic is specifically reflected in the actions taken by various members of the community to support the entrepreneurial process, such as making bank loans to startups, passing favorable legislation, welcoming new members and including them in social and economic networks, etc. If an area is going to be successful in encouraging entrepreneurship, the entire community must support it.

The emerging literature on entrepreneurial communities offers a smorgasbord of ideas and prescriptions about what it takes to foster business entrepreneurship in a community. Much of it draws upon case studies of communities that are widely perceived to be successful in spawning and sustaining entrepreneurial activity—Silicon Valley in northern California, Route 128 in Boston, the Research Triangle in North Carolina, and Emilia Romagna in Italy, among others. This literature cites the importance of "social capital" to the success of communities that have created environments that foster entrepreneurship (Putnam, 1993; Flora et al., 1997; Lichtenstein, 1999; Lyons, 2002). This social capital may be in the form of regional networks among entrepreneurs and their companies, as in Silicon Valley (Saxenian, 1996). It may take the form of geographically based clusters of businesses by industrial sector a la Route 128 (Porter, 2000). It might also manifest itself in partnerships between the community's private and public sectors, as in the case of Tupelo, Mississippi (Grisham, 1999).

Other researchers emphasize different factors. Florida (2002) asserts that human capital is the key to an "entrepreneurial society." He cites the diversity of the local population as an essential ingredient to a community's ability to attract and retain business activity. He believes that communities must adopt policies that yield investment in skilled people, that encourage immigration from elsewhere, that provide an infrastructure for human and business development, and that bring the public and nonprofit sectors into the entrepreneurial mix. Rogers and Larson (1984) and Malecki (1997) have also argued for the importance of nurturing human capital development as a strategy for enhancing local entrepreneurial activity.

Feldman (1994) uses the example of Baltimore to make the point that a strong research university (Johns Hopkins) alone does not ensure an entrepreneurial environment. She argues that an entire "innovative infrastructure" must also be in place, including such elements as a critical mass of activity in one or more industrial sectors, adequate business support services, and a culture of encouraging entrepreneurship. Sirolli (1999) argues for the importance of personal relationships in encouraging entrepreneurial activities in a community. Specifically, he advocates a function he calls an "enterprise facilitator," the purpose of which is to find prospective entrepreneurs, encourage them to pursue their dreams, counsel them, and connect them to other sources of assistance.

These discussions have identified a number of factors that seem to contribute to local entrepreneurial success. Yet, these factors are like unassembled pieces of a puzzle. The question remains, "How does one go about building an entrepreneurial community?"

At the local level, the answer to this question has been to engage in *enterprise development*. In the next section, we examine this strategy and its relationship to community development.

What is Enterprise Development?

Koven and Lyons (2003, p. 100) define enterprise development as "...assistance to entrepreneurs in support of the creation, growth and survival of their businesses." It is an economic development strategy that seeks to create a supportive environment in which new ventures can flourish. In this way, it is viewed by many to be the strategy of choice in the pursuit of entrepreneurial communities.

The infrastructure for pursuing enterprise development includes a host of nonprofit, private, and public organizations—entities that we call "service providers" or "assistance providers." Among these organizations are youth entrepreneurship programs, microenterprise programs (342 programs in the United States as of 1999), business incubators (over 950 in North America), manufacturing networks, entrepreneurship networks, small business development centers (over 63 centers in the United States with over 1,100 service locations), angel capital networks, venture capital clubs and funds, revolving loan funds, Service Corp of Retired Executives (SCORE) chapters, and technology transfer programs, to name but a few. Most communities or regions boast one or more of these entities.

Enterprise development lends itself well to community economic development for several reasons. First, it is a strategy that targets development, not simply growth for its own sake. Second, the focus is on developing local companies in order to build local wealth. Third, it is economically sustainable because local companies tend to use local inputs, they export goods and services and import income to the community, and they tend to remain loyal to their community of origin, being less likely to be lured away to another community (Koven & Lyons, 2003).

Despite its intentions, enterprise development has, thus far, failed to consistently produce entrepreneurial communities, as evidenced by the fact that examples of success in the U.S. are few in number and limited in impact. The next section addresses the reasons behind this disappointing performance.

Why Enterprise Development as it is Currently Practiced Fails to Build Entrepreneurial Communities

Over the last twenty years, we have worked with close to one thousand entrepreneurs and more than one hundred entrepreneurship assistance providers on a variety of applied and action research projects. On the basis of these experiences and data, we have diagnosed at least eight shortcomings of the current approach to enterprise development as practiced in the United States that limit our country's ability to create entrepreneurial communities.

1. Activities are tool-driven, not needs-focused.

2. Activities are fragmented and categorical.

3. There is too little focus on execution.

4. The learning cycle is broken.

5. The focus is placed on the business, not the entrepreneur.

6. There is a missing function – responsibility for the community's supply of entrepreneurs.

7. Funders, not clients, drive the operations.

8. The impact is not scalable.

In the following section, we examine each of these shortcomings.

Shortcoming #1: Tool-Driven, not Needs-Focused

Most enterprise development activities are driven by the use of a particular tool, rather than by meeting a particular entrepreneurial need. In other words, they are supply rather than demand driven. The process for adopting a new activity usually involves the discovery of an approach or program that is being used someplace else and seems to be working. A decision is then made to bring that tool whole cloth, or with only minor modification, to the community searching for solutions.

The belief that proposed enterprise development programs will work is frequently based on the fact that they have been tried elsewhere and have received a lot of attention, not on the basis of proven success nor demonstrated demand (either latent or expressed). Without being grounded in the needs of entrepreneurs, many initiatives are hit or miss affairs—solutions in search of a client base.

A recent study of enterprise development activities in the state of Maine conducted by the Kauffman Foundation demonstrates the conflict between the perspectives of entrepreneurs and service providers. While service providers were convinced that they were providing what entrepreneurs needed, entrepreneurs were not. They believed that providers were promoting solutions they had to offer, rather than what entrepreneurs needed (Kayne, 2002).

In another case, a minority-oriented community development venture fund closed its doors after ten years, having only completed six deals in that time. The post mortem indicated that there was insufficient demand. In reality, the fund was providing a higher level of service than many minority entrepreneurs in the community were prepared to use at the time. We believe these examples are fairly common. They occur because the voice of the customer—the entrepreneur—is missing.

Rarely are enterprise development programs initiated on the basis of a rigorous analysis of the needs of actual, prospective or potential entrepreneurs in the community. Usually the need that the proposed solution is designed to address is assumed, and whatever case is made for funding only involves demonstrating the program's feasibility. Where needs assessments are attempted, they suffer from a number of serious flaws that make the validity of their conclusions questionable.

One problem is that entrepreneurial needs are almost never framed precisely or researched in ways that enable them to be properly proven. For example, the answer by entrepreneurs to a question about their need for financing, or whether or not they would be willing to utilize below-market priced space, would obviously be "yes." But whether or not an entrepreneur would claim to be willing to use a resource or a program is not the issue. The issue is whether the need represents a significant obstacle to the entrepreneur's success and development. In the case of space, for example, a more precise and useful question would be, "Is the unavailability and unaffordability of space a significant obstacle to starting or growing your business? How and in what way?"

In the current approach to enterprise development, assessments, when conducted, are generally very selective and arbitrary in their choice of entrepreneurial needs to be examined. For example, financial needs are given a great deal of attention, whereas marketing needs are relatively ignored. In the United States, as compared to many other countries, internal obstacles—those that have to do with the entrepreneur's willingness and ability to use a particular resource—are often a more serious problem than the accessibility of resources. However, this class of obstacles is largely ignored in enterprise development.[1] We believe the reasons for this situation have to do with the experience and perspectives of the individuals or organizations undertaking the assessment. This behavior may be the result of unintentional bias or an emphasis on activities that are easier to perform or where the necessary expertise is more readily available. It may also be a result of the fact that the field (at least until recently) has lacked an approach to diagnosing needs that is both multi-dimensional and comprehensive.[2]

Entrepreneurial needs are difficult to determine for several reasons. First, entrepreneurs cannot always clearly articulate the needs they have; they understand the symptoms of the problems they are experiencing, but not always the cause. Second, most entrepreneurs do not sufficiently trust the individuals asking the questions, whom they do not know personally, to be honest about their most important problems and needs. Third, surveys are rarely effective in getting useful answers. Either there are communications issues that cannot be overcome by an arms-length format, such as confusion over the meaning of the terms used in the questionnaire, or the issues are too complex and messy to lend themselves to such a simple format. Surveys also fail to capture the difference between what entrepreneurs say and what they actually do. In our experience working with entrepreneurs, we often find that the exact nature of the need cannot be determined until an action is taken to address the problem and the results observed.

Finally, as a group, entrepreneurs (both actual and prospective) are often difficult to reach—they are not always visible (some operate informally until their business is more developed), easy to find even when they are known to exist, nor willing to cooperate. They also are not organized, so there is no intermediary that can help in the process of collecting information.

Shortcoming #2: Fragmented and Categorical

Enterprise development activities are fragmented and categorical in terms of the needs addressed and the population served. Most service providers specialize in a particular functional area or on a particular population, without anyone having responsibility for the individual business or the community as a whole.

The issue is that business problems are complex and multi-dimensional. They are not always amenable to a simple, single solution nor are they exclusively financial, marketing, managerial, or operational in nature. At best, specialized approaches tend to produce partial solutions; in the worst cases, they contribute to the failure of the firm by doing the right things, but in the wrong order.[3]

These service providers tend to function in remarkable isolation of one another within their local communities, an isolation that is reinforced by the fact that each provider has its own culture, jargon, operating practices, professional associations, performance standards, and funding streams. Entrepreneurs in these communities face a disjointed and ad hoc collection of agencies. Any effort to integrate their services must be undertaken by the entrepreneurs themselves, if they possess the awareness and the skills necessary to do so (abilities that are rare among all but the most skilled and experienced entrepreneurs).

Notwithstanding the increasing calls to link financial assistance with technical assistance (and the initial attempts to do so), the fragmentation in enterprise development is truly staggering. Paul Reynolds and Sammis White, two leading entrepreneurship researchers, report for example, "In the summer of 1992, it was possible to identify at least 456 programs providing assistance in 28 different categories, for a total of 752 distinct offerings in Wisconsin" (Reynolds & White, 1997, p. 27).

While the issue of fragmentation in enterprise development has not received any detailed treatment by scholars (largely because the research tends to focus on individual tools or programs), it is a hot topic in the business community, and to a more limited extent, among the service providers themselves. What entrepreneurs see when they look at these offerings is a maze, with no entry point and no clear exit. The result is confusion about where to go for assistance and underutilized services whose impact is far less effective than it could be (Rosenfeld, p. 25).

Another source of fragmentation comes from differences among providers in the populations of entrepreneurs they serve within the community. Certain service providers, like microenterprise programs or targeted incubators, may focus on a broad array of needs but serve only one type of firm or entrepreneur. In some cases, specialization by client population makes sense; in others, it is highly problematic. For example, under pressure from sponsors for immediate results and self-sufficiency, some programs focus on "high-impact clients" (Bates, 1995; Servon and Bates, 1998). This leads them to work exclusively with high-growth ventures (usually technology-oriented) referred to as "gazelles" that are expected to generate very substantial results (i.e., revenues and jobs) in extremely short periods of time. We believe that this practice, cynically referred to as "creaming" or "skimming," is growing.

There are a number of serious problems with this approach:

1. It is extremely difficult to pick winners on the basis of gross generalizations such as which sector is "hot" (e.g., wireless, biotechnology, telecommunications, etc.).[4] Serious misallocation of resources invariably occurs under these conditions.

2. Firms that demonstrate the potential for high-growth are usually able to secure both funding and technical assistance from private sector sources within the community or outside of it. By working with such firms, non-profit economic development agencies are competing directly with the private sector and diverting scarce resources away from other entrepreneurs who need them and have fewer options for securing them.

3. A dynamic economy requires firms of various sizes representing different market segments. By focusing exclusively on one group, the rest are ignored. It is the equivalent of suggesting that we field an entire team of quarterbacks because, as the most important position, it is the only one that matters. That begs the question, "Who is going to catch the ball?"

4. Even if such a strategy succeeds in helping grow a small number of high-impact companies, it has limited effect on the other firms in the community. In other words, this strategy lacks what we refer to as a "developmental multiplier"—any direct benefits to, or influences on, other entrepreneurs or stakeholders in the community.

5. This approach excludes potential clients who might require more effort or time to produce results. It involves reaping rather than sowing, working with firms that are ripe and whose assets are ready to be mined or extracted rather than investing in growing new ones. It favors quick returns rather than patient capital.

6. It breeds a winner-take-all mentality, in which everyone else is considered to be losers.

There is definitely a role within a community for such an approach; the problem is that it is often pursued as a solitary strategy. If successful, the results can be quick and perhaps significant, but they will be short-term and short-lived. The question is, "What will the community do for its next act?" This strategy, moreover, has increasingly become non-viable. The major complaint of providers with a "high-impact" focus is that there are not enough entrepreneurs in the community with whom to work. This conclusion is simply not true. There are plenty of entrepreneurs, just not enough which fit the providers' highly exclusive definition.

Underlying such statements about the limited supply of entrepreneurs is a deeply held and often unexamined belief that entrepreneurship is innate and as a result, the supply is fixed. If individuals must be born with the "right stuff" in order to be successful entrepreneurs, any strategy that involves sitting back, waiting to see who rises to the top and focusing one's resources only on those candidates is eminently sensible. This thinking, which we believe is seriously flawed, does, however, help makes sense of the intensely unproductive competition, the duplication of effort as well as the major gaps in the availability of certain kinds of services that we observe among enterprise development service providers in many communities.

In contrast to this belief that entrepreneurship is innate, we argue that entrepreneurship is a skill that can be developed; and therefore, entrepreneurs are made and not born (Shefsky, 1994). Efforts can be made to increase the supply and to improve the quality of entrepreneurs in a community. There is a workable alternative to chasing gazelles; it involves building a pipeline of entrepreneurial talent and successful companies.

There are other forces of enterprise development fragmentation at work in our communities as well. Microenterprise programs and certain types of inner-city business incubators, for example, have an exclusive focus on low-income individuals. This emphasis serves to balance the extreme focus just discussed; and yet, this approach too, in isolation, has its limitations. Graduates of these programs have reported being satisfied with their experience; but are left afterwards with a sense of being in "limbo," not having anywhere to go for support in their next stage of development.

For example, a microenterprise program in the southeast United States provided excellent support to its clients in the start-up phase; however, when these clients were ready to move to the next level of business development, the program did not have the capacity to assist them in meeting the accompanying set of new challenges. Despite the fact that some of these companies had been in business for as many as eleven years, they were still stuck in the start-up phase, and their entrepreneurs had no idea where else to go for help that they could afford.

Some foundations, in keeping with their philanthropic missions, tend to unwittingly exacerbate this fragmentation by their exclusive emphasis on "low-income communities." They want people to work their way out of this stratum and be able to join the economic mainstream. To do so, members of the community need a pipeline or a ladder from where they presently are to where they want to be. Yet, many such programs limit their attention to members of this segment of the economy. With the best of intentions, this merely creates a path to nowhere. Without any linkage to the broader economy, low-income entrepreneurs will continue to be isolated and enjoy limited success.

Similarly, sectoral strategies have their benefits (e.g., certain economies of scale, collective content expertise, etc.), but at the same time become negative when the firms and participating service providers operate exclusively within these silos, unwilling to interact with other segments of the economic community. Such exclusivity reduces the opportunity to capture business opportunities that can exist between sectors as well as those that cut across different markets.

Shortcoming #3: Too Little Focus on Execution

A third problem with enterprise development today is that there is insufficient focus on execution. Far too much attention and resources are devoted to studying the problems and talking about ideas, rather than implementing them. Many reports describe the nature of the problems, document their impact, but contain no actionable recommendations.

Each year, various gurus crisscross the country to offer their analyses or prescriptions and then walk away leaving their listeners inspired, but struggling to figure out how to make use out of the concepts they have just paid so dearly to hear. There is a certain magical, black box quality to many of these proposals. They are strong on vision, but devoid of details about how to implement or operationalize them.

It is this vast gap between ideas and execution that must be closed. The critical, but missing, piece is the ability to turn ideas into reality. The first step is to begin to value this activity more fully. As one person has suggested, we should stop giving prizes for forecasting rain and, instead, give them only for building the ark.

Shortcoming #4: The Broken Learning Cycle

The field as a whole has failed to use its experiences, of both successes and failures, to build a body of action-usable knowledge about what works, why and under what conditions in order to improve the practice of enterprise development. This is another reason why the discussion tends to stay focused on ideas; the knowledge of what is learned in practice is rarely articulated, captured, organized or disseminated. For a variety of reasons, this know-how remains largely hidden.

One example of this problem is the numerous attempts to identify a set of "best" practices. We believe this effort is fundamentally misguided, because there are no practices that are best for everyone, in all cases, at all times. Instead, the goal should be to identify "successful" practices and to specify the conditions under which they are or have been successful. The difference in terminology is more than just a matter of semantics. Like everything in life, certain practices work "best" under particular conditions, and it is those conditions that must be specified as a part of the description of how the practice works. Information about these conditions is invariably absent in these efforts. As a result, the field continues to lack a more scientific basis for enabling people to make better choices among various alternatives, given the different and unique circumstances they face.

Shortcoming #5: Focus on the Business, not the Entrepreneur

The focus of enterprise development efforts is on the business, not the entrepreneur. They are not one and the same, and the lack of attention to the entrepreneur, as distinct from the business, has become a source of failure. Service providers can provide numerous stories where the proper assistance was delivered but it had no impact on the business at all, because (as is commonly recognized after the fact), the entrepreneur was either unwilling or unable to take the necessary actions to grow the business.

The entrepreneur drives the business, and when he or she does not—by not doing the right thing or by letting the business drive them—the venture is in danger of failing (Gerber, 1995). Successful investors recognize that the right entrepreneur is the key to success, because a skilled entrepreneur can succeed even if the product or service is not exactly right, where a less skilled entrepreneur can kill a business even with the perfect offering.

When service providers focus exclusively on the business, they are missing half the equation and in some respects, the more important half. Not only must they attend to the entrepreneur, they must insure that there is a fit between the business opportunity and the skill set of the entrepreneur as well.

The focus on the business both contributes to and is reinforced by the short-term, arms-length interaction between service providers and their clients. It also causes service providers to lose sight of the fact that, such transactions by themselves are incapable of producing deep and substantial changes in entrepreneurial skills and ability—in other words, in transforming individual business talent and community economies to higher levels of performance. To accomplish that, a deep and longer-term relationship with the entrepreneur is required.

Shortcoming #6: The Missing Function: Responsibility for the Community's Supply of Entrepreneurs

Under current conditions, no one in the community is responsible for the community's supply of entrepreneurs. Enterprise development programs are essentially reactive in nature. They typically wait for individuals to start a business and to walk through the program's doors asking for assistance.

What is missing is any effort to create customers for enterprise development services by influencing both the quantity and the quality of the entrepreneurs in the community.

This function of creating a pipeline of entrepreneurs is a transformational, rather than transactional, undertaking; that is, it involves work that is long-term and developmental. As a result, it cannot be the responsibility of the service providers, but must be the role of an entirely new entity that bears responsibility for enterprise development at the community-wide level.

Shortcoming #7: Funders, not Clients, Drive the Program

A number of problems in enterprise development today are caused by the fact that funders, not the clients, drive the program. This arrangement, also common in fields such as social service and education where clients are limited in their ability to pay, distorts the operations and shifts the focus from the needs of the clients to the priorities of those who write the checks. This results in:

- Funding for bricks and mortar projects that offer ribbon-cutting opportunities, but not for the soft costs of programs, such as staffing highly skilled enterprise development positions. For example, local, state and federal governments provide generously for the construction and rehabilitation of incubator facilities, but little, if anything at all, for the costs of delivering management and technical assistance.

- Funding for new initiatives and pilots, but little for replication or to expand successful programs (Schorr, 1997).

- Decreases over time in on-going operational support, regardless of demand, based on the argument that enterprise development activities should be self-sufficient.

- Funding for activities that produce quick results (e.g., recruiting of branch plants that pick up and move in search of even more favorable tax climates), rather than long-term outcomes (e.g., home-grown enterprises that stay). "Indeed, a 1998 survey found that entrepreneurial development programs accounted for less than 1 percent of the more than $2 billion in annual state economic development investments" (NASDA, 1998).

Shortcoming #8: Impact is not Scalable

Enterprise development is rarely done on a scale that is sufficient to create any significant impact on the community's economy. Yet, if creating entrepreneurial communities is our goal, then scale becomes crucial. Our efforts must have community-wide impact. Because of the fragmentation discussed above, the impacts tend to be incremental, generated on a service provider-by-service provider basis. Because no one is responsible for the entire community, no one is tallying impacts across service providers in order to ascertain a total impact. Furthermore, the manner in which enterprise development is done makes it cost-prohibitive to scale it up. Most programs serve a very small clientele and as a result, their impact is rather limited.

What Must We Do to Build Entrepreneurial Communities?

There are at least five critical strategies for building entrepreneurial communities:

1. Take a systems approach to enterprise and community development
2. Customize the enterprise development system for each community
3. Focus on developing entrepreneurs
4. Develop new roles, skills, and tools
5. Operate as a "transformation business"

In this section, we explore each of these strategies.

Strategy #1: Take a systems approach to enterprise and community development

A major reason for the shortcomings in this field is that enterprise development does not operate as a system whose performance is greater than the sum of its parts. In some communities, critical components are missing; others may have all of the parts, but they are operating in isolation of one another and achieving limited impact.

Enterprise development is not thought of as a system. Even the terminology itself sounds strange, much as referring to the "health care system" might have sounded more that 30 years ago. But in fields such as health care, education, and social services, the need to create a system out of disparate programs and agencies is at least well recognized in principle, if not yet achieved in practice.

Communities need to take a systems approach to enterprise and community economic development. This means two things: that enterprise development programs must work with businesses in a holistic rather than a piece-meal fashion and that they must work with and for the entire community, not just a select part of it.

Many enterprise development professionals genuinely believe that they are taking a systems approach or are making the effort. But as explained in the previous section, this is simply not the case. However, we do believe that in many communities, practitioners are being asked to do so.

Communities are constantly looking for the "magic bullet" or the "holy grail—the one new initiative that will single-handedly solve all of their economic problems. In many cases, these enterprise development programs are being asked to achieve the impossible or to achieve the possible under impossible conditions. Business incubators, just to take one example, are often called upon to reuse old industrial facilities and revitalize abandoned areas by working with small, high-risk start-up enterprises. They are supposed to charge these firms below market rates while operating free of outside financial support and, at the same time, to provide clients with a high-level of technical and management assistance. Finally, incubator managers are often held accountable for generating jobs and tax revenues when they have no control over the business decisions that produce these outcomes. Such expectations are simply unrealistic.

The 1980s and 1990s witnessed a steady parade of new initiatives—enterprise zones, empowerment zones, business incubators, manufacturing networks, industrial districts, cluster development initiatives, peer-lending groups, community venture funds, etc.—all pursued with these same hopes and promises. Each new solution, in turn, was accompanied by great fanfare and high expectations and then faded into the background as it proved to be incapable of accomplishing the impossible—exhibiting a certain faddishness that continues to plague the field.

At the same time, we have repeatedly observed ambitious public entrepreneurs who take on these assignments with the primary goal of establishing model programs that would bring accolades to themselves and their sponsors. These initiatives then become competitions for attention, fueled by a talent for publicity, not performance. In these situations, such individuals act alone, under the belief that they can do it better than and without the help of anyone else in the community and under the need to do so in order to garner all of the glory. We refer to this phenomenon as the "messiah syndrome."[5] This behavior often results in program failure, professional burnout and disillusionment and individuals who leave the field, usually at the point that they have finally learned enough to make a substantive contribution.

Why do these public entrepreneurs (many of whom are incredibly dedicated and energetic) engage in such behavior? We believe it has to do with flaws in the current system, not the participants. This is the nature of the game. The premise of the game is that there is only room within the community for one service provider at the top. This ultimately leads to self-defeating, competitive, and non-systemic behavior.

This occurs when a single program or service provider attempts to assume the responsibility or is improperly given the burden for a mission that should belong to the entire enterprise development "system." Given the partial and obviously limited focus of each provider (as explained in the previous section), the result of the provider's efforts can never be sufficiently global. The claim that a single program is or should be benefiting the whole community, all the while operating in a manner that can never be holistic, is a setup for failure.

Individual programs have their benefits and their place within the community's enterprise development system. However, each operation needs to be seen in the context of the community as a whole. The partial perspectives and competition must be replaced by an integrated system in which each participant has their role to play—complementing one another in a synergistic manner. Only when that happens will enterprise development become a system capable of benefiting the entire community, not simply the few clients in a single program.

Strategy #2: Customize the enterprise development system for each community

Each community must customize its enterprise development system to meet their own needs and circumstances. Since no single program will fulfill all of a community's needs, an enterprise development system will have to be assembled from a variety of possible programs or program elements. Although components may be common to other communities, the complete recipe for each will be unique. It is critical that the enterprise development activities selected be linked to and result in community development. Enterprise development is focused on incubating businesses (and also, we would argue, entrepreneurs). However, for this to result in community development, it must be done in a way that will lead to the transformation of the entire community's economy, not just some small and select segment.

Enterprise development activities must be selected on the basis of their ability to provide both direct benefits to the client population and have an economic as well as "developmental" multiplier or impact on the rest of the community. This can be achieved for example, by focusing on enterprises that trade outside of the community or have the potential to be tightly linked operationally with existing firms.

Strategy #3: Focus on developing entrepreneurs

Communities should concentrate their efforts on developing a supply or pipeline of entrepreneurs capable of building successful companies and improving their ability to successfully identify and capture new market opportunities. Development is a competency, an ability to deal with new circumstances:"It is an increase in capacity and potential, not an increase in attainment" (Ackoff, 1981, p. 35).

The quantity and quality of the community's entrepreneurs are the crucial factors in determining how entrepreneurial it is and has the potential to be in the future. The supply of entrepreneurs is not something that should be taken for granted, and there are many things that can be done to develop them (see Lichtenstein & Lyons, 2001).

Enterprise development is an investment in a community's future. The challenge is to strike a proper balance between investments in the present and the future. One example that highlights this challenge comes from the corporate world. In the early 1960s, the DuPont Corporation of Wilmington, Delaware, launched a new ventures program in order to identify and invest in new market opportunities. In 1970, they scrapped the program, after its detractors successfully argued that the return was insufficient to justify their investment. A subsequent study of DuPont's sales in 1982 showed that the 60-70 lines of business started by the new ventures program in the 1960s accounted for over 50 percent of the company's total profits and 50 percent of its cash flow

(Pinchot, 1985). Investments in the future take time to pay off. Being developmental in nature, such investments require a different decision-making calculus than that used for quick returns.

In order to build entrepreneurial communities, we must proactively engage as well as invest in a set of activities that are focused on developing entrepreneurs who can capture new market opportunities, not simply on preserving the success of existing businesses.

Strategy #4: Develop new roles, skills, and tools

Building entrepreneurial communities requires a new set of skills, roles, strategies, and tools. Missing from the current system is someone with the responsibility for creating and managing the supply or pipeline of entrepreneurs and new ventures within the community. This "incubation" function—through its control of various enterprise development activities and its focus on new versus existing business or revenue—should be accountable for the community's economic future.

Strategy #5: Operate as a "transformation business"

This incubation function should be evaluated based on the efficiency, effectiveness, equitability, and sustainability of its performance, as well as the scale of impact on the community's economy. These criteria clearly indicate that the enterprise development system must be operated as a highly specialized business whose bottom line is defined by the quantity and quality of entrepreneurial and community transformations it produces.

The unique nature of this enterprise development system's business is defined by a new type of economic offering. According to Pine and Gilmore (1999), there are five different types of economic offerings whose value increases in relation to one another: commodities, goods, services, experiences, and transformations.

An example illustrates the differences among these offerings. When they first appeared, the value of business incubators to entrepreneurs was claimed to consist of low-cost (below market) space—a commodity whose only source of value was the price. Slowly, it was recognized that incubators provided additional benefits or "goods"—flexible leasing terms, a variety of sizes, shared physical resources—that were not readily available. Then, incubators began to provide business services—e.g., business planning, accounting, and office support. More recently, entrepreneurs have begun to recognize the value of the experiences they have in incubators—the opportunity to interact with peers and advisors (Lichtenstein, 1992). The next, newly emerging level of economic offering is to facilitate entrepreneurs in developing the necessary skills to build successful companies—in other words, to guide entrepreneurial transformations (Lichtenstein & Lyons, 2001).

CONCLUSION AND IMPLICATIONS FOR ACTION

Success in building entrepreneurial communities can produce jobs, wealth, personal development, and an overall improvement in quality of life. But enterprise development as it is currently practiced, fails to build such communities because it is tool-driven, fragmented, improperly focused, not scalable, and unaccountable to the entire community.

Building entrepreneurial communities involves more than simply implementing one or a number of current enterprise development programs. If we are truly serious about building entrepreneurial communities, we must make the following critical changes:

- Take a systemic approach to our enterprise and community development efforts by creating a community-wide enterprise development system.

- Customize our enterprise development system to the specific needs of our community.

- Focus our efforts on developing a supply or pipeline of highly skilled entrepreneurs capable of building successful companies. We must also institutionalize these efforts, so that the community can sustain a constant flow of entrepreneurial activity.

- Develop new roles, skills, and tools for managing and implementing our enterprise development system.

- Operate this system as a "transformation business"—one that seeks to transform our entrepreneurs, their companies and, ultimately, the community's economy.

None of these changes will be easy to implement, nor will the process be quick. It will require leadership from the public and private sectors of our communities. It will require political will to stay the course while the enterprise development system is designed, staffed, and becomes productive. A community-wide entity will need to be created to facilitate the integration of these activities. Throughout this process, the community's vision of its desired outcome will need to be continuously maintained.

Although space does not permit an in-depth description, many of the strategies presented here are or have been implemented in a number of different settings: a service providers network for minority entrepreneurs in Louisville, Kentucky; a social-capital building initiative in Philadelphia among more than 150 inner-city manufacturers; peer networks among high-tech entrepreneurs in Philadelphia; analyses of enterprise development service providers in Asheville, North Carolina, and Advantage Valley, West Virginia; and production networks among garment industry micro-enterprises in Johannesburg, South Africa. These initiatives are at various stages in their development. The impacts of these new strategies are just beginning to appear and detailed case studies are in preparation.

An entrepreneurial community is one in which everyone—residents, business people, politicians, and government officials—think and act entrepreneurially. Merely exhorting people to behave in this manner will not make this happen. Building an entrepreneurial community requires a conceptual framework as well as a practical operating system that helps people to understand the larger vision, their role in achieving the vision, and the rules for successfully interacting with one another to achieve this outcome.[6]

NOTES

1. These include self-awareness, accountability, emotional, capability and creativity obstacles. See Chapter 2 of Incubating New Enterprises (Lichtenstein and Lyons, 1996) for a complete discussion.

2. See Incubating New Enterprises (Lichtenstein and Lyons, 1996) for such a diagnostic tool; it is the only comprehensive approach to assessing entrepreneurial needs of which we are aware.

3. In several cases, we are aware of technical assistance efforts to implement cellular manufacturing methods on a production line in order to improve efficiency and throughput time. These particular efforts resulted in the bankruptcy of the client because the project was undertaken without first identifying whether the improvements were something that would help them keep existing customers or win new ones. They were not, and the firms were unable to recover from making such a substantial and ineffective investment. The proper procedure would have been to first assess their market and customers and then to determine the appropriate production configuration.

4." Even after extensive due diligence and monitoring, many VC investments yield disappointing returns: One study of venture capital portfolios by Venture Economics, Inc. reported that about 7 percent of investments accounted for more than 60 percent of the profits, while fully one-third resulted in a partial or total loss." (Bhide, 2000:145). More commonly cited is a statistic that no more than 1 in 100 venture capital investments yield a home run – that is, significant returns on investment.

5. We have been present in meetings where sponsors have urged program managers to seek publicity for having a "model" program, even before the program had opened its doors to clients! In other situations, program managers have been urged to become the number one source for entrepreneurial assistance in their community or to go out and find exemplary clients (entrepreneurs that are already far along on the road to success) and then claim them for credit with sponsors.

6. See the following sources for more information on one such system: Lichtenstein, G. A. and T. S. Lyons (2001). The entrepreneurial development system: Transforming business talent and community economies. Economic Development Quarterly, 15, 1, 3-20; Lyons, T.S. (2002). The Entrepreneurial League System,: Transforming your community's economy through enterprise development Washington, DC: Appalachian Regional Commission; Lyons, T.S. 2003. Policies for creating an entrepreneurial region. Proceedings of the Main Streets of Tomorrow: Growing and Financing Rural Entrepreneurs Conference, Kansas City, MO: Federal Reserve Bank of Kansas City.

REFERENCES

Ackoff, R. L. 1981. *Creating the Corporate Future*. New York: John Wiley and Sons.

Argyris C., R. Putnam, & D. McLain Smith. 1985. *Action Science*. San Francisco, CA: Jossey-Bass Publishers.

Bates, T. 1995. Why do minority business development programs generate so little minority business development? *Economic Development Quarterly* 9(1): 2-14.

Bhide, A. V. 2000. *The Origin and Evolution of New Businesses*. Oxford University Press.

Bourdieu, P. 1990. *Outline of a Theory of Practice*. Great Britain: Cambridge University Press.

Bourdieu, P., & L. D. C. Wacquant. 1992. *An Invitation to a Reflexive Sociology*. Chicago, Illinois: University of Chicago.

Dabson, B., C. Rist, & W. Schweke. 1994. *Bidding for Business: Are Cities and States Selling Themselves Short?* Washington, DC: Corporation for Enterprise Development.

Feldman, M. P. 1994. The university and economic development: The case of Johns Hopkins University and Baltimore. *Economic Development Quarterly* 8(1): 67-76.

Flora, J. L., J. Sharp, B. L. Newlon & C. Flora. 1997. Entrepreneurial social infrastructure and locally initiated economic development in the non-metropolitan United States. *The Sociological Quarterly* 38(4): 623-645.

Florida, R. 2002. *The Rise of the Creative Class.* New York: Basic Books.

Gerber, M. E. 1995. *The E-myth Revisited: Why Most Small Businesses Don't Work and What to Do About It.* New York: HarperCollins.

Grisham, V. L., Jr. 1999. *Tupelo: The Evolution of a Community.* Dayton, OH: Kettering Foundation Press.

Harrison, B. & S. Kanter. 1978. The political economy of states' job creation business incentives. *Journal of the American Institute of Planners* 44(4): 424-435.

Kayne, J. 2002. *Promoting and Supporting an Entrepreneurship-based Economy in Maine.* Augusta, ME: Ewing Marion Kauffman Foundation and Entrepreneurial Working Group/Maine Small Business Commission.

Klein, B. H. 1977. *Dynamic Economics.* Cambridge, Massachusetts: Harvard University Press.

Koven, S. G., & T. S. Lyons. 2003. *Economic Development: Strategies for State and Local Practice.* Washington, DC: International City/County Management Association.

Lewin, K. 1951. *Field Theory in Social Science.* New York: Harpers & Brothers Publishing.

Lichtenstein, G. 1992. *The Significance of Relationships in Entrepreneurship: A Case Study of the Ecology of Enterprise in Two Business Incubators.* Unpublished doctoral dissertation, University of Pennsylvania, Philadelphia.

Lichtenstein, G. A. & T. S. Lyons. 1996. *Incubating New Enterprises: A Guide to Successful Practice.* Washington, DC: The Aspen Institute.

Lichtenstein, G. A. & T. S. Lyons. 2001. The entrepreneurial development system: Transforming business talent and community economies. *Economic Development Quarterly* 15(1): 3-20.

Lichtenstein, G. A. 1999. Building social capital: A new strategy for retaining and revitalizing inner-city manufacturers. *Economic Development Commentary* 23(3): 31-38.

Lyons, T. S. 2002. Building social capital for rural enterprise development: Three case studies in the United States. *Journal of Developmental Entrepreneurship* 7(2): 193-216.

Lyons, T. S. & R. E. Hamlin. 2001. *Creating an Economic Development Action Plan: A Guide for Development Professionals,* Revised and Updated Edition. Westport, CT: Praeger.

Malecki, E. J. 1997. *Technology and Economic Development: The Dynamics of Local, Regional and National Competitiveness.* Reading, MA: Addison-Wesley.

Millenson, M. L. 1997. *Demanding Medical Excellence.* Chicago: University of Chicago Press.

National Association of State Development Agencies. 1998. *State Economic Development Expenditure Survey.* Washington, D.C. NASDA

Pinchot, G. 1985. *Intrapreneuring.* New York: Harper & Row.

Pine, B. J., & J. H. Gilmore. 1999. *The Experience Economy.* Boston: Harvard Business School Press.

Porter, M. E. 2000. Location, competition, and economic development: Local clusters in a global economy. *Economic Development Quarterly* 14(1): 15-34.

Putnam, R. D. 1993. The prosperous community: Social capital and economic growth. *Current* October(356): 4-9.

Reynolds, P. D., & S. B. White. 1997. *The Entrepreneurial Process: Economic Growth, Men, Women and Minorities*. London: Quorum Books.

Rogers, E., & J. Larson. 1984. *Silicon Valley Fever*. New York: Basic Books.

Rosenfeld, S. 2002. *Just Clusters*. Carrboro, NC: Regional Technology Strategies.

Saxenian, A. 1996. Inside out: Regional networks and industrial adaptations in Silicon Valley and Route 128. *Cityscape* 2(2): 41-59.

Schelling, T. C. 1978. *Micromotives and Macrobehavior*. New York: W. W. Norton & Co.

Schon, D. A. 1987. *Educating the Reflective Practitioner*. San Francisco: Jossey-Bass.

Schon, D. A. 1983. *The Reflective Practitioner*. New York: Basic Books.

Schorr, L. B. 1997. *Common Purpose: Strengthening Families and Neighborhoods to Rebuild America*. New York: Doubleday.

Servon, L. J. & T. Bates. 1998. Microenterprise as an exit route from poverty: Recommendations for programs and policy makers. *Journal of Urban Affairs* 20(4): 419-441.

Sirolli, E. 1999. *Ripples from the Zambezi*. Gabriola Island, BC, Canada: New Society Publishers.

Shefsky, L. E. 1994. *Entrepreneurs Are Made Not Born*. New York: McGraw-Hill.

Whyte, W. F. 1986. On the uses of social science research. *American Sociological Review* 51: 555-563.

Whyte, W.F., D. J. Greenwood, & P. Lazes. 1991. Participatory action research: Through practice to science in social research. Pp. 19-55 in W. F. Whyte (ed.), *Participatory Action Research*. Newbury Park: Sage Publications.

An Effective Process for
Rural Planning

Martin G. Anderson and Ralph A. Catalano

CONCLUSIONS

Results of the MIDNY pilot program in Central New York indicated that rural concerns can be meshed into institutionalized planning, providing those holding such concerns can effectively plug into county and regional planning processes utilized by professional planners.

However, experiences in the six-year effort pointed to the desirability of greater flexibility in planning processes, when planning is expanded from an urban oriented focus to counties and regions. The project also demonstrated a need for vastly more involvement of non-traditional planners, either on planning staffs or available in a counseling capacity concerning natural resource management and economic problems of rural areas.

Community education, as carried out by Cooperative Extension's MIDNY Project in the five-county region, helped focus attention on rural problems. It provided opportunities for productive interaction between professional planning offices and numerous agencies and organizations concerned with rural interests.

BACKGROUND

Despite the systemic relationship between the "urban crisis" and the little publicized problems of rural areas, professional planners have given little attention to rural areas. Also, planners in the past have given little consideration to the interrelationship between the city and its rural hinterland. This oversight is not a result of inadequate information, as geographers, economists, and others have written on it extensively.

Rather, this lack of sensitivity seems to be inherent in two factors: (a) the planners' roots in architecture, and (b) planning's reform ethic of the late 19th and early 20th century,

This is a summary of a paper presented at the annual meeting of the Community Development Society, Columbus, Ohio, August 1, 1972. Mr. Anderson is an Extension Community Resource Development Specialist, Cornell University. Dr. Catalano is an Associate Professor, University of California, Irvine, Calif. The presentation was made by Mr. Anderson, based on a paper that he and Dr. Catalano prepared jointly. The sixteen page mimeograph report is available from either author as MIDNY—Case Study #2, *An Effective Process for RURAL PLANNING*.

which focused on alleviating the political and physical corruption of the American city.

City planning in America very early became the "City Beautiful Movement." This focus, fed by prominent planners of the early 20th century, developed a preoccupation with the aesthetic impact of the man-made environment, which planning inherited from its architectural forebearers. With this bias, the "comprehensive plan" considered primarily physical determinants, focusing especially on an orderly arrangement of urban land uses.

Simultaneously, social reformers tended to see the city as the source of all evil, and the rural areas as the faunt of all virtue. Rural areas were viewed by planners as "undeveloped land" or "open space," rather than vital element in the whole system that was a city-hinterland unit. The assumption that rural areas were healthy bastions of American individualism was fortified by the early conservation movement. This movement was championed by the natural resource professionals, whose intent was to preserve rural areas from urban corruption.

Planners' preoccupation with the city was reinforced and institutionalized in the past decade by the creation of the "701" program. This program created a great demand for planners, and a proliferation of planning schools which taught skills and theories germaine to 701 planning.

THE CHALLENGE

Recent legislation, focusing on problems of non-metropolitan regions, has revealed a lack of knowledge and experience in rural planning. Insight into non-metropolitan planning is critically needed. Politicians, interest groups, and others have applied pressure to change traditional planning processes to better meet special needs of rural areas.

Also, planners and other professionals concerned with natural resources in rural areas, have recently attempted to team up to plan comprehensively for entire regions, recognizing the interrelationship between the city and its hinterlands. While seemingly desirable, these efforts have frequently been frustrated by conflicting ideologies and incompatible agency goals and objectives.

For example, planners and community educators in the Central New York experiment soon discovered that *comprehensive planning* and *community development* are different processes. Planning is a city-born concept, designed especially to control and direct impending growth. Community development in this country has frequently been utilized in rural areas, often designed to stimulate economic growth and development in communities bypassed by progress. Because of differences in op-

erational techniques, formal training of the professionals involved, and the differing ideology and theoretical underpinning,
these two processes frequently are in conflict.

Essentially, the MIDNY experience demonstrated that a
combination of comprehensive planning and community education, going on simultaneously but independently, was effective. It utilized advantages of each phenomenon. The key to
success was close working relationship, and forced linkages between the two processes on a problem basis.

COMMUNITY EDUCATION CAN PLAY A ROLE

The MIDNY experience indicates that traditional planning
processes will fall short of meeting needs of rural areas. Also,
commonly used implementation tools—such as land use zoning,
building codes, and subdivision regulations—have little relevance to many rural settings. They will meet strong resistance
when applied to problems of declining economic growth, insufficient services, and inadequate public facilities.

Central New York experiments indicate that public education can be used to raise the consciousness of a community to
the point where it recognizes and seeks to activate its self-
interests in public decision making. Leaders of rural interest
groups must be sensitized to the fact that public planning is crucial to their interests; that today's planning decision precipi-
tates the forces which create tomorrow's crises. This was essentially the role of the MIDNY Project in its six-year pilot effort.

THE MIDNY APPROACH

The MIDNY approach capitalized on a recognition that
elected officials and other leaders of small communities, made
day to day incremental decisions. The decision-making process
utilized in rural areas required a constant flow of information,
on a problem by problem basis—as contrasted to the "master
plan" approach.

MIDNY'S educational activities brought together, on crucial regional issues, persons who could influence decisions from
six distinct vantage points—that of promotion, service, regulation, financing, education, and planning. Numerous agency ad
hoc committees from among these disciplines functioned constantly, interacting with planning staffs on a broad array of
problems. These committees guided activities of Cooperative
Extension, and other out-of-school educational efforts.

Though it operated in an urbanizing region, the Central
New York development model seemed adaptable to non-metropolitan regions. This belief was strengthened by a special study
conducted in Southern Illinois near the conclusion of the MIDNY
pilot program (see Case Study #11).

Community education in Central New York triggered a significant increase in relevant communication among elected officials, planning offices, local organizations, and agency professionals. This fostered a working rapport and trust for planning. Planning itself was altered by this increased interaction, and became acceptable to a variety of organizations and agencies that worked with rural people.

This, in turn, improved public decisions that local leaders made in legislative deliberations, and the day to day operation of programs. Focus was diverted from "the plan" to the process of planning as a way to deal with issues and every day community problems.

MIDNY's experiences indicate that planners in non-metropolitan areas must address a planning process to perceived needs of rural leaders, and tailor it to their way of solving problems. In other words, planning must be flexible to fit existing decision making processes of rural communities, and facilitate the involvement of many service agencies and interest groups.

Results of the Central New York experience, written up in a series of case studies and working papers on specific educational activities, should prove helpful to others struggling with the problem of developing an effective planning process for rural regions.

DEVELOPING A COMMUNITY PERSPECTIVE ON RURAL ECONOMIC DEVELOPMENT POLICY

By Glen C. Pulver

ABSTRACT

There is a growing economic disparity between rural and urban areas. To be effective, policy aimed at improving rural employment and income must recognize the great variations that exist in local development opportunities. The objectives of a comprehensive rural economic development policy should include the concerns of both the farm and nonfarm rural economies and resource transitions—people and capital—from one economic use to another. Community development practitioners can play a critical role in helping rural volunteer leaders assess their conditions, acquire necessary knowledge from external sources, and act as catalysts and facilitators in the execution of economic development policy. This paper outlines the changing rural economic base, the factors affecting development prospects, general policy objectives, and the role of the community development practitioner.

INTRODUCTION

There is a growing economic disparity between the people who live in rural America and those who reside in urban America. Rural America, home to nearly one-fourth of the country's people, has lower incomes, fewer job opportunities, and higher unemployment and underemployment rates than does urban America. Those who live in rural America are more apt to be in poverty or live in substandard housing than are their urban counterparts (Eberts, 1986). As a result, national, state, and local policymakers, community development practitioners, farmers, business people in small towns, rural residents, and others are deeply concerned about what can be done to improve rural economic conditions (Extension Committee on Organization and Policy, 1986; Economic Research Service, 1987).

Much of the widening difference between rural and urban areas is attributed to recent declines in farm income and in the value of farmland (Sommer & Hines, 1988). Although agriculture remains a

Glen C. Pulver is a professor in the Department of Agricultural Economics at the University of Wisconsin–Madison.

critical industry (21.2 percent of the jobs in the United States are agriculturally related (Schluter & Edmundson, 1986), the personal income generated by farming is a small share of total personal income in even the most farm-dependent counties (Pulver & Rogers, 1986). Attributing the current rural income situation to the farm crisis alone misses other serious causes of the problem. While policy focused solely on improving farm prices may have a positive effect on farm family incomes, a narrowly focused rural development policy ignores the fact that related nonfarm government decisions at the national, state, and local levels may also reduce the economic well-being of rural areas. Those who live in rural areas are similarly dependent on employment in manufacturing, construction, mining, forestry, and the service-producing industries and incomes from social security, dividends, interest, and rent (Bender et al., 1985).

The purpose of this paper is to provide an outline of the factors that are important in establishing a set of objectives for a comprehensive rural economic development policy. The first part of the paper focuses on the changing economic base of rural America. The second part provides an indication of the factors affecting rural development prospects, while the third section outlines a set of general rural economic development policy objectives. The paper concludes with a discussion of the role of community development practitioners in policy development.

THE CHANGING ECONOMIC BASE OF RURAL AMERICA

Rural America has a complex economy with diverse sources of employment and income. For well over fifty years, the people of the United States have received a relatively small proportion of their personal income from farming (Bender et al., 1985). Although the number of U.S. farm operations reached its maximum in 1916 (Lacy & Bogie, 1986), by 1929, only 8.8 percent of total U.S. personal income came from farming (U.S. Department of Commerce, 1984). Farm earnings are essentially net farm income, with provisions for inventory valuation and capital consumption adjustments. Farm earnings hovered between 6 and 8 percent of total personal income for a number of years, reaching nearly 10 percent in the late 1940s. Since then the relative share for farm earnings has declined almost continuously, falling to 1.3 percent of total U.S. personal income in 1982 (U.S. Department of Commerce, 1984).

Farm earnings do not reflect the total importance of agriculture because many people are involved in providing inputs to and processing products from America's farms. Approximately one out of three jobs in nonmetropolitan counties of the U.S. are agriculturally related—14.7 percent on farms, 1.2 percent in input industries, 6.0 percent in processing industries, and 8.5 percent in businesses retailing and wholesaling food and fiber (Hines et al., 1986).

Agricultural industries are also important employers in urban communities (Salant et al., 1987). Farmers purchase trucks, farm machinery, fuel, fertilizers, and other inputs that are often produced in large cities. Farm products are also processed and distributed there. The economic well-being of agriculture continues to be extremely important to the long-run vitality of much of America. Farmers and agricultural industries are important sources of income and employment.

In recent years the incomes of many farm families have become tied to nonfarm sources. Over 40 percent of the farmers in nonmetropolitan counties currently work off the farm over 100 days a year (Petrulis, 1985). The 1.5 million farm operations with annual gross farm incomes of less than $40,000 are almost totally dependent upon nonfarm income (Findeis, 1985). Many of the 700,000 farm operations with gross farm incomes over $40,000 also receive a substantial amount of nonfarm income (Findeis, 1985). Much of this nonfarm employment has little connection to agriculture. The economic health of the nonfarm sector in rural America is important to the family incomes of many farmers.

In 1982, the U.S. Department of Agriculture classified the 2,443 nonmetropolitan counties in the country by economic dependence (Ross & Green, 1982; Bender et al., 1985). In 1979, the year of peak farm earnings in the United States, the people in the 702 most farm-dependent counties received 19.8 percent of their total personal income from farming (Bender et al., 1985). Dividends, interest, and rent accounted for 17.6 percent, transfer payments for 14.5 percent, and other nonfarm sources for 48.1 percent of total personal income. The bulk of these counties are in the Plains states, with the remainder scattered in states in the Southwest and Southeast (Pulver & Rogers, 1986).

The economic future of rural America remains closely tied to the success of the goods-producing sector because it remains a prime source of income and employment. Government policies and individual decisions that affect the capacity of rural areas to be internationally competitive in farming, forestry, manufacturing, and mining are vital. Rural economic conditions will be adversely affected by a loss in the global market share of these industries. (Sharp changes in social security benefits, interest rates, or government expenditures may have an even more profound effect than shifts in the goods-producing sector.)

The growing need for rural people to rely on the service-producing sector for growth in employment and income is the critical new variable. Nearly 100 percent of U.S. net job growth since 1980 has been in this sector (National Commission on Employment Policy, 1982). If rural areas can be competitive in attracting service-producing industries (such as tourism, computing and data processing, nursing and personal care, and business services) and high-technology-based manufacturing industries, then their futures are bright. If not, life in rural America is likely to become more depressed.

DEVELOPMENT PROSPECTS IN RURAL AREAS

Regional economists have studied the factors that are important to industrial location. While most of these studies have focused on traditional goods-producing industries, some insights have been gained regarding service-producing industries and new high-technology manufacturers (Ady, 1986; Premus, 1986). Five variables appear critical to the location and growth of the goods- and service-producing industries: access to knowledge, access to capital, access to telecommunications, access to transportation, and access to a high-quality living environment (Pulver, 1988).

Access to Knowledge

The application of higher levels of technology and more-frequent adjustments in firm operation and organization (both farm and non-farm) are vital if the United States is to remain competitive in an international economy. This will require better-educated proprietors and workers who are more apt to possess the required managerial and technical skills and, in most cases, are more flexible to changes in the workplace.

Start-ups and expansions of small businesses are generating an increasingly larger portion of American jobs (Report of the President, 1987). The 1980s have been heralded by some as the age of the entrepreneur (*Inc. Magazine*, 1985). Access to management knowledge and skills is essential to those with an entrepreneurial inclination. Most will need specific guidance in writing business plans, developing marketing projections, and establishing effective management procedures.

The generation of new technology can, in and of itself, foster economic growth. The creation of new products and new ways of doing things is essential to sustained economic vitality (Vaughan et al., 1986). Regions where research on and development of new technologies is encouraged are often the "hotbeds" of business creation and expansion.

Access to Capital

Capital access is essential to economic growth. Accessibility problems often occur in more-rural regions. Difficulties tend to arise in the following cases: in start-ups of business types unfamiliar to local financial intermediaries; when there are limited physical assets; when the capital seeker is unknown to the lender; in faster-growing firms; in somewhat larger firms in smaller markets; and with long-term unsecured loans (Combs et al., 1983).

Access to Telecommunications

The advent of the information age will have a profound effect on rural areas (U.S. Department of Commerce, 1988). Within a few years, it is expected that low-cost communication linkages will be a fundamental part of the operation of all industries. It will still be possible to operate outside of these telecommunications systems, but only at a higher cost.

Developments in telecommunication technology continue to reduce the data-transfer cost disadvantage of rural areas relative to urban areas (U.S. Department of Commerce, 1988). This improves the possibility that rural locations will be selected for information-dependent industries. Fiber-optic networks now being built across the country appear to offer even lower-cost means of transmitting large quantities of data. These lines may affect future economic growth in the same way that rivers, rails, highways, and airports have in the past.

Access to Transportation

Access to high-quality transportation systems remains an important industrial location variable. In recent years, proximity to interstate highways and airline facilities has grown in importance. Manufacturing firms ship large quantities of products by trucks. Airline travel is increasingly important to business managers and sales personnel (Ady, 1986; Premus, 1986). The nearly completed interstate highway system has reached directly into many rural areas that are otherwise relatively remote. The steady growth in airport improvements and the development of feeder airlines has had a similar effect.

Two critical transportation matters will influence the development prospects of more-remote rural areas. First, interstate highways— including bridges and important access roads—are deteriorating rapidly (Johnson et al., 1987). If a commitment to repair the highway system is not made, rural areas will become progressively remote.

Second, deregulation of the airlines, aimed at returning the industry to a more free-market-oriented economy, has had a stark effect on the relative competitiveness of most rural areas. The cost of flying between major U.S. cities has been sharply reduced relative to the costs incurred when flying to or from smaller communities.

Access to a High-Quality Living Environment

People throughout the country have come to expect that they can find a way to make a living in communities that offer a high-quality living environment. Many prefer life in more-remote rural regions, but most want ready access to good schools, excellent health care, physical security, recreational and cultural opportunities, satisfactory housing and public amenities, clean air and water, and an appropriately aesthetic setting (Ady, 1986; Premus, 1986; Smith & Pulver, 1981).

There is great variation among rural communities in access to knowledge, capital, telecommunications, transportation, and a high-quality living environment. The most severe impacts from current income and/or employment reductions are being felt by goods-producing-dependent, relatively remote areas such as the farming communities of the Plains, the mining towns of the West, and the small mill towns of the Southeast. People who live in rural areas within easy commuting distance to cities with populations of 20,000 to 30,000 people or more have less difficulty finding alternative employment. These cities appear to offer sufficient access to the critical factors that provide a base for the location and expansion of high-technology manufacturing and service-producing businesses—the growth industries of the 1980s and 1990s (Pulver, 1988).

Some of America's most productive agricultural land is found close to very urbanized regions. While a family's income from farming may be severely affected by reduced agricultural product prices, this is often counteracted by nonfarm sources of income that are stable or increasing. In some cases, the off-farm jobs may attract rural family members into urban employment. The employment opportunities of families living within easy commuting distances of cities are generally greater than those of families in more remote regions. Likewise, the economic development options of small towns near urban centers are drastically different than those for communities farther away from these centers. The great variation in economic dependency and regional remoteness presents a major problem in establishing an effective rural development policy.

Local community development practitioners must be aware of unique resource conditions and existing access to critical development variables. Each community's specific situation will define its realistic opportunities. Community residents must have an understanding of the specific types of industries that can locate within existing resource conditions. This will allow them to invest their energy in stimulating the growth or location of industries that offer real hope for development. For example, those rural areas within easy commuting distance of urban areas may be able to stimulate the growth of or attract a wide range of businesses, including computer and data processing services, personnel supply services, and office and computing machine manufacturing. Community development practitioners in more-remote regions will have fewer options. Among them will be industries such as tourism, nonresidential contract construction, and nursing and personal care services (Cotter & Pulver, 1987).

Some of the critical industrial location variables are policy-sensitive and may often be modified by local action. For example, community leaders may develop capital pools that stimulate the formation and/or expansion of local businesses. Educational programs may be supported that improve the quality of local business management and, consequently, the capacity of existing firms to be economically competitive over the long run. Housing, outpatient health care, and other services focused on the concerns of the elderly may improve the local living environment, thereby keeping that group's spending power in the rural community.

The primary burden for outlining local rural economic development policy lies in the hands of community decision makers. A recent study sponsored by the National Governors' Association found that economic growth in rural counties is the result of "sustained, broadly based local economic development activities" (John et al., 1988, p. 50). State and national leaders, both public and private, make choices that have significant economic influences on every region; but in the end, local community leaders must respond to those influences as best they can.

RURAL POLICY OBJECTIVES

Specific rural economic development strategies need to be built on a framework of clearly articulated policy. Actions must be predicated on rationalized objectives if economic goals are to be met. Webster defines the word policy as "a definite course or method of action selected from among alternatives and in light of given conditions to guide and determine present and future decisions" (Merriam-Webster, 1984, p. 910). Policy choices are influenced by a combination of individual and collective values, knowledge and interpretation of facts, and expected consequences of specific actions (Deavers, 1987).

Although values and opportunities affecting economic objectives may vary widely across the country, there is a common framework for policy formulations. A comprehensive rural economic development policy at the national, state, and local levels should include three concerns: the farm economy, the nonfarm rural economy, and rural resource transitions from one economic use to another.

Farm Policy

The cornerstone of policy aimed at improving the well-being of most rural areas is the maintenance of a healthy agricultural economy. Specific policy objectives could be to:

1. assure an adequate supply of food and fiber to the United States and other available world markets;
2. provide reserves for natural disasters without penalty to producers;
3. assure a reasonable rate of return to resources employed in farming and agriculture-related industries;
4. find new opportunities for the production of crops for nonfood uses;
5. identify substitutes for imported products that might be produced in rural areas;
6. increase the economic value of products and services produced in rural areas;
7. improve the competitive efficiency of American agriculture through increased management efficiency on and off the farm;
8. continue the development and adoption of general wealth-improving production and marketing technology;
9. allow for the necessary long-run structural adjustments on and off the farm; and
10. protect the natural environment for the benefit of future generations.

A parallel set of objectives could be established for those rural regions that are primarily dependent on forestry, fishing, or mining.

Nonfarm Economic Development Policy

The survival of farm families and people in more-remote communities depends on the expansion of nonfarm income and employment opportunities. Those rural communities in which economic growth can be stimulated from sources such as tourism, manufacturing, retirement populations, or service-producing industries may provide ample opportunities for those who need additional income or are leaving farming, forestry, or mining altogether. Specific policy objectives could be to:

1. stimulate the growth of private sector employment and income in rural areas;
2. assure an adequate economic and fiscal base capable of supporting fundamental private and public community institutions (e.g., churches, hospitals, schools, and roads);
3. improve the operating efficiency of private and public community institutions;
4. allow for long-run structural adjustment in the nonfarm economy;
5. insure that public decisions do not place rural areas at a competitive disadvantage (e.g., deregulation, privatization, monetary policy, government expenditures, and international trade regulations); and
6. protect the environment from permanently destructive economic activities.

Rural Transition Policy

The need to ease the transition of resources (human and capital) from their current uses (farming, forestry, mining, durable goods manufacturing, and related businesses) to more productive uses will continue. Specific policy objectives could be to:

1. provide temporary income assistance in times of economic stress for those with a realistic future in farming or other rural-based industries;
2. improve access to job counseling and training;
3. establish transition income-support programs for those who must leave farming, forestry, and mining;
4. stimulate early recognition by individuals of the need to leave farming, forestry, and mining;
5. provide psychological and human support services; and
6. maximize the human resource potential of all rural residents through education and health care.

To be effective, rural economic development policies must be rationalized at all political levels—that is, national, state, and local policies should not be at cross purposes. Some objectives can be attacked at the local level; others can be addressed more effectively at state and national levels. For example, local government units can improve access to job counseling and training and provide some psychological and human support services, but state and national governments will probably have to carry the major burden for providing temporary income assistance in times of economic stress. It is important that local, state, and national policies be complementary and supportive rather than contradictory and competitive.

Public policies that pit producers of one product against another (e.g., cranberries versus mint as a condiment with lamb) or one region against another (e.g., southern milk producers versus midwestern milk producers) add little to everyone's net benefit. Care should be taken not to suggest generalizable solutions from efforts that can promise assistance to only a few (e.g., fireplace logs from oat straw). This is not to discourage improvements in the efficiency of existing firms, new uses for existing products (e.g., biodegradable containers from farm crops), research on new products and new markets, and other efforts that offer the hope of improved economic well-being throughout the United States. There are important roles for leaders at all levels in policy development. State and local leaders are responsible for establishing rural development policy that maximizes the economic prospects of specific states and localities; yet, their efforts should remain consistent with general national policy objectives.

THE ROLE OF THE COMMUNITY DEVELOPMENT PRACTITIONER

Community development practitioners in rural areas have a particularly critical role to play in establishing economic development policy. A clear assessment of community goals and existing resource conditions is necessary as a foundation for policy development. A knowledge of realistic opportunities for employment and income growth, acquirable external resources (private funds and public programs), and prospective outcomes of a wide range of strategies for action is vital. Rural regions are generally at a disadvantage in carrying out an appropriate assessment of local conditions and acquiring necessary new information when compared to urban areas. This is because local government officials, community organizations, business people, farmers, and other individuals in rural America generally have a narrower knowledge base and are a greater distance from specialized sources of information. In addition, they possess a smaller economic and fiscal base with which to finance the acquisition of needed information.

In urban areas, large economic development staffs are hired to provide appropriate community assessments and technical knowledge. Specialists are employed in the areas of public finance, business management, industrial development, entrepreneurship, tourism promotion, job training, minority representation, and citizen participation. In small towns and villages, the responsibility for community economic development lies in the hands of a group of volunteers. These volunteers are usually fully employed in occupations such as farmers, school teachers, hardware store owners, and nurses. As a consequence, there are great differences between urban and rural areas in the capacity to develop effective policy.

Because of the limited economic base with which to hire specialists, volunteers must establish economic development policy in rural areas. This has the potential advantage of better serving the interests of the people as a whole, rather than those of a specialized economic development bureaucracy, if the volunteers truly represent the interests of the broader community.

In rural areas, especially, community development practitioners can serve as catalysts in bringing together diverse interests to develop rational economic development policy. They can provide guidance and support in developing mechanisms to assess community goals, needs, and resources. They can also serve as critical bridges between external information sources and local government, community organizations, business leaders, farmers, and other individuals. This can be done through community education and technical assistance that focuses on specific community concerns. Performing these roles, community development practitioners help local leaders develop comprehensive action plans aimed at meeting their specific policy objectives for farms, nonfarm businesses, and individuals in transition. The major burden for executing the action plans remains on the shoulders of community volunteers. Community development practitioners can, however, serve as facilitators of this local effort.

SUMMARY

The future of rural America is in question. The growing disparity between rural and urban economic well-being has generated great interest in rural development among those with a strong interest in maintaining a prosperous, rural living environment. At the same time, an increasingly diverse rural economy has complicated national policy choices. Farming, which once dominated most rural economies, is now only one of a number of critical income sources. Manufacturing, other nonfarm employment, and retirement incomes are vital to the economic health of many regions.

Once reliant primarily on the natural resource base, rural Americans now find their futures increasingly dependent on access to knowledge, capital, telecommunications, transportation, and a high-quality living environment that includes factors such as health care. A positive future is not assured. A healthy farm economy will influence the immediate employment prospects of less than half of the people who call rural America home. The economic revitalization of rural America, especially in the more-remote areas, will require the careful actualization of a comprehensive rural development policy. A comprehensive policy includes objectives relating to the farm economy, the nonfarm economy, and the transition of human and other resources from old to new uses.

Clearly stated and widely supported policy objectives can provide direction for an array of specific rural economic development strategies. These strategies should link policy objectives to public programs and private actions that provide access to critical economic development factors such as knowledge, capital, telecommunications, and transportation. Policy objectives can also serve as a basis for evaluating the urban/rural consequences of other public or private initiatives that have no direct rural economic development intentions (i.e., deregulation of transportation). Community development practitioners have a vital role to play in working with local volunteers to rationalize and act on an economic development policy that best fits the needs and opportunities of each specific, rural area.

With a comprehensive rural economic development effort, both public and private, there is a high probability of improved economic well-being across rural America. Without it, continued hit-and-miss actions will be futile, lead to great frustration, and assure the continuing growth in disparity between urban areas and much of rural America—especially between urban areas and more-remote regions of the nation.

REFERENCES

Ady, Robert M. Criteria used for facility location. Pp. 72–84 in N. Walzer and D. L.
    1986   Chicoine (eds.), *Financing Economic Development in the 1980s*. New York: Praeger.
Bender, Lloyd D., Green, Bernal L., Hady, Thomas F., Kuehn, John A., Nelson, Marlys,
    1985   Perkinson, Leon B. & Ross, Peggy. *The Diverse Social and Economic Structure of Nonmetropolitan America*. Rural Development Research Report No. 43.

Washington, DC: U.S. Department of Agriculture, Economic Research Service.

Combs, Robert P., Pulver, Glen C. & Shaffer, Ron E. *Financing New Small Business*
1983   *Enterprise in Wisconsin.* Madison, WI: University of Wisconsin College of Agriculture and Life Sciences.

Cotter, Catherine M. & Pulver, Glen C. Metropolitan-nonmetropolitan locational bias-
1987   es of high-growth industries. Unpublished paper. Madison, WI: University of Wisconsin College of Agriculture and Life Sciences.

Deavers, Kenneth L. Choosing a rural policy for the 1980s and 90s. Pp. 377–395 in
1987   *Rural Economic Development in the 1980s.* Washington, DC: U.S. Department of Agriculture, Economic Research Service.

Eberts, Paul. Economic development in rural America: Situations, prospects, and pol-
1986   icies. Pp. 529–546 in *New Dimensions in Rural Policy: Building Upon Our Heritage.* Joint Economic Committee, Congress of the United States. Washington, DC: U.S. Government Printing Office.

Economic Research Service. *Rural Economic Development in the 1980s.* Washington, DC:
1987   U.S. Department of Agriculture.

Extension Committee on Organization and Policy. *Revitalizing Rural America.* Madison,
1986   WI: University of Wisconsin Cooperative Extension.

Findeis, Jill. The growing importance of off-farm income. *Farm Economics.* University
1985   Park, PA: Pennsylvania State University.

Hines, Fred K., Green, Bernal L. & Petrulis, Mindy. Vulnerability to farm problems
1986   varies by region. *Rural Development Perspectives* 2(5):10–14.

Inc. Magazine. Your world will never be the same. 7(April):4.
1985

John, DeWitt, Batie, Sandra S. & Norris, Kim. *A Brighter Future for Rural America.*
1988   Washington, DC: National Governors' Association.

Johnson, Thomas G., Deaton, Brady J. & Segarra, Eduardo. *Local Infrastructure In-*
1987   *vestment in Rural America.* Boulder, CO: Westview Press.

Lacy, A. Wayne & Bogie, David W. America's farm population: Historical changes
1986   and recent trends. Pp. 98–113 in *New Dimensions in Rural Policy: Building Upon Our Heritage.* Joint Economic Committee, Congress of the United States. Washington, DC: U.S. Government Printing Office.

Merriam-Webster. *Webster's Ninth New Collegiate Dictionary.* Springfield, MA: Merriam-
1984   Webster, Inc.

National Commission on Employment Policy. *The Work Revolution.* 8th Annual Report.
1982   Washington, DC.

Petrulis, Mindy F. Effect of U.S. farm policy on rural America. *Rural Development*
1985   *Perspectives* 1(3):31–34.

Premus, Robert. Attracting high-tech industry and jobs: An assessment of state prac-
1986   tices. Pp. 55–71 in N. Walzer and D. L. Chicoine (eds.), *Financing Economic Development in the 1980s.* New York: Praeger.

Pulver, Glen C. The changing economic scene in rural America. *The Journal of State*
1988   *Government* 61(1): 3–8.

Pulver, Glen C. & Rogers, Glenn R. Changes in income sources in rural America.
1986   *American Journal of Agricultural Economics* 68(5):1181–1187.

Report of the President. *The State of Small Business.* Washington, DC: U.S. Government
1987   Printing Office.

Ross, Peggy J. & Green, Bernal L. Procedures for developing a policy-oriented clas-
1982   sification of nonmetropolitan counties. U.S. Department of Agriculture, Economic Research Service, EDD Staff Report No. AGES 850308.

Salant, Priscilla, Saupe, William, Green, Bernal & Carlin, Tom. Which Wisconsin
    1987   counties will be affected most by the farm crisis? *Economic Issues*, No. 103.
              Madison, WI: University of Wisconsin–Extension.
Schluter, Gerald & Edmundson, William. How to tell how important agriculture is to
    1986   your state. *Rural Development Perspectives* 2(3):32–34.
Smith, Stephen M. & Pulver, Glen C. Nonmanufacturing business as a growth alter-
    1981   native in nonmetropolitan areas. *Journal of the Community Development Society*
              12(1):33–47.
Sommer, Judith E. & Hines, Fred K. *The U.S. Farm Sector.* Washington, DC: U.S.
    1988   Department of Agriculture, Economic Research Service.
U.S. Department of Commerce. *State Personal Income 1929–82* Washington, DC: U.S.
    1984   Department of Commerce.
U.S. Department of Commerce. Ensuring telecommunications and information ser-
    1988   vices for rural America. *NTIA Telecom 2000: Charting the Course for a New
              Century.* Washington, DC: U.S. Department of Commerce.
Vaughan, Roger, Pollard, Robert & Dyer, Barbara. *The Wealth of States.* Washington,
    1986   DC: Council of State Planning Agencies.

COOPERATIVES IN RURAL COMMUNITY DEVELOPMENT: A NEW FRAMEWORK FOR ANALYSIS

By Kimberly Zeuli, David Freshwater, Deborah Markley and David Barkley

ABSTRACT

Although cooperatives are viewed as an important vehicle for community development, the relationship between cooperatives and communities is a neglected research issue. Because of this neglect, no framework for analysis of the relationship between cooperatives and communities exists. We present case studies of non-agricultural cooperatives in rural areas that provide some general insights into the innovative activities of successful cooperatives in rural community development. The case studies help define a new framework for analyzing the complete impact and efforts of cooperatives as community development agents. In contrast to the typical unifunctional and multifunctional categorization of cooperatives, our framework identifies two main categories of cooperative community development activities: unintentional, by simply organizing a business as a cooperative, and intentional, by creating community development programs. Cooperatives in this latter group are further sub-divided according to how closely the development activity is related to their core function.

INTRODUCTION

In 1995, the International Cooperative Alliance, the organization that represents cooperatives globally, adopted an additional (seventh) guiding principle for cooperatives: "concern for community," sending the message that cooperatives should work for sustainable community development.[1] As Wilkinson & Quarter (1996) insightfully note, the addition of this principle made the implicit link between cooperatives and communities explicit. The potential for cooperatives to play a more vital and direct role in community development was also recognized by a group of cooperative development practitioners in the United States. They adopted the following principle for their profession in 1994: "Cooperatives are development tools and should promote both social empowerment and economic goals" (Patrie, 1998, p. 11). The crucial question that remains to be answered is how cooperatives can accomplish this task. Our research on innovative, non-agricultural cooperatives involved in rural development informs a new framework that helps answer this question.

Kimberly Zeuli is an Assistant Professor in the Department of Agricultural and Applied Economics at the University of Wisconsin-Madison. David Freshwater is a Professor in the Department of Agricultural Economics at the University of Kentucky. Deborah Markley is Co-Director of the Center for Rural Entrepreneurship, Chapel Hill, North Carolina. David Barkley is a Professor in the Department of Applied Economics and Statistics at Clemson University.

Cooperatives are viewed as potentially important vehicles for community development since they can solve local problems by mobilizing local resources into a critical mass, and by virtue of being locally owned and controlled, cooperatives can keep profits and responsibility in the hands of local citizens. More than this, the cooperative structure has the potential to create more substantial social and economic benefits within a community than non-cooperative firms. The structure, or the very nature of cooperatives, it is argued, makes them more community-oriented, because they can pursue different objectives than purely profit-oriented firms (Fairbairn et al., 1995; Wilkinson & Quarter, 1996).

Nearly a decade after the call for cooperatives to become more intentionally community-oriented (Patrie, 1998; Wilkinson & Quarter, 1996), it seems an appropriate time for analyzing the role today's cooperatives are playing in community development. More specifically, how do they contribute to rural community development? The relationship between cooperatives and communities is a neglected research issue. Most studies of cooperatives in rural areas focus on the impacts of agricultural cooperatives, still the most prevalent rural cooperatives (Leistritz, 1997; Merrett & Walzer, 2001; Trechter & King, 2001). The significant potential for non-agricultural cooperatives in rural communities has been recognized in several related studies (Bhuyan & Leistritz, 2000; Fulton & Ketilson, 1992; Lorendahl, 1996; Nadeau & Thompson, 1996), but no comprehensive analysis of their activities in the United States has been undertaken.[2] Because of this lack of inquiry, no framework for *analysis* of the relationship between cooperatives and communities exists. Fulton and Ketilson (1992) provide some theoretical models to explain cooperative behavior in communities, and Wilkinson and Quarter (1996) offer a theoretical framework that describes the process of developing cooperatives in a community development context. While both offer important insights, they do not offer a framework for examining the actual impacts and intentions of cooperatives regarding community development.

The results of our analysis provide practitioners, policymakers, and scholars of both community development and cooperatives with not only a better understanding of the multifaceted role cooperatives can and do play in rural community development, but also insight into the factors that characterize successful efforts. Our findings illustrate how cooperatives can be used within community self-development initiatives, as another way to create locally owned small businesses, an alternative to the more familiar industrial recruitment strategy.[3] Although research has documented that both strategies can create more jobs and increased local economic activity in communities (Flora et al., 1992; Green et al., 1990; Loveridge, 1996), the appeal of self-development lies in its process, which typically includes broader community involvement than other strategies (Sharp & Flora, 1999).

The balance of this article is organized as follows. The second section provides a brief description of the research methods. The third section comprises a synthesis of past research on the role of cooperatives in local development, which establishes a number of different ways that cooperatives have been instrumental in improving community conditions. This information was used to construct a tentative analytical framework that was then more fully developed inductively, using the results of our case study research. The framework is presented in the fourth section and then amplified in the fifth section by using case studies as illustrations. We finally conclude with a review of our findings, focusing on factors for success and the implications for community development.

RESEARCH METHODOLOGY

We contacted cooperative development centers, university cooperative centers, and state cooperative trade associations to help us identify innovative non-agricultural cooperatives involved in rural development activities. An effort was made to find cooperatives in different regions across the United States and in sectors that had the greatest potential to stimulate local economic growth. While consumer and service cooperatives, such as those involved in housing, day care, and groceries, play important support roles in a local economy, they are not major engines of economic growth. We chose cooperatives that were either directly engaged in activities that led to a significant share of sales to non-local customers, or cooperatives that had direct links to firms that serve external markets. Thus, we followed a traditional "export-base" orientation in selecting the set of case studies. Since an important goal of our research was to use the cases to help describe more generally the different ways that cooperatives foster community development, we selected cooperatives that were engaged in variety of development activities and that had entered those activities for different reasons. Our final criterion was to choose cooperatives that represented relatively successful business ventures. Failed co-ops would have been less useful for this research since the primary purpose was to identify a set of factors or conditions that enable cooperatives to be *successful* rural economic development agents.

Ultimately, we chose to study fourteen cooperative organizations.[4] The case studies, conducted in 2001, involved visits to the cooperatives and detailed interviews with their managers, board members, and key community individuals. Qualitative and quantitative data gathered through the interviews and secondary sources of information included general information on the cooperative and community, its rationale for engaging in community development, a description of its community development activities, and feedback on how the co-op affected its community. A case study approach was chosen because it provides more depth and a richness of understanding that is often lacking in empirical analysis based upon secondary data. Case studies are especially useful in exploratory analysis, allowing scholars to gather information on subjects that have not been previously analyzed (Yin, 1989).

Only nine of the case studies are discussed in this paper (listed in Table 1). Three cases were omitted in order to keep the discussion as cogent as possible. They represented new opportunities for the cooperative model, but they were

Table 1. Cooperative Case Studies

Name of Cooperative	Location	Description
Extrinsic Community Development Cooperatives		
Flathead Electric Cooperative	Kalispell, Montana	Industrial park development
Pee Dee Electric Cooperative	Florence, South Carolina	Industrial park development
Central Iowa Power Cooperative	Cedar Rapids, Iowa	Venture capital program
Rural Electric Cooperative	Lindsay, Oklahoma	New house construction company
Northern Electric Cooperative	Opheim, Montana	Purchase of a small local bakery
Inherent Community Development Cooperatives		
The North Coast Co-op	Arcata, California	Full service grocery store
Rural Wisconsin Health Cooperative	Sauk City, Wisconsin	Rural health service cooperative
Community Cooperatives		
Garrett Rural Information Cooperative	Garrett County, Maryland	Internet service provider
Foodworks Culinary Center	Arcata, California	Business incubator program

not actual cooperatives. Two additional cases, which we judged to be less innovative in terms of activity and organizational structure, were also excluded, primarily for sake of brevity.[5]

COOPERATIVE INVOLVEMENT IN COMMUNITY DEVELOPMENT: A NEW FRAMEWORK

Within the current body of literature, cooperatives are generally divided among those that are unifunctional and others that are multifunctional (MacLeod, 1997; Wilkinson & Quarter, 1996).[6] As described by Melnyk (1985), unifunctional cooperatives focus on meeting the specific needs of their members but not on broader community issues; they reflect the individualistic tendencies of modern society. Multifunctional cooperatives serve both their members as well as the broader community. They are concerned with achieving a dual bottom-line: financial and social (Fairbairn et al., 1995). Cooperatives in the United States, especially agricultural cooperatives with their explicit focus on providing member returns, are almost always placed in the unifunctional category. Our case study research results, however, suggest this categorization is inappropriate and its generality provides a limited perspective for analyzing the relationship between cooperatives and communities. We posit an alternative typology of cooperatives from a community development perspective (Figure 1). The distinction between intentional and unintentional cooperatives will be fleshed out in this section.

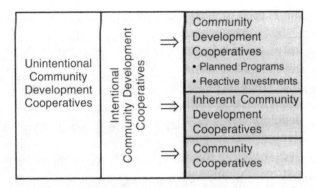

Figure 1. A New Typology of Cooperatives from a Community Development Perspective

As with any business structure, cooperatives provide goods and services while generating jobs and taxes for the community, as well as income for the business owners. However, since cooperative owners (members) are generally local residents, the community often retains a greater share of the business profits than in the case of investor-owned firms whose shareholders may be scattered across the country, or in the case of smaller partnerships and sole proprietorships, whose profit sharing is limited to only a few. Cooperatives can also challenge the domination of local monopolies by offering competitively priced products and services (Fulton & Ketilson, 1992).

In addition to these economic benefits, cooperatives generate positive social influences within their communities. Individuals who serve on boards of cooperatives develop skills in business management, communication, and group problem-solving that can be used in other organizations. Educational opportunities are often extended to members who do not serve on the board and are provided in areas beyond the core business (Torgerson, 1990); a duty to educate members is a traditional cooperative principle. Thus, cooperatives can play an important role in developing a capacity in training local leadership. Since cooperatives comprise local people working collectively towards a common mission, they also have the potential to foster community cohesion. The process of creating cooperatives can be very inclusive, involving many different stakeholder groups within a community (Walzer & Merrett, 2001).[7] Cooperatives often provide vital local meeting places where people have a chance to interact—a key factor in community building (Fulton & Ketilson, 1992; Wilkinson, 1990). Anecdotal evidence suggests that cooperatives help towns maintain a sense of community (Fulton & Ketilson, 1992).

These social and economic contributions are largely *unintentional*, unplanned outcomes emerging from the process of organizing and operating a cooperative. As Egerstrom (2001) states, today's agricultural cooperatives are created to provide economic benefits for their members; "community economic development is a by-product of cooperative development" (p. 73). Nadeau and Wilson (2001) refer to these social and economic benefits as "community externalities," the "consequences of [cooperative] development that affect the local community" (p. 65). In sum, cooperatives included in the unintentional category of our new taxonomy have no community development objectives; their local impact is related to the business and structure of the cooperative only.

In other instances, cooperatives are directed to be more *intentional* about community development, i.e., they have explicit community development objectives and invest their resources in efforts that serve the broader community. The cooperatives that fit in this category can be further subdivided into three groups: (1) extrinsic community development cooperatives, (2) inherent community development cooperatives, and (3) community cooperatives (Figure 1). Again, the subdivision is based primarily on the cooperatives' community development objectives and activities. *Extrinsic community development cooperatives* invest in development activities separate from the core business of the cooperative; they do not directly meet the needs of their members, but they are expected to increase local economic activity and thereby create additional future demand for their core function. Many of these investments are in what might be termed "platform for development" functions, including the provision of broadly used services (such as cable television), more housing or industrial sites for firms, and general programs to attract, retain, and expand business. Rural towns in the Midwest have been steadily losing retail stores over the last two decades resulting in fewer jobs, taxes, and ultimately the decline in population (Ayres, Leistritz, & Stone, 1992). To offset these trends, local cooperatives that depend on local demand often initiate community development programs (Stafford et al., 1989). For example, rural electric and utility cooperatives may sponsor distance-learning technologies in rural schools, finance the building of physical infrastructure, and make direct equity investments in local businesses (Freshwater, 1998; Stafford et al., 1989; Thompson, 2002).

While this type of cooperative community development activity is planned, programmatic, and largely proactive, in other cases cooperatives may engage in these activities on an ad-hoc basis, in reaction to a community crisis. For example, local agricultural cooperatives frequently purchase non-related (and often not very profitable) stores (e.g., bakeries, car washes, and auto parts) in their towns (Duffey, 1990; Stafford, 1990). Typically, they are the buyers of last resort; without their purchase the stores would close and community residents would be forced to find the same services in another town (Fairbairn et al., 1995; Stafford, 1990). Thus, these reactive investments tend to occur in activities or sectors in which cooperatives lack prior experience and core competency (e.g., an electric cooperative purchasing a bakery or a grain marketing cooperative operating a tire dealership).

The co-op members may recognize not only a personal inconvenience if they fail to act, but also the long-term negative economic and social impacts that failed businesses impose on their community, including (although they may be very indirectly related) their cooperative. In general, since cooperative owners are also community residents, they are still acting rationally when they choose to accept lower profits or decreased benefits from their co-op investment if the tradeoff provides an important service or product in the community (Enke, 1945; Fulton & Ketilson, 1992; Fairbairn et al., 1995). However, non-cooperatives and enterprises owned by non-local investors are likely to be guided by shareholder profits, unless one assumes they are altruistic. This argument explains why cooperatives (owned by investors who cared more about the service than the profits) were historically the major providers of electricity and telephone service to sparsely populated rural areas in the United States. Recent empirical research by Bhuyan and Leistritz (2000) and Fulton and Ketilson (1992) further support this premise. Both studies found various types of cooperative businesses that were created because other types of firms were unwilling to provide the goods and services. Reactive investments should be distinguished from non-reactive investments in which co-ops invest in a local business for strategic business purposes. When the decision to invest is forward looking, there is a greater opportunity to act strategically and choose investments with greater potential to benefit the local community.

In contrast to co-ops in the extrinsic community development category, other cooperatives pursue community development as a more integrated function of their overall activity. These aptly labeled *inherent community development cooperatives* have no separate community development subsidiaries or programs. Indeed, within these types of cooperatives, it should be impossible to separate the core activity of the cooperative from its community development objectives. Such cooperatives have been established by a group of people to fill some normal business function that is either absent or inadequately provided (e.g., housing and credit), but that function is also an integral part of that community's development. For instance, a housing cooperative provides affordable housing for the group of individuals who created the co-op, and it adds more affordable housing within the community in general. Therefore, this category of cooperatives challenges the underlying assumption supporting the unifunctional-multifunctional paradigm. Certainly, housing cooperatives could also be created from the "top-down" by local governments or community development organizations. In that case, however, those cooperatives would belong in our third category of cooperatives—*community cooperatives*.

At the other end of the spectrum of community orientation, some cooperatives are created with the primary objective of serving the community. These *community cooperatives* provide specific goods or services primarily dictated by the broad social and economic development needs of the community. Both the core activity and the cooperative organizational form are chosen primarily for their ability to serve community development. MacLeod (1997) calls such cooperatives "community business corporations." In his words, they "indicate a class of business that is specifically set up for the purpose of improving the local community ..." instead of "creating dividends for shareholders" (p.

114). They are characteristically developed by individuals within a community who seek to address a community development issue (i.e., they are organized from the "top-down" rather than "bottom-up").

Perhaps the most well known example of a community cooperative is Mondragon in the Basque region of Spain. The Mondragon "experiment" in community economic reform has grown into a complex of cooperatives that comprise over 100 individual businesses (MacLeod, 1997). Other notable cases include the Evangeline region in Prince Edward Island, Cheticamp in Nova Scotia, Emilia Romagna in Italy, and the kibbutz of Israel.[8] Each of these cases represents an integrated system of co-ops working together within a distinct geographic space to meet collectively the needs of the community (Wilkinson & Quarter, 1996). Less well known, but similar in concept, are the "community cooperatives"—designed to meet diverse social and economic community objectives—in Great Britain, Canada, and Sweden (Lorendahl, 1996; Storey, 1982).[9] Our case studies highlight another type, independent community cooperatives (i.e., they are not part of a larger cooperative network) that are engaged in a single business.

CASE STUDIES

The following discussion briefly summarizes the findings from each case study in the context of the alternative typology of cooperatives described above (figure 1). All of the cases (by virtue of our selection criteria) represent intentional community development cooperatives. The brief synopsis for each co-op highlights the characteristics that place them in one of the three intentional community development categories (and thus helps illustrate the categorization process) as well as the factors behind their success. Success is defined as their ability to meet their objectives, but it does not reflect their total community development impact. Four rural electric extrinsic community development cooperatives, all of which have planned community development programs, will be summarized first: Flathead Electric Cooperative, Pee Dee Electric Cooperative, Central Iowa Power Cooperative, and Rural Electric Cooperative. They are followed by a single case of an extrinsic community development cooperative making an ad-hoc, reactive investment: Northern Electric Cooperative. Two cases epitomize inherent community development cooperatives: North Coast Cooperative, a food cooperative, and Rural Wisconsin Health Cooperative, which provides an array of services to its 28 member hospitals. The final pair of case studies represents community cooperatives: Garrett Rural Information Cooperative, an Internet service provider, and the Foodworks Culinary Center, a business incubator.

Extrinsic Community Development Co-ops (Planned Programs)

The primary mission of Flathead Electric Cooperative and Pee Dee Electric Cooperative is to provide competitive and reliable electric service to their members in Montana and South Carolina, respectively, although both cooperatives also pursue economic development objectives. For example, in its mission statement, Pee Dee declares that it is dedicated to "the active participation in economic development and the recruitment of jobs and opportunities for the citizens of the Pee Dee region."[10] In response to both missions (the provision of power and economic development), both co-ops have developed industrial parks to recruit and retain businesses in the communities they serve. The businesses they help to sustain clearly increase the demand for electric power, thus increasing the co-op's customer base, as well as stimulating the local economy. In 1995, Flathead Electric created the Evergreen Rail Industrial Park (ERIP), approximately 40 acres of land adjacent to its headquarters in Kalispell, Montana. Pee Dee Electric's community development efforts are more comprehensive, and they date back to the 1980s with the establishment of a 300-acre industrial park in Marion County, South Carolina, and a subsidiary (Pee Dee Electricom) that provided digital satellite technology to the region. Pee Dee Electricom now serves as the co-op's property development arm. It is developing Commerce City, a 700-acre industrial park in Florence, South Carolina, that will serve a six county area labor market.

Flathead and Pee Dee were able to successfully develop their industrial parks because of the strong and established relationships both had developed within their communities. In the case of Flathead, the city of Kalispell had been buying its power from another utility. Because the sewage treatment plant in Kalispell was near peak capacity, the city had placed restrictions on further local development. Flathead was given permission to develop ERIP because of Flathead's close ties to the community and its previous contributions to community development. Pee Dee was able to broker a partnership with area city and county governments jointly to support the park; the government agencies viewed the cooperative as a vital part of the region with no "ulterior" motives. A particularly innovative aspect of Pee Dee's development effort was to incorporate local universities and community colleges into the process of recruiting prospective employees into the firm. Both cooperatives have taken a cautious approach in developing their industrial parks, which seems to be another essential factor in their success. By developing the industrial park's infrastructure in phases (on demand), they are not unduly risking their members' equity.

The Central Iowa Power Cooperative (CIPCO), an electric generation and transmission company based in Cedar Rapids, Iowa, operates a comprehensive economic development program that includes business recruitment, land development, a construction management enterprise, and the management of the Iowa Capital Corporation (ICC), a subsidiary venture capital firm. A significant barrier to business growth in rural areas is lack of equity capital. Equity capital is necessary not only to create new business ventures, but also to finance business expansion (Gaston, 1990; Parker & Parker, 1998). Innovative rural equity institutions have been created in some regions to fill this need, although not all have been successful (Barkley et al., 2001). An equity institution modeled as a cooperative theoretically could help avoid the problems some traditional venture capital institutions face as they try to balance financial and development objectives. Since a cooperative may not require the same rate of return on its investments as an investor-owned firm, it might choose to make an investment that is beneficial to the community and not just to the bottom line.

ICC was initially created and capitalized by CIPCO, Corn Belt (another Iowa generation and transmission cooperative), and the state government in 1991. Several years after ICC was established, CIPCO bought out the other two partners. Originally, ICC had two funds, one for CIPCO and one for Corn Belt, because they had different investment goals and criteria. Corn Belt was primarily interested in investments to boost economic development in its service area. CIPCO's principal objective, however, was to make investments with a high potential rate of return; the location of the investment was a secondary concern. CIPCO continues to manage ICC with the objective of maximizing the internal rate of return, suggesting it is not fully committed to community development and thus contradicting the theoretical advantage of cooperative venture capital firms. CIPCO has even drawn from ICC revenue to cover costs in its core generation and transmission business in spite of the wishes of ICC directors, who would rather use more of its revenue to increase the venture capital pool to a more efficient size.

Another barrier to rural economic development is a shortage of affordable housing. To address this problem, a group of eight rural electric cooperatives in Oklahoma jointly developed a plan in the 1990s to form a new housing construction and property development cooperative. After considerable discussion, they abandoned the plan, in part because existing state law prohibited cooperatives to proceed with a joint subsidiary cooperative, and in part because the mechanics of coordinating such an investment were formidable. In addition, several cooperatives balked at the cost of capitalizing such a large company. Nevertheless, despite these setbacks, Rural Electric Cooperative (REC), a rural electric distribution cooperative located in Lindsay, Oklahoma, decided to proceed independently with a scaled down version of the plan and created Country Living Homes (CLH), a corporate subsidiary, in 2000. CLH is a housing construction firm that specializes in building steel framed homes in rural areas of Oklahoma. REC had developed three subsidiaries before CLH, including one that provided better television service to its members. REC is interested in creating subsidiaries that provide products and services that are not readily available in rural areas.

In the four preceding cases, the cooperatives or their subsidiaries operated their community development programs either as separate business entities (subsidiaries) or as distinct programs within their cooperatives. Further, the programs do not directly meet the needs of their members, but they are expected to increase local economic activity and thereby create additional future demand for their core function. The programs are all proactive and planned, conceived to meet a well-established need in a specific rural area.

Extrinsic Community Development Co-ops (Reactive Investments)

In contrast to the preceding cases of planned programs in Extrinsic Community Development cooperatives, the following case represents a distinctly different approach: reactive investment. Northern Electric Cooperative (NEC), a rural electric cooperative with headquarters in Opheim, Montana, bought Granrud's Lefse Shack in 1997 when the owners wanted to retire and sell the business but no local buyer emerged. The Lefse Shack is a small bakery that specializes in the production of lefse, traditional Norwegian potato bread. Although the Lefse Shack is a relatively small business, it remains one of the larger employers in the town of Opheim. The loss of the 27 jobs it provided would have been significant. The Lefse Shack had been a family business in Opheim for over twenty years, and the owners wanted the business to stay in town; therefore, they turned down offers from investors outside the state who wanted to relocate the business. They sold the business to NEC for a price significantly less than the amounts offered by the out-of-state investors and financed a considerable portion of the sale. The Lefse Shack is a profitable business that generates modest annual returns for NEC.

This case represents a successful example of the entry of an existing cooperative into a new, unrelated enterprise. Because the Lefse Shack is a small firm that produces a single product with a well-established market, it was relatively easy for NEC to maintain those operations. The cooperative was not required to learn a great deal about the production or marketing of lefse. In addition, NEC was able to provide accounting, legal, and other business services at lower rates than the Lefse Shack was able to obtain before the sale.

Inherent Community Development Co-ops

In contrast to the preceding five cases highlighting extrinsic cooperatives, we shall look at inherent community development cooperatives and how they pursue community development as a more integrated function of their overall activity. They have no separate community development subsidiaries or programs, and the division between the core activity of the cooperative and its community development objectives should be almost imperceptible. Two examples of cooperatives within this category are presented in this section.

Located in Arcata, California, North Coast Cooperative (NCC) is a consumer food cooperative with two successful full-service grocery stores. NCC offers some positive (unintentional) externalities: it is an important source of employment for local townspeople in Arcata, which is a small and relatively economically depressed town, and NCC acts as a competitive yardstick, keeping prices down and product selection high (especially locally grown food) at other area grocery stores.

NCC was established in 1973 to provide a simple bulk distribution system of natural foods for a small group of members. In addition, NCC has always worked with local agricultural producers to build supply chains and improve the diversity and quality of local food production. Today, it is the largest purchaser and retailer of local organic produce in the area. The co-op has, therefore, been able to provide its members with a better variety of local products while investing in local farms and supporting a deteriorating agricultural sector. And in perhaps what is a more common gesture by local consumer cooperatives than is recognized, NCC operates a foundation, the Co-op Community Foundation that donates money to a wide variety of community organizations and causes, providing much needed equity for cash-poor organizations. Members can donate directly or sign over their cash discount and/or patronage refund to the foundation. Since the co-op began, it has given over $855,000 to help fund local community events, programs, and projects. NCC's devotion to the community, its ability to grow and yet stay in the same physical location, and its continuity in management are all factors in its success.[11]

A second example of an inherent community development cooperative is the Rural Wisconsin Health Cooperative (RWHC), located in Sauk City, Wisconsin. It was established in 1979 to help relatively small rural hospitals in south central Wisconsin share services, especially in terms of efficient staffing. It was one of the earliest models of cooperation among rural hospitals in the United States. The interdependence between rural health care and rural development is widely recognized, and RWHC has helped increase the likelihood of survival for small rural hospitals. It offers important services that its 28 member hospitals would have difficulty obtaining at a similar quality and cost. Through RWHC's formal and informal networking opportunities, the hospitals share information and strategies for resolving workforce problems. Advocating for rural health policy regionally and nationally is a strategic priority at RWHC; the manager is well known in the rural health policy arena and devotes a substantial amount of time working on these issues. The co-op's board and management believe that their primary activities (i.e., serving its members directly) support and provide credibility for their efforts to advocate health care and rural development.

RWHC is a good example of how well a cooperative structure might be used in an area where other forms of organization are more common (e.g., trade associations and non-profit organizations). Although a different form of business may have been able to deliver the same services, the founders of RWHC believed the cooperative form offered advantages in ensuring collective and equitable governance among members and better direct ownership links between the hospitals and RWHC. The cooperative succeeded in part because of its flexibility, altering its mix of services to meet the changing needs of members, as well as having member and management support for advocacy. Its ability to do so was a function of experienced and stable leadership (the manager helped to create the co-op), a stable, relatively small and homogeneous membership, and regular communication among parties.

COMMUNITY COOPERATIVES

Two examples of community cooperatives are presented here. Since they were both established by community leaders to meet specific community development objectives, they illustrate this category nicely. In the early 1990s, administrators at Garrett Community College (GCC), located in Mountain Lake Park, Maryland, realized that their students and the community at large needed improved local Internet access. At the time, the only access to the Internet was through long distance dial-up service that was both slow and expensive. The College administrators recognized that better and cheaper Internet services would give their students and community residents access to "virtual" or distance learning courses as well as other services and information not available in the area. It was also hoped that the technology would attract off-site workers from the Washington D. C. area. College and other local business leaders created the Garrett Rural Information Cooperative (GRIC), an Internet service provider (ISP), in 1998.

Many rural cooperatives offer broadband telecommunication services because they provide "rural areas access to many of the services once confined to larger population centers—services that are becoming…vital to the economic health of America's heartlands" (Thompson, 2002, p. 12). GRIC is unique because a group of community leaders started it as an independent cooperative. A cooperative model was chosen for GRIC because it retained local ownership and control within the community and because it avoided potential problems for GCC associated with creating an investor-owned firm. GCC provided an initial home for GRIC, and it still houses the server, computer equipment, and technicians (who also work for GCC). The ISP industry is now dominated by a small number of large national firms with enough capital to make substantial investments in technology subject to rapid obsolescence. Consequently, the opportunities for a small ISP have diminished, and GRIC faces the challenge of having either to make a major capital investment to keep pace with current technology or to dissolve the business. In addition, GRIC has had difficulty creating a cooperative identity among its members. Most members, as well as the current management, have little knowledge about the co-op model, and they are uncertain of its benefits. Local citizens, therefore, would probably be unlikely to continue their patronage of the co-op if a large national Internet service provider offered lower cost service.

The second example of a community co-op case has followed a similar development path. In 1989, an economic development study of the Arcata, California area recommended that the best replacement for lost timber and fishery income was specialty food manufacturing. At the time, however, there was no commercial kitchen space available. The local economic development organization, the Arcata Economic Development Corporation (AEDC), decided to create an incubator for small food processing companies with additional space for a shared community kitchen. AEDC hoped the incubator would stimulate demand for local farm products, as well as create more local jobs and income. The Foodworks Culinary Center, established in 1991, was structured as a cooperative to encourage incubator tenants (the co-op members) to work together to capture joint procurement and joint marketing efficiencies. When it was created, AEDC believed that the members would take over the facility after about five years, which did not happen. Although about a dozen businesses graduated and moved into the community, many of the original members are still located in the incubator. AEDC is now trying to sell the facility, which ceased being a cooperative in 1998. It currently houses eleven companies with over 60 employees.

Although all the tenants are engaged in some form of food processing, there are very few synergies among them. The founders at AEDC assumed they could find common interests by virtue of all being food processing firms. The businesses, however, identify more with their product than the general food business, and thus, the intended opportunities for collaboration and joint activity never materialized. Further, the members were more interested in developing their own businesses than in strengthening and managing the cooperative. Indeed, their focus on personal business profitability encouraged behavior that was incompatible with the viability of the cooperative.

CREATING SUCCESSFUL COMMUNITY DEVELOPMENT COOPERATIVES

Community cooperatives, such as those created by the Arcata Economic Development Corporation and Garrett Community College, illustrate the primary benefit of community-driven enterprises; they offer creative solutions to community development issues while maintaining some level of community ownership and control. The drawback of such enterprises is the high likelihood of failure associated with cooperatives organized from the top-down. Since the members are not involved in the creation of the cooperative, they may never truly feel a sense of ownership and loyalty, as in both of our cases (GRIC, the ISP, and the Foodworks incubator). This estrangement means that once the co-op is no longer needed (e.g., other ISPs move into the area) or when the returns from individual efforts outweigh the common good (e.g., business profits exceed co-op benefits), the cooperatives will have difficulty retaining their member support. Some cooperatives may serve a short-term purpose, and thus, they should develop a clear exit strategy. It is important for leaders of cooperatives to realize that changing conditions might ultimately require divesting the business when either the initial objectives have been met or the cooperative is unable to supply the level of capital required for continued growth and viability.

Another important observation gleaned from these case studies is that community support for the cooperative development venture is essential to its viability and success, regardless of the reason for engaging in the activity.[12] This observation was especially evident in the industrial parks created by rural electric cooperatives. The parks could not have been created without the support of the local community, especially the local government. In some cases, local cooperatives may have a competitive advantage over non-cooperatives seeking to undertake the same enterprise (especially if the non-cooperatives firms are not local). The industrial park initiatives and Northern Electric Cooperative, which purchased the Lefse Shack, benefited from such competitive advantage. Clearly, cooperatives will have an easier time gaining community support when they purchase an existing business that has no other potential buyers than when they enter into a business that places them in direct competition with other locally owned firms.

The characteristics that make cooperatives valuable vehicles to enhance local community development can also create challenges. For example, finding internal support for a cooperative's community development activity can be difficult when those efforts do not directly complement the cooperative's core mission. This was the case for the original partners in the Oklahoma housing construction cooperative and the Iowa venture capital fund. Some cooperatives can be very conservative in deciding which activities to back with their member equity. This caution may reflect management's unwillingness to take risks with member capital since it serves at the pleasure of the board (Fairbairn et al., 1995). Further, large cooperatives with diverse memberships may not be able to convince enough members to support a community venture if the benefits are limited to a small segment of the membership, i.e., those living within a certain community (Fairbairn et al., 1995).

If cooperatives attempt to manage or purchase a new or existing business (reactive investments) without prior knowledge of the industry, they may be confronted with another set of challenges. The cooperative may become engaged in an activity that requires a disproportionate commitment of time and resources, perhaps in a sector where the co-op has no core competency. The case of Northern Electric Cooperative, which was able to operate a specialized bakery successfully, suggests an important exception to this rule. Limited knowledge of an industry may not be harmful if the business being purchased is successful and simple, with well-established markets and experienced employees. In those cases, the businesses may be able to continue to thrive with little involvement from the cooperative.

Although, overall, our cases show that cooperatives can be extremely effective and creative in fostering rural community development, creating new cooperatives may not always be optimal or viable. As demonstrated in both the Country Living Homes and Iowa Capital Corporation cases, the original cooperatives were abandoned in part because of differing objectives among the project partners. The Foodworks case illustrates the difficulties that can arise with community leaders who want to develop a cooperative, but who have no actual knowledge of the industry to which they are applying the model. Without such knowledge, revenue estimates and ideas about how the cooperative should function may be completely erroneous. In the Foodworks case, the cooperative failed, but the business idea (the incubator) was viable.

CONCLUSIONS

The case studies analyzed for this research provides some general insights into the innovative activities of today's non-agricultural cooperatives in rural communities. They helped inform a new typology for analyzing the complete community development efforts of cooperatives. In contrast to the typical unifunctional and multifunctional categorization of cooperatives, our framework identifies two main categories of cooperative community development activities: unintentional, for example, a business organized as a cooperative, and intentional. Cooperatives in this latter group can be further sub-divided according to how closely the community development objectives match with their core function. Three sub-groups were identified: (1) cooperatives that pursue activities extrinsic to their core mission; (2) cooperatives that inherently engage in community development activities; and (3) cooperatives that are created to explicitly address community development.

Our results point to the flexibility of cooperatives as an organizational form and show they can play numerous roles in community development. There are clear differences in why and how cooperatives engage in community development activity. These differences reflect the capacities of the cooperative and the community, and most importantly the specific environment at a given time. It is important to recognize that there are many practical and theoretical reasons why a cooperative may not pursue community social or economic objectives that do not neatly translate into increased member returns from the cooperative (Fairbairn et al., 1995; Olson, 1971). These reasons include limited cooperative resources (management time, expertise, and capital) to take on additional activities, limited links between the members and the rest of the community (which reduces their incentive to engage in community development activity), and/or an inability to identify a useful role that falls within the capacity of the cooperative. Thus, only a subset of cooperatives is in a position to actively invest in community development activities.

The relationship between cooperatives and communities is even more complex than perhaps what this article allows the reader to believe; the firm and the community influence each other, creating a certain level of interdependence (Fairbairn et al., 1995; Merrett & Walzer, 2001). We hope that future research will expand our framework to understand the complete relationship better and in turn will guide cooperative efforts in community development successfully. As direct federal assistance for rural development declines and as agriculture plays a smaller role in the rural economy, the potential for cooperatives to play a more vital and direct role in rural economic development increases. Consequently, it becomes more important for scholars, stakeholders, community advocates, and the public to understand the characteristics of cooperatives that can promote community development more effectively.

END NOTES

1 Cooperatives vary greatly in their adoption and interpretation of these principles. The degree to which they subscribe to them is sometimes used to classify forms of cooperatives. In spite of this, the principles still play a role in the organization and operation of cooperatives.

2 Bhuyan and Leistritz (2000) conducted a comprehensive survey of non-agricultural cooperatives that was not restricted to rural areas. Although their results provide significant and useful information, they did not focus on the impact these cooperatives had on their communities.

3 The principle behind self-development is that local residents use local financial resources to retain, expand, or stimulate the formation of new locally owned and controlled firms (Green et al., 1990; Sharp and Flora, 1999).

4 The complete case studies are reported in K. Zeuli, D. Freshwater, D. Markley, and D. Barkley, "Non-agricultural Cooperatives in Rural Areas: 14 case studies." University of Wisconsin Center for Cooperatives, Case Study No. 1, June 2003.

5 The five excluded cooperatives are as follows: Northwinds Publishing Company, Great Falls, Montana; Northcoast Artists, Fort Bragg, California; Salmon Trollers Marketing Association, Fort Bragg, California; Locally Owned Business Organization, Grand Junction, Colorado; Northern Colorado Water Conservancy District, Loveland, Colorado.

6 The concept sometimes gets blurred with the idea of single sector and multi-sector businesses, which doesn't accurately reflect the core distinction.

7 Some agricultural cooperatives challenge this premise. The so-called new generation cooperatives, which have limited or closed membership policies, may also be divisive by virtue of their exclusivity (Zeuli, 2001). The location of agricultural processing companies, regardless of business structure, frequently divides rural communities. Many residents fear the potential pollution (air, water, and noise) will outweigh any positive economic impacts.

8 The Antigonish Movement in Canada, which promoted the formation of cooperatives as a means for community residents to create their own local development, is a well-known historical example connecting cooperatives and community development (MacPherson, 1979).

9 A similar type of cooperative, called Emerging Cooperatives, were created in the US during the 1960s by communities to serve the needs of the economically, politically, and educationally disadvantaged (Williams, 1974).

10 The complete Pee Dee mission statement can be found on their web site: http://www.peedeeelectric.com.

11 The senior management has been with the enterprise since its early days and has been able to grow with the organization.

12 The importance of community support in cooperative development is also supported by other studies (Fairbarin et al., 1995; Merrett & Waltzer, 2001; Wilkinson & Quarter, 1995).

REFERENCES

Ayres, J., L. Leistritz, & K. Stone. 1992. Rural retail business survival: Implications for community developers. *Journal of the Community Development Society* 23(2): 11-21.

Barkley, D. L., D. M. Markley, D. Freshwater, J. S. Rubin, & R. Shaffer. 2001. *Establishing Nontraditional Venture Capital Institutions: Lessons Learned.* P2001-11A. The Rural Policy Research Institute, University of Missouri, Columbia.

Bhuyan, S., & F. E. Olson. 1998. Potential Role of Non-agricultural Cooperatives in Rural Development: A Report on Focus Group Studies Conducted in North Dakota. North Dakota State University, Department of Agricultural Economics, Ag. Econ. Report No. 383 (January).

Bhuyan, S., & F. L. Leistritz. 2000. Cooperatives in non-agricultural sectors: Examining a potential community development tool. *Journal of the Community Development Society* 31(1): 89-109.

Duffey, P. 1990. Northeast Wisconsin cooperative finds home community best site for expansion. *Farmer Cooperatives* (October): 14-18.

Egerstrom, L. 2001. New generation cooperatives as an economic development strategy. Pp. 73-90 in C.D. Merrett and N. Walzer (eds.), *A Cooperative Approach to Local Economic Development*. Westport, CT: Quorum Books.

Enke, S. 1945. Consumer cooperatives and economic efficiency. –*American Economic Review* 35:148-155.

Fairbairn, B., J. Bold, M. Fulton, L. H. Ketilson, & D. Ish. 1995. *Co-operatives and Community Development: Economics in Social Perspective*. Saskatoon, Saskatchewan: Centre for the Study of Co-operatives, University of Saskatchewan.

Flora, J. L., G. P. Green, E. A. Gale, F. E. Schmidt, & C. B. Flora. 1992. Self development: A viable rural development option? *Policy Studies Journal* 20:276-288.

Freshwater, D. 1998. Utility cooperatives as a source of equity finance: Montana examples. University of Kentucky, Department of Agricultural Economics, Staff Paper No. 386.

Fulton, M. & L. H. Ketilson. 1992. The Role of Cooperatives in Communities: Examples from Saskatchewan. "*Journal of Agricultural Cooperation* 7: 15-42.

Gaston, R. J. 1990. Financing Entrepreneurs: The Anatomy of a Hidden Market. In R. D. Bingham, E. W. Hill & S. B. White (eds.), *Financing Economic Development: An Institutional Response*. Sage Publications.

Green, G. P., J. L. Flora, C. B. Flora, & F. E. Schmidt. 1990. Local self-development strategies: national survey results. *Journal of the Community Development Society* 21(2): 55-73.

Leistritz, F. L. 1997. Assessing local socioeconomic impacts of rural manufacturing facilities: The case of a proposed agricultural processing plant. *Journal of the Community Development Society* 28:43-64.

Lorendahl, B. 1996. New cooperatives and local development: A study of six cases in Jamtland, Sweden. *Journal of Rural Studies* 12(2): 143-150.

Loveridge, S. 1996. On the continuing popularity of industrial recruitment. *Economic Development Quarterly* 10(2): 151-158.

MacPherson, I. 1979. *Each for All: A History of the Co-operative Movement in English Canada, 1900-1945*. Toronto: Macmillan.

MacLeod, G. 1997. *From Mondragon to America: Experiments in Community Economic Development*. Sydney, Nova Scotia: University College of Cape Breton Press.

Merrett, C.D. & N. Walzer (eds.). 2001. *A Cooperative Approach to Local Economic Development*. Westport, CT: Quorum Books.

Melnyk, G. 1985. *The Search for Community*. Montreal: Black Rose Books.

Nadeau, E. G., & D. J. Thompson. 1996. *Cooperation Works*! Rochester, MN: Lone Oak Press.

Nadeau, E. G., & C. Wilson. 2001. New generation cooperatives and cooperative community development. Pp. 55-71 in C.D. Merrett and N. Walzer (eds.), *A Cooperative Approach to Local Economic Development*. Westport, CT: Quorum Books.

Olson, M. 1971. *The Logic of Collective Action: Public Goods and the Theory of Groups*. Cambridge, MA: Harvard University Press.

Parker, E. & P. T. Parker. 1998. Venture Capital Investment: Emerging Force in the Southeast. *Economic Review* (Fourth Quarter): 36-47.

Patrie, W. 1998. *Creating 'Co-op Fever': A Rural Developer's Guide to Forming Cooperatives*. USDA, RBS Service Report 54.

Sharp, J.S., & J.L. Flora. 1999. Entrepreneurial social infrastructure and growth machine characteristics associated with industrial-recruitment and self-development strategies in nonmetropolitan communities. *Journal of the Community Development Society* 30(2):131-153.

Stafford, T. H. 1990. Agricultural Cooperatives and Rural Development. *American Cooperation*: 81-88.

Stafford, T. H., A. D. Borst, D. A. Frederick, T. Gray, A. A. Jermolowicz, & R. K. Mahoney. 1989. *Cooperatives and Rural Development*. USDA, Agricultural Cooperative Service.

Storey, R. J. 1982. Community co-operatives—a Highlands and Islands experiment. Pp.71-86 in J. Sewel & D. O'Cearbhaill (eds), *Cooperation and Community Development*. Galway: Social Sciences Research Centre.

Thompson, S. 2002. Closing the gap. *Rural Cooperatives* (July/August):12-16.

Torgerson, R. E. 1990. Human capital: Cooperatives build people, also. *Farmer Cooperatives* 57(July):2.

Trechter, D. and R. King (eds.). 2001. *The Impact of New Generation Cooperatives on Their Communities*. USDA, RB-CS, RBS Research Report 177.

Walzer, N. & C.D. Merrett. 2001. Introduction. Pp. 1-10 in C.D. Merrett & N. Walzer (eds.), *A Cooperative Approach to Local Economic Development*. Westport, CT: Quorum Books.

Wilkinson, K. 1990. *The Community in Rural America*. Westport, CN: Greenwood Press.

Wilkinson, P. & J. Quarter. 1996. *Building a Community-Controlled Economy: The Evangeline Co-operative Experience*. Toronto, OT: University of Toronto Press.

Williams, T. T. 1974. The role of low-income rural cooperatives in community development. *American Journal of Agricultural Economics* (December):913-918.

Yin, R. 1989. *Case Study Research*. London: Sage Publications.

Zeuli, K. A. 2001. Business Attraction as a Rural Community Development Tool: Arguments for More Comprehensive Evaluations. In D. Bruce & G. Lister (eds.), *Rising Tide: Community Development Tools, Models, and Processes*. Sackville, NB Canada: Rural and Small Town Programme.

Rural development policy in the United States: a critical analysis and lessons from the "still birth" of the rural collaborative investment program

Beth Walter Honadle*

The development of a comprehensive rural development policy in the United States has been stymied repeatedly. A number of factors account for the low salience of rural development on the domestic policy agenda, from misconceptions about the economic composition of rural areas to the pitting of agriculture against broader rural development constituencies. The Rural Collaborative Investment Program (RCIP) from the 2008 "Farm Bill" is used to illustrate how the latest attempt to give rural communities and regions the capacity to tailor rural development programming to serve local needs ultimately failed due to a prohibition on spending funds to implement the legislation. The RCIP was essentially a stillborn policy because Congress never appropriated the funds needed to give it life. This article suggests that a better approach to advancing comprehensive rural development in the United States is to avoid placing "Rural Development" policy as a stand-alone initiative under the US Department of Agriculture. Instead, major programs in health, education, housing, the environment and other substantive areas should be designed in ways that meet the needs of rural communities and places.

The purpose of this article[1] is to critically analyze the prospects of the latest rural development legislation for reaching its potential. The Food, Conservation, and Energy Act of 2008 ("the 2008 Farm Bill"[2]) was enacted in June 2008. The rural development title of the legislation authorized the new Rural Collaborative Investment Program (RCIP). The goal of the RCIP was for rural areas to define their own regions and apply for funding to support the development and implementation of strategies to address self-identified needs (Edelman, 2008). The RCIP was viewed by its supporters as a flexible, bottom-up approach to rural development—and a departure from decades of broken promises and unfulfilled mandates.

The intergovernmental nature of the issues in rural development policy has been described as a gathering "perfect rural storm" by Fluharty. He referred to three rural

---

*Email: beth.honadle@uc.edu

frameworks that challenge rural policy-making, including "the rural dilemma in American federalism":

> While much has been written regarding federal devolution of public policies, programs and funding, in reality we are at the end of a 25-year shift in interjurisdictional relationships. Though many rural advocates believe greater state-level control over programs, personnel and funding works to the advantage of rural areas, this outcome remains uncertain. (Fluharty, 2003, p. 5)

From a different point of view, one study of the Community Development Block Grant (CDBG) program's implementation in one state concluded that:

> Nebraska, and likely other rural states, have taken the HUD [US Department of Housing and Urban Development] Small Cities CDBG program ... and modified it to also address the development issues and needs of rural communities. ... Clearly the Small Cities CDBG program benefits rural communities. (Blair, Deichert, & Drozd, 2008, p. 128)

This finding echoed findings from a decades earlier study of another HUD program, the Urban Development Action Grant (UDAG) program. Based on case studies of ten nonmetropolitan communities that had received Action Grants, this study found that "the UDAG program has been flexible in accommodating differences in economic development needs as perceived locally" (Honadle, 1987, p. 53).

So, it is against a mixed backdrop of earlier rural development programs and programs that were not targeted specifically at rural areas, but served state- or locally-identified rural development goals nonetheless, that the RCIP program was put forth as the latest Federal approach to rural community development. The outcome of this endeavor was a "still birth" program in which a full-term program failed to draw its first breath due to a lack of the basic necessity of life—Federal funding.

The analysis in this paper leads to the conclusion that this program was not funded primarily due to a lack of funds across-the-board because of the current economic situation. The position this paper takes is that rural development was singled-out within the Farm Bill for de-funding. This article also argues that, by continuing to use the USDA as the "home" for rural development, policy makers perpetuate the misconception of "rural" and "agricultural" as being synonymous.

A logical framework

Tracing the logic of a policy is a useful way to assess programs and policies (Kumar 1995; McLaughlin & Jordan, 1999). When these initiatives fail to reach stated goals, using a logic model is a way of showing the exact cause of the breakdown. A logical framework helps to answer fundamental questions such as "*can* it work?" and isolates missing links that may be preventing implementation from going according to plan. The late John Brandl, an experienced policymaker and public policy scholar, urged academics to examine the theoretical basis for their expectations so that they would obtain the desired results from government programs. Specifically, he challenged academics to ask, "[W]hat is the theory behind this thing? Why should we expect this to work?" and to consider whether sometimes the "theory" is nothing more than "wishful thinking" (Brandl, 2001, p. 5).

This paper borrows ideas from a simple logical framework originally developed by the Agency for International Development for program evaluation to analyze the implementation—or, more accurately, non-implementation of the RCIP. This logical framework provides a convenient (albeit oversimplified) way of explaining the recurring failure to have a *funded* rural development policy. A key assumption necessary to achieve the goals of various initiatives has not been met—namely that the programs have been funded. The basic framework is depicted as a series of steps leading up to the attainment of the overall goal as follows:

$$input \rightarrow output \rightarrow purpose \rightarrow goal$$

In short, by the *purposeful* application of *inputs*, certain activities will take place that convert those inputs or resources into *outputs* (goods, services, programs) and that—by doing this—an identifiable *goal(s)* will be achieved. Of course, for these if-then propositions to produce identifiable results (captured by "objectively verifiable indicators"), certain *assumptions* must hold. Using the framework one can trace the apparent logic of the RCIP.

Input

Inputs are merely the raw materials that go into a process in which they will be converted to outputs (goods and services). In this case, the inputs from the RCIP would be funding and technical assistance. According to the Economic Research Service of the US Department of Agriculture:

> Title VI of the 2008 Farm Act replaces the RSIP with the Rural Collaborative Investment Program (RCIP), which will create a national institute to provide technical assistance in administering the program. RCIP is authorized to award grants to regional boards that represent self-identified multicounty regions (which must meet certain population-based eligibility standards) and that propose projects meeting certain standards, including addressing regional development issues. Grants can be issued either for planning or implementing development strategies, and grants can pay operating costs of the local development organization heading up the regional effort. Longterm loans may be provided to eligible community foundations to assist in implementing the regional investment strategies. RCIP is authorized to receive $135 million for fiscal years 2009–2012.

Output

The program's logic posits that if the above-named inputs are provided, then certain outputs will result. Those outputs are primarily inter-jurisdictional partnerships, which would come about because the Federal government had provided essential inputs. In other words, the federal dollars would be a carrot that coaxed rural governments to work in concert toward the betterment of rural regions.

The program is the latest initiative in a series of attempts to develop a comprehensive, well-funded rural development policy in the US. The underlying logic of the program is that by providing resources, incentives, and technical assistance to rural communities and local governments to help them form inter-jurisdictional partnerships, those rural communities will be more successful in leveraging resources (volunteers, philanthropy, state and local funds, private investment) and implement locally-driven strategies and projects. The theory is that if rural regions have ample financial resources (incentives), they will be more likely to carry out local plans more democratically and sustain ambitions developed at the grassroots.

There is nothing evidently wrong with the theory of the programs that the US Congress has passed in the last two Farm Bills (2002 and 2008). A reasonable argument could be made that the most recent Farm Bill addressed some of the deficiencies previous rural development programs had not addressed in a comprehensive way. There have been piecemeal and incremental attempts to deal with access to existing Federal rural development resources, to coordinate the programs across many Federal agencies with programs intended to serve rural clientele, and to target the resources to places in most need (the "worst first" approach embodied in structures such as economic development regions of the Economic Development Administration of the US Department of Commerce). There have also been top-down approaches to delineate regions (among the most notable of these would be the Tennessee Valley and the Appalachian Region).

The Federal government has tried using sectoral policies to support industries that are based in rural areas (agriculture, forestry, and mining, for example) on the logical fallacy that this would lead to general prosperity and well-being in rural communities. The error of this approach was that resources are transferred to relatively well-off individuals and corporations and do not have the effect of lifting up disadvantaged rural people and achieving the community development ideals of the people who live in those places.

In short, the logic of the latest rural development program—in *theory*—seemed to avoid some of the shortcomings of a generation of initiatives. Rather than using the proverbial "cookie-cutter" to stamp out uniform strategies that may not suit each region's conditions, the RCIP was going to provide the "dough" (pun intended) so that rural areas could develop their own recipes with outside expertise and the technical assistance available through the national institute to advise and support these locally conceived initiatives. In other words, it would decentralize programming and build local capacity (Honadle, 1981) for realizing their objectives in an era of devolution (Honadle, 2001a). Regions would have incentives to form functional regions[3] that were of the shape, size, and character that fit the needs of the community. It was correctly assumed that the clustering of industries, institutions, and governmental units would be diverse, so an appropriate Federal role was to be the catalyst. Leading experts in the rural development field advocate for public encouragement of regional economic partnerships (Drabenstott, 2003; Markley, 2009).

In addition, some of the practical problems of combining "cooperative federalism" and regionalism have been understood for decades. Among these are the fact that regions are made up of states or portions thereof and the fear on the part of state "partners" that their power might be weakened by regionalization. Moreover, "regions do not have a formal legal position in the American federal system as do the states" (Carnathan, 1973, p. 15).

Furthermore, a more decentralized, regional approach can be justified by research suggesting that modern counties have evolved considerably in recent years. Benton (2003) succinctly summarized this trend by writing, "Simply put, new research has documented the pivotal role that counties play as leaders in and models for multi-jurisdictional issues and the more positive and 'equal partner' role played by counties in state-county relations" (pp. 23–24). There is also a body of theoretically sound empirical research on the correlates of successful collaboration (Dedekorkut, 2003).

The crux of the matter is that no money has been expended on the newly minted programs which offered a window of opportunity for changing relationships in rural development policy implementation. The main policy vehicle for rural development in the US is out of gas. It is stalled out and going nowhere. Paradoxically, the 2002 Farm Bill *mandated* the Rural Strategic Investment Program (RSIP), but the agricultural appropriations bills required to implement the program—to literally allow the US Department of Agriculture to write the regulations needed in order to spend the money—forbade USDA from spending the money. Congress went so far as to ensure that these programs would never be implemented by writing into the General Provisions of the agricultural appropriation legislation explicit and unambiguous language that "(Sec. 735) Prohibits fund use to carry out the rural strategic investment program [*sic*]" (Consolidated Appropriations Act, 2005).

In 2008 the Farm Bill replaced the RSIP with the RCIP (see Reeder (2008) for a comparison of the two programs), which not only allowed for flexible regional development strategic planning and implementation, but included funding for a "National Institute" at USDA to provide technical assistance to regions in administering the program. However, unlike the RSIP, the RCIP was a discretionary—not mandatory—program. This twist meant that rural interests had to make the case for funding each year because it was not a mandated program. (But, the problem with the mandated program was that the money was authorized, but language in the appropriations bill specifically prohibited the writing of regulations for implementing the program.)

Instead of being put toward rural development programming, the money in the Farm Bills has consistently gone to commodities, conservation, food and nutrition interests, which are better at winning the battles for appropriations.

Explaining the recurrent federal rural development stalemate

The unequivocal failure to put in place a meaningful rural development policy was predictable. Even before the current financial problems that are tightening resources in most discretionary spending, and even conceding that there are policy advocates in other substantive areas that also make a convincing case that "we have no national policy" there are so many factors that work against having a rural development policy. The surprising thing would be if there *were* a national rural development policy (ignoring, for sake of argument, the cogent point that doing nothing is also a policy choice).

Figure 1 is a diagram representing the context for rural development policymaking in the US. This model includes the major features of the environment that commonly impinge on the formation and implementation of rural development policies (Honadle, 1993; Honadle, 2001b). It portrays rural development policy as being heavily influenced by an inaccurate rural image; the common misperception that rural and urban interests are necessarily in conflict; the steady decline in the rural population in the US; the Congressional committees and bureaucratic structures (which tend to reinforce the outdated image of rural areas as being synonymous with agricultural areas); and interest groups.

Note that the circle depicting interest groups is divided into agricultural and nonagricultural interests. It shows a downward pointing arrow from agricultural

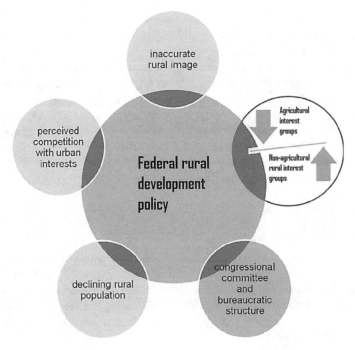

Figure 1.   The environmental context for rural development policy in the United States.

interest groups who are able to exert pressure to thwart more comprehensive rural development policies. The nonagricultural interest groups (represented by towns and townships, counties, regional development organizations, and so on) are shown as the less powerful interest "complex" (or coalition) that are attempting to raise *rural* development policymaking holistically rather than through a sectoral policy that is targeted to one industry.

Inaccurate rural image

The model that policymakers have of rural areas is not an accurate depiction of reality. The reasons for the perpetuation of the iconic rural community with family farms, a wholesome environment, and a bustling main street peopled with characters from a 1960s sitcom or reading primer from the same time are many. Through popular culture such idealized generalizations exist. The myth forms the impression that rural areas do not have problems or that they are so minimal as to be of lower priority than urban areas, which are obviously places that have poverty, crime, underachieving schools, and other problems that rural areas do not experience. Moreover, many rural communities are faring better than national averages in many respects (Isserman, Feser & Warren, 2009).

Agricultural versus nonagricultural rural interest groups

The lobbyists for large, multinational agricultural producers are very good at making their case for subsidies to make agriculture more competitive. In every Farm

Bill negotiation, they outmaneuver the nonagricultural interest groups. That is why their relationship is depicted in Figure 1 as opposing forces with the agricultural interests having the upper hand.

In recent years the nonagricultural groups representing rural America in the politics surrounding the landmark legislation setting the course for the next several years of expenditure by USDA (mostly) have tried to pull together to compete for their slice of the pie. Perhaps this effort is too little or too late to make a difference at this point. Calling itself the Campaign for a Renewed Rural Development (Rowley, 2007), more than 550 community and economic development, healthcare, education, local government, and entrepreneurship groups signed on to a letter to Senator Tom Harkin (IA) urging him to ensure full funding for the rural development title of the 2008 Farm Bill.

Congressional committee and bureaucratic structure

Fragmentation of policymaking in Washington is not unique to rural development. However, it is certainly an important impediment to consolidating support for a viable rural development policy. For this reason, it is worth considering—now more than ever—an approach that cuts across the structures that vertically make policies on everything from health to education to workforce development to economic development to transportation. While there are fragments of those policy arenas found in many places in the Federal establishment, even the casual observer knows where the hearts of those efforts reside, just as it is obvious to everyone whose interests are supreme in the halls of the USDA and in the committees of Congress dedicated to agriculture.

Declining rural population

Numerically, the cards are stacked against rural America having a putative rural development policy and the trend is not in its favor. As Redlin, Wright and Redlin (2007) have stated, "There has been one inescapable truth in rural regions of America in the last 50 years. Rural Americans are leaving" (p. 153). For only a brief time in the last two centuries did rural areas grow faster than urban areas. It was a blip, an aberration, a short-term phenomenon that took place in the 1970s. This really was noteworthy, because it was the first time in over 150 years that the truly rural places were actually growing in population. But, this was partly due to some "boom" industry that later "went bust." Since then, growth has been more the result of sprawl from the edges of metropolitan areas. The implication of this is that the representation in Congress has shifted toward suburban areas and away from rural areas. No end to this trend is in sight.

Perceived competition with urban interests

The belief that rural and urban interests are somehow antithetical is based, at least in part, on misunderstandings. For instance, if urban areas need workers and rural people need jobs, rural and urban interests might agree on the need for safe, reliable, affordable transportation. Besides, many of the problems and needs are the same— poverty, crime, water and air quality, education, programs for youth, access to childcare, access to the Internet, and high-quality, affordable healthcare are of interest to constituents regardless of their geographic region. The difference is sometimes that the *cause* of the problem (for instance, agricultural run-off polluting wells rather than industrial waste polluting the source of urban water) may be different. At other times, the difference is in *how* these issues should be addressed through public intervention. A more densely populated urban area has economies of scale and geographic proximity, among other distinguishing features, which provide a different context for producing public goods from those in more sparsely populated (rural) areas (Honadle, 1985).

One published research article that explicitly explored the question of a rural-urban conflict over environmental policy found that there were differences in support for environmental protection. However, it found that demographic variables and economic condition were better predictors of the level of support for environmental policy than whether an area is urban or rural. More generally, the author of this study discussed the "considerable disagreement in the literature over explanations for differences in levels of support ... between urban and rural areas. In fact, there is disagreement over whether such a split even exists" (Salka, 2001, p. 45).

Summary of the policy environment and its implications

These factors can explain conceptually the continuing absence of a rural development policy that has funding. This is not saying that there should be a policy or that one is not needed nor is it judging the actions of the individuals and organized interests who have fought long and hard for the passage and implementation of a rural development policy. If there is one takeaway lesson it might be that the Farm Bill is not the vehicle for achieving the desired outcome. It is simply not the mechanism through which the goals and objectives of rural development advocates can be realized. Experience with the two most recent Farm Bills makes that conclusion rather clear.

Another variable that makes regional rural development policy development more challenging than in many other countries is our federal system of government. Were the US a unitary system it would be easier to impose an approach centrally. The downsides to this approach in a country as diverse as the US should be apparent. There are important differences in governance structures from state to state, which affects the assignment of public sector functions and how they are financed, among other implications. Within and among states there is marked variation in values, culture, industrial base, geography, history, and other features. To draw a comparison from the European experience, Börzel described the challenges of Europeanization and federalism and found that autonomous regions have more to lose from centralization than do subnational authorities having strictly administrative functions (Börzel, 2000, p. 19).

Current prospects for rural development policy

According to experts in economic development, "the federal government has been adopting more regionally and locally targeted economic development strategies. ... [N]ational economic development policies targeting localities are not new. ... [A] plethora of ... programs aimed at underdeveloped rural areas are now an important part of the pattern of American life" (Blakely, & Leigh, 2010, p. 50).

In some respects rural development policy in the US parallels the way that policies evolve piecemeal in many other areas of endeavor. In a reflection on federalism and US water policy Gerlak recently made this observation:

> There is no real national water policy in the United States but rather fragmented, incremental crisis-driven policy. The federal-state relationship is at the heart of this conflict. A struggle between national supremacy and local autonomy pervades water management. (Gerlak, 2006, p. 231)

Thus, it may be a rather ordinary lament that there is no real national policy for a number of substantive issues.

However, rural development policy has been fraught with some extraordinary challenges. (For an objective historical treatment of rural development policy in the United States, an extensive source is by Roth, Effland, and Bowers, updated 2008.) In earlier decades the federal government offered "coordination" (Radin, 1992), "access," "targeting" and other approaches that were frequently little more than slogans and repackaging of existing programs for a serious attempt to make rural development policy (Honadle, 1993; 2001b). In the past decade there have been some attempts to encourage bottom-up development through locally organized regions in order to take advantage of entrepreneurial clusters and commonality of purposes that make sense across the diverse circumstances of "rural America." The RSIP and the RCIP programs from the 2002 and 2008 Farm Bills respectively were rather similar and they met with identical fates—non implementation.

The reasons for this are clear and compelling: the preeminence of agricultural interests in getting their way with each Farm Bill at the expense of rural development; the decline of the rural population; the disconnected structure of Congressional committees and agencies with the potential to craft a comprehensive rural policy; the pitting of rural against urban; and the persistence of the classical image of rural America—together—make for an environment that is not conducive to the development of a rural development policy that matches reality.

The logic underpinning the most recent rural development titles of the Farm Bills has been reasonably sound and supportable by research. What have been lacking are the will and the funding to carry out these programs. It is hard to conceive of the outcome changing as long as rural development advocates pin their hopes and their efforts on a bill that, by its very name, is all about agriculture. It seems highly unlikely—unless the environment changes drastically—that rural development will suddenly emerge as a national policy priority.

A recent article in this journal explored the dismal prospects for comprehensive rural development policy in the US from a sociological perspective. Its authors observed that rural areas face formidable challenges in competition for resources. They succinctly captured the crux of the problem as follows:

> ... [I]n American politics, authorizing legislation is separated from appropriating legislation and funding. Legislation is broad-brush, whereas implementation is largely dependent on political will, the availability of money, and implementing regulations and procedures. This means communities should actively negotiate federal resources on a yearly basis. Often this is unrealistic given the existing capacity of rural communities and the way resource decisions are made at the federal level. (Padt & Luloff, 2009, p. 240)

More than 20 years ago a well-versed, experienced practitioner and scholar of rural development policy at the USDA wrote:

> [I]f having a policy means having a systematic approach to reaching defined objectives, the US has had no rural policy. The objectives of federal rural efforts have never been settled on, and approaches to rural problems continue to be unsystematic. (Long, 1987, p. 15)

The same observation can be made today. While the rhetoric and photo-opportunities (see Johnston, 2009) may suggest that there is a change in tone, without the money to back up the gestures, it may just be more lip service. Last summer President Barack Obama announced his administration's "Rural Tour."

> The President announced yesterday that [Secretary of Agriculture, Tom Vilsack] will be leading the Administration's rural tour, which will be visiting rural communities across the country over the coming weeks and months. At each event [the Secretary] will try to provide information about how the USDA and the Obama Administration are affecting the lives of rural Americans.
>
> And just as importantly, I want to listen to the thoughts, concerns and stories about each community's vision for its future. We will collect ideas about how the USDA could be better serving these communities. (White House Briefing Room Blog, 2009)

The US is fighting wars in Iraq and Afghanistan, healthcare reform has been the top domestic priority, and the Federal government is immersed in efforts to bring the country back from the brink of the worst economic recession of at least a generation through banking regulation, public works projects, an overhaul of the automotive industry, and an overhaul of the financial system is under way. At the time of this writing, urgent issues related to pollution from a catastrophic oil spill in the Gulf are making environmental issues more salient. So, the ascendance of other priorities over rural development notwithstanding, as of last summer it appeared that the current Administration was furthering the tradition of talking about rural development and the spokesperson for this agenda was the Secretary of Agriculture. Without the President himself behind rural development to rally broad-based support for a more comprehensive set of programs to bolster rural communities, it is virtually impossible to conceive of a comprehensive rural development strategy emerging in the next decade. Perhaps the rural "tour" was a way for the current administration to stop and ask for directions in the development of the Obama policy on rural development. On 4 May 2010 the Secretary of Agriculture announced that USDA will host a "National Rural Summit." According to Secretary Vilsack, "I visited dozens of communities in 20 states while leading President Obama's Rural Tour—an effort to engage in a more robust dialog with folks living in rural America. In those visits I saw that there is more opportunity in rural American today than at any time in decades—but that we need to embrace new strategies to help drive that revitalization" (White House Briefing Room Blog, 2010).

Meanwhile, it appears that the Obama administration is attempting to integrate rural development into other substantive policies. According to the White House issue page headed "Rural" (White House Issues, *Rural* 2010), the current administration is promoting the American Recovery and Reinvestment Act (ARRA) as the vehicle it has used to make progress in rural development. Using ARRA funding, the progress claimed includes supplemental assistance benefits to low-income rural families; a variety of rural development activities, including rural water and waste water projects, broadband infrastructure, and rural business programs (among others); biofuels research and development; and farm disaster assistance.

Relevant to the community development perspective, the current White House's "Guiding Principles" on the rural issue is as follows:

> President Obama believes in nurturing strong, robust, and vibrant rural communities. These communities also safeguard our environmental heritage, supply our food, and play a growing role in science and innovation. Today, rural communities face numerous challenges but also enormous economic opportunities. President Obama believes that together we can ensure a bright future for rural America. He will work to help family farmers and rural small businesses find profitability in the marketplace and success in the global economy. (White House Issues, *Rural*, 2010)

The rhetoric seems to focus on rural communities and links the strength of those communities to the environment, food, science and innovation. The administration lists are (in order): farm and rural economic development; the development of rural broadband services; the promotion of rural America's leadership in renewable energy; investment in rural teachers; and support for rural community colleges.

It appears for now that this administration is continuing the tradition of placing responsibility for rural development with the USDA. If past experience is any indication of what to expect, this approach will tend to equate rural development with promoting agriculture. It will be interesting to see if the Rural Tour and the upcoming National Rural Summit will lead to announcement of the latest presidential "national rural development policy."

Normative endnote

One of the reviewers of the original submission of this manuscript asked for some discussion of the "right" vehicles for advancing rural development policy. This concluding section is intended to address this request. Trying to use the Farm Bill to advance rural development made it unlikely that the RCIP would be supported with funds, in part, because the agricultural interests would block expenditure on the program. As long as the Federal government continues to place the development and implementation of rural development policy at the US Department of *Agriculture*, there will always be a tendency for policy to reflect the adage that "what's good for agriculture is good for rural America." An analysis done nearly two decades ago showed that the legacy of the previous several administrations' formally announced rural development initiatives were little more than attempts to foster coordination, client access, efficiency and other goals geared to management. These are all necessary and good things to do. However, the recommendation from that analysis was that, rather than pinning hopes on yet another unfunded Rural Development policy (with a capital "R" and a capital "D"):

> Perhaps the best thing for rural advocates to do ... is to show how helping rural areas could help solve the urban crisis at the same time and to help policy makers, at all levels, have a better appreciation of rural values and needs. ... This will not result in a separate, identifiable rural development policy for the United States, but it may make all of the federal departments a better resource for rural constituents. (Honadle, 1993, p. 236)

This perspective is still valid. The US should be developing policies that develop people and support community and economic development that reflect national priorities and local needs. The emphasis on schools, community colleges, broadband, and so on, are not "Rural Development" issues. They are issues for the United States' future. By ensuring that rural places are not disadvantaged in housing, environmental protection, public safety, and other substantive areas of public policy, rural development (measured by things like educational attainment, jobs, income, shared prosperity, civic engagement, and so forth) are more likely to be successful than if we continue to take the narrow focus of agriculture as the way of achieving rural development.

Going back to the logical framework, if one continues to put inputs (staff, loans, grants, and the like) into agricultural programs, then the outputs (farm subsidies and so on) will be for the purpose of helping farms be more profitable. If the goal is to develop agriculture in the US, this is not necessarily wrong. But, if the goal is to have strong, healthy rural communities with a diverse economic base and better standards of living in areas like education, recreation, healthcare, and housing, it will take a more comprehensive approach. One step would be to require impact statements that assess the effects of major policies on rural people and communities with recommendations for ensuring that those policies do not unintentionally hinder rural communities' partaking of the benefits of programs. This would include program guidelines that were flexible enough to accommodate the context of rural communities with their lower population densities and distances from major cities.

Notes

1. The author would like to acknowledge a number of people who provided valuable information and insights that contributed to the writing of this article: Charles W. Fluharty, Vice President for Policy Programs, Rural Policy Research Institute, University of Missouri; Colleen Landkamer, Blue Earth County (Minnesota) Commissioner; Jason Boehlert and Amy Linehan, Legislative Director, and Amy C. Linehan, Legislative Representative, National Association of Development Organizations; M. Louise Reynnells, USDA Rural Information Center; Richard Reeder, USDA Economic Research Service; and David Sears, USDA Rural Development.
2. Throughout the paper the author uses the conventional shorthand, the Farm Bill, to refer to the enacted (i.e., no longer a bill) Federal legislation containing programs and budget authorization to fund programs having to do with agriculture, conservation, food and nutrition, rural development, and other broad functions of the USDA.
3. It is beyond the scope of this paper to explore the normative implications and potential trade-offs between decentralization and inequalities between and among regions. See, for example, Morgan's analysis of how the replacement of centralized regional policies with devolved regional policies does not address regional inequalities in the United Kingdom (Morgan, 2006).

References

Benton, J.E. (2003). Looking backward and ahead: The evolution of an agenda for county government research. *Presented at a special workshop on The American County: A Research Agenda*. Athens, Georgia: University of Georgia, Carl Vinson Institute of Government. June 4–6, 2003. Retrieved from http://www.cviog.uga.edu/ncsc/benton.pdf.

Blair, R., Deichert, J., & Drozd, D.J. (2008). State rural development policy: The role of the Community Development Block Grant program. *Journal of Public Budgeting, Accounting & Financial Management, 20*(1, Spring), 108–132.

Blakely, E.J., & Leigh, N.G. (2010). *Planning local economic development: Theory and practice*. Thousand Oaks, CA: SAGE.

Börzel, T.A. (2000). From competitive regionalism to cooperative federalism: The Europeanization of the Spanish State of the Autonomies. *Publius: The Journal of Federalism*, *30*(Spring): 17–42.

Brandl, J.E. (2001). *The role of the academy in policy formation and critique* (PB2000/01). Bowling Green, OH: Center for Policy Analysis and Public Service, Bowling Green State University.

Carnathan, R.D. (1973). *Experiment in regional federalism: Implementation of the appalachian regional development act of 1965 in Georgia, North Carolina and Tennessee*. Doctoral dissertation: University of Tennessee.

Consolidated Appropriations Act (2005). The Library of Commerce Thomas. Retrieved from http://thomas.loc.gov/cgi–bin/bdquery/D?d108:6:./temp/ ~ bdz4ax:@@@D:&summ2=m&.

Dedekorkut, A. (2003). *Determinants of success in interorganizational collaboration for natural resource management*. Doctoral dissertation, Florida State University.

Drabenstott, M. (2003). Rural America's new economic frontier. *State Government News* (June/July), 8–11.

Edelman, M.A. (2008). Title VI Rural Development. 2008 National Extension Farm Bill Education Conference. Kansas City, Missouri. Airport Hilton. PowerPoint presentation. Retrieved from http://www.agrisk.umn.edu/uploads/ARL03710.ppt.

Fluharty, C.W. (2003). The rural policy question. *State Government News* (June/July), 5–11.

Gerlak, A.K. (2006). Federalism and US water policy: Lessons for the twenty–first century. *Publius: The Journal of Federalism*, *36*(Spring), 231–257.

Honadle, B.W. (1981). A capacity–building framework: A search for concept and purpose. *Public Administration Review*, *41*(5), 575–580.

Honadle, B.W. (1985). Small is different: Public Administration as if rural areas and small jurisdictions mattered. *Municipal Management* (Summer), 179–185.

Honadle, B.W. (1987). Federal aid and economic development in nonmetropolitan communities: The UDAG program. *Publius: The Journal of Federalism*, *17*(4), 53–63.

Honadle, B.W. (1993). Rural development policy: Breaking the cargo cult mentality. *Economic Development Quarterly*, *7*(August), 227–236.

Honadle, B.W. (2001a). Theoretical and practical issues of local government capacity in an era of devolution. *Journal of Regional Analysis & Policy*, *31*(1), 77–90.

Honadle, B.W. (2001b). Rural development policy in the United States: Beyond the cargo cult mentality. *Journal of Regional Analysis & Policy*, *31*(2), 93–108.

Isserman, A.M., Feser, E., & Warren, D.E. (2009). Why some rural places prosper and others do not. *International Regional Science Review*, *32*(3), 300–342. Retrieved from http://irx.sagepub.com/cgi/reprint/32/3/300 on 2/26/2009.

Johnston, E. (2009). Vilsack envisions strong USDA–NACo partnership. *CountyNews* March 23, 2009. Retrieved from http://naco.org/CountyNewsTemplate.cfm?template=/Content Management/ContentDisplay.cfm&ContentID=30340.

Kumar, K. (1995). Measuring the performance of agricultural and rural development programs. *New Directions for Evaluation*, *67*(Fall), 81–91.

Long, R.W. (1987). Rural development policy: Rationale and reality. *Publius: The Journal of Federalism*, *17* (Fall), 15–31.

Markley, D.M. (2009). Capitol hill hearing testimony: Rural development. 31 March 2009. Retrieved from http://www.rupri.org/Forms/Markley_Testimony_March09.pdf

McLaughlin, J.A., & Jordan, G.B. (1999). Logic models: A tool for telling your program's performance story*Evaluation and Program Planning*, *22*(1), 65–72.

Morgan, K. (2006). Devolution and development: Territorial justice and the north–south divide. *Publius: The Journal of Federalism* (Winter): 189–206.

Padt, F.J.G., & Luloff, A.E. (2009). An institutional analysis of rural policy in the United States. *Community Development*, *40*(3), 232–246.

Radin, B.A. (1992). Rural development councils: An intergovernmental coordination experiment. *Publius: The Journal of Federalism* (Summer), 111–127.

Redlin, M.M., Wright, A., & Redlin, B. (2007). Development and entrepreneurship. In G. Aguiar (Ed.), *Government in the countryside*. Dubuque: Kendall/Hunt Publishing Company.

Reeder, R. (2008). *2008 Farm Bill Side–By–Side. Title VI: Rural Development. US Department of Agriculture, Economic Research Service*. Retrieved from http://www.ers.usda.gov/FarmBill/2008/Titles/TitleVIRural.htm.

Roth, D., Effland, A.B.W., & Bowers, D.E. (2008). *Federal rural development policy in the twentieth century.* Beltsville, Maryland: USDA Rural Information Center. Retrieved from http://www.nal.usda.gov/ric/ricpubs/rural_development_policy.html.

Rowley, T.D. (2007). Can you hear rural America now? Washington, DC. National Association of Counties, Campaign for a Renewed Rural Development press release. May 18, 2007. Retrieved from http://www.ruralcampaign.org/news–press/commentary–opinion/2007/05/18/can–you–hear–rural–america–now/.

Rural Collaborative Investment Program of the *Food, Conservation, and Energy Act of 2008.* US Code. Public Law 110–246. §6028.

Salka, W.M. (2001). urban–rural conflict over environmental policy in the western United States. *American Review of Public Administration, 31*(1), 33–48.

White House Briefing Room Blog. 2009. *Strengthening Rural Communities: USDA Kicks Off Rural Tour.* Posted by Tom Vilsack, July 1, 2009. Retrieved from http://www.whitehouse.gov/blog/USDA–kicks–off–rural–tour/.

White House Briefing Room Blog. 2010. *A Summit to Discuss the Future of Rural America.* Posted by Tom Vilsack, May 4, 2010. Retrieved from http://www.whitehouse.gov/blog/2010/05/04/a–summit–discuss–future–rural–america.

White House Issues. 2010. *Rural.* Retrieved from http://www.whitehouse.gov/issues/rural.

ACHIEVING SUSTAINABLE ECONOMIC DEVELOPMENT IN COMMUNITIES

By Ron Shaffer

ABSTRACT

The options available for communities to work toward sustainable community economic development are explored through four fundamental elements of community economic development theory. Sustainable community economic development is about changing perceptions and choices regarding community resources, markets, rules, and decision-making capacity. The idea of new knowledge and reframing issues is offered as a method to create new options. The dimensions of time, space, marginalized social-economic groups, and dynamic economies broaden the concept of sustainable development beyond the more traditional physical-biological definition.

INTRODUCTION

Community developers are increasingly struggling with fundamental questions about whether their efforts will have continuing impact and not unintentionally foreclose future options for community residents. The idea of sustainability is advanced to capture this struggle. While the concept of sustainability is influenced substantially by one's values, this paper uses four fundamental elements of community economic development theory to explore the options available for communities to work toward sustainable community economic development.

Sustainable community economic development is about changing perceptions and choices regarding community resources, markets, rules, and decision-making capacity. The idea of integrating new knowledge and reframing issues is a method to create new options. By understanding these forces, the community improves its capacity to manipulate them to the community's advantage. The dimensions of time, space, marginalized social-economic groups, and dynamic economies broaden the concept of sustainable development beyond the more traditional physical-biological definition. The balance of the paper explores the substantial shift in our conceptualization of development, and the necessary

Ron Shaffer is Professor of Agricultural Economics and Community Development Economist, University of Wisconsin–Madison/Extension. An earlier version of this paper was shared at the International Conference on Issues Affecting Rural Communities, Townsville, QLD Australia, July 14, 1994.

conditions for sustainable community economic development. The paper does not reach conclusions, but attempts to summarize the thinking of one person trying to give personal meaning to an important question facing communities and those who work with them.

THE PARADIGM SHIFT

In many respects sustainable development represents a shift in paradigms about how development occurs and which aspects of development are crucial. Table 1 offers two contrasting paradigms about how our socio-economic-biological system works. No small part of the current sustainability debate is about which paradigm most accurately reflects the conditions of today and desires for tomorrow. The distinctions in Table 1 are exaggerated to expose what I believe to be the different perspectives and move us toward some general ideas regarding sustainable development.

The elements in Table 1 represent parts of two alternative views of how we frame the question of community economic development and indicate both how it will occur and the likely outcomes. These differences are not new. The first more visible appearance probably occurred in the 60s, when communities, neighborhoods, community activists, and public officials started to deal with the initiatives of the Kennedy–Johnson Administrations.

The old paradigm can be summarized in terms of more of the same, techno-logical fixes, everyone will naturally benefit, and little connection among the elements of the community and elsewhere. The new paradigm suggests that there will be substantial transformations in how we do business; social interactions and networks are substantial parts of the fixes; conscious efforts are required to insure those we seek to help are actually helped; and the connections among all of us are stronger and often more indirect than we realize.

While these ideas have ebbed and flowed in the academic literature, policy debates, and community meetings, the emergence of the interest in sustainable development has given some legitimacy and renewed attention to how commu-nity economic development occurs and what outcomes we expect. Several themes come together in helping me make some sense of what this means in my professional career and how I might work with communities exploring their choices. The ideas contained in the concept of sustainable development help me look at how a community's economy is organized, what are key components, and how it changes over time.

Sustainable Development

In defining sustainable development, most analysts start with the World Commission on Environment and Development (Brundtland Report) definition of sustainable development as "that which ensures the needs of the present are met, without compromising the ability of future generations to meet their own

Table 1. Paradigms Describing Community Economic Development

Old	New
Growth is preeminent (more of the same)	Development is preeminent (long-term transformation)
Benefits of growth will naturally trickle down and out to others	Equity considerations require conscious policy efforts
Individuals are wise and all-knowing	Individuals can comprehend only part of what is happening and needed
Technological change is either always good or will solve most problems	Technological change is only one of many possible solutions, and may not even be one of the better choices
Tomorrow will look like today	Tomorrow may look like today, but certainly no guarantee
Externalities of space, time, and class typically of minor concern and likely to take care of themselves	Externalities of space, time, social groups must be explicitly considered
Dynamic economies are growing	Dynamic economies are creating new choices, reframing of issues, changing perceptions of markets and resources, changing values
Socio-economic-biological elements are largely independent or can be treated that way	Socio-economic-biological elements are so interdependent that failure to consider linkages creates problems

needs" (1987, p. 9). The balance of the Brundtland Report emphasizes management and control over development, plus a holistic approach to problem solving. This is a perspective most community developers feel reflects their values. An overlooked aspect of the report is recognition that "development is not a fixed state of harmony,[1] but rather a process of change in which the use of resources, direction of investments, orientation of technological development, and institutional change are made consistent with future as well as present needs" (World Commission, 1987, p. 9).

Part of the dilemma facing many of us is that the definition remains fluid. One expansion of the Brundtland definition includes

> . . . a system that secures effective participation in decision making, provides for solutions that arise from disharmonious development, and is flexible and has the capacity for self-correction. . . . a production system that respects the obligation to preserve the ecological base for the future while continuing to search for new solutions (Sustainable Rural Communities Committee, 1991, p. 6).

---

[1] Schumpeter (1983) defines development as *creative destruction*.

The addition of disenfranchised groups in decision making is an important advancement. While their involvement in the actual decision making may not be a reality, the inclusion of their interests and perspectives in the choices considered is paramount. This dimension is particularly crucial to community developers.

The importance of time becomes significant when considering that many families and communities are having increased difficulty earning an acceptable standard of living and are experiencing an increasing sense of marginalization. This sense certainly places a premium on decisions favoring this generation and attempting to capture the "good life."[2]

For community developers, this idea of time and sustainable development should not imply maintaining or returning to some nostalgic recollection of how things once were. A form of nostalgic misdirection is that every community and its historic role should be protected from outside forces and has a right to survive. Rather, greater emphasis needs to be put on the future and what may be possible with respect to maintaining options or choices for the future.

To close this section, Dykeman's (1990, p. 6–7) definition of sustainable community economic development is particularly helpful.

> . . . those communities that manage and control their destiny based on a realistic and well thought through vision. Such a community based management and control approach requires that a process be instituted within the community that effectively uses knowledge and knowledge systems to direct change and determine appropriate courses of action consistent with ecological principles. The process must be comprehensive and address social, economic, physical, and environmental concerns in an integrated fashion while maintaining central concern for present and future welfare of individuals and the community.

SUSTAINABLE COMMUNITY ECONOMIC DEVELOPMENT

Figure 1 displays the essence of my conception of how community economic development occurs.[3] The nodes in Figure 1 represent four significant elements that influence the economic change of a community (Shaffer, 1989). The diagram could be better displayed as a hologram, in motion with different images at different angles.

Two elements of Figure 1 that transcend the sustainability discussion are the need to be comprehensive in the strategies of change (Pulver, 1979) and the need

---

[2] For some marginalized groups the "good life" is rising above subsistence (Rural Sociological Society, 1993).

[3] Wilkinson (1991) and others argue that developing the social system called a community is far more important than just the economic dimensions of that community. The present discussion is limited to sustaining the economic dimensions of the community rather than the general concern of sustaining the community, but they are inseparable ideas.

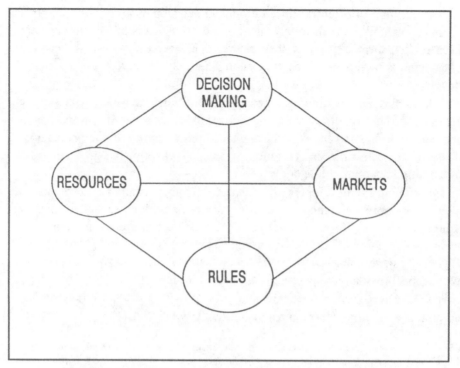

Figure 1. Crucial elements of community economic development.

to incorporate the various components of the community's economy in problem definition and the creation of options (Shaffer, 1989).

The resource node reminds us of the need to incorporate capital (financial, buildings, public infrastructure, housing), labor (workers, skills, educational outcomes), and technology (management systems, waste disposal or production, skill requirements) as important aspects of the community. Some policies communities create within this node include industrial parks, revolving loan funds, vocational training, management training, and low/moderate housing. The resource node can be thought of as the supply aspect of community's economy. It is the ability of the community to produce the desired goods and services.

The market node represents the demand side of community's economy. It is the nonlocal and local markets in which the community operates. These nonlocal markets could be international, in the next state, or in the next county. This is the export base idea of community economic development that probably best represents the old logic in Figure 1. It also represents the sense of how community economies change for an alarming portion of community and economic developers. The efforts to attract businesses to the community are the most obvious community policies emerging from this node. It is important, however, not to ignore the local market form. The local market generally affects community residents most directly. It relates to what goods and services are available locally, customer relations, store hours, parking, and ADA access. Shopper surveys, mainstreet renovation, and parking facilities are examples of local market focus community activities.

The aspects of the community's economy contained within the rules node are the more visible legal and the less visible cultural/values structures. Examples of visible legal structures include zoning, housing safety, taxing, forms of business organization, inheritance transfers, contracts, and utility regulation. The less visible cultural/value aspects of rules are the standards of conduct that are encouraged or accepted. A recent example of this element is the communitarianism ideas present in such work as Etzioni (1993). The recent work by Putnam (1993) and the Floras (1993) on social capital is another form of the less visible cultural/value dimensions.

The decision making node involves leadership, which most community developers would feel is their *entrée*. While leadership captures some parts of this node, it really is much more comprehensive than typically found in the leadership literature. This node clearly includes distinguishing between symptoms and problems, implementation of action efforts, and how internal and external forms of knowledge are integrated.

Sustainable community economic development is about changing perceptions and choices regarding community resources, markets, rules, and decision-making capacity. While not obvious in Figure 1, sustainable development requires the use of accumulated knowledge (both scientific and experiential) to reframe questions that change the set of perceived options available. *Sustainable* must not be redefined into meaninglessness, but the choices we make regarding the four nodes of Figure 1 and their definition go a long way in making sustainable development attainable.

A dynamic economy adds the important aspect to sustainable development— recognition of the changing circumstances in which the community functions. These changes can be depletion or revaluation of a resource (e.g., groundwater, mineral deposits, scenic vistas), technological changes (e.g., genetic engineering, fiber optics), market shifts (e.g., aging population, single parent families, working couples, shifts in defense spending), changes in political-economic institutions (e.g., eligibility for federal programs, discharge standards, NAFTA/GATT) or economic structure (e.g., transnational corporations, relative decline of manufacturing employment). These changing economic circumstances alter the choice set for community response. Sustainable communities recognize these changes and create responses that allow the community to maintain and improve its economic position now and through time.

Four characteristics are associated with communities which appear to be economically sustainable (Shaffer, 1991). They are, in no order of importance: a slight level of dissatisfaction; a positive attitude toward experimentation; a high level of intra-community discussion; and a history of implementation. In a few words, communities that demonstrate the qualities of sustainability believe they, and they alone,[4] make and/or control their own destiny. This recognizes that while individual communities are given different economic circumstances (resources, economic structure, access to markets, growth of local markets), the sustainable community will capture the economic possibilities available.

Sustainable community economic development means using new knowledge to create new choices and options through time regarding the nodes in Figure 1. Now resources take on new meanings including assimilative capacity, marginalized groups, nonrenewable resources, lower energy use technology, and different skill sets for people. Likewise, markets start including buying locally whenever possible, recycling, consuming green products, and green lifestyles. Decision-making capacity now adds sensitivity about the biosphere, sensitivity about inter-generational implications, sensitivity about marginalized groups, and sensitivity about spatial flows. The rules of the economic game now include discharge permits and markets, compensation to people adversely affected, development impact hearings, and taxes on transboundary environmental use.

The themes that emerge from the expanded definition of sustainable community economic development lead to policies that explore how to increase community self-reliance, increase niche marketing (i.e., less volume, more value), increase ecological awareness (e.g., diversification of production from mono-culture, recycling wastes or reducing waste stream), change labor and management relations, and increase demands on knowledge and creativity.

Necessary Conditions For Sustainable Development

Economists contend that a major theme in sustainable community economic development is the externality of decisions and actions. Externalities can be both positive and negative, but are generally not accounted for in the market prices used to allocate resources across groups, space, and time.

In sustainable community economic development, time and future generations are explicitly brought into consideration for decisions and actions. If decisions and actions adversely affect future generations then current prices need to reflect that. To assert that time is important begs the question: relative to what? To argue that some resources should be preserved for the future does not answer the economic questions of what alternatives are foregone—now or in the future. Who is being impacted by the choice of preserving a resource? The end result of this blanket acceptance of future over present value could lead to the sacrificing of current legitimate interests for undefined future legitimate needs. Either condition leads to equally inappropriate decisions.

Another externality is that the benefits and costs of a decision or action are distributed spatially to separate groups, minimizing the possibility that market

---

[4] The term *alone* is used to place responsibility on ourselves, not on others or external institutions. It does *not* mean isolation in action or response.

prices will create self-correcting signals. So, rather than getting corrective feedback, the system becomes self-reinforcing. The interaction between urban and rural economies is an example of spatial flows. Changes in urban markets (e.g., natural or artificial fibers, use of rain forest wood) and rules (e.g., water quality standards, prevailing wage standards) often play out in rural economies in a perverse manner. The transboundary flows of sulphur dioxide, ozone-depleting chemicals, or poorly educated migrants are other examples of externalities over space and time.

An aspect of sustainable community economic development that appears to have generated little direct discussion is the Schumpeterian (1983) idea that development is "creative destruction" with the associated economic dynamics that creates winners and losers. The sense of gains/losses may only be relative, but often is absolute (i.e., displaced worker, family, community).[5] The inability of some adversely affected groups to contribute to decisions leads to reinforcing patterns of shifting burdens to those groups. Economists deal with this in statements about needed adjustments (migration, training, identifying new business opportunities) in a dynamic economy. It is insufficient to expect the market to handle many of the noneconomic aspects of these adjustments given asset fixity, family, gender, education, personal traits, age and race (Hite & Powell, 1993).

Some suggest that people consciously make short-run non-sustainable decisions and even imply that the economic system discourages longer term sustainable development choices. The reality is that we often do not know what the full range of options and their implications are and often do not face the choices at the same time. A minimum precondition for sustainable development is an active effort to acquire and improve access to knowledge regarding the range of choices available and their implications. This will require a substantial personal and societal investment to create a culture that explores alternatives.

SUMMARY

In summary of my thinking to this point, sustainable development explicitly recognizes increasing limits (biological/physical), given past and current economic/cultural/social norms and knowledge. It is not absolute; relative to shifting constraints, it embodies different forms of capital (i.e., renewable and nonrenewable), and has the capacity to accommodate change. Sustainable development incorporates linkages between economic and ecological issues and is sensitive to distribution across generations (time), space, socio-economic groups, and economic sectors.

---

[5] An example of gains/losses and creative destruction is contained in the recent ending of the cold war. Most would agree that it represents a structural transformation and opens a host of new choices, but some communities, tied to the defense industry, obviously see themselves as losing.

Recognizing that changing norms, knowledge, technology, and markets lead to shifting needs for capital, labor, and space, I contend that sustainable community economic development is less a natural/physical/biological and more an institutional phenomenon. Sustainable development is less an issue of technical feasibility, and more an issue of what policies, behaviors, and institutions are required to achieve it in practice. Have we framed the questions appropriately? For example, energy is associated with economic growth,[6] so it has been assumed that we must increase energy use to have economic growth. If we adopt energy conserving technology or if we adopt new product configurations (lower hydrocarbon content), we can conserve energy usage and still have growth and development.

The preceding example exemplifies the importance of re-framing questions from either/or to multiple options. The paradigm shifts (see Table 1) that must occur include reframing the growth/non-growth dichotomy; market/state directed dichotomy, and the assumption that since marginalized groups will not improve their relative position, absolute growth is the only choice available. There is a need to explore new procedures with new partners. For example, collaboration rather than competition becomes the guiding principle (Bryson & Crosby, 1992). Some of the new processes that sustainable communities will need to master include negotiation and conflict management skills. A crucial component is accumulating and incorporating new knowledge into the choices considered and made (Buxbaum & Ho, 1993).

Sustainable development, in its most admirable form, consciously reminds us that the system we are dealing with is complex (e.g., time, marginalized groups, and externalities) and that the stock of resources (e.g., physical, social, human capital) used to produce the outputs desired is both nonrenewable and renewable. It is not a "no growth" concept, but one in which different forms of growth are encouraged. It recognizes that a dynamic economy is not a euphemism for growth, but refers to changing choices, reframing issues, changing perceptions of markets and resources, and changing values. Nostalgia is replaced with the reality of changing needs and functions. Insistence on maintaining some historic view (e.g., production processes or community role) will only delay making needed choices. Economic choices are guided by both market and nonmarket (including intergenerational) values. There is concern about how change is creating increased disenfranchisement based on gender, skills, ethnicity, space, or economic status. The pursuit of sustainability implies an effort to increase access to decision making and to provide a fuller array of knowledge for decision making.

---

[6] Energy is also associated with development, to the extent electricity transforms how we conduct our lives.

SELECTED REFERENCES

Bryson, John M. & Barbara C. Crosby. 1992. *Leadership for the Common Good*. San Francisco: Jossey–Bass Publishers.

Buxbaum, Stephen, & Robert Ho. 1993. *Innovation and Collaboration: Challenges for State Rural Development Councils*. Aspen, CO: Aspen Institute.

Dykeman, Floyd W. 1990. Developing an understanding of entrepreneurial and sustainable rural communities, in F. W. Dykeman (ed.) *Entrepreneurial and Sustainable Communities*. Sackville, NB: Rural Studies and Small Town Research and Studies Programme, Department of Geography, Mount Allison University.

Etzioni, Amitai. 1993. *The Spirit of Community: Rights, Responsibilities, and the Communitarian Agenda*. New York: Crown Publishers.

Flora, Cornelia B., & Jan L. Flora. 1993. Entrepreneurial social infrastructure: A necessary ingredient. *The Annals of the American Academy of Political and Social Science* 529 (September): 48–58.

Hite, James, & Roy Powell. 1993. Economics of the hinterland. Unpublished manuscript. Clemson University and New England University.

Pulver, Glen. 1979. A theoretical framework for the analysis of community economic development policy options. In Gene Summers & Arne Selvik (eds.), *Nonmetropolitan Industrial Growth and Community Change*. Lexington, MA: Lexington Books.

Putnam, Robert D.. 1993. The prosperous community: Social capital and public life. *The American Prospect* 13: 35–42.

Rural Sociological Society. 1993. *Persistent Poverty in Rural America: Rural Sociological Society Task Force on Persistent Rural Poverty*. Boulder, CO: Westview Press.

Schumpeter, J.A. 1983. *The Theory of Economic Development*. New Brunswick, NJ: Transaction Books.

Shaffer, Ron. 1991. Building economically viable communities: A role for community developers. *Journal of the Community Development Society* 21(2): 74–87.

Shaffer, Ron. 1989. *Community Economics: Economic Structure and Change in Smaller Communities*. Ames, IA: Iowa State University Press.

Sustainable Rural Communities Committee. 1991. *Sustainable Rural Communities*. Guelph, ONT: University of Guelph.

Wilkinson, Ken P. 1991. *The Community in Rural America*. Westport, CT: Greenwood Press.

World Commission on Environment and Development. 1987. *Our Common Future*. Oxford: Oxford University Press. (Generally referred to as the Brundtland Commission).

WHAT DOES "SMART GROWTH" MEAN FOR COMMUNITY DEVELOPMENT?

By Tom Daniels

ABSTRACT

Sprawling patterns of dispersed residential and commercial development are seen as wasteful of land, expensive to service, automobile-dependent, environmentally harmful, and, ultimately, community-defeating. The state of Maryland has enacted a package of "Smart Growth" programs to promote more compact development by targeting public infrastructure and providing financial incentives in designated growth areas. It is hoped that this strategy will result in less sprawl, higher density development, greater use of mass transit, a pedestrian orientation, more closely-knit communities, and a higher quality of life. But smart growth will succeed only if people in designated growth and redevelopment areas are able to improve the economic, social, and physical aspects of their communities. Smart growth must build the capacity of community residents to undertake land use planning and solve community problems. Otherwise, additional policies will be needed to link smart growth and community development.

INTRODUCTION

Sprawling commercial and residential development has become the leading land use concern in the United States (Freilich, 1999; Sierra Club, 1998). Sprawl has produced unbalanced growth as suburban areas expand out into the countryside and inner cities and older suburbs suffer from disinvestment (Orfield, 1997). New infrastructure in the form of sewer and water facilities, schools, and roads must be built to service the new suburban development while older infrastructure in the inner cities and older suburbs deteriorates. In addition, sprawl has increased dependence on the automobile and foreign energy supplies, assaulted air and water quality, produced look-alike places without identity or uniqueness, and resulted in the conversion of millions of acres of farmland, forestland, and natural areas (Natural Resources Conservation Service, 2000).

Tom Daniels, Professor, Department of Geography and Planning, State University of New York at Albany, Albany, NY.

Community interaction is necessary for social well-being (Wilkinson, 1991). But in 1990, the national census showed that for the first time, more Americans were living in suburbs than in central cities (U.S. Department of Commerce, 1991). One consequence of this "suburban nation" has been reduced social cohesion, sense of community, and social capital as people are more isolated in cars and separated between suburbs and central cities (Putnam, 1995, 2000). This social separation hinders the ability of people who share a common territory to devise and implement collective solutions to the social, economic, and environmental problems caused by sprawl (Bridger & Luloff, 1999).

In short, sprawl has brought profound and often hasty changes to many communities across America. Ultimately, sprawl is reducing America's quality of life through a pattern of growth that is not economically, environmentally, or socially sustainable over the long run (Ewing, 1997). Responses to curb sprawl must include greater social interaction as a fundamental goal. The ability of communities to control sprawl and offer attractive land use and economic alternatives are predicated upon active public participation in decisions about growth, re-development, and natural resource protection.

Community Development, Sustainable Development, and Smart Growth I

Community development means improving the economic, social, and physical aspects of community life among a group of people who share a common territory. It also focuses on building the capacity of local people to work together to solve local problems and address issues. Community development must be a continuous process so that past gains are retained and further improvements and problem solving are realized. Thus, it embodies the concept of sustainable development in which intergenerational equity is achieved by meeting the needs of future generations as well as those of the current generation.

Bridger and Luloff (1999) identify two types of sustainable development. The first type involves a goal of constrained growth. While growth is still a primary objective, it must be limited spatially or in the rate of increase. Growth presents a host of problems, especially in maintaining the health and functions of ecosystems. The second type of sustainable development features the protection of natural resources both for food and fiber production and ecological stability.

By combining community development and sustainable development, sustainable communities "meet the economic needs of their residents, enhance and protect the environment, and promote more humane local societies" (Bridger & Luloff, 1999, p. 381). At the same time, these communities strive for social justice through housing opportunities, access to public services, minimizing class and racial spatial separation, and empowering people to participate in decision-making. The overall result is sustainable community development.

Sprawl threatens sustainability by reducing the capacity of people to work together for community development and increasing the fiscal and environmental challenges they face. Urban areas and inner ring suburbs lose population, social cohesion, and economic vitality, and suffer physical blight as people move to the outer suburbs (Rusk, 1996). In the new and growing suburbs, newcomers and established residents clash over social roles, open farm and forest lands are converted to houses and commercial development, and infrastructure costs and property taxes soar as new public facilities are built to serve the growing population (Daniels, 1999a). At the same time, suburban property values increase and land use controls are used to keep out lower income people (Orfield, 1997).

By contrast, compact cities with at least modest population and economic growth hold the promise of greater social involvement and physical and economic improvement. Likewise, suburbs that are growing (but not rapidly) should be better able to accommodate that growth spatially, fiscally, and socially. Hence, compact development focused on improving existing cities, suburbs, and villages is more likely than centerless sprawl to promote social and economic fulfillment and durable, cohesive communities.

"Smart growth" has emerged as a set of land use planning incentives and principles that attempt to promote sustainable development by constraining growth through channeling it into existing settlements and adjacent growth centers. At the same time, it is aimed at protecting rural natural resources, in particular farmland and environmentally-sensitive areas. Still, smart growth implies that it is possible to enjoy robust economic growth and accommodate population growth (Glendening, 1997).

It is important to note that there is no one "smart growth" plan or program. Communities must define what smart growth means to them and identify who stands to gain or lose if the community adopts such an approach. Community residents should determine if any, some, or all elements of a smart growth approach are appropriate for them as they attempt to shape their future appearance, development patterns, and social interaction (see Table 1). This flexibility is necessary for communities to respond to different local opportunities and constraints. Moreover, smart growth in particular, and land use planning and community development in general, are not passing fads; they require a long-term commitment of the private and public sectors to achieve success.

Gainers and Losers from Sprawl and Smart Growth

Smart growth can also be seen as an attempt to tame the "urban growth machine" that drives urban and suburban sprawl (Logan & Molotch, 1987). Logan and Molotch differentiate between the use value or utility of place, and the exchange value of property in the market. Use value and exchange value may be at odds or they may reinforce each other (Swanstrom, 1993). Swanstrom warns that an emphasis on economic development—increasing incomes, property tax base, and jobs—can simply drive up exchange values (i.e., the price of real estate) and force out lower income groups. Similarly, Logan and Molotch argue that an emphasis on increasing exchange values tends to favor corporate and landowning elites. Yet, Swanstrom observes that use values and exchange values can reinforce each other, especially for corporations, when the corporations have made large investments in a community.

The purpose of smart growth is to enhance use value and exchange values in existing settlements. Use value will increase if people live near their work and thus avoid traffic congestion, and can walk to stores, offices, and schools. Exchange value will increase if brownfields are remediated and developed and if public investments are made in new and improved infrastructure. That is, existing settlements will become better places to live—socially, environmentally, and economically. Yet, there is no guarantee a priori that smart growth alone will actually enhance social institutions or community interaction. In the countryside, the preservation of land through the purchase of conservation easements is a voluntary way to buy off the "unearned increment" of the exchange value of land from landowners so that the use value for farming or open space is equated with exchange value (Daniels, 2001). In effect, in the countryside, the smart growth approach is aimed at maintaining the status quo.

Land use planning and land use decisions are primarily the domain of local governments, and they affect the appearance and functioning of communities far into the future. But state and federal funding programs for highways, schools, housing, and sewer and water facilities can substantially influence the location and intensity of local land uses.

Local land use planning is a political process that influences both use value and exchange values, and hence is subject to influence from four major interest groups: politicians, owners of potentially developable land, developers, and the public-at-large of home-owning taxpayers and renters. How do the four main interest groups interact in such a way that sprawl results? Politicians rely substantially on campaign contributions to get elected and re-elected. Developers have a long record of contributing to local politicians. In turn, local politicians have often been accused of serving primarily the interests of developers and land speculators who seek to profit from land development activity (Bridger, 1992; Bridger & Harp, 1990; Logan & Molotch, 1987). Journalist Robert Heuer describes the relations between local politicians and developers as the "civic-industrial complex" a force that also includes financial institutions and the media (Daniels & Bowers, 1997).

Homeowners and owners of developable land, such as farmers, typically have large portions of their wealth tied up in real estate. Whereas homeowners are usually limited in what they can do with their land, owners of open land have more options. They may continue to keep the land in its open condition for farming, forestry, or natural areas, or they may seek to develop the land for a more intensive use, or sell it to a developer. When the exchange value of open land in the market (e.g., development) exceeds its use value (e.g., farming), the landowner has a financial incentive to sell the land for development. The exchange value of open land increases as rural lands become more accessible from cities and suburbs, and as government regulations allow more intensive development in rural areas. For instance, road construction makes rural lands accessible, and the extension of sewer and water facilities enables intensive development. Zoning that allows residential development with on-site septic systems and private wells also encourages sprawl. In other words, it is not surprising to see communities that have open land zoned for fairly intensive development that would benefit local landowners, even though sprawl would occur (Daniels, 1999a).

The public-at-large of homeowners and renters has concerns about local property taxes: the cost of owning a home and rental rates are affected by property taxes. The public-at-large wants adequate public services, but at an affordable cost. Politicians recognize that they can get re-elected in part by keeping property taxes under control. As a result, many growing suburban governments have a pro-growth bias as they compete to attract land uses—commercial, industrial, and high-end residential—that generate more in property tax revenues than they demand in public services. This practice is better known as <u>fiscal zoning</u>. In the process, one local government tries to lure away tax base from other local governments, and low-income people are discouraged from moving in (Orfield, 1997). The location of new development and its contribution to sprawl are not as much a concern as broadening the property tax base.

Perhaps the largest financial incentive that promotes sprawl is the mortgage interest deduction, which is worth tens of billions of dollars each year (Daniels, 1999a, 1999b). Many Americans have shown a preference for living in the rural-urban fringe on one- to ten-acre lots in houses of more than 3,000 square feet (Daniels, 1999a; Ewing, 1997). These houses have been ridiculed as McMansions, taco bells, and starter castles, but they embody a financial strategy of maximizing exchange value in which one's house has become a major investment vehicle. The strategy is to buy as much house and land as possible to maximize the mortgage interest deduction, build up equity while paying off the mortgage, and buy property in an area with good appreciation potential (i.e. the rural-urban fringe or an upscale suburb). Wealthier people have more income with which to buy a large house with a large mortgage, and the mortgage interest deduction is worth more to them. And larger houses on larger lots generate more in property taxes, which appeals to the local politicians.

In addition, state and federal spending for roads, schools, and sewer and water facilities are directed to growing suburbs. Orfield (1997) shows that residents of central cities and inner suburbs are in effect subsidizing the wealthier growing suburbs. These growing suburbs—called the "favored quarter" by Orfield—are capturing the majority of new jobs at the expense of inner cities and older suburbs. Moreover, many suburban governments continue to use large-lot residential zoning and discourage multi-family housing, resulting in a deep racial divide and segregation by income between the suburbs and central cities (Orfield, 1997; Rusk, 1999).

In short, politicians, developers, and landowners in growing suburban communities benefit from sprawl. Homeowners in central cities and inner suburbs do not, nor do renters in growing suburbs. The public-at-large loses by having to pay for new infrastructure in growing suburbs while the infrastructure in cities and older suburbs deteriorates. Also, despite the attempt by growing suburbs to attract high-end housing, several cost of community services studies have shown that most new residential development does not pay its way (Daniels & Bowers, 1997).

Smart Growth, Maryland Style

The term "smart growth" first appeared in the American media in 1997, during the debate over so-called "Smart Growth" legislation in Maryland (Maryland Office of Planning, 1997). Other states, such as Oregon (1973) and Florida (1985), have long required local governments to draft land use plans consistent with statewide goals. But Maryland emphasized the need to create financial incentives to curb the sprawling pattern of low-density residential development and arterial strip commercial development, spilling outside of existing cities and villages. This pattern was seen as using more land than necessary, and expensive to service. For instance, journalist Neal Peirce estimated that Maryland would save $100 million if children could walk to school, rather than use buses (Peirce, 1997). A smart growth pattern would promote more compact and cost-effective development through "creating high density, mixed-use and pedestrian oriented development that promotes efficient land use and increases transit ridership" (Maryland Office of Planning, 1997, p. 31). In addition, smart growth would help achieve sustainable community development by improving existing communities to be economically vibrant, physically attractive, and socially cohesive over the long run.

The Maryland smart growth legislation has five main components.

1. Priority funding areas. This requires county, city, and village governments to identify priority growth areas both within and adjacent to existing settlements. The local governments must then submit their proposed growth areas to the Maryland Office of Planning for review, negotiation, and approval. The state then targets its grants and loans for public sewer, water, schools, and housing to the designated growth areas. A county could allow a residential or commercial development to be built outside of a growth area, but there would be no state funding available for infrastructure.

2. The Brownfields Redevelopment Program is aimed at resolving landowner liability issues and helping to fund the clean-up and re-development of urban industrial sites that had been contaminated with hazardous waste.

3. The Job Creation Tax Credit Act offers income tax credits to business owners who create at least 25 jobs in a Priority Funding Area.

4. The Live Near Your Work Program provides a minimum of $3,000 for people who purchase homes in older neighborhoods and near their jobs.

5. The Rural Legacy Program. Outside of the growth areas, Maryland established a Rural Legacy Program to buy environmentally sensitive land and development rights to farmland. The program has been funded at $500 to $600 million over the next 15 years (Young, 2000). This funding supplements the state's farmland preservation program, which since 1977 has preserved over 180,000 acres.

The Rural Legacy Program is aimed at preserving 250,000 acres. A further benefit is that many counties have employed agricultural zoning to limit residential development in the countryside. If sufficient rural land can be preserved or restricted, then sprawl will be largely contained by the location of infrastructure.

In 1998, Maryland Governor Parris Glendening issued an executive order called the Smart Growth and Neighborhood Conservation Policy requiring state agencies to focus on locating and maintaining their facilities in central business districts and revitalization areas, and to consider the impact of projects on mass transit potential (Johnson, 1999).

Lessons from Maryland's Smart Growth Approach

Maryland's experience has already shown that smart growth incentives alone are not sufficient to produce desirable growth patterns, or sustainable community development. Effective local land-use regulations, public participation, and social capital are also important. One case in particular illustrates the Achilles heel of the Smart Growth approach. In Queen Anne's County on Maryland's Eastern Shore, county officials approved a 150,000 square foot Wal-Mart store outside of any Priority Funding Areas (Montgomery, 2000). Local opponents of the Wal-Mart have claimed that the location of the new store violated the county's long-range growth plan. But the local zoning allowed the Wal-Mart, and the developers agreed to pay $21 million in road and sewer improvements. The state was powerless to stop the project because no state funds were being used to extend public services or make road improvements. While the county stands to benefit from the Wal-Mart's property tax revenues, the large store may cause severe traffic problems and take retail trade away from nearby communities (Montgomery, 2000).

There are three main community development strategies: self-help, technical assistance, and conflict. The Maryland approach to smart growth relies heavily on technical assistance and funding from the state. But smart growth is more likely to be successful in those communities that are able to help themselves.

Communities that can achieve a consensus about future growth and development and implement effective land use planning can make better use of the state incentives. For instance, Baltimore County, Maryland has very tough, sprawl-fighting agricultural zoning at one dwelling per 50 acres. In addition, the county uses a rural-urban demarcation line to keep sewer and water lines out of the farming area. The county also has preserved almost 30,000 acres of farmland through conservation easements. The Rural Legacy program to preserve farmland and other rural lands will be effective in Baltimore County because of the existing planning efforts. Existing settlements in the county, such as Towson, the county seat, will benefit as Priority Funding Areas. In short, in Baltimore County, the state's technical assistance for smart growth will mesh well with the current local planning for smart growth.

It is naïve to think that good land use planning and community development can occur without any conflict. But poor land use planning and lack of community development often are the result of apathy on the part of the public-at-large and narrow self-interest on the part of developers and politicians.

The Maryland experience suggests that communities will be better able to plan their futures and be more rewarding places to live and work if they learn to work together through the Priority Funding Areas process. An important lesson is that in metropolitan America, the region is now the community (Daniels, 1999b; Rusk, 1993).

A local community does not exist in isolation; it is both an actor in a regional setting and acted upon by other communities. As Wilkinson notes there are "patterns of interaction that cross jurisdictional borders" (Wilkinson, 1991, p. 35). For instance, many public services now extend across several communities, such as sewer and water facilities, solid waste disposal, regional high schools, and transportation networks. At the same time, several types of private development, such as regional shopping malls, large residential subdivisions, office parks, and industrial parks can be described as "developments of regional impact." Decisions about the location of public facilities and large private developments need to be made with input from all of the communities that would be affected.

Given the size of regions, and the multitude of local communities, outside intervention may be needed to remove barriers to community development (Wilkinson, 1991). Often a state role is needed to help communities to work together and ensure adequate public involvement in decision-making to enact land use plans, ordinances, and infrastructure investments that promote coordinated development (Maurer, Forsyth, & Whipple, 1999). At the same time, regional tax base sharing, such as is practiced in greater Minneapolis-St. Paul, and regional fair share of low- and moderate-income housing as required in New Jersey can help to counteract the tendency to create well-to-do suburban enclaves (Daniels, 1999b). Regional governments, such as Portland's Metro, or regional councils, such as the Met Council of metropolitan Minneapolis-St. Paul or Metropolitan Planning Organizations that make decisions on transportation planning, will be needed to make decisions on land use and infrastructure that transcend local communities. Also, the preservation of land for open space or active farming on a regional scale can help to channel development toward existing settlements, as well as limit sprawl.

Maryland has committed a substantial amount of money to promote smart growth, especially for purchasing development rights to rural land through the Rural Legacy program. The acquisition of development rights marks an important new direction for communities. Traditionally, land use planning in America has meant planning for development. The Rural Legacy program emphasizes planning for long-term land preservation as well, which can influence the location and pace of development.

Finally, Maryland's smart growth approach embodies a confidence in being able to accommodate population growth without sacrificing environmental quality or social cohesion. But smart growth will not happen overnight. The proof will be how well Maryland communities and counties are able to absorb the projected 1.6 million additional residents expected between 2000 and 2025 (U.S. Department of Commerce, 1997).

Refining the Smart Growth Approach

Maryland was by no means the first state to tackle growth management, and there is no single "smart growth" blueprint. But the Maryland legislative effort seemed to coalesce a nationwide personal and business dissatisfaction with the dispersed settlement and commercial patterns of metropolitan growth. For example, in California, sprawl has been recognized as a drag on growth, harming both use values and exchange values America (Bank of America et al., 1995).

While Maryland's Smart Growth approach has several attributes that discourage sprawl and encourage economic development and physical improvements, other states and local governments have adopted refinements of the smart growth approach that deserve consideration for furthering the social aspects community development.

Regional tax base sharing. Local governments compete for development in order to expand their property tax base. This competition promotes premature commercial development and sprawl. Regional property tax sharing in which communities pool at least some of their tax revenues can decrease the competition for tax base, and reduce the polarization between "have" and "have-not" communities. So far, only greater Minneapolis-St. Paul has a regional property tax sharing program (Orfield, 1997).

Regional cooperation. Local units of government will need to learn to work together because many land use and community development issues transcend individual city, suburban, and county boundaries. Transportation, solid waste, public sewer and water, and future growth are all issues that point to the need for regional responses. Greater Portland, Oregon is the nation's only elected regional government, encompassing three counties and 24 municipalities. Metro Portland has control of regional land use planning, transportation, and utility development (Daniels, 1999b). A regional, democratic approach to land use and public services can help avoid a duplication of services in several communities as well as compel communities to cooperate on the location of services and development. This greater interaction is key to social well-being (Wilkinson, 1991).

Good urban design. The smart growth model emphasizes a land use pattern of compact cities and suburbs surrounded by countryside that is devoted primarily to farming, forestry, and open space (see Table 1). Cities and suburbs must become attractive places to live and work in order to minimize sprawling development out into the countryside. One key to making cities and suburbs more desirable places is good design. The New Urbanism movement among architects and planners arose in the early 1990s as an attempt to produce physical designs that translate into a high quality of community life, based on a human scale of buildings, a slower pace with a pedestrian-orientation, a mix of residences, commercial space, and public parks, and a distinct edge between built-up areas and the countryside (Calthorpe, 1993). All of these features tend to promote social interaction.

To promote good design principles, community residents can work together to draft design guidelines and appoint design review boards for the review of development proposals. Zoning ordinances that allow a mix of residential and commercial development will also be essential. Historic preservation and the re-use of older buildings can be very helpful in bringing in new businesses and residents and creating tourist attractions.

One criticism of the New Urbanism is that it has largely been limited to upscale residential communities, such as Kentlands in Gaithersburg, Maryland, a suburb of Washington, DC. New Urbanism needs to occur as redevelopment projects within existing cities. For instance, HUD's HOPE VI low-income housing projects are embodying low-rise New Urbanist design, replacing the high-rise housing projects of Urban Renewal. Moreover, isolated New Urbanist projects may not achieve region-wide changes in land use, transportation, or social cohesion. For instance, critic James Kunstler described Kentlands as "embedded in one of the worst suburban crudscapes in America" (Kunstler, 1996, p. 189).

Urban and village growth boundaries. Several communities have worked with neighboring communities or the surrounding county to draft urban or village growth boundaries (Daniels, 1999b). Typically, the area inside the growth boundary has enough buildable land to accommodate development needs for the next 20 years. Infrastructure—such as public and private sewer and water,

Table 1. Smart Growth Principles and Practices.

Principle	Practice
1. Compact Settlements	1. Targeted Infrastructure Investment Growth Boundaries
2. Good City and Village Design with Mixed Uses, Pedestrian Orientation, and Mass Transit	2. Design Review Ordinances Ordinances, Zoning Ordinances That Allow Mixed Residential and Commercial Uses, Transit Oriented Development
3. A Mix of Housing for All Income Levels	3. Fair Share Housing Legislation By State
4. Private Re-investment in Downtowns	4. Brownfields Clean-up Historic Preservation
5. Protection of Farmland, Forestland, and Natural Areas	5. Land Protection Zoning, Purchase, Donation, and Transfer of Development Rights, Use-Value Property Taxation, Growth Boundaries, and Rural Residential Zones

schools, and major roads—is located inside the boundary. The growth boundary may be expanded as needed over time. It induces a more compact style of growth that is cheaper to service than sprawl, and retards the premature development of rural lands. Since the early 1973 the state of Oregon has required that all of its cities and counties agree on growth boundaries. The State of Washington adopted a similar requirement in its 1990 Growth Management Act. Growth boundaries are also found in Durham, North Carolina, Virginia Beach, Virginia, Sonoma County, California, and Lancaster County, Pennsylvania, among others (Daniels, 1999b). A major challenge is to induce a large majority of future growth occur inside the boundaries and at densities that will not cause boundaries to fill up rapidly, and to make living within the growth boundaries socially, environmentally, and economically attractive.

Fair share housing. Smart growth and community development must be inclusive. Compact cities and suburbs must accommodate a variety of income groups and hence provide affordable housing. To do this, state fair share housing legislation is needed. Such legislation has been passed in Oregon (1973) and New Jersey (1985) (Porter, 1997). Suburbs, for example, must zone for multi-family housing, not just large single-family house lots.

Mass transit. Cities and suburbs must develop reliable mass transit that is tied to compact, walkable, mixed-use settlements. Oregon is pioneering the creation of "transit-oriented developments" that combine a mix of residential and commercial developments with mass transit (Calthorpe, 1993). One purpose of the transit-oriented developments is to create greater social interaction.

Community Development and Smart Growth II

America faces a possible increase of more than 115 million people between 2000 and 2050 (U.S. Department of Commerce, 1997). If this additional population is to enjoy good shelter, employment opportunities, recreational sites, and social relations, new land use patterns must emerge and sustainable community development must become a priority. Bridger and Luloff (1999) judge sustainable communities according to five goals: increasing local economic diversity, greater self-reliance, a decrease in the use of energy and an increase in the recycling of waste, protection of biodiversity and natural resources, and social justice in housing and living needs, and access to public services.

Maryland's smart growth effort is clearly aimed at greater economic diversity through the Jobs Credit Program, the Brownfields Redevelopment Program, and the targeting of state infrastructure dollars to the Priority Funding Areas. Greater self-reliance is not likely to be a goal of smart growth, especially in metropolitan areas. Linkages through transportation, infrastructure and regional cooperation are seen as more important. In fact, Bridger and Luloff admit that community self-reliance may be "little more than a romantic longing for a mythical past" (1999, p. 382).

The Live Near Your Work Program and the promotion of mass transit will help to reduce energy use. More compact forms of development and urban revitalization will reduce automobile-dependence. The Brownfields Program serves to recycle old industrial sites into productive commercial, residential, or industrial space. The Rural Legacy Program in conjunction with the state farmland preservation program promotes the conservation of natural resources in the countryside. Finally, by focusing state infrastructure investments within Priority Funding Areas, people in existing communities will have greater access to public services.

Smart growth suggests that financial incentives and land use planning can create a healthy, attractive environment along with a vibrant economy and well-adjusted, productive citizens. But community development includes building capacity for people to work together to promote a sense of community, nurture a caring attitude about the community, and to resolve economic, social, and environmental problems (Claude, Bridger, & Luloff, 2000). If smart growth principles and programs are not carried out over the long run, they run the risk of being merely a sporadic reaction to a perceived problem (Wilkinson, 1991).

Successful community development and good land use planning are mutually reinforcing and stand the test of time. Successful smart growth and community development efforts depend on inclusiveness, trust, and cooperation among interest groups. This social capital is the basis of public involvement in formal and informal decision-making (Flora, 1998). Building social capital is essential for effective, equitable, and long-term land-use planning. Otherwise, with the public removed, the "civic-industrial complex" of politicians, developers, and major landowners will dominate and continue to produce sprawl.

CONCLUSIONS

Decisions about where to develop and when are made by thousands of local governments and millions of people each year. The smart growth movement has value in getting people to look at how their communities function internally and within a region, how they are growing, and what steps are needed to shape that growth. It aims to provide financial incentives to create more compact development that is cheaper to service, less land consumptive, and more attractive than sprawl. But smart growth will need to foster community participation and decision-making capacity to ensure long-term implementation of smart growth principles and programs.

Planners and community developers would be naïve to think that smart growth incentives and land-sue planning techniques can be implemented without conflict. Many local politicians, developers, and landowners have benefitted from sprawl. In general, the public-at-large stands to benefit from smart growth in lower infrastructure costs, less conversion of rural land, the revitalization of cities and inner suburbs, and possibly greater social cohesion and democratic decision-making.

Community development is ultimately aimed at human fulfillment. America's communities will continue to grow and change in the new millennium. How they grow and where they grow will greatly influence the sense of community, economic opportunities, environmental quality, and quality of life they are able to offer. While some incentives and direction from the state may be necessary, those communities in which the public participates in the planning and decision-making process the more likely they will produce smarter growth and sustained social capital.

REFERENCES

American Planning Association. 1998. *Growing Smarter: Legislative Guidebook: Model Statutes for Planning and the Management of Change, Phases I & II*, Interim Edition. Chicago: Planners Press.

Bank of America, Greenbelt Alliance, California Agency of Natural Resources, and the Low Income Housing Fund. 1995. *Beyond Sprawl*. San Francisco, CA.

Bridger, J. C. 1992. Local elites and growth promotion. Pp. 95-113 in D. Chekki (ed.), *Research in Community Sociology*. Greenwich, CT: JAI Press.

Bridger, J. C., & A. Harp. 1990. Ideology and growth promotion. *Journal of Rural Studies* 6: 269-277.

Calthorpe, P. 1993. *The Next American Metropolis*. Princeton, NJ: Princeton University Press.

Bridger, J. C., & A.E. Luloff. 1999. Toward an interactional approach to sustainable community development. *Journal of Rural* Studies 15(4): 377-387.

Claude, L. P., J. C. Bridger, & A.E. Luloff. 2000. Community well-being and local activeness. Pp. 39-45 in P. Schaeffer and S. Loveridge (eds.), *Small Town and Rural Economic Development*. Westport, CT: Praeger.

Daniels, T. L. 1999a. What to do about rural sprawl? Paper presented at the American Planning Association Conference, Seattle, WA, April 28, 1999.

Daniels, T. L. 1999b. *When City and Country Collide: Managing Growth in the Metropolitan Fringe*. Washington, DC: Island Press.

Daniels, T. L. 2001. Coordinating opposite approaches to managing urban growth and curbing sprawl: A synthesis. *American Journal of Economics and Sociology* 60(1): 229-243.

Daniels, T. L., & D. Bowers. 1997. *Holding Our Ground: Protecting America's Farms and Farmland*. Washington, DC: Island Press.

Ewing, R. 1997. Is Los Angeles style sprawl desirable? *Journal of the American Planning Association* 63(1): 107-126.

Flora, J. L. 1998. Social capital and communities of place. *Rural Sociology* 63(4): 481-506.

Freilich, R. H. 1999. *From Sprawl to Smart Growth*. Washington, DC: American Bar Association.

Glendening, P. 1997. A new smart growth culture for Maryland, Annapolis, MD. At www.op.state.md.us/smartgrowth.

Johnson, D. 1999. Maryland, in S. Meck et al., *Planning Communities for the 21st Century*. Chicago: American Planning Association.

Kunstler, J. H. 1996. *Home From Nowhere: Remaking Our Everyday World for the 21st Century*. New York: Simon & Schuster.

Logan, J. R., & H. L. Molotch. 1987. *Urban Fortunes: The Political Economy of Place*. Berkeley: University of California Press.

Maryland Office of Planning. 1997. *Smart Growth and Neighborhood Conservation Initiative*. Annapolis, MD.

Maurer, G., K. Forsyth, & M. Whipple. 1999. *Making Smart Growth Smarter*. Annapolis, MD: Chesapeake Bay Foundation and 1000 Friends of Maryland.

Montgomery, L. 2000. Maryland land-use weapon backfires. *The Washington Post*, May 14, 2000, pp. C1, C5.

Natural Resources Conservation Service (NRCS). 2000. *1997 National Resources Inventory*. Washington, DC: U.S. Government Printing Office.

Orfield, M. 1997. *Metropolitics*. Washington, DC: Brookings Institution.

Peirce, N. 1997. Maryland's smart growth law: A national model? Washington Post Writers Group, Washington, DC, April 20, 1997.

Porter, D. 1997. *Managing Growth in America's Communities*. Washington, DC: Island Press.

Putnam, R. D. 1995. Bowling alone: America's declining social capital. *Journal of Democracy* 6(1): 65-78.

Putnam, R. D. 2000. *Bowling Alone: The Collapse and Revival of American Community*. New York: Simon and Schuster.

Rusk, D. 1993. *Cities Without Suburbs*. Washington, DC: Woodrow Wilson Center Press.

Rusk, D. 1996. *Baltimore Unbound: A Strategy for Regional Renewal*. Baltimore, MD: The Abell Foundation.

Rusk, D. 1999. *Inside Game, Outside Game: Winning Strategies for Saving Urban America*. Washington, DC: Brookings Institution.

Sierra Club. 1998. *Sprawl Report*. San Francisco, CA: Sierra Club, See, www.SIERRACLUB.ORG/transportation/sprawl/sprawl_report/index.html.

Swanstrom, T. 1993. Beyond economism: Urban political economy and the post modern challenge. *Journal of Urban Affairs* 15(1): 55-78.

U.S. Department of Agriculture. 1999. *1997 Census of Agriculture*. Washington, DC: U.S. Government Printing Office.

U.S. Department of Commerce, Bureau of the Census. 1991. *1990 Census of Population*. Washington, DC: U.S. Government Printing Office.

U.S. Department of Commerce, Bureau of the Census. 1997. *Demographic State of the Nation*. Washington, DC: U.S. Government Printing Office.

Wilkinson, K. P. 1991. *The Community in Rural America*. Westport, CT: Greenwood Press.

Young, R., Assistant Director, Maryland Office of State Planning. Personal communication, February 28, 2000.

An Interactional Approach to Place-Based Rural Development

Jeffrey C. Bridger and Theodore R. Alter

Rural America is in the midst of the most far-reaching transformation in our history. Globalization and other forces are fundamentally altering the economic landscape and erasing many traditional sources of employment and income; in such an uncertain environment, economic development has become more important and more complicated than ever. Unfortunately, rural policies have not kept pace with the times, and there is growing recognition that what worked in the past is not effective in a global economy. In place of traditional approaches to rural development, there is an emerging consensus that we must create strategies that enhance regional/place competitiveness. In this paper, we explore this strategy, identify some of its most serious shortcomings, and propose an interactional approach that integrates economic, environmental, and social well-being.

Rural America is in the midst of the most far-reaching and rapid transformation in our history. Globalization is fundamentally altering the economic landscape and erasing many of the better sources of income and employment. Manufacturing, which is still the most important economic sector, has declined markedly in recent years. In 2005, manufacturing accounted for approximately 12 percent of all jobs in nonmetropolitan counties. This represents a sharp drop from 1976, when almost 19 percent of the rural workforce was employed in manufacturing (United States Department of Agriculture, 2006). And although manufacturing has stabilized over the last two years, the picture varies considerably by region and industry. Parts of the Northwest, for instance, are continuing to shed jobs in timber and other natural resource industries (Whitener & Parker, 2007).

Many agriculturally dependent communities have also fallen on hard times. Small farms have been disappearing for decades, but losses have been accelerated by changes in the structure of U.S. agriculture, especially the decisive shift away "…from the production of commodities to finely graded products and a shift from spot and futures markets to contracts" (Drabenstott, 2001, p.10). Instead of producing generic commodities for sale

Jeffrey C. Bridger: Senior Research Associate, Department of Agricultural Economics and Rural Sociology, Penn State University, 814-863-8631, jcb8@psu.edu. Theodore R. Alter: Professor of Agricultural, Environmental, and Regional Economics, Department of Agricultural Economics and Rural Sociology, Penn State University, 814-863-8640, talter@psu.edu.

the open market, many farmers have become the first link in vertically integrated supply chains which coordinate production, processing, marketing, and consumption (Buttel, 2003). As this consolidation continues, more and more farms will be forced out of business. Nowhere can this be seen better than in the pork industry, which experts estimate will be dominated by fewer than forty supply chains in just a few years. Only a small fraction of the nation's 100,000 hog farmers will receive production contracts (Drabenstott, 2001). The remainder will be forced to shift to another commodity or seek alternative sources of income and employment.

Supply chains are also changing the geography of U.S. agriculture. Because it is more efficient to reduce the distance between production and processing, farms are increasingly locating near processing facilities. The poultry industry, for instance, is concentrated around processing facilities in the South, the mid-Atlantic, and the upper Midwest. As this process gains momentum, clusters of agricultural production will replace the dispersed settlement pattern that has historically characterized agriculturally dependent rural areas. In fact, as the declining number of farm-dependent counties indicates, geographic reorganization is already occurring. In 1990, 618 of the nearly 2,000 nonmetropolitan counties were farm-dependent. By 2000, only 420 nonmetropolitan counties were still relying on agriculture for 15 percent or more of earnings (Ghelfi & McGranahan, 2004). As these counties have lost their farms, they have also lost banks and other businesses. And in many historically farm-dependent counties, matters have been made worse by a lack of alternative employment opportunities (Ghelfi & McGranahan, 2004).

Even in those rural locations where jobs are available, they tend to pay less than in urban areas. And the wage gap between rural and urban America has widened in recent years. In 2006, median weekly earnings for rural workers were only 84 percent of the average for their metropolitan counterparts (Whitener & Parker, 2007). And in some sectors of the rural economy, wages are actually declining. For instance, workers in the meat packing and processing industry have seen their wages fall by 30 to 40 percent since 1990 (Brueggemann & Brown, 2003; Drabenstott, 2001). This trend is particularly troubling because meat packing and processing is the largest employer in the rural manufacturing sector.

Figures from the 2000 census underscore the economic problems facing rural America. Between 1990 and 2000, 25 percent of nonmetropolitan counties lost population. Remote, agriculturally dependent counties were most likely to lose people, especially young people. Over half of these counties had fewer people in 2000 than in 1990, and in over a third of these places, the loss exceeded 5 percent (McGranahan & Beale, 2002). During the same period, many rural counties with natural amenities or within commuting distance to metropolitan areas experienced moderate growth. These divergent population trends reflect a pattern of uneven development that is fostering increasing spatial inequality and threatening the security of many rural communities (Drabenstott, 2001; Falk & Labao, 2003; Harvey, 1996).

In such a dynamic and uncertain environment, economic development has become more important and more complicated than ever. Unfortunately, rural policies have not kept pace with the changes described above. At the federal level, we have never had a coherent policy for rural America. Instead, we have implicitly equated rural with agriculture and relied on agricultural subsidies and selective infrastructure investments that ultimately benefit a small segment of the population. At the state and local levels, a variety of industrial recruitment and retention strategies continue to dominate efforts to stimulate rural economies. The problem with these approaches is that in a global economy, rural America no longer has the competitive advantage it once did. In the past, abundant natural resources, low-cost land, and relatively cheap labor gave rural areas an edge over their metropolitan counterparts. Today, corporations can search the globe for the most profitable place to do business. In this context, it is both expensive and risky to offer tax breaks and other incentives to lure footloose industries that can easily relocate to lower-cost foreign locations (Drabenstott, 2001).

Although no single strategy has emerged to replace traditional approaches to economic development, there is an emerging consensus that enhancing community or regional competitiveness will be key to the future of rural America:

> More and more policy experts agree that rural policy in the 21ˢᵗ century must center on enhancing the competitiveness of places. In short, rural America needs a policy focused on geography, supporting economic development in defined geographic areas. Place policy supports a community's ability to compete in the new economy by highlighting and accentuating community attributes that are attractive to households and firms. The attributes are sources of strength from which a community provides economic opportunity and value. Put another way, these strengths define a place's competitive advantage (Johnson, 2001:2).

In this paper, we begin by describing place-based economic development in more detail. Following this, we examine some of the problems associated with place competitiveness. Finally, we draw on an interactional approach to social organization (Bridger et al., 2002; Luloff & Bridger, 2003; Wilkinson, 1991) to create a more comprehensive place-based policy framework that integrates economic, environmental, and social well-being.

Place Competitiveness as Rural Development

Economists have not traditionally paid much attention to why certain activities happen in certain places, preferring instead to develop models where locations are portrayed, in Krugman's (1991, p.2) words, as "… dimensionless points within which factors of production can be instantly and costlessly moved from one activity to another." The reality, of course, is not so simple. Location clearly does matter. Consider, for example, the case of Dalton, Georgia (Krugman, 1991). In 1895, a teenager named Catherine Evans made a bedspread as a wedding gift. But this was no ordinary bedspread. It utilized a technique called tufting. Over the next few years, Miss Evans made several of these bedspreads, and in 1900, she perfected a technique for locking the tufts into the backing. After this discovery, she began to sell the bedspreads, and a local handicraft industry sprang up in the area. For the next few decades, tufting was done exclusively by hand. But after World War II, a machine was developed for producing tufted carpets, which were much cheaper than the woven carpets commonly in use at the time. With its workforce skilled in tufting, Dalton was able to capitalize on this advance and soon many small carpet manufacturers popped up in the area, together with supporting businesses that specialized in dyes and carpet backings. Over the next several decades, Dalton emerged as the carpet capital of America.

Until recently, economic development policy has for the most part ignored the experience of places like Dalton where some unique characteristic has been the key to their success. In fact, policy has been designed largely to flatten the landscape. While investments in education, infrastructure improvements, and industrial sectors might be targeted at different locations, the actual intent is to minimize the differences between places and create a system in which individuals (rather than places) have the maximum chance for success (Johnson, 2001).

Now, policy analysts are focusing on the features that distinguish places from one another and asking how these differences might be harnessed to foster more sustained growth and development (Johnson, 2001). Obviously, places differ from one another in myriad ways. At the most basic level, there are attributes there are largely "given" and beyond the control of local leaders or residents. These include physical qualities such as distance from other communities, climate, scenery, and natural resource endowments. They also include previous developments such as highways, railroads, and other infrastructure investments. Finally, population characteristics (age structure, educational attainment, and ethnicity) can be features that are that difficult to change over the short run.

In addition to these more or less fixed attributes, there are other characteristics which can be modified. Leadership capacity and local governance, for instance, can be strengthened in ways that enhance competitiveness. Workforce development can be aligned with emerging market opportunities, polluted environments can be remediated, and new infrastructure investments can be made. And in many places, unique historical and cultural attributes can be mobilized for development efforts:

> The communities have a history and culture that may not be fully expressed. This history and culture as well affects what the community or region can be or how it can change. The idea here is path dependence, where we are and will be is a function of where we have been….what a community can and will be is with the wisdom and culture of the local people and reflective of what has occurred in the past…Much of this wisdom and the cultural uniqueness of places is resident in the local people – a part of the social capital of the community (Johnson, 2001, p. 3).

Proponents of place-based development argue that the key to success hinges on making the most of "…the unique package of differentiating factors that add value to the region or community or its products" (Johnson, 2001, p. 3). This process involves a number of steps. First, both fixed and malleable assets must be identified. These assets must then be analyzed with an eye toward identifying how they truly differentiate a place. The idea is to create strategies that build on local uniqueness in ways that enable places to carve out an economic niche in the global market. Ideally, places will sort themselves out in a way that results in a more diverse and economically stable landscape. Instead of competing for the same pool of manufacturing jobs, for instance, places will be offering unique products or services matched to local assets.

This approach to economic development differs dramatically from previous strategies. Instead of trying to level the playing field, a place-based approach must by definition be community and/or region-specific. In short, this kind of development is an "inside job" by local actors and organizations (Wilkinson, 1991). External resources will be needed, but the real work will have to be done at the local level.

Barriers to Place-based Competitiveness

In theory, a place-competitive approach to rural development seems viable – especially in light of the economic trends described above. In practice, there are a number of potential obstacles that must be overcome. First, it is doubtful that capitalizing on local uniqueness will remedy past patterns of uneven development. While regional/place-based approaches to rural development may foster a more equitable distribution of jobs and income, there is no guarantee that they will. In fact, a narrow focus on place competitiveness may reinforce or exacerbate existing patterns of uneven development. Historically, this has certainly been the case:

> Small, pre-existing differences, be it in natural resources or socially constructed endowments, get magnified and consolidated rather than eroded by free market competition. The coercive laws of competition push capitalists to relocate production to more advantageous sites and the special requirements of particular

forms of commodity production push capitalists into territorial specialization... Agglomeration economies...generate a locational dynamic in which new production tends to be drawn to existing production locations (Harvey, 2006, p.98).

In other words, places that are already in a privileged position because of geography, natural resource endowments, infrastructure, proximity to transportation routes, or a variety of other factors, tend to prosper, while their less well-endowed counterparts fall behind. And as Harvey (2006, p.109) points out, the landscape that results from this process is marked by a "...hierarchy of power and interests such that the richer regions grow richer and the poor languish in indebtedness."

Matters are further complicated by differences in local capacity for action. Every element of a place competitiveness strategy, from identifying an economic niche to retraining the workforce, to creating complementary clusters of firms, places heavy demands on local institutions. To take just one example, consider the level of technical expertise needed to identify a potential economic niche. At the very least, this requires a thorough understanding of regional economic assets and trends and how these relate to emerging opportunities in the global market. And once a potential niche is identified, a host of additional issues must be addressed, ranging from workforce development, to infrastructure requirements, to financing strategies. Few communities – especially rural communities – have the resources or leadership to undertake such a complicated venture. Once again, it is the places that are already most developed that are likely to be in a position to most successfully leverage local assets.

Even so seemingly a straightforward task as drawing on local history and cultural traditions in ways that add value to the region raise complicated issues that are not adequately addressed in much of the recent writing on place competitiveness. One of the biggest problems is that places do not have just one history or one culture. Consider, for instance, the case of Lancaster County in Pennsylvania's historic "Dutch Country." The story most people know of Lancaster County revolves around the Amish and their simple, agrarian lifestyle. But there are other stories that can be told about this place, including one in which the County is a bastion of growth and entrepreneurial capitalism. As one local reporter explained, "Lancaster is a community with a dual personality...One personality glorifies capitalism....There are few communities in Pennsylvania, perhaps in the U.S., that match Lancaster Countians in their belief in free enterprise, the preeminence of the businessman and economic growth. The other half of the split personality longs for preservation, old-fashioned things and quaint ways. This is the homeland of the plain people, a conservative sect that gets about in horses and buggies in the supersonic age" (Klimuska, 1988, p. 14).

Most communities have these kind of competing heritage narratives, which are best defined as selective representations of the past that feed into and are partially driven by the sentiments and interests of contemporary residents (Bridger, 1996). And for this reason, heritage narratives are never politically neutral. In fact, they are frequently mobilized to position different groups to support lines of action that result in an inequitable distribution of costs and benefits. In Lancaster County, the Amish story has been pitted against the entrepreneurial narrative in a protracted struggle over land use and economic development strategies that has helped shape the region's developmental trajectory (Bridger, 1996).

As this example illustrates, local history does not necessarily provide guidance for place differentiation. Place construction (and reconstruction) is a cumulative and messy process that involves material, discursive, and symbolic practices in ways that are unpredictable and fraught with deep-seated conflicts over the interpretation of history, culture and identity (Bridger, 1996; Harvey, 1996; Molotch et al., 2000).

Over time, all of these elements interact to create physical and cultural environments that affect current and future possibilities. Even places like Santa Barbara and Ventura, California, that have similar climates, environmental assets, and demographic characteristics, can proceed along very different trajectories that leave them with very different options for future economic development opportunities (Molotch et al., 2000). Santa Barbara has come to approximate "…development experts' ideal – a 'learning community' on the forefront of information, technology, and leisure services…," while Ventura "… more nearly typifies the qualities that preoccupy critics of U.S. urban places" (Molotch et al., 2000, p.797). What the experiences of these two communities suggest is that even when places have similar assets, a variety of forces, ranging from local power structures to historical accidents, affect the ability to capitalize on them.

Place and Social Well-Being

While the emphasis on place is a welcome shift, the problems identified above point to the need for a more holistic framework. And perhaps more importantly, a broader perspective is needed because place competition, as currently conceived, does not adequately address the non-economic factors that impact the local quality of life. In our view, place competitiveness has a role to play but only as one component of a multi-faceted strategy. As a first step in sketching such an approach, it is important to specify the relationship between place and individual and social well-being, because this underlies the rationale for an alternative policy.

As many observers (Leach, 1999; Meyrowitz, 1985; Zukin, 1991) have noted, the role of place in social life has become increasingly uncertain in the wake of globalization and the rapid changes it has spawned. Places that once seemed invincible suddenly find themselves vulnerable to economic, financial, and physical shifts over which they have no control. The stability and permanence we associate with specific places have been fundamentally undermined. Zukin (1991, p.8) likens this change to the "Great Transformation" that happened in England during the 18th and 19th centuries (Polyani, 1957). In Zukin's view, abstract market forces have both separated people from social institutions and "…have overpowered specific forces of attachment identified with place" (Zukin, 1991, p. 4). Meyrowitz (1985) goes so far as to argue that place no longer matters in today's world. And Leach (1999, p.8) writes of a placeless society - a world in which "we live longer but emptier, without those nurturing habitats or places which remind us where we came from and, therefore, who we are."

Despite this alarmist rhetoric, there is reason to doubt that place has become less important. The meaning of place may have changed, and our relationship to specific places may have become more contingent and complicated (Bridger & Alter, 2006). But as Agnew (1987, p.33) argues, for most people, place continues to play an important role in the social construction of meaning:

> The strongest forms of bonding are still local: a village or a town, particular valleys or mountain…Common experiences engendered by the forces of "nationalization" and "globalization" are still mediated by local ones. Most people still follow well-worn paths in their daily existence. Though "national" or "global" issues have increased in number and significance relative to local ones, they take on meaning as they relate to local agendas…all issues, whatever their source or pervasiveness, are meaningful or important only in the context of outlooks derived from everyday life.

In short, place, and experience in place, are fundamentally implicated in our understanding of the world. As Casey (1993, p.307) puts it, "Where we are has a great deal to do with who and what we are…Where something or someone is, far from being a casual qualification, is one of its determining properties. As to the *who*, it is evident that our innermost sense of personal identity…deeply reflects our implacement." To be more specific, our experience of place, and the interactions that occur in specific places, affect individual and social well-being in important ways.

The first and most fundamental connection between place and well-being stems from the simple fact that the locality is where the individual and society intersect. The family, of course, is the first point of contact between the child and the larger world. But this is a sharply limited form of contact, and one that "…screens and conveys selected information and selected demands from the outside world" (Wilkinson, 1991, p.77). The local society, by contrast, provides the opportunity to experience a wider range of people and institutions, and thus represents a tangible manifestation of the larger social order. This is important for well-being because the quantity and quality of available interpersonal contacts provide the raw material for social interaction. And as Wilkinson (1991) argues, it is a truism that well-being depends crucially on the ability to interact with a broad range of other people.

To fully appreciate this relationship, consider the opportunity structure for interaction in rural localities. Many of our rural communities lack a complete table of social organization. Consequently, people must travel to different places to meet many of their daily needs. In such a situation, the locality becomes primarily a place of residence only, "… as relatives and neighbors who are strongly tied to one another have few mutual contacts in their separate involvements outside the place of residence" (Wilkinson, 1991, p.114) Available contacts tend to be repeated and become what Granovetter (1973) calls "strong ties." On the surface, the prevalence of strong ties would seem to foster well-being because they promote solidarity and can be a source of financial and other resources. But at the same time, the lack of weak ties among a population makes it difficult to create linkages between clusters of strong ties. Without these linkages, it is difficult to create a holistic local society and develop the range of relationships that foster well-being.

There is also evidence to suggest that because living in a rural location creates an opportunity structure for certain forms of contact, it fosters a unique set of social problems. The idea here is that different kinds of social disruptions tend to be associated with different types of interpersonal contacts (Wilkinson, 1991). Robberies and other violent crimes tend to be committed by strangers or non-intimates. Homicides, on the other hand, are more likely to be committed by an intimate associate of the victim (Paulozzi et al., 2002). Other problems such as suicide and child abuse are frequently associated with isolation from social networks (De Leo & Spathonis, 2004; Paulozzi et al., 2002). And while it is difficult to say for sure that rurality is at the root of these problems, it does appear that the fragmented social structure of many rural areas contributes to certain forms of social disruption. Among white males, for instance, suicide rates are consistently higher in rural areas (Kaplan & Geling, 1998).

These interpersonal issues point to another important way in which locality-based interaction affects well-being: it is the setting for the emergence and development of the self. As Mead (1934) argued long ago, the self does not exist as an entity lodged within the isolated individual; selves take on meaning only through the relationships in which we are embedded: "It is the social process itself that is responsible for the appearance of the self; it is not there as a self apart from this type of experience" (Mead, 1934, p.142).

In Mead's framework, the self first arises in interactions with specific others. Later, as we come into contact with a wider range of people and groups, our concept of self is influenced by these interactions as well. Mead (1934, p.155) calls this the generalized other and claims that this "…social process influences the behavior of the individuals involved in it and carrying it on…for it is in this form that the social process or community enters as a determining factor into the individual's thinking." In the course of this process, we develop bonds with specific and generalized others, and, by taking the role of the other, we become aware of the role we play in social interaction and what it means to be a social being. Hence, the self, as it arises out of social interaction, connects the individual with society by creating a bond of shared meaning. Or, as Mead (1934, p.162) puts it, "There are certain common responses which each individual has toward certain common things, and insofar as those common responses are awakened in the individual when he is affecting other persons, he arouses his own self. The structure, then, on which the self is built is this response to all, for one has to be a member of a community to be a self."

Mead's theory of the self was not explicitly tied to place. The generalized other, for instance, simply refers to social processes and activities within which specific interactions occur, regardless of location. In today's world, there are many ways to interact with other people across vast distances, and these interactions obviously also affect the ongoing construction of the self. At the same time, the vast majority of people continue to have most of their being and existence in specific geographic locales. People who share a common territory tend to interact with one another, even as they participate in more far-flung networks (Bernard, 1973; Bridger et al., 2002; Oldenburg, 1999; Wilkinson, 1991). And these patterns of interaction have a profound effect on how we understand and relate to one another. Duncan (1999, p.193) provides a powerful example of this in her description of how the class structure and social stratification in parts of the rural South have undermined civic culture and constrained social mobility:

> The structure of daily life that takes shape over time is taken for granted. Because new ideas and new resources rarely penetrate this environment that the powerful have deliberately kept closed off – worlds apart – from the larger society, people form their cultural tool kit in the context of the relationships and norms they know. Their immediate social context shapes who they become and how they see their options, both as individuals and as a community.

For better or worse, place, social interaction, and well-being are inextricably linked. In fact, they are mutually dependent on one another. As Gieryn (2000, p.467) argues, "...place stands in a recursive relationship to other social and cultural entities: places are made through human practices and institutions even as they make those practices and institutions...Place mediates social life; it is something more than just another independent variable."

The Interactional Approach to Development

This conceptualization of the relationship between place, social interaction, and well-being suggests a unique approach to development. In addition to focusing on jobs and income, development must facilitate other conditions that support individual and social well-being. From an interactional perspective (Bridger & Alter, 2006; Bridger et al., 2002; Bridger &Luloff, 1999; Luloff & Bridger, 2003; Wilkinson, 1991) this is best accomplished by enhancing the capacity of residents to create a holistic local society by strengthening the political, economic, social, and environmental dimensions of the places they live – and the connections between them.

In contrast to human ecology and systems approaches to social organization, the interactional perspective views local life in more fluid and processual terms. The various actors that give form and texture to places are more or less organized as unbounded fields of interaction (Bridger et al., 2002). In most localities, for example, it is possible to identify a number of social fields that are concerned with different issues ranging from environmental protection to social services to workforce development.

In order for a place to "hang together" as a local society, there must be some mechanism that connects the acts which occur in these special interest fields into a discernable whole.

This is accomplished by a broader, more inclusive "community" field, which like other social fields is comprised of actors, agencies, and associations. The key difference is that the community field does not pursue a single or narrow set of interests. Instead it creates linkages between the actions and interests of other social fields:

> The community field cuts across organized groups and across other interaction fields in a local population. It abstracts and combines the locality-relevant aspects of the specialized interest fields, and integrates the other fields into a generalized whole. It does this by creating and maintaining linkages among fields that are otherwise directed toward more limited interests. As this community field arises out of the various special interest fields in a locality, it in turn influences those special interest fields and asserts the community interest in the various spheres of local social activity (Wilkinson, 1991, p.36).

The actors and actions that comprise the community field coordinate the more limited and more narrowly focused actions that occur in other social fields. The community field is a linking device that covers many substantive areas and harbors "…memory traces… through which something like a social structure can transpose itself from one time or institutional realm to the next." The community field helps to bridge "…the somewhat ineffable 'betweenness' of people's subjective experiences and the objective realities of locale" (Molotch et al., 2000, p.794). In the course of this process, the community field creates a larger whole - one that is unbounded, dynamic, and emergent. As it builds linkages across different domains of local life, the community field provides the interactional milieu upon which individual and social well-being depend. And as these relationships are strengthened, they simultaneously enhance the capacity of local residents to address common issues and problems that inevitably cut across interest fields.

Because of the important role the community field plays in well-being, from the interactional perspective it is *the* primary focus of development efforts. Indeed, the entire process of development can be viewed as a process of developing the community field (Bridger & Luloff, 1999; Luloff & Bridger, 2003; Wilkinson, 1991). Obviously, the interactional processes that give rise to and are subsequently shaped by the community field are in a continuous state of change. This means that the community field is also in constant flux as actors and organizations come and go, different interests arise and assert themselves, and outside forces impinge on local life. Thus, the community field is variable over time; at one moment it may be strong, at a later date it may be weak. But regardless of its state at a particular time, the main goal of development is to strengthen and institutionalize the community field by building from more narrowly focused fields of interaction to find points of intersection that can be used to enhance local capacity to solve problems.

It is important to note that from this perspective, development does not depend on objective measures of success. Indeed, trying to accomplish some goal is enough to qualify as development. To require success not only ignores the fact that many forces other than purposive actions contribute to change, it also misses the point that "…development is a process rather than an outcome of social interaction… Development exists in the action that is undertaken with positive purpose" (Wilkinson, 1991, p.94). Indeed, the mere fact that people have taken an action to improve local life contributes to local capacity and enhances well-being, because the action itself helps to build the linkages that are the essence of the community field.

Recent research supports this assertion. In a study of four small communities in Pennsylvania, Claude et al. (2000) found that in those places that displayed high levels of activeness, residents rated community well-being higher than residents in communities that success but low levels of activeness.

Conclusion: Toward a Holistic Place-Based Development Policy

Taking this as a general description of the development process, we are now able to more clearly specify what an interactional approach to place-based development would entail. First, and most obviously, there must be an explicit focus on building linkages between interactional fields in ways that contribute to individual and social well-being. In practical terms, this means strengthening the relationships between the economic, social, environmental, and political dimensions of local life. To take just a couple of examples, workforce development should be closely tied to emerging economic trends and job opportunities, and safe, affordable child care should be provided to enable low-income workers to participate fully in the economy. In short, an effective place-based policy will identify relationships between a wide range of issues and interests, and develop plans that build on these connections to create balanced and healthy communities.

Achieving this kind of balance also requires that such activities as innovation, entrepreneurship, job creation, infrastructure improvement, and business retention are tied to the broader process of developing the community field. Here it is useful to draw a distinction between development *in* the community and development *of* community. Job creation and the other instrumental activities listed above are examples of development in the community. In contrast, development of community is oriented toward building the structure of the community field by creating connections between special interest fields and enhancing problem-solving capacities.

In many communities, there is an obvious need for better jobs and higher incomes. At the same time, though, focusing too heavily on these sustenance issues misses the important contribution that development of community makes to well-being. Moreover, when growth is pursued as *the* answer to rural problems, without careful consideration of how it affects other aspects of life, the results are often environmentally and socially disruptive (Bridger, 1996; Wilkinson, 1991). Effective development is a broad and multifaceted process that requires both development *of* community and development *in* the community.

Leadership is crucial to achieving this goal. Unfortunately, leadership development programs do not always promote the common good. In many instances, leadership skills contribute more to the lives and careers of individuals than they do to the local capacity to solve problems. And when leadership programs focus heavily on specific issues and topics, they may actually hinder broad development efforts (Bridger & Alter, 2006). By including insights from the interactional perspective in leadership development curricula, it is possible to build individual skills while fostering local capacity to address issues and problems. For instance, leadership development can focus on building the skills needed to identify potential connections between interactional fields, promoting actions that provide mutual benefits across fields, and facilitating concerted actions across groups and organizations. Participants could also learn about the phases and roles associated with community actions and how these provide opportunities to strengthen lines of communication and build capacity (Wilkinson, 1991).

Currently, there are no development policies in the U.S. that are capable of easily incorporating the interactional perspective – primarily because they are preoccupied with economic growth. In contrast, the latest framework for rural development under the common agricultural policy (CAP) in the European Union (EU) explicitly considers many of the issues raised in this article. One component of this policy, which was initiated in the 1990s, presented disadvantaged rural areas with an opportunity to establish Local Action Groups and collaborate "…in order to construct a territorial identity that would meet their of the issues raised in this article. One component of this policy, which was initiated in the 1990s, presented disadvantaged rural areas with an opportunity to establish Local Action Groups and collaborate "…in order to construct a territorial identity that would meet their own needs as well as those of the policy controllers (the EU), and the political agendas of any regional or national government intermediaries" (Ray, 1999, p.260). In other words, it actively encouraged residents to build the linkages that contribute to the development of the community field.

CAP rural development policy further strengthens the community field through four strategically interdependent initiatives (European Union, 2006). The first focuses on ensuring the competitiveness of agriculture through increased efficiency, strengthening orientation toward markets, and taking advantage of opportunities for economic diversification. The second set of activities fosters sustainable management and use of agricultural lands and forests, ensuring the preservation and enhancement of natural resources, landscapes, and associated amenities and services. The third focuses on strengthening the broader economy to promote environmentally sustainable employment opportunities and a better quality of life. Finally, the Leader Community Initiative works to enhance local leadership, emphasizing the importance of building capacity and encouraging community action within and across the other arenas of activity to update and create new, locally driven development plans.

Obviously, EU rural development policy cannot simply be imported to the U.S. – rural Europe and rural America are different in many ways. But what is applicable to the American experience is the emphasis on local participation, empowerment, and strengthening the community field. Incorporating these elements into place-based rural development policy will require a major shift in our thinking. For too long, we have ignored the relationship between place and well-being, focusing instead on constantly generating wealth with little concern for the physical and social settings in which we live. Indeed, there has been an implicit assumption that economic growth will simply translate into all sorts of other benefits. And up to a certain level this is probably true. Indeed, for most of human history, more did mean better. As McKibben (2007, p.45) puts it, "When More and Better shared a branch, we could kill two birds with one stone." Now, there is mounting evidence that the unmediated pursuit of economic growth can reach a point of diminishing returns and undermine the very conditions that are essential for ecological, individual, and social well-being (Wilkinson, 1991; Bridger & Luloff, 1999; McKibben, 2007).

If we hope to create better places, our state and federal policies must provide rural areas with the incentives and the resources to create more holistic local societies – societies which provide the interactional opportunities that are crucial to individual and social well-being. In some instances, this might entail the creation of more local jobs. But it will also require building new institutions and strengthening the connections between organizations and social fields (Alter et al., 2007). And while this will ultimately depend on the efforts of local people, we need a coordinated and comprehensive rural policy framework – at the federal, state, and local levels – that removes barriers to effective local action.

References

Agnew, J.A. (1987). *Place and politics.* Winchester, MA: Allan and Unwin.

Alter, T.R., Bridger, J.C., Findeis, J., Kelsey, T.W., Luloff, A.E., McLaughlin, D.K. & Shuffstall, W.C. (2007). *Strengthening rural Pennsylvania: A rural policy agenda for the commonwealth.* Report to the Brookings Institution.

Bernard, J. (1973). *The sociology of community,* Glenview, IL: Scott, Foresman and Company.

Bridger, J. C. (1996). Community imagery and the built environment. *Sociological Quarterly*

Bridger, J.C, & Luloff, A.E. (1999). Toward an interactional approach to sustainable community development. *Journal of Rural Studies* 15(4):377-387.

Bridger, J.C., Luloff, A.E., & Krannich, R.S. (2002). Community change and community theory. Pp. 9-22 in A.E. Luloff and R.S. Krannich (eds.), *Persistence and change in rural communities.* New York: CABI Publishing.

Brueggeman, J., & Brown, C. (2003). The decline of industrial unionism in the meatpacking industry. *Work and Occupations* 30(3):327-360.

Buttel, F. H. (2003). Continuities and disjunctures in the transformation of the U.S. agro-food system. Pp. 177-189 in D.L. Brown and L.E. Swanson (eds.), *Challenges for rural America in the twenty-first century.* University Park, PA: Penn State University Press.

Casey, E.S. (1993). *Getting back into place: Toward a renewed understanding of the place-world.* Bloomington, IN: Indiana University Press.

Claude, L.P., Bridger, J.C., & Luloff, A.E. (2000). Community well-being and local activeness. Pp. 39-45 in P.V. Schaeffer and S. Loveridge (eds.), *Small town and rural economic development: A case study approach.* Westport, CT: Praeger Publishers.

De Leo, D., & Spathonis, K. (2004). Culture and suicide in late life. *Psychiatric Times,* Vol. XX [electronic version] retrieved 12/2/05 from www.psychiatrictimes.com.

Drabenstott, M. (2001). New policies for a new rural America. *International Regional Science Review.* 24(January):3-15.

Duncan, C.M. (1999). *Worlds apart: Why poverty persists in rural America.* New Haven, CT: Yale University Press.

European Union. (2006). *Fact sheet: New perspective for EU rural Development.* Brussels, Belgium: European Communities.

Falk, W.W., & Labao, L.M. (2003). Who benefits from economic restructuring? Lessons from the Past, challenges for the future. Pp. 152-165 in D.L. Brown and L.E. Swanson (eds.), *Challenges for rural America in the twenty first century.* University Park, PA: Penn State University Press.

Ghelfi, L., & McGranahan, D. (2004). One in five rural counties depends on farming. *Amber Waves* 2(3) June.

Gieryn, T.F. (2000). A space for place in sociology. *Annual Review of Sociology.* 26:463-496.

Granovetter, M. (1973). The strength of weak ties. American Journal of Sociology 78 (6): 1360-1380

Harvey, D. (1996). *Justice, nature, and the geography of difference.* Oxford, UK: Blackwell Publishers.

Harvey, D. (2006). *Spaces of global capitalism: Towards a theory of uneven geographical development.* New York: Verso.

Johnson, S. (2001). Exploring policy options for a new rural America: conference synthesis. Pp. 185-193 in *Exploring policy options for a new rural America.* Kansas City, MO: Center for the Study of Rural America, Kansas City, Federal Reserve Bank of Kansas City.

Kaplan, M.S., & Geling, O. (1998). Firearm suicide and homicide in the United States: regional variations and patterns of gun ownership. *Social Science and Medicine* 46(9):1227-1233.

Klimuska, E. (1988). *Lancaster County: The Ex-garden spot of America?* Lancaster, PA: Lancaster New Era.

Krugman, P. (1991). *Geography and trade.* Cambridge, MA: The MIT Press.

Leach, W. (1999). *Nation of exiles: The destruction of place in American life.* New York: Pantheon Books.

Luloff, A.E., & Bridger, J.C. (2003). Community Agency and Local Development. Pp. 203-213 in D.L. Brown and L.E. Swanson (eds.), *Challenges for Rural America in the twenty first century.* University Park, PA: Penn State University Press.

McGranahan, D.A., & Beale, C.L. (2002). Understanding rural population loss. *Rural America* 17(4):2-8.

McKibben. B. (2007). *Deep economy: The wealth of communities and the durable future.* New York: Times Books.

Mead, G.H. (1934). *Mind, self, and society: From the standpoint of a social behaviorist.* Edited by C.W. Morris. Chicago: University of Chicago Press.

Meyrowitz, J. (1985). *No sense of place: The impact of electronic media on social behavior.* New York: Oxford University Press.

Molotch, H., Freudenburg, W., & Paulsen, K.E. (2000). History repeats itself, but how? City character, urban tradition, and the accomplishment of place." *American Sociological Review* 65(December):791-823.

Oldenburg, R. (1999). *The great good place.* New York: Marlowe and Company

Paulozzi, L.J., Saltzman, L.E., Thompson, M.P. & Holmgreen, P. (2002). *Surveillance for Homicide Among Intimate Partners – United States, 1991-1998.* Centers for Disease Control [electronic version] retrieved 12/2/05 from www.cdc.gov/mmwr/preview/mmwrhtml/ ss5003.ai.htm

Polyani, K. (1957). *The great transformation.* Boston: Beacon Press.

Ray, C. (1999). Endogenous development in the era of reflexive modernity. *Journal of Rural Studies* 15(3):257-267.

United States Department of Agriculture, Economic Research Service. (2006). Rural Employment at a Glance.

Whitener, L.A., & Parker, T. (2007). Policy options for a changing rural America." *Amber Waves.* May 2007. Retrieved from http://www.ers.usda.gov/AmberWaves/May07SpecialIssue/ Features/Policy.htm

Wilkinson, K.P. (1991). *The community in rural America.* New York: Greenwood Press.

Zukin, S. (1991). *Landscapes of power: From Detroit to Disneyland.* Berkeley, CA: University of California Press.

Measuring community development: what have we learned?

Andy S. Blanke and Norman Walzer

Since the 1960s, community development organizations in the public and nonprofit sectors have become increasingly conscious of the impact of their work in light of finite financial resources and a growing range of policy concerns. This article briefly reviews the history of outcome measurement in community development organizations and describes innovative and emerging measurement practices used to improve public policy. It also outlines key ingredients in successful measurement systems, especially the importance of linking the measures to the strategic planning process. Two prevalent models of outcome measurement are described: universal measures where quantitative data are used to assess progress toward goals common to many communities and contingent measures where qualitative data indicate progress toward goals unique to one community. Common themes among the measurement practices include technical assistance provided by national or regional grantors, a triple bottom line measurement focus, and reduction of measurement cost through secondary data or inexpensive case study methodology.

Introduction

A growing interest in improving local decisions about investments in development projects has motivated economic and community development practitioners to find more precise information about documented outcomes. Past efforts have often focused on recording the number of jobs created or retained and the amount of private investment following a public intervention (Ammons, 2012; Blakely & Leigh, 2010). Public and private agencies alike now want more specific documentation regarding results, so they can choose among alternative strategies to promote local development (Madan, 2007; Moynihan, 2008).

The interest in better accountability is part of a larger initiative dating back to Federal legislation, such as the Government Performance and Results Act in 1993 that pushed Federal agencies to set goals and strategies and to track outcomes (Plantz, Greenway, & Hendricks, 1997). More recently, foundations and funding agencies want to determine that their spending generates significant results (Phillips, 2003). Likewise, the growing professional management practices and tighter budgets in local government agencies further intensified the pressures for better measures and accountability, including using trend data to monitor or evaluate effectiveness (Moynihan, 2008). At the same time, community development organizations internationally have addressed the United

*Corresponding author. Email: ablanke1@niu.edu

Nations' Millennium Development Goals, including priorities such as poverty reduction, expanded access to education, and environmental sustainability (United Nations, n.d.).

The interest in better measurement practices extends well beyond assessing the impact of a specific program, however. Community leaders are interested in monitoring overall conditions and finding ways to integrate decisions about health care, jobs, environmental issues, and other characteristics important in healthy communities (Blakely & Leigh, 2010; Hoffer & Levy, 2010). Thus, some communities have turned to a "dashboard" concept that includes data on health, housing, environmental issues, and other factors affecting livability or quality of life (Community Indicators Consortium, 2013; Wilder Research, 2009). Much work has been done on dashboards, especially in the field of public health, as demonstrated by the Kids Count (Annie E. Casey Foundation, 2013) and County Health Rankings (Robert Wood Johnson Foundation, 2013) initiatives. Other areas have built indicators to compare across cities or regions (Boston Indicators Project, 2012; Rockford Region Vital Signs, 2012).

Common among successful initiatives has been a clear vision and set of consistent goals, targets, and desired outcomes that can lead to changes resulting from successful community interventions (Walzer & Hamm, 2012). Frequently, goals include increasing decision-making capacity, building social capital, and preserving natural resources. However, especially in the field of community development with broadly defined goals, reaching a clear consensus about measurable outcomes and indicators can be difficult. Nonetheless, progress has been made toward developing and using consistent performance measures, as the number of cities working with indicators expanded and their experiences were shared (Community Indicators Consortium, 2013).

This article describes major issues involved in measuring community development outcomes and ways they can affect policy responses to improve conditions. The first section examines key elements in designing a measurement system, along with a brief history of outcome measurement practices. Next is a review of the literature on measurement approaches and their alignment with the key components, including examples of innovative and successful measurement issues. The final section presents lessons learned and how they can be implemented in other areas.

Historical interest in measurement

Interest in measuring community development activities gained popularity in the 1960s, as the US Department of Health and Welfare (now the Department of Health and Human Services) began studying quality of life on a national scale (Phillips, 2003). By the 1970s, some large cities paid more attention to local quality of life issues such as health and education, as demonstrated by New York City's 1973 Scorecard Project (Phillips, 2003). State governments also became involved when, in 1977, the State of California published a guide for local governments to compile indicators of social phenomena, although the guide was not widely used after 1980.

In the late 1980s and early 1990s, environmental concerns became more prominent on lists of community development issues. Seattle, Washington was an early city that tracked progress regarding sustainable community development in a report using several sustainability indicators published in 1993 (Hart, n.d.). Traditional indices of population change and economic growth were supplemented by environmental indicators. Examples included the number of days each year with healthy air quality as defined by a regional environmental agency and the percentage of pedestrian-friendly city streets (Sustainable

Seattle, 1993). Since 1993, more than 90 cities have adopted measurement practices based on those in Sustainable Seattle (Sustainable Seattle, n.d.).

However, during the 1990s, these practices were limited mainly to metropolitan areas (Center for Building Better Communities, 2001). Communities that adopted outcome measurement systems were those with access to technical expertise including professional management and trained financial staff to monitor performance indicators (Ammons, 2012).

In decades leading to the 1990s, many municipal governments regularly reported performance information (Ammons, 2012). Most of the information provided, though, was limited to outputs such as number of employees and clients. So although some communities had prior experience in outcome measurement before the 1990s (Phillips, 2003; Plantz et al., 1997), it was relatively uncommon.

In the 1990s, driven by the National Performance Review under US President Clinton, professional associations developed standards to encourage more widespread measurement practices. The Governmental Accounting Standards Board and the International City Management Association both published guidelines for reporting services delivered and performance levels (Ammons, 2012). One of the first communities to adopt measures of service outcomes was Portland, Oregon, using indices such as citizen perceptions of public safety and children's preparedness for kindergarten in the county relative to the state (Bernstein, 2002). Other places adopting community indicators at this time were also mostly larger cities with more technical expertise (Ammons, 2012).

Initiatives to measure community development became more common in rural areas in the 2000s (Phillips, 2003). The Central Texas Sustainability Indicators Project and the Pueblo Community Indicators Project in 29 communities in Colorado are such examples (Phillips, 2003). In the Central Texas project, six counties pooled resources to develop a shared vision and measure progress toward that vision. In the Pueblo Community project, local organizations received financial and technical assistance from a statewide foundation focused on expanding access to health care (Phillips, 2003). External technical assistance has been important in encouraging communities to begin designing and monitoring outcome indicators (Forster-Gills, 2012; Langlois, 2010).

Today, the focus of community development measurement remains much as it has since sustainability became a topic measured alongside social and economic concerns. What has changed is that communities, overall, have access to more technical resources to design their own metrics. Large nonprofit organizations have started initiatives to help rural communities measure their performance. Examples include the Measuring Community Wealth project sponsored by the Ford Foundation (Hofffer & Levy, 2010), the Vibrant Communities (VC) Canada initiative (Forster-Gills, 2012) sponsored by several research and nonprofit organizations, and Minnesota Compass (Wilder Research, 2009) sponsored by multiple corporate and regional foundations. These and other examples are discussed in more detail later in this article.

Key components of outcome measurement

Economic and community development practitioners realized that their disciplines have some common goals (Blakely & Leigh, 2010) and are linked to overall community well-being (Hart, 2012). In some instances, they have incorporated the seven capitals: financial, built, natural, individual, intellectual, social, and political (Flora & Flora, 2004). Likewise, development practitioners recognize that prosperity requires communities to address social, environmental, and economic issues (Slaper & Hall, 2011).

Beyond a simple reference to social, environmental, and economic issues, outcome measurement systems must be based on clearly defined goals. A formal community visioning or planning process can identify policy goals that are then converted to policy options or strategies. The planning or visioning process should include citizens, local government staff, business leaders, and representatives of community-based and non-profit organizations (Walzer & Hamm, 2012). The planning or visioning process is also crucial in gaining support from citizens and public officials, which is a key to the success of the measurement system (Posovac, 2011). Each goal typically includes specific and implementable strategies, the progress of which can be documented with relevant, cost-effective, and diverse indicators (Figure 1).

Designing and monitoring indicators are at the heart of an effective measurement and evaluation system because they provide operational meaning to the goals in the minds of policy-makers and the public. Especially important in designing indicators is to gain a consensus among policy-makers and the public about what each indicator means, as well as its importance to the overall well-being of the community (Burd-Sharps, Guyer, & Lewis, 2011). Policy-makers may resist allocating time to developing community indicators because the process is considered costly in time and effort and may not lead directly to improvements in community conditions. However, opportunities to reduce the cost of developing indicators exist, such as using case study methodology (Forster-Gills, 2012), drawing indices from secondary data sources such as state agencies (Gallagher & Putiak, 2010), and adopting indices that have succeeded in other communities (Success Measures, 2012).

Finding suitable indicators is not the most difficult task since many lists of indicators are readily available (Success Measures, 2012; Yellow Wood Associates, 2009). More difficult is matching the indicators to conditions in a specific community so that changes in policies effectively guide policy decisions (Anderson, 2005). This process is covered during strategic planning, which involves engaging key stakeholders in

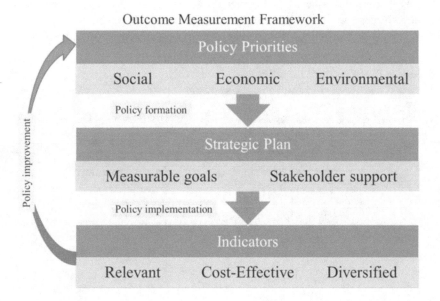

Figure 1.   Components and process of outcome measurement.

discussions about long-term outcomes desired, short-term actions that can be taken toward those goals, and indicators that will accurately show progress or change (Posovac, 2011). Thus, indicators must raise awareness of issues, engage stakeholders in actions, inform decisions, and measure progress toward long-term goals (Hart, 2012).

Key to success in measurement is obtaining buy-in and commitment to a common set of indicators and agreement on what they mean. The LOGIC framework differenti- ates between inputs, activities, outputs, outcomes, and impacts, and underlies several measurement systems discussed in this article (W.K. Kellogg Foundation, 2004). Espe- cially important, however, is having a manageable number of consistent and unambigu- ous indicators to monitor. Likewise, including stakeholders in the selection process increases their acceptance (Burd-Sharps et al., 2011; Posovac, 2011). A telling sign of an indicator's acceptance is its incorporation into policy decisions and practices, includ- ing financial management (Gallagher & Putiak, 2010). The process of designing and monitoring indicators becomes a cost without much benefit to the community develop- ment organization if it does not lead to an improvement in service delivery (Ammons, 2012).

Effective measurement and evaluation systems push decision-makers into a systems thinking environment, because many aspects of the community are interrelated. If the workforce is not adequate, the economic sector will not perform well, and so on. There- fore, the indicators must recognize this interdependency and help policy-makers track changes over time toward the long-term goals. Focusing on only one or two indicators misses other essential components of community well-being (Flora & Flora, 2004).

Also, the indicators must be diversified at each stage of the implementation process, which requires different types of information. Hart (2012) classified indicators into three groups. System indicators reflect overall community performance. Program indicators show the performance of specific policies or strategies. Action indicators inform the daily decisions of individuals, businesses, and other organizations. Hollander (2002) argued that successful indicators have nine characteristics including: validity, relevance, reliability, measurability, clarity, comprehensiveness, cost-effectiveness, comparability, and attractiveness to the media (Figure 2). Of special importance is an indicator's cost-effectiveness and clarity. If data used are not cost-effective to collect and easy for

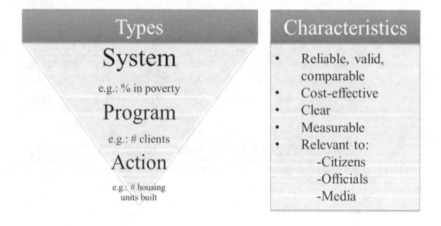

Figure 2.   Types and characteristics of outcome measures.

citizens to understand, community developers may not see value in allocating time to collect performance information (Phillips, 2003).

To summarize, outcome evaluation systems are designed to represent the results or outcomes of community policies and identify avenues for policy improvement. The measurement process stems from a community's commitment to improving social, economic, and environmental conditions. Policies and programs for improving community conditions emerge from the strategic planning process, where all stakeholders engage in a dialog to identify shared, measurable goals. An effective planning process creates indicators that are meaningful to citizens and officials, can be collected regularly at a reasonable cost, and cover a range of goals important to the community. Effective measures can guide policy improvements and a re-evaluation of policy priorities.

Community development measurement approaches

Measuring outcomes remains a challenge for many community development organizations. A widely held belief among development practitioners is that each community has unique goals, so progress is difficult to measure using only one scale (Dorius, 2011). Unlike economic development, which has a more clearly defined set of goals including employment and income growth or tax base expansion, the goals for community development more often vary by city (Blakely & Leigh, 2010). Although community development advances the goals of economic development (Blakely & Leigh, 2010), community development also includes the empowerment of population groups with specific needs.

Dorius (2011) argues that the root of the evaluation problem comes from a lack of a common definition of community development. He reviewed the community development literature and interviewed 40 representatives of large funding agencies such as the W.K. Kellogg Foundation and the Urban Institute to find a consensus on this topic. He suggested that community development success be "measured in terms of poor citizens gaining the skills and confidence required to overcome social barriers to economic success, and community institutions making policy decisions and resource commitments that help sustain such success-seeking behavior" (Dorius, 2011, p. 274). In other words, community development can be defined as the process of integrating disadvantaged citizens into the local economy to create community wealth (Hoffer & Levy, 2010).

The definition of community development stated by Dorius (2011) brings in other community development frameworks such as the seven capitals of community wealth mentioned previously (Hoffer & Levy, 2010). By definition, economically engaging disadvantaged citizens include a social and economic dimension of community improvement. Long term, this definition of community development includes an environmental component as well, since natural capital is a part of community wealth.

Given the broad definition of community development, two broad strains of thought have emerged as to how outcomes can best be monitored. Some academics and practitioners have proposed allowing each community to decide its own approach to economically engage disadvantaged citizens, with each community creating a set of indicators for its goals (Patton, 2011; Stoecker, 2005). Others have proposed a universal, operational model for creating community wealth (Flora & Flora, 2004; Hoffer & Levy, 2010). In this approach, the same indicators are used to address social issues important in all communities. Each of these approaches is briefly discussed in the next section, recognizing that measurement practices often include many other scenarios as well.

Contingent models of measurement

The need for outcome measurement as a means of accountability, as well as the perceived need for community-specific definitions of success, has caused funders of community development organizations to design participatory outcome measurement approaches (Stoecker, 2005). In these models, communities decide on the types of changes desired as an outcome of a program. Then, community participants identify outcome measures that are highly relevant to their interests (Posovak, 2011). Through participatory evaluation, development organizations determine whether programs have succeeded based on their clients' terms, recognizing that participatory measures can be difficult to compare across cities (Dorius, 2011).

The VCs model in Canada where social service providers in cities describe the ways they expect to improve the lives of citizens and then write case studies detailing their progress toward that end is an example of participatory outcome measurement (Forster-Gill, 2012). Another example is the Success Measures toolkit provided by NeighborWorks America, which allows communities to select and monitor indices from hundreds of possible performance measures, based on the priorities of residents (Success Measures, 2012).

The process of measuring community development outcomes remains difficult, even when detailed evaluation plans are used. The traditional method of outcome evaluation by an external consultant can also create problems (Preskill & Beer, 2012). As supposed neutral observers, evaluators cannot inform service providers of ways to improve programs until a report is presented at the end of the study period, even if the program's success may hinge on immediate corrections (Preskill & Beer, 2012). In addition, reports from external consultants may be interpreted as evidence that a program is ineffective and should lose funding, even though reports were submitted before project outcomes could be observed. For these reasons, a traditional program evaluation may not work well, even if the community development organization has the resources to do so.

The Developmental Evaluation (DE) model was created to measure community development outcomes when the expected results of a program are unclear (Patton, 2011). Under the DE approach, evaluators collect and report information to program administrators periodically, rather than in a year-end report. To provide timely information on progress and challenges in a program, developmental evaluators regularly collect qualitative data and promptly report findings. Unlike traditional models of evaluation based on a fixed goal, DEs are conducted assuming that program goals can change (Patton, 2011). For example, DE was used in the J.W. McConnell Family Foundation's YouthScape Initiative described later (Preskill & Beer, 2012).

The DE model prioritizes responsiveness over quantitative and/or statistical rigor. The rationale is that outcomes for some programs may not be statistically measurable in a reasonable time frame, but funders require *some* demonstration of accountability from the programs they support (Preskill & Beer, 2012). DE is best used when development activities occur in uncertain contexts. For example, DE is desirable when a program has not been evaluated previously. Another example where DE is useful is when a program has been evaluated in the past but in contexts that were not generalizable, such as when a rural community adapts promising practices that have been tested mainly in cities.

The participatory and developmental models of evaluation both imply that community development outcomes are best measured on a case-by-case basis. Stoecker (2005) argued that if every community's needs and goals are unique then communities should decide their own performance measures. In these models, no indicator applies to all communities, but a universal process exists for identifying goals in each community. An alternative approach is a model that measures community development outcomes based on goals relevant to all communities.

Universal models of measurement

In 2008, the Ford Foundation sponsored an initiative to promote sustained wealth creation in rural communities (Hoffer & Levy, 2010). Toward this goal, strategies for increasing community wealth were developed based on the Community Capitals Framework (CCF) proposed by Flora and Flora (2004). For each component, programs that expand a community's capital were labeled as investments and the outcomes of those programs were classified as investment income (Hoffer & Levy, 2010). This model of community wealth was designed to be applicable to all communities and has led to successful development initiatives such as the Central Appalachian Network (CAN) (Allen & Watson, n.d.) described below.

The CCF includes seven capitals: financial, built, natural, individual, intellectual, social, and political (Flora & Flora, 2004). This framework was designed as a way to identify the common characteristics of socially, economically, and environmentally sustainable communities. Natural capital refers to a community's natural resources that provide economic opportunity and enhance quality of life. Cultural or intellectual capital refers to a community's ability to encourage innovation, reflected in part by its diversity. Built capital refers to physical infrastructure. Individual capital refers to the skills, knowledge, and experience citizens have that enable gainful employment. The CCF was developed based on observations of prosperous rural communities in the Andes Mountains, but the framework has since then been applied to successful development efforts in the USA (Emery & Flora, 2006; Hoffer & Levy, 2010).

The CCF is based on the premise that increasing stocks in one of the seven capitals in a community could increase stocks in the other capitals (Emery & Flora, 2006). Conversely, decreasing stocks in one capital may lead to further decreases in other capitals (Myrdal, 1957). An example of both phenomena occurring is the case of the Nebraska Hometown Competitiveness program (Emery & Flora, 2006). In rural Nebraska communities, job losses from farm consolidation resulted in population declines and falling personal incomes impeding wealth transfer across generations (Emery & Flora, 2006). However, programs focused on building networks between rural residents and community development consultants from regional nonprofit and research organizations led to increased social capital, which increased rates of youth entrepreneurship, restoring population, and employment growth (Emery & Flora, 2006).

An advantage of the CCF is that it encourages community developers to consider the outcomes of their work from social, economic, and environmental perspectives. While financial implications of a program usually receive frequent attention, impacts on social capital, natural resources, and public health are often not documented as heavily.

Unlike contingent measurement models, universal models imply that community development can be linked to outcomes that are universally desirable, such as public health and sustainability, even if the means to those ends vary. Both universal and contingent models of evaluation have been used in innovative ways by community development organizations, suggesting merit in both approaches.

Several examples of outcome measurement systems in community development that have succeeded in improving an organization's policies or practices while also taking steps to ensure cost-effectiveness are described next. These examples have received attention in the literature on community development, often highlighted in recent scholarly studies or presentations, or as featured communities in the Community Indicators Consortium. The following cases are sorted by those that more closely fit a universal or contingent model of measurement, although in many instances, mixed methods have been applied. The framework of contingent versus universal methods is used for simplicity and contrast, although the practices include elements of both.

Contingent measurement approaches

Three examples of innovative contingent measurement approaches are presented next, along with lessons learned that may be used by other agencies.

J.W. McConnell family foundation – YouthScape initiative

The YouthScape Initiative was designed to increase participation of teens and young adults in local government decision-making. Five cities participated in the project and each hired a part-time developmental evaluator. Evaluators attended program events such as youth-led art marathons and interviewed stakeholders before and after each event. Stakeholders interviewed participating youth, community volunteers, and local government management staff. The five evaluators held monthly conference calls with a national evaluator from the Foundation to identify behavior patterns from the observers' case studies. The national evaluator then synthesized information from the calls into quarterly reports regarding challenges, successes, and opportunities created by the YouthScape Initiative (Cawley, 2010).

According to the YouthScape program manager, the quarterly reports were useful in correcting tensions that could have ended the program prematurely (Cawley, 2010). For example, in certain cities, evaluators convinced client organizations to train or replace employees in specific positions that were points of concern as identified in the evaluators' observations and interviews (Langlois, 2010).

In another example, DE reports helped refine one program participant's funding guidelines (International Institute for Children's Rights and Development [IICRD], 2010). Community foundations were not accustomed to funding arts programs managed by teenagers and needed to revise their requirements with each round of funding. Grantors acknowledged difficulties obtaining adequate financial information from young grantees. Comments from these grantors were used to clarify reporting requirements and explain to youth grantees the need to keep receipts (IICRD, 2010). According to developmental evaluators' observations, an estimated 1000 people between age 13 and 30 were involved in managing grants from YouthScape. Cultural events funded through these grants were attended by an estimated 10,000 participants (IICRD, 2010).

Some, but not all, of the key components of outcome measurement were included in the YouthScape Initiative. The measures included social and environmental concerns because the goal was to incorporate disengaged youth into local economies. However, environmental concerns were not explicitly identified. The DEs used for YouthScape were found to be relevant and cost-effective, since communities hired one consultant to write case studies and they received quarterly reports that were useful in improving youth programs.

Broward County, Florida – Children's Services Council

Broward County was recognized in an international Community Indicators Consortium competition for community indicators and performance measurement in 2009. The use of performance measurement for social services in Broward County dates back to the 1990s when it created a Children's Strategic Plan to coordinate the activities of disparate and overlapping child-service agencies (Gallagher & Putiak, 2010). Since then, the CSC has incorporated performance measures into its annual budget (Gallagher & Putiak, 2010).

Indicators include the number of abused or neglected children per 1000 residents under age 18 and rates of juvenile delinquency per 100,000 residents. These measures flow from the CSC's strategic plan and are used as discussion points in annual budget retreats, showing that the performance measures help shape organizational policy. As an example of how community indicators influenced the CSC budget, documented decreases in the child abuse and juvenile delinquency rates caused the CSC to increase funding for after-school programs because these programs were shown to yield expected results (Gallagher & Putiak, 2010). Other indicators included changes in the percentage of adoptions finalized within 24 months of client children being removed from homes (Gallagher & Putiak, 2010) and reductions in teacher turnover rates (CSC, 2011).

Several conditions allowed the CSC to adopt performance management when other community development organizations might not. First, the CSC secured external funding and expertise to develop a measurement system. Consultants were hired with a grant from the Florida State Department of Children and Families, Alcohol, Drug Abuse, and Mental Health. Second, the data used in Broward County's indicators came mainly from state and federal agencies such as the Centers for Disease Control and Prevention and the Florida Department of Education (Gallagher & Putiak, 2010), which reduced the cost of monitoring indicators. Finally, leadership within the CSC supported adopting community indicators and performance measures (Gallagher & Putiak, 2010).

VCs Canada

VCs Canada is an initiative, created by the Institute for Community Engagement, the Caledon Institute for Social Policy, the J.W. McConnell Family Foundation, and 13 cities in Canada to reduce poverty (Forster-Gill, 2012). The cities participating in VC used the same three-part approach to measure their progress toward that end. First, communities developed their own theories of change, describing how they expected to improve the lives of residents.

Next, communities wrote brief case studies describing their efforts to reduce poverty, including how the programs addressed the issues and outcomes expected of the program in the future. Finally, communities wrote semi-annual reports providing information on the number of clients receiving services, number of organizations providing services, and an annual narrative describing the progress of poverty reduction initiatives in each community.

This approach to performance measurement was useful for participating communities because it encouraged social service providers to develop and refine theories of change based on the changing concerns of residents (Forster-Gill, 2012). The VC measurement model was also useful for researchers and policy-makers nationally because the content of the reports could be used to identify common themes behind effective or innovative poverty reduction programs.

The main disadvantage of the VC approach to measurement is that it provided a volume of data that were difficult for researchers to manage (Forster-Gill, 2012). Common themes in the reports published can be obtained only through content analysis, since the quantitative information provided is on number of clients and service organizations.

The VC model has become increasingly popular since it began in 2002. As of 2013, committees in 84 Canadian municipalities have participated in VC, and 11 provinces have created poverty reduction strategies based on common themes from the VC reports (Forster-Gills, 2012). From a practical standpoint, the VC model is attractive because social service providers can avoid most of the confusion surrounding outcome measurement. Since service providers are not required to decide on specific statistical indicators and are asked only to write brief stories about their efforts, they are more likely to allocate time to using the VC measurement system (Forster-Gills, 2012).

The measurement model used in VC includes most of the key components of an outcome measurement system. For one, the VC approach allows communities to plan strategically and identify common goals. This is accomplished in the first step of the evaluation as communities identify their specific theories of change. This model also allows community developers to obtain relevant information in a cost-effective manner requiring short case studies that illustrate expected program results and progress. The semi-annual reports by communities identifying opportunities for program improvement also inform policy.

At the same time, indicators in this model do not always cover social, economic, and environmental concerns. Each participating community has a theory of change with at least some social and economic goals in mind. However, because VC focuses mainly on poverty reduction, environmental issues are not necessarily included. In addition, since each report is based primarily on case studies and secondarily on a simple count of service providers and clients, the range of indicators provided is relatively narrow.

The VC model differs from the performance measurement system used in Broward County, but each program has succeeded in its own right. The CSC developed its measurement system independently, whereas multiple participants in VC developed plans with external technical assistance. In the VC case, indicators are mainly qualitative and are reviewed semi-annually for policy improvements. In the CSC case, most indicators are quantitative and are used to assign annual budget priorities. Under the VC model, measurement costs were reduced by giving evaluators a prompt for writing simple case studies and reducing the need for quantitative skills. In the CSC approach, measurement costs are reduced by obtaining indicators from data compiled by state and federal agencies.

Universal measurement approaches

Examples of projects that include mainly universal measurement approaches are presented in this section.

Boston indicators project

Started in 1998, the Boston Indicators Project was designed to measure progress toward shared goals for community development in the greater Boston region of Massachusetts. The project is coordinated by The Boston Foundation (TBF), the region's community foundation.

The Boston Indicators Project includes indicators for 10 sectors: civic vitality, transportation, cultural life, economy, education, energy and environment, health, housing, public safety, and technology. The project includes 150 indicators for 70 goals and the biennial reports that will be published until 2040. Goals included in the indicator project are based on Boston's Civic Agenda, which was developed in meetings of regional leaders and community development experts facilitated by TBF (Boston Indicators Project, 2012). Project partners represent the public, private, and nonprofit sectors, including the City of Boston, the Metropolitan Area Planning Council, and economic consulting firm Planet-TECH Associates (Boston Indicators Project, 2012).

Improvements in civic vitality are measured in part by the number of foreign-born residents with post-secondary education and number of racial and ethnic minorities that started businesses or were elected to public office. Improvements in transportation access are measured in part by residents' transportation costs as a percentage of income and the concentration of housing units within a quarter mile of public transit stations. Indices of cultural life include the supply of dedicated artist housing and the number of free events by neighborhood. Progress toward environmental goals is measured partly by the number of buildings certified by the US Green Building Council and the number of days when Boston beaches are fit for swimming (Boston Indicators Project, 2012).

The Boston Indicators Project requires no primary data collection; all indicators are compiled from data already collected by state, federal, and local organizations. Therefore, the project is cost-effective. The indices are organized under specific goals in each subject area, showing that the indicators are linked to a strategic plan. The BIP demonstrates a triple bottom line measurement focus in that it includes explicit social, economic, and environmental goals. The indicator project was not designed for one specific organization or program, and the outcomes measured have been impacted by policies within the Boston metropolitan area. The project website includes a Hub of Innovation showing case studies of local programs that address one or more Civic Agenda goals (Boston Indicators Project, n.d.). As an example, for transportation improvements, a bicycle sharing program was initiated to ease traffic congestion and make Boston more pedestrian-friendly.

Minnesota compass

In 2008, the Wilder Research Foundation, in conjunction with the Bush Foundation, started a system to track trends in community development across the State of Minnesota (Bush Foundation, n.d.). Minnesota Compass provides information on trends in numerous economic and community development issues including public safety, economic disparities, health, housing, and transportation. Indicators were selected for each issue based on input from development practitioners, business leaders, and policy researchers.

Advisory groups were formed to identify indicators that predict future policy needs, can be influenced by public policy, are understandable to users, and can be collected regularly and reliably with a limited budget (Wilder Research, 2009). Several main indicators were selected on each issue. For example, transportation conditions are measured by spending on transportation as a share of personal income, traffic injury and fatality rates, and a community's percentage of bridges classified as obsolete or dangerous. Economic disparity is measured by median household income for people over age 64 by race and gender. Annual data on each indicator are available by county and city with a population of more than 20,000, as well as for seven regions within the state.

Unlike typical outcome measurement systems, Minnesota Compass is not based on a specific organization's strategic plan. Instead, the indices were selected based on the expressed concerns of public officials, businesses, and academics. However, the indices provided are based on what development stakeholders find most relevant regarding social, environmental, and economic policy concerns. The indices fit with the strategic goals of a variety of organizations, and the Minnesota Compass website (Wilder Research, 2009) has an "Ideas at Work" section for each measurement topic that lists organizations using the indices.

As an outcome measurement system, Minnesota Compass is cost-effective since time-series data for most indicators have already been compiled at the county or regional level. However, the data are not always current because they are not regularly collected for some variables. Currently, indicators provided by Minnesota Compass work best for systems-level indices used in a needs assessment, rather than to show outcomes for a recent program.

Central Appalachian Network

The CAN is a coalition of nonprofit organizations in Kentucky, Ohio, Tennessee, Virginia, and West Virginia dedicated to maintaining a prosperous farming community in the Appalachian region (Allen & Watson, n.d.). The network provides an array of services that keep regional farmers integrated into broader supply chains. Some of the organization's activities include providing grants to farms and small businesses to improve their productivity and establish networks between farmers and wholesalers.

CAN uses an outcome measurement system based on the CCF (Allen & Watson, n.d.). Gains in the Appalachian region's financial capital were measured by an increase in the average income of farmers selling to wholesalers. Improvements in natural capital were measured in acres of farmland preserved and protected from development. Built capital was measured by structures constructed with CAN grant money to help businesses such as a facility to freeze meats processed from regional farms. Gains in social capital or the building of relationships were evident as restaurants began featuring locally purchased foods on their menus and as other purchasing companies began extending loans to suppliers.

CAN's measurement system stems from a strategic commitment to improve communities socially, economically, and environmentally. The network's mission is to create wealth and reduce poverty while conserving the environment (Allen & Watson, n.d.). Indicators of the seven capitals used by CAN also relate to the organization's strategic plan, since they were designed to measure a triple bottom line (Hoffer & Levy, 2010).

An assortment of strategies for reducing the cost of measurement is reflected in the outcome indicators. Some indicators are observable naturally as part of the organization's operations. For instance, the number of facilities constructed to aid farmers is measured by following up with recipients of CAN grants. When secondary data are not readily available, case studies are used to reduce cost. Evidence of restaurants incorporating local crops into their menus is anecdotal, but indicates increased social capital.

Lessons learned

Several lessons can be learned from the approaches to measuring community development examined in this article. Models that are primarily universal or contingent can guide decisions by community development practitioners regarding local changes. However, they involve differences in costs and the extent to which policy changes are based on unique characteristics in a community.

Financial or technical assistance from external sources is often necessary for a measurement system to succeed. Without this support, community development organizations may not deem the cost of measurement worthwhile. The CSC, for example, did not adopt its indicators until it had obtained state funding to hire a consultant. Several examples previously discussed involved state or national organizations providing resources at the local level. The J.W. McConnell Family Foundation provided on-site evaluators for the YouthScape Initiative and Minnesota Compass provided indices for community development organizations statewide.

Communities should measure outcomes using available data sources when possible to reduce the measurement costs. Broward County's performance measurement system is based heavily on data from state and federal sources. Several of the Ford Foundation's dimensions of community wealth are measurable using information from state and federal sources, as are the performance measures used in the Broward County CSC. Quantitative data can be a powerful component of outcome measurement systems, providing generalizable observations about a program's ability to increase the seven capitals of community wealth. When data from state or federal agencies are available, they can be used without additional monitoring costs for the communities involved. However, qualitative indices have considerable advantages as well.

Qualitative information should be used when quantitative indicators are not readily available. While secondary data are useful, they may not always be timely. For instance, data for indices in Minnesota Compass are sometimes unavailable for the previous two years. In other cases, quantitative indicators may not be suitable simply because a community has not identified a specific measure. Development evaluation has been used in instances where communities did not have one outcome indicator but nevertheless needed feedback on service providers' performance in a timely fashion. Local data from state and federal sources may take a year to compile and make available (Gallagher & Putiak, 2010), but an evaluator can conduct several interviews and report on findings within weeks (Preskill & Beer, 2012).

Making a community indicator relevant to decision-makers precedes adding statistical complexity. Ideally, outcome measures lead to policy improvements, so the measures used must be clear and timely for policy-makers. In DEs, such as those conducted for the YouthScape Initiative in Canada, evaluators collected most of the information from regular interviews so that service providers received timely feedback on their performance. The indicators provided by Minnesota Compass were selected based on inputs from businesses, community development practitioners, and academics. The Children's Services Council in Florida integrated the performance measurement system into its budget because the system was championed by the organization's leadership.

Another lesson is that the triple bottom line approach to measurement is not always apparent. Some measurement systems discussed earlier, such as Minnesota Compass and the capitals used by the CAN, include indices for social, environmental, and economic goals. In some cases, the focus on environmental issues is less apparent. Community development initiatives may underreport their impacts by not documenting gains in environmental capital (Hoffer & Levy, 2010).

Perhaps the largest change in measurement practices has been a growing realization that community developers are not alone in documenting their successes. The availability of technical assistance for outcome measurement has expanded since the 1970s when the State of California published a guide for local governments to compile data on social conditions. Today, nonprofit and research organizations with a national focus guide community development organizations in tracking their performance. Examples include the VCs Canada partnership that uses a DE model with client communities and the Ford Foundation that provides grants for organizations to create and measure community wealth.

Ideally, an outcome measurement system would include elements of contingent and universal models, utilizing both qualitative and quantitative indices. In the early stages of a project or program, DE informs policy-makers and citizens of the initiative's challenges and successes. This allows for successful implementation and is especially helpful when timely quantitative data are unavailable. As community development initiatives mature and data become available for the program's earlier years, universal indices could provide a detailed retrospective of the program's ability to increase community wealth. Evaluation of quantitative growth in the seven capitals could then be used to inform the adoption of further changes in the community development organization's practices.

Much work has been done to make outcome measurement systems more accessible in terms of relevance to policy and cost-effectiveness. Community leaders interested in monitoring the effects or results of their intervention programs have the technical resources available. There is no question that monitoring results and outcomes will become a growing part of community and economic development efforts especially during continued fiscal austerity. Linking the progress toward goals into policy changes will always be difficult but fortunately, many agencies exist to help with these efforts.

References

Allen, K., & Watson, T. (n.d.). *Wealth creation in action: CAN takes the wealth creation approach and runs with it.* Retrieved June 7, 2013, from http://www.creatingruralwealth.org/wealth-crea-tion-approach/wealth-creation-in-action/

Ammons, D. (2012). *Municipal benchmarks: Assessing local performance and establishing community standards* (3rd ed.). Armonk, NY: M.E. Sharpe.

Anderson, A. (2005). *The theory of change: A practical guide to theory development.* Washington, DC: The ASPEN Institute Roundtable on Community Change. Retrieved August 21, 2013, from http://www.dochas.ie/Shared/Files/4/TOC_fac_guide.pdf

Annie E. Casey Foundation. (2013). *Kids count.* Retrieved from http://www.aecf.org/MajorInitia-tives/KIDSCOUNT.aspx

Bernstein, D. (2002). City of Portland, Oregon: Pioneering external accountability. *GASB SEA research case study.* Norwalk, CT: Governmental Accounting Standards Board.

Blakely, E. J., & Leigh, N. G. (2010). *Planning local economic development: Theory and practice* (4th ed.). Thousand Oaks, CA: Sage.

Boston Indicators Project. (2012). *City of ideas: Reinventing Boston's innovation economy.* Retrieved from http://www.bostonindicators.org/shaping-the-future/~/media/92727AB2F0834 6D79D14E4B99122353F.pdf

Boston Indicators Project. (n.d.). *Hub of innovation.* Retrieved from http://www.bostonindica-tors.org/shaping-the-future/hub-of-innovation

Burd-Sharps, S., Guyer, P., & Lewis, K. (2011). *Metrics matter: A human development approach to measuring social impact.* San Francisco, CA: Federal Reserve Bank of San Francisco.

Bush Foundation. (n.d.). *Navigating data with compass.* Retrieved from http://www.bushfounda-tion.org/solutions/resources/compass

Cawley, J. (2010). *YouthScape: A funder's perspective.* Montreal, Quebec: J. W. McConnell Family Foundation.

Center for Building Better Communities. (2001). *Hernando County economic development plan.* Gainesville, FL: University of Florida, Urban and Regional Planning Department.

Children's Services Council. (2011). *2010–2011 annual report.* Tamarac, FL: Children's Services Council.

Community Indicators Consortium. (2013). *Indicator projects.* Retrieved from http://www.communityindicators.net/projects

Dorius, N. (2011). Measuring community development outcomes: In search of an analytical framework. *Economic Development Quarterly, 25,* 267–276.

Emery, M., & Flora, C. (2006). Spiraling-up: Mapping community transformation with the community capitals framework. *Community Development, 37*, 19–35.

Flora, J. L., & Flora, C. B. (2004). Building community in rural areas of the Andes. In R. Atria & M. Siles (compilers), *Social capital and poverty reduction in Latin America and the Caribbean: Towards a new paradigm* (pp. 523–542). Santiago Chile: Economic Commission for Latin America, Caribbean University, & Michigan State University.

Forster-Gill, D. J. (2012). *Vibrant Communities Canada: Measuring impact.* Retrieved from http://www.slideshare.net/socialfinance/vibrant-communities-canada-measuring-impact

Gallagher, S., & Putiak, G. (2010). Making children's lives better: Integrating community indicators and performance measures in Broward County, Florida. *Community Indicators Consortium real stories series.* Issaquah, WA: Community Indicators Consortium.

Hart, M. (2012). *Community change, community vitality and measurement. Bush Foundation.* Retrieved from http://www.bushfoundation.org/community-vitality-measures-meeting

Hart, M. (n.d.). *Sustainable seattle. Sustainability measures.* Retrieved from http://www.sustainablemeasures.com/node/242

Hoffer, D., & Levy, M. (2010). *Measuring community wealth.* Report for the Wealth Creation in Rural Communities project of the Ford Foundation. St. Albans, VT: Yellow Wood Associates.

Hollander, J. (2002). Measuring community: Using sustainability indicators in Devens, Massachusetts. *Planners' Casebook, 39*(Winter), 1–7.

International Institute for Children's Rights and Development. (2010). *YouthScape final report. Learnings and impact.* Retrieved August 21, 2013, from http://www.youthscape.ca/YouthScape%20FINAL%20REPORT%20Final%2030%206%2010.pdf

Langlois, M. (2010). *Developmental evaluation report: A trek through the YouthScape landscape.* Retrieved from http://www.mcconnellfoundation.ca/assets/Media%20Library/Reports/YouthScape%20DE%20final%20report.pdf

Madan, R. (2007). *Demystifying outcome measurement in community development.* Boston, MA: Harvard Joint Center for Housing Studies.

Moynihan, D. (2008). *The dynamics of performance management: Constructing information and reform.* Washington, DC: Georgetown University Press.

Myrdal, G. (1957). *Economic theory and underdeveloped regions.* London: Duckworth.

Patton, M. Q. (2011). *Developmental evaluation: Applying complexity concepts to enhance innovation and use.* New York, NY: Guilford Press.

Phillips, R. (2003). *Community indicators. American Planning Association Planning and Advisory Service Report Number 517.* Retrieved from http://www.planning.org/pas/reports/subscribers/pdf/PAS517.pdf

Plantz, M., Greenway, M., & Hendricks, H. (1997). Outcome measurement: Showing results in the nonprofit sector. *New Directions for Evaluation, 75*, 15–29.

Posovac, E. (2011). *Program evaluation: Methods and case studies* (8th ed.). Upper Saddle River, NJ: Prentice Hall.

Preskill, H., & Beer, T. (2012). *Evaluating social innovation.* Washington, DC: FSG & Center for Evaluation Innovation.

Robert Wood Johnson Foundation. (2013). County health rankings & roadmaps. Retrieved October 16, 2013, from http://www.countyhealthrankings.org/

Rockford Region Vital Signs. (2012). *About our vital signs.* Retrieved August 21, 2013, from http://www.ourvitalsigns.com/

Slaper, T., & Hall, T. (2011). Triple bottom line: What is it and how does it work? *Indiana Business Review.* Retrieved August 22, 2013, from http://www.ibrc.indiana.edu/ibr/2011/spring/article2.html

Stoecker, R. (2005). *Research methods for community change: A project-based approach.* Thousand Oaks, CA: Sage.

Success Measures. (2012). Measurement tools. Retrieved August 20, 2013, from http://www.successmeasures.org/measurement-tools

Sustainable Seattle. (1993). First set of indicators. Retrieved August 22, 2013, from http://www.sustainableseattle.org/programs/regional-indicators/133-first-set-of-indicators

Sustainable Seattle. (n.d.). History. Retrieved from http://www.sustainableseattle.org/whoweare/history

United Nations. (n.d.). Millennium development goals. Retrieved from http://www.un.org/millenniumgoals/

Walzer, N., & Hamm, G. F. (2012). *Community visioning programs: Processes and outcomes*. New York, NY: Routledge.

Wilder Research. (2009). *The Minnesota compass – The data*. Retrieved from http://www. mncompass.org/about/the-data.php#.UZp-o6KKpF8

W.K. Kellogg Foundation. (2004). *Logic model development guide*. Battle Creek, MI: Author.

Yellow Wood Associates. (2009). *Connecting goals, indicators, and measures; Planning for measurement; Using the results of measurement; Getting to action steps*. St. Albans, VT: Author.

Index